CW01498125

The Collected Courses of the
Series Editors: Profess
Fordham Law School, New York;
Professor Marise Cremona
Professor Bruno de Witte, and
Professor Francesco Francioni,
European University Institute
Florence
Assistant Editor: Anny Bremner, *European University*
Institute, Florence

VOLUME XVI/4
Access to Justice as a Human Right

The Collected Courses of the Academy of European Law
Edited by Professor Gráinne de Búrca, Professor Marise Cremona,
Professor Bruno de Witte, and Professor Franceso Francioni.
Assistant Editor: Anny Bremner

This series brings together the Collected Courses of the
Academy of European Law in Florence. The Academy's mission is to
produce scholarly analyses which are at the cutting edge of the two
fields in which it works: European Union law and human rights law.
A 'general course' is given each year in each field, by a
distinguished scholar and/or practitioner, who either examines the
field as a whole through a particular thematic, conceptual, or
philosophical lens, or who looks at a particular theme in the context
of the overall body of law in the field. The Academy also publishes
each year a volume of collected essays with a specific theme in each
of the two fields.

Access to Justice as a Human Right

Edited by

FRANCESCO FRANCIONI

Academy of European Law
European University Institute

OXFORD
UNIVERSITY PRESS

OXFORD
UNIVERSITY PRESS

Great Clarendon Street, Oxford OX2 6DP

Oxford University Press is a department of the University of Oxford.
It furthers the University's objective of excellence in research, scholarship,
and education by publishing worldwide in

Oxford New York

Auckland Cape Town Dar es Salaam Hong Kong Karachi
Kuala Lumpur Madrid Melbourne Mexico City Nairobi
New Delhi Shanghai Taipei Toronto

With offices in

Argentina Austria Brazil Chile Czech Republic France Greece
Guatemala Hungary Italy Japan Poland Portugal Singapore
South Korea Switzerland Thailand Turkey Ukraine Vietnam

Oxford is a registered trade mark of Oxford University Press
in the UK and in certain other countries

Published in the United States
by Oxford University Press Inc., New York

British Library Cataloguing in Publication Data

Data available

Library of Congress Cataloging in Publication Data

Data available

Typeset by Newgen Imaging Systems (P) Ltd., Chennai, India
Printed in Great Britain
on acid-free paper by
Biddles Ltd., King's Lynn

ISBN 978-0-19-923308-3
ISBN 978-0-19-923309-0 (pbk.)

1 3 5 7 9 10 8 6 4 2

Acknowledgements

I am grateful to the many people who contributed ideas and support in bringing this volume to publication. My thanks go especially to the authors—Rory Stephen Brown, Fionnuala Ní Aoláin, Catherine Redgwell, Natalino Ronzitti, Martin Scheinin, Eva Storskrubb, and Jacques Ziller—for their presentations at the Academy's summer course and their contributions to this book. Many thanks to Bruno De Witte, and Marise Cremona for their contribution of ideas and constant support in the organization of the Academy courses. For financial support, thanks go to the Commission of the European Community. I owe special thanks to Anny Bremner for her efficient and careful work as assistant editor of this series, and to Barbara Ciomei and Mario Mendez who have assisted at various stages of the editorial process. Finally, I would like to thank the OUP staff, especially John Louth, Hayley Buckley, and Alex Flach, for their patient and pro-active interaction with the authors.

Florence, July 2007.

Contents

Table of Cases

INTERNATIONAL

NATIONAL

Argentina

Australia

Canada

Greece

Italy

Japan

Philippines

Switzerland

United Kingdom

Table of Legislation

Table of Treaties and Other Relevant Instruments

BILATERAL TREATIES AND AGREEMENTS

NATIONAL INSTRUMENTS

France

United States

List of Abbreviations

General

ADR	alternative dispute resolution
ATCA	Alien Tort Claims Act (US)
CPR	Civil Procedure Rules (UK)
ECE	Economic Commission for Europe
ECHR	European Convention on Human Rights
FSIA	Foreign Sovereign Immunities Act of 1976 (US)
GA Res	General Assembly Resolution (UN)
HRC	Human Rights Committee (UN)
ICC	International Criminal Court
ICJ	International Court of Justice, the Hague
ICRC	International Committee of the Red Cross
ICSID	International Centre for the Settlement of Investment Disputes
ICTR	International Criminal Tribunal for Rwanda
ICTY	International Criminal Tribunal for the Former Yugoslavia
IHL	international humanitarian law
IHR	international human rights
ILC	International Law Commission
ILO	International Labour Organization
ITLOS	International Tribunal for the Law of the Sea
KFOR	Kosovo Force (NATO)
NAFTA	North American Free Trade Agreement
NATO	North Atlantic Treaty Organization
NGO	non-governmental organization
OAS	Organization of American States
OSCE	Organization for Security and Co-operation in Europe
PCIJ	Permanent Court of International Justice
SC Res	Security Council Resolution (UN)
UNCAT	United Nations Convention Against Torture
UNCC	United Nations Compensation Commission
UNCED	United Nations Conference on Environment and Development
UNCITRAL	United Nations Commission on International Trade Law
UNMIK	United Nations Mission in Kosovo
WSSD	World Summit on Sustainable Development

Publications

CLJ	Cambridge Law Journal
Col HRLR	Columbia Human Rights law Review
Col LR	Columbia Law Review
EHRLR	European Human Rights Law Review
EJIL	European Journal of International Law
ELJ	European Law Journal
ELR	European Law Review
Ford ILJ	Fordham International Law Journal
Harv Env LR	Harvard Environmental Law Review
HRLJ	Human Rights Law Journal
HRLR	Human Rights Law Review
HRQ	Human Rights Quarterly
ICLQ	International and Comparative Law Quarterly
IJHR	International Journal of Human Rights
ILM	International Legal Materials
IRRC	International Review of the Red Cross
IYHR	International Yearbook of Human Rights
IYIL	Italian Yearbook of International Law
JIA	Journal of International Arbitration
JICJ	Journal of International Criminal Justice
JILE	Journal of International Law and Economics
JTLP	Journal of Transnational Law and Policy
LJIL	Leiden Journal of International Law
LQR	Law Quarterly Review
Mich JIL	Michigan Journal of International Law
Mich LR	Michigan Law Review
NYU JILP	New York University Journal of International Law and Politics
Stan JIL	Stanford Journal of International Law
Tex ILJ	Texas International Law Journal
YLJ	Yale Law Journal

Notes on Contributors

Rory Stephen Brown is currently a doctoral researcher at the European University Institute in Florence, Italy. He is Editor-in-Chief of the European Journal of Legal Studies, a lecturer in European Union Law at the Scuola di Lorenzo de' Medici in Florence, and a non-practising barrister. He has published in the fields of European human rights law, international law, and international studies. His current research investigates the effect of state responses to terrorism on law.

Francesco Francioni is Professor of International Law and Human Rights at the European University Institute, Florence, and at the Law Faculty of the University of Siena. He is a Director of the Academy of European Law and General Editor of the *Italian Yearbook of International Law*. Professor Francioni is a member of the American Law Institute and of the Executive Board of the European Society of International Law. He has been a member of the Italian delegation at many diplomatic conferences and international negotiations, particularly in the field of environmental law and cultural heritage. He has given courses at the Hague Academy of International Law (1995), Cornell Law School (1983–86), Texas Law School (1988–2005), and Oxford University (1999–2003).

Fionnuala Ní Aoláin is concurrently Professor of Law at the University of Ulster's Transitional Justice Institute in Belfast, Northern Ireland, and the Dorsey and Whitney Chair in Law at the University of Minnesota Law School. She is co-founder and Associate Director of the Transitional Justice Institute. Professor Ní Aoláin is the recipient of numerous academic awards and honours including a Fulbright scholarship, the Alon Prize, the Robert Schumann Scholarship, a European Commission award, and the Lawlord fellowship. Her teaching and research interests are in the fields of international law and human rights law. She has published extensively in the fields of emergency powers, conflict regulation, and sex-based violence in situations of conflict. In 2003, she was appointed by the Secretary-General of the United Nations as Special Expert on promoting gender equality in times of conflict and peace-making. In 2004, she was nominated by the Irish government to the European Court of Human Rights, the first woman and the first academic lawyer to be thus nominated. Professor Ní Aoláin's book, *Law in Times of Crisis*: *Emergency Powers in Theory and Practice* (with Professor Oren Gross, 2006) was awarded the 2007 American Society of International Law Certificate of Merit.

Catherine Redgwell is Professor of International Law at University College London, having previously held positions at the Universities of Oxford, Nottingham, and Manchester. She is also Joint General Editor of the International and Comparative

Law Quarterly. Professor Redgwell's research interests lie in the public international law field, especially international energy law and international environmental law, in which she has published widely. Forthcoming publications include co-authoring, with Professor Alan Boyle, the third edition of Birnie and Boyle's *International Law and the Environment* (Oxford University Press) and as co-editor and contributor to *Beyond the Carbon Economy* (Oxford University Press).

Natalino Ronzitti is Professor of International Law, LUISS University School of Law, Rome, Italy. He has been legal adviser to the Permanent Representative of Italy to the Conference on Disarmament (Geneva), consultant with the Italian Ministry of Foreign Affairs and Ministry of Defence, and member of the Italian delegation at several diplomatic conferences. He has been lecturer and guest professor at several universities and institutions abroad, including the Hague Academy of International Law. Professor Ronzitti is the author of numerous publications of public international law and is a member of the board of editors of the *Italian Yearbook of International Law*, the *International Spectator*, and the Journal of Conflict and Security Law.

Martin Scheinin is Professor of Constitutional and International Law at Åbo Akademi University, where he is also Director of the Institute for Human Rights. He leads the Nordic School in Human Rights Research, which is a cooperative framework for doctoral studies in the field of human rights in the five Nordic countries. From 1997 to 2004 he was a member of the Human Rights Committee under the International Covenant on Civil and Political Rights. Currently he serves as the United Nations special rapporteur on human rights and counter-terrorism. As of 1 September 2008, he will join the European University Institute as Professor of Public International Law.

Eva Storskrubb received her LL Lic at the University of Helsinki and her PhD at the European University Institute, Florence. Dr Storskrubb's research interests lie in civil and commercial dispute resolution, and she has particularly focused on comparative civil procedure as well as the Europeanization of civil procedure. She has published various articles and book chapters, and is currently practising law.

Jacques Ziller is Professor of Comparative Public Law at the European University Institute, on secondment from the Université de Paris 1 Panthéon-Sorbonne. He teaches public law, among others French procedural law of administrative courts, comparative law, and European law. He has published numerous books and articles on comparative public law, EU law, and administrative sciences.

1

The Rights of Access to Justice under Customary International Law

FRANCESCO FRANCIONI[1]

I. THE DEVELOPMENT OF ACCESS TO JUSTICE IN CUSTOMARY LAW

A. Introduction

In international law, as in any domestic legal system, respect and protection of human rights can be guaranteed only by the availability of effective judicial remedies. When a right is violated, access to justice is of fundamental importance for the injured individual and it is an essential component of the system of protection and enforcement of human rights. As a term of art, however, access to justice has acquired a variety of meanings. In a general manner it is employed to signify the possibility for the individual to bring a claim before a court and have a court adjudicate it. In a more qualified meaning access to justice is used to signify the right of an individual not only to enter a court of law, but to have his or her case heard and adjudicated in accordance with substantive standards of fairness and justice. In this second meaning it provides a standard of review of the administration of justice in the state where the infringement of a right has occurred. Finally, in a narrower sense, access to justice can be used to describe the legal aid for the needy, in the absence of which judicial remedies would be available only to those who dispose of the financial resources necessary to meet the, often prohibitive, cost of lawyers and the administration of justice. In the course of this chapter I will deal only with the first two meanings. In particular, my intention is to assess whether an individual right of access to justice has emerged under customary international law, and, if so, its scope and the limits to its exercise.

This essay is divided into three parts. In the first part I will examine access to justice as it first appeared in customary international law, ie as a subset of

[1] The author gratefully acknowledges the valuable research assistance provided by Eniko Horvath and Kathrin Scherr and the useful comments and suggestions made on an earlier draft of this chapter by Mario Mendez and Rory Brown, doctoral candidates at the EU.

the law of state responsibility for injuries to aliens. In this context we can find the early development of the right of access to justice in connection with claims by individuals whose rights were breached in a state other than that of their nationality. Here, access to local justice is at the same time the object of a right, guaranteed under the international standard of treatment of aliens, and of a legal duty, or legal onus, in as much as it constitutes a prerequisite for the exercise of the right of diplomatic protection by the national state of the alien. Besides the law on the treatment of aliens, the individual right of access to justice emerges in international law also in connection with the progressive development in the twentieth century of the capacity of private persons to bring a claim before international tribunals and a variety of international bodies, such as war claims commissions and mixed commissions, which foreshadow the contemporary development of judicial institutions where private persons have the right of direct access to justice at the international level.

The second part of this essay will examine the development of access to justice in the context of the international law of human rights. It will address (1) whether today there is an obligation under general international law for every state to guarantee individual access to justice as a human right, regardless of diversity of citizenship; (2) the scope of this obligation; and (3) how it is implemented in practice. In addressing these questions, account will be taken of the fact that access to justice is guaranteed as a legal right in virtually all universal and regional human rights instruments, since the 1948 Universal Declaration,[2] as well as in many national constitutions.[3] Despite treaty and state practice supporting the individual right of access to justice, a number of questions and obstacles remain with respect to its effective implementation. In particular, it is not sufficient to proclaim such right formally if its actual enjoyment is not guaranteed by a system of fair and impartial administration of justice, something that remains problematic in many countries, as the practice of the European Court of Human Rights and the Human Rights Committee will clearly show.[4] Another question to be addressed in this part is the extent to which the nature of the substantive right, for the infringement of which redress is sought, may influence the strength of the claim for access to justice in the event of its infringement. Does a breach of a *jus cogens* norm create a corresponding non-derogable right of access to justice, or can the recourse to court be subject to limitations in exceptional circumstances, such as those invoked for the defence of democratic societies against terrorism?

The third part of this chapter will be devoted to an examination of the norms and doctrines which may constitute an obstacle to the exercise of the individual right of access to justice. Whether we construe access to justice as treaty based

---

[2] See Universal Declaration of Human Rights, Art 10, GA Res 217 A (III), UN Doc A/810 (1948) 71.

[3] See Storskrubb and Ziller, ch 6 below.

[4] For a detailed examination of the case law of these two bodies, see Scheinin, ch 4 below.

or generally applicable under customary international law, its effective enjoyment remains hindered by conflicting norms of international law or by specific domestic law doctrines. This is evident with regard to sovereign and diplomatic immunities, which continue to shield perpetrators of human rights abuses, and with regard to doctrines of non-justiciability, forum non conveniens, or lack of jurisdictional nexus, which in different ways limit the competence of domestic courts to provide a remedy to victims of human rights violations.

As in other areas of international law, in these cases the individual's right of access to justice may suffer from restrictions and may need to be balanced against other rights and other legitimate interests of the international community.

B. Use of the Term 'Access to Justice'

In its ordinary usage, the term 'access to justice' is a synonym of judicial protection. Thus, from the point of view of the individual, the term would normally refer to the right to seek a remedy before a court of law or a tribunal which is constituted by law and which can guarantee independence and impartiality in the application of the law. This definition is obviously a rather restricted one: it is premised on the concept of the rule of law and of the constitutional separation of powers, where courts are independent of the executive and have the power and responsibility to interpret and apply the law independently. This condition, which is typical of the systems of constitutional democracies, might at first sight be considered only a feature of the Western legal tradition,[5] in as much as it does not obtain in the totality of contemporary domestic legal systems. However, even if we may concede that international law leaves a wide margin of discretion to states in the administration of justice, nevertheless a general acceptance of such notion of justice can be evinced from the human rights instruments adopted since the establishment of the United Nations. In particular, it can be found in Article 8 of the 1948 Universal Declaration,[6] Article 6(1) of the European Convention on Human Rights (ECHR)[7] and Article 25 of the American Convention,[8] as well as

---

[5] 'A society in which the observance of the law is not assured, nor the separation of powers defined, has no constitution at all.' Article 16 of the French Declaration of the Rights of Man of 1789, art 16. See also Charter of Fundamental Rights of the European Union, Art 47, para 2, which stresses the requirements of fairness, publicity of the hearings, impartiality and independence of the judge: 'Everyone is entitled to a fair and public hearing within a reasonable time by an independent and impartial tribunal previously established by law. Everyone shall have the possibility of being advised, defended and represented.'

[6] See n 1 above.

[7] 'In the determination of his civil rights and obligations or of any criminal charge against him, everyone is entitled to a fair and public hearing within a reasonable time by an independent and impartial tribunal established by law . . .', European Convention of Human Rights and Fundamental Freedoms, 1950 (CETS No 005) Art 6(1).

[8] American Convention on Human Rights, 1969 (1144 UNTS 123) Art 25 (Right to Judicial Protection): '(1) Everyone has the right to simple and prompt recourse, or any other effective recourse,

Article 7.1 of the African Charter on Human and Peoples' Rights[9] and Article 47 of the Charter of Rights of the European Union.[10]

Within the general meaning of access to justice as the right to a judicial remedy before an independent court of law, a narrower and more technical definition of justice can be found in the constitutions of countries that had past experiences of non-democratic regimes or periods of systematic violations of civil liberties. In these constitutions the term 'justice' is sometimes understood as the 'natural judge', ie the court or tribunal which is pre-constituted to hear a given class of civil or criminal cases, as opposed to ad hoc or special tribunals, often used as instruments of the executive in the pursuit of political objectives.[11]

By contrast, a broader meaning of the term justice is the one which is inclusive of those remedies offered by competent public authorities, which are not courts of law but can nevertheless perform a dispute settlement function. This is the case with administrative or legislative agencies which—without presenting the formal pre-requisite of judicial independence—are engaged in some form of administration of justice. Naturally, whether these authorities are capable of dispensing effective justice with the objectivity and impartiality required in a democratic society depends on each particular case and on the way in which they operate. What is important, for the purpose of the following analysis, is to recognize that, from the point of view of international law, states enjoy a wide latitude of freedom in the organization of their domestic system of leal remedies. What counts, for the purpose of the right of access to justice, is that such remedies are effective and that they provide fair and impartial justice in a way that is equivalent to that provided by remedies that are *stricto sensu* judicial. This is confirmed by some specific provisions of human rights treaties, such as Article 2(3) of the International Covenant on Civil and Political Rights (ICCPR), which speaks of remedies provided by 'judicial, administrative or legislative author-ities', as well as by Article 13 of the ECHR, which requires an 'effective remedy before a national authority', without any further qualification.

A more complex question is whether the concept of justice used in this chapter may include those forms of 'alternative' or 'private ' justice that are becoming more

---

to a competent court or tribunal for protection against acts that violate his fundamental rights recognized by the constitution or laws of the state concerned or by this Convention, even though such violation may have been committed by persons acting in the course of their official duties.'

[9] African Charter on Human and Peoples' Rights, 1981 ((1982) 21 ILM 58) Art 7.1: 'Every individual shall have the right to have his cause heard. This comprises: (a) The right to an appeal to competent national organs against acts of violating his fundamental rights as recognized and guar-anteed by conventions, laws, regulations and customs in force; (b) The right to be presumed innocent until proved guilty by a competent court or tribunal; (c) The right to defence, including the right to be defended by counsel of his choice; (d) The right to be tried within a reasonable time by an impartial court or tribunal.'

[10] See Storskrubb and Ziller, ch 6 below.

[11] The notion of the 'natural judge' can be found in the Italian Constitution, art 25 (published in *Gazzetta Ufficiale* n 298, 27 December 1947, and in the German Basic Law of 1949, art 101.

and more widespread in some advanced societies, such as Europe and the United States, as a substitute for adjudication. Such forms of alternative justice, generally denominated 'alternative dispute resolution' (ADR), are the response to the excessive formalism and increasingly prohibitive costs of ordinary justice. They are one of the many manifestations of the rise of spontaneous social organization in response to the increasing technicality and unsustainable length of judicial proceedings. It would be wrong to consider these methods of dispute resolution as an idiosyncratic phenomenon and a temporary trend in the rich world. On the contrary, on the one hand they rediscover traditional forms of dispute settlement that may present the added value of a high degree of spontaneous compliance, because they are rooted in social structures and in customary law; on the other hand, they are a specific reflection of the general crisis of the welfare state, a crisis that is mainly one of the increasing cost and inefficiency of the bureaucratic apparatus of justice and of consequent distrust on the part of the ordinary citizen. In this perspective, the contemporary trend to 'privatize' justice in certain areas, such as business relations and family law, is the expression of a real social need and we can expect that this trend will stay and expand in the future. The question, for the purpose of our discussion, is, therefore, not whether ADR can be included or not in the definition of 'justice'—because certainly it provides a more expeditious and less costly alternative to traditional justice; but whether it is designed and monitored in such a way as to guarantee equal access, proper expertise of the professionals involved, sustainable costs, and, most important, a timely and high quality justice so as to satisfy accessibility and effectivity in accordance with the principle of equal protection of the law.

C. The Individual Right of Access to Justice in General International Law

Having clarified in a general manner the meaning of 'access to justice' in the context of the present discussion, we can now turn to the examination of the legal basis and scope of the corresponding right under general international law.

At the outset, it may be useful to remember that, according to the orthodox positivist view, international law is a system of law governing inter-state relations, in which only states have 'rights', and obligations, including the right to bring a claim before a court or an arbitral tribunal. For sovereign states, such right is contingent upon the consent of the state against which the claim is directed, since no *a priori* compulsory dispute settlement mechanism is conceivable in a legal order based on sovereignty. This narrow view of international law is consistent with the Statute of the International Court of Justice (ICJ), which is open only to states,[12] and with the theories advanced by Anzilotti,[13] Triepel,[14] Strupp,[15] and

---

[12] The ICJ's Statute, Art 34(1) reads as follows: 'Only states may be parties in cases before the Court.'

[13] See D Anzilotti, *Corso di Diritto Internazionale* (1912).

[14] See von H Triepel, *Völkerrecht und Landesrecht* (1899).

[15] See K Strupp, *Theorie und Praxis des Völkerrechts* (1925).

other champions of legal positivism and of dualism, and later with the views of some eminent representatives of legal realism—such as Quadri[16]—who relentlessly denied that individuals, and private persons in general, may have the capacity to be rights holders and duty bearers under international law. Of course, even before the contemporary developments in the area of international human rights, eminent jurists such as Duguit, Scelle, Kelsen, and others had challenged the state-oriented approach to international law and advocated a 'monist' conception of the relationship between the international and the domestic legal order. This entailed a progressive development of the role of individuals and their emancipation from being mere 'objects' of the law to becoming legal 'subjects' capable of asserting rights at the international level. The same conclusion, although through a different intellectual process, is reached by the sociological school of international law, which proceeds from a deconstruction of the state as a primary subject of international law and focuses on law as a 'process' of continuous adaptation to societal needs, and on 'participants' rather than 'subjects' in order to highlight the liberal perspective of law as a social process where human beings are active members of the organization of society through law, rather than passive subordinates to pre-constituted legal authority and the formal sources of the law.[17] In spite of the great importance of these theories from the point of view of the intellectual history of international law, their influence on the reality and practice of international law has remained rather limited: states and unions of states have continued to be the primary actors in international relations for most of the last century, and even today they continue to enjoy a near monopoly in relation to the capacity to bring claims before international mechanisms of dispute settlement.[18]

This being the case, it would be foolish, however, to deny today that individuals and private persons in general have certain rights and obligations under international law. The progressive development of international human rights law has endowed every person with the abstract capacity to invoke international

---

[16] See R Quadri, *Diritto internazionale Pubblico* (1968).

[17] See MS McDougal, HD Lasswell, and WM Reisman, 'The World Constitutive Process of Authoritative Decision' (1967) 19 Journal of Legal Education 253; R Higgins, *Problems and Process: International Law and How We Use It* (1995).

[18] Even the most recent mechanisms of international dispute settlement, such as the WTO Dispute Settlement Body and the International Tribunal for the Law of the Sea (ITLOS), are open, with some limited exceptions, only to states; and private persons, who are the beneficiaries of the treaties under which such mechanisms are established, can obtain judicial protection only through the intermediary of their national state or another state which can demonstrate *locus standi*. Besides, individuals and private parties may continue to find obstacles to effective judicial remedies because of the impossibility for them to invoke the international treaties of which they are beneficiaries. The long running saga concerning the enforcement of GATT and WTO norms in the Community legal order can be seen as testimony to this. Most recently, the ECJ in its *Van Parys* decision of March 2005 rejected review of the compatibility of a Community measure vis-à-vis WTO norms even where a Dispute Settlement Body decision had concluded that the Community measure was in breach of WTO obligations and the compliance period had expired (OJ, C 106, 30 April 2005, 4).

law, customary law, and treaty law against a state, including the national state, which is responsible for an abusive exercise of its governmental powers. Under specific human rights treaties—such as the European and the Inter-American Conventions—this abstract capacity translates into a concrete right of access to international judicial remedies before the competent organs for the supervision and enforcement of the human rights obligations undertaken by the state parties. Similarly, in the area of international economic law, a nearly universal network of investment treaties creates rights for private entities directly enforceable under international law.[19] In the field of consular relations, the ICJ has recognized the right to consular assistance for aliens charged with a criminal offence as a true 'individual right', independent of the parallel state right to exercise diplomatic protection, and has gone as far as to hold that a breach of such right entails the obligation to provide the affected individual with proper reconsideration of his or her case in fresh criminal proceedings.[20]

Yet, even if it is easy to recognize that the human person today is the holder of rights under international law, the question remains as to whether and to what extent the present inter-state structure of international law may pose obstacles to the ability of the individual to assert such rights directly before domestic or international remedial bodies. This question is central to the theme of this chapter. But it would be wrong, and certainly misleading, to try to answer it in absolute and unconditional terms[21] by reference to the old and inconclusive discussion as to whether individuals are entitled or not to an international personality. Rather than focusing on the formal criterion of the international personality, the existence of an individual right of access to justice must be assessed on the basis of an objective examination of international law. International practice in this respect reveals first of all that access to justice in domestic law is a prerequisite for the exercise of the international right of diplomatic protection of nationals who have suffered injuries abroad.[22] Besides, and most important, international practice shows a process of continuous change and adaptation of international norms and principles to the new realities where private actors—individuals, as well as economic, scientific, and technological entities—are increasingly participating in the process of law formation, law enforcement, and adjudication at the international level. If we look at international law from this evolutive perspective, it becomes apparent that nothing in its legal nature and structure is inherently incompatible with the conceptualization

---

[19] See eg International Centre for the Settlement of Investment Disputes (ICSID), North American Free Trade Agreement (NAFTA), etc.

[20] *Case Concerning Avena and Other Mexican Nationals (Mexico v United States of America)* Judgment of 31 March [2004] ICJ Rep 128.

[21] In the negative, see Lord Denning in *Gouriet v Union of Post Office Workers and Ors* [1977] 3 All ER 70; in the positive, and with emphasis on the transformative process of the international community, see R Pisillo Mazzeschi, *Esaurimento dei ricorsi interni e diritti umani* (2004).

[22] For an in-depth analysis of the principle of prior exhaustion of local remedies in the context of human rights, see Pisillo Mazzeschi (n 21 above).

of the individual right of access to justice.[23] On the contrary, as we shall see, international practice shows that this right has already emerged and is exercised independently or in cooperation with the national state of the affected individual. At the same time it would be wrong to jump to the conclusion that international law has already undergone a structural transformation so as to be a universal law or global[24] law today, where individuals can claim access to justice and especially to international remedies as a matter of right and in all circumstances. In the present structure of international law, human organization is modelled on the pattern of sovereign states, and human beings continue to be subject to state authority and national jurisdiction.[25] Therefore it is essential for the purpose of this chapter to proceed with some caution in the reconstruction of the right of access to justice under general international law. First, we need to distinguish between domestic and international remedies, recognizing that the individual right of access to justice must primarily be ensured within the domestic legal system where the violation of human rights has occurred. Secondly, it is essential to examine carefully the conditions and circumstances under which an opening of international remedies is necessary and recognized as a matter of human rights under international law. Thirdly, it is important to remain aware of possible risks or abuses that may derive from too broad a construction of the right of access to justice, of the inevitable limitations that it is bound to suffer in the present state-centred structure of international law, and of the consequent need to avoid the risk of its exercise turning into a destabilizing, and even destructive, element of the normative and institutional architecture of the international society.[26]

With these caveats in mind, we can now turn to the examination of the origin and evolution of the right of access to justice, first in relation to the emergence of the concept of 'denial of justice' in customary law on the treatment of aliens, and then in relation to the progressive development of a limited capacity of individuals to bring claims before international organs, especially war compensation commissions and minority commissions, since the beginning of the twentieth century.

---

[23] In this sense see R Higgins, 'Conceptual Thinking about the Individual in International Law' in R Falk *et al* (eds), *International law: a Contemporary Perspective* (1985) 479; F Orrego-Vicuna, *International Dispute Settlement in an Evolving Global Society* (2004) 29 *et seq*. See also F Durante, *Ricorsi individuali ad organi internazionali: contributo alla teoria della personalità internazionale dell'individuo* (1958).

[24] See Pisillo-Mazzeschi (n 21 above) 16 *et seq*.

[25] On the complex interplay between individual rights and state rights from the point of view of the actionability of legal remedies of the former, see A Cassese, 'Individuo (dir. Internazionale)' in *Enciclopedia del Diritto*, (1971) Vol XXI, 184, 189; G Strozzi, *Interessi Statali e interessi privati nell'ordinamento internazionale* (1977) 114.

[26] These notes of warning are sounded by Christian Tomuschat, especially in relation to individual claims of reparation against states for gross violations of human rights involving thousands or millions of potential claimants. See C Tomuschat,
in A Randelzhofer and C Tomuschat (eds), *State Responsibility and the Individual: Reparation in Instances of Grave Violations of Human Rights* (1999) 1.

D. Access to Justice as a Right of Aliens

Before the emergence in the second part of the twentieth century of the modern law of human rights, the question of an individual right of access to justice arose, under international law, mainly in the context of the law of state responsibility for injuries to aliens. Under this law, a person deemed to be a victim of some wrong-doing abroad could invoke the customary rules on the treatment of aliens and seek appropriate redress before the local courts or administrative organs. In the event of lack or inadequacy of local remedies, the alien could seek the protection of his or her national state, which in turn could espouse the individual's claim and resort to diplomatic protection of its national on the basis of an alleged 'denial of justice'. In this sense, access to justice was and remains a component of the complex system of guarantees to aliens recognized under the law of state responsibility for injuries to nationals of another state, and constitutes the indispensable condition for the operation of the rule of prior exhaustion of local remedies.

However, it must be observed that under this particular branch of international law the alien would enjoy a limited and qualified right of access to justice. First, such right would exist only in relation to the state in whose territory the alien has suffered the alleged injury; no right to judicial protection is guaranteed under international law in a third state, for which, in principle, the legal relationship between the alien and the defendant state would be irrelevant. Secondly, no individual right of access to justice would exist at the international level, since, once local remedies failed, diplomatic protection by the national state would 'transform' the individual claim into a state claim with the effect of almost nullifying the role of the individual in the international remedial process. This situation is well expressed in the classic case of the *Mavrommatis Palestine Concessions*, where the Permanent Court of International Justice (PCIJ) ruled that 'by taking up the case of one of its subjects and by resorting to diplomatic action or international judicial proceedings on his behalf, a State is in reality asserting its own right—its right to ensure in the person of its subjects, respect for the rules of international law'.[27] This approach, although perfectly coherent with the positivist tradition of international law as a system of rules created and applied by sovereign states, is quite unsatisfactory from the point of view of the individual who seeks access to justice. Once the original claim is transformed into a state claim, the state is free to espouse it or not, depending on considerations of political power and expediency rather than law and justice; the original injury to the individual becomes secondary to the primary damage suffered by the state and consisting in the alleged breach of international law; the compensation eventually received as a result of diplomatic interposition remains at the discretionary disposal of the state, and may never reach the individual claimant. Besides, the theory of transformation of the private claim into a governmental claim entailed that international remedies could be

---

[27] PCIJ Rep Series A No 2 (30 August 1924) 12.

maintained only as long as the beneficiary of the diplomatic protection continued to be a national of the protecting state. A change of nationality would be fatal to the claim because the protecting state would loose its *locus standi* under the classic rule of continuity of nationality.

It is not difficult to see how this approach results in a panoply of legal contradictions and in a totally unsatisfactory response to the need for the provision of effective judicial remedies to an individual who has suffered injuries abroad. It is because of these contradictions and shortcomings that, as we shall see below, alternative methods to diplomatic protection have been devised under specific treaty regimes and in contemporary international practice where individuals and private persons in general have gained direct access to international remedial processes. At the same time a reconsideration of diplomatic protection has been undertaken at a theoretical level by the International Law Commission to take into account the influence of the law of human rights on the traditional rules on the protection of aliens.[28] But before we examine these developments, it is necessary to see what the scope of the right of access to domestic justice is under the international law of aliens.

E. Access to Domestic Justice

If it is clear that the classical rules on the treatment of aliens have not, so far, guaranteed an individual right of access to international justice, with regard to domestic justice such right is an integral part of the guarantees provided by the international standard on the treatment of aliens. In the language of the law of diplomatic protection, access to justice for the alien who has suffered an injury is so fundamental that 'denial of justice' has come to define the very breach of the rights of aliens and sometimes it has been used in a broad sense as a synonym of denial of the substantive standard of fair and equitable treatment guaranteed to aliens by international law.[29] Of course, the meaning of denial of justice that is of interest to us for the purpose of the present discussion is rather the procedural one, that is the meaning which indicates the denial of the right of access to, or the lack or unavailability of, appropriate judicial or other remedies in the territorial state.

But what are the precise legal obligations of the territorial state with regard to the alien's right of access to justice? Is the territorial state simply bound to make available local machinery to adjudicate the alien's claim in accordance with local law and legal process? Or is that state obliged to guarantee aliens judicial protection

---

[28] ILC, John Dugard, 'First Report on Diplomatic Protection' (7 March 2000) UN Doc A/CN.4/506; 'Second Report' (28 February 2001) UN Doc A/CN.4/514; 'Third Report' (7 March 2002) UN Doc A/CN.4/523; 'Fourth Report', (13 March 2003) UN Doc A/CN.4/530; 'Fifth Report' (4 March 2004) UN Doc A/CN.4/538; 'Sixth Report' (11 August 2004) UN Doc A/CN.4/546; and the 2005 and 2006 reports.

[29] See, for instance, the arbitral award in the case *Robert E Brown (US v UK)* (1923) 6 RIAA 120.

of a certain quality so as to measure up to the international standard of fair and equitable treatment and of effective protection?

The former, minimalist view was typical in the past of the Latin American tradition and was inspired by the heritage of the Calvo doctrine, which was adopted in the domestic law and in the constitutions of many Latin American states in the nineteenth and twentieth centuries.[30] Its formulation can be found in several official manifestations of Latin American practice. For example, M Guerrero, the Salvadorian Rapporteur on the topic of state responsibility for the Committee of Experts for the Progressive Codification of International Law, concluded on this point: 'Denial of justice is therefore a refusal to grant foreigners free access to the courts instituted in a State for the discharge of its judicial functions, or the failure to grant free access, in a particular case, to a foreigner who seeks to defend his rights, although, in the circumstances, nationals of the State would be entitled to such access'.

This position was restated, as late as 1961, in the Report of the Inter-American Juridical Committee in the following terms:

The obligation of the State regarding judicial protection shall be considered as having been fulfilled when it places at the disposal of foreigners the national courts and the legal remedies essential for implementing their rights. The State cannot initiate diplomatic claims for the protection of its nationals nor bring an action before an international tribunal for this purpose *when the means of resorting to the competent courts of the respective State have been made available.*[31]

It is easy to see how this very formal and narrow conception of access to justice can be a mockery of the individual right to a remedy, if the opening of the courts is followed by disguised discrimination, intentional delay, or other gross deficiency in due process. Access to justice is not simply access to the courts, but availability of a system of fair and impartial justice the effectiveness and legitimacy of which may be reviewed under the international standard on the treatment of aliens. For this reason a much better definition of access to justice and of denial of justice is the one which can be found in Article 9 of the Harvard Draft on state responsibility for injuries to aliens: 'Denial of justice exists when there is a denial, unwarranted delay or obstruction of access to courts, gross deficiency in the administration of judicial or remedial process, failure to provide those guarantees which are generally considered indispensable to the proper administration of justice, or a manifestly unjust judgment. An error of a national court which does not produce manifest injustice is not a denial of justice.'[32]

---

[30] For an exhaustive analysis of these laws, see E Borchard, *Diplomatic Protection of Citizens Abroad* (1915) or, *The Law of International Claims* (1915) Part IV, ch VII.

[31] Report of the Inter-American Juridical Committee, cited in M Whitman, *Digest of International Law*, 1973, Vol VIII, 727 (emphasis added).

[32] 'The Law of Responsibility of States for Damage Done in their Territory to the Person or Property of Foreigners' Supplement: Codification of International Law (1929) 23(2) AJIL 131, 134.

This definition reflects much better the nature and function of the right of access to justice under the customary law on the treatment of aliens. It is the essence and the aim of this law to guarantee aliens a decent level of treatment by the territorial state and to ensure that in the event of an injury the affected aliens can have access to effective remedial process. The effectiveness of the remedy, however, cannot be determined solely by reference to local law and on the basis of the formal criterion that no impediment existed to the alien's access to a court or other local agency; it must be determined in the light of a standard of fair and effective administration of justice, which ultimately depends on the international norms and principles on the treatment of aliens. So, it is not enough that the territorial state opens its courts to the adjudication of aliens' claims. This state must ensure that the adjudication process respects the rule of law and provides effective remedies to the injured alien. As a minimum, the procedure and the decision of the court must not be in violation of domestic law or be in conflict with treaty obligations of the forum state or with customary international law; there must be no unconscionable delay of justice or manifest discrimination against the alien. By the same token, denial of justice would occur when the judicial process has been arbitrarily controlled by the executive or tainted by corruption.

The right of access to justice as outlined above provides guarantees for aliens in relation to claims they maintain against the territorial state or its public authorities as well as in relation to disputes with private citizens. In the latter case, it is axiomatic that access to justice is conditioned upon the existence of a valid jurisdictional title, based on a territorial, personal, or other nexus with the territorial state. However, there may be cases in which the mere invocation of a lack of jurisdiction does not absolve the territorial state from its international obligation to provide a remedy. This is particularly true when there is no alternative forum for the alien to address[33]—as in the case of a tort action against the territorial state or its public agencies, which would meet the exception of immunity in a foreign court—or where there is an unjustifiable refusal to grant protection on the basis of the strict application of local law. International practice shows that in this case the technical argument of lack of jurisdiction has not prevented the finding of denial of justice.[34]

---

[33] In this sense, see C De Visscher: 'Ce qui importe, au point de vue du droit international, c'est qu'il se trouve au moins un tribunal competent pour examiner la demande au fond. S'il ne s'en trouve aucun, la declaration d'incompétence, même rendue conformement à la legislation interne, fera apparaitre les defectuosités de l'organisation judiciaire' (op cit quoted in A Freeman, *The International Responsibility of States for Denial of Justice* (1938) 228).

[34] The case law of international tribunals on this point is vast. See, for instance, the *Ruden* case, (US v Peru) 1870, where the claimant sought damages for the burning and destruction of his property by a mob and the judicial authority refused to provide a remedy because of the government's refusal to authorize actions against the Treasury. JB Moore, *History and Digest of the International Arbitrations to Which the United States Has Been a Party* (1989) 1653 *et seq*. See also the *Johnson* case arising from the same factual situation, ibid 1656. In the *Tagliaferro* case the lack of jurisdiction had been invoked by the territorial state (Venezuela) on the ground that civil courts had no power to review the acts of the military, which in this case had

Even apart from arbitrary refusal to exercise jurisdiction, an alien seeking redress before a local tribunal may encounter financial obstacles. This is the case when access to local courts is contingent upon the payment of security for cost, the so-called *cautio indicatum solvi*. Up to the first half of the twentieth century, this condition was generally considered to be compatible with the international standard on the treatment of aliens to the extent that it aimed at defraying the costs involved in the litigation to which the alien was a party and to guarantee equality of status as between the parties, in view of the fact that aliens may not have assets in the forum to satisfy an adverse judgment.[35] In the arbitral and diplomatic practice of the same period, the requirement that the alien file a security bond was often enforced even in the presence of specific treaty provisions binding the contracting parties to grant 'free access to courts' to citizens of the other party. The arguments in support of this restrictive view were that the territorial state could not provide 'even a meritorious foreign claimant with pecuniary aid which his own government might decline to afford',[36] and the characterization of the security bond as a procedural measure which could not be considered as a limitation on the right of access to justice.[37] Despite these justifications, it is evident that the exaction of bonds or other deposits or fees for judicial costs can *de facto* nullify the alien's right of access to justice if the amount of the payment is exorbitant or in any case prohibitive for the claimant. For this reason, recent practice shows a progressive obsolescence of this requirement and the recognition of the principle of equal access to courts for aliens and nationals alike. Today, this principle has been codified in Article 14 of the United Nations Covenant on Civil and Political Rights[38] and by Article 47 of the Charter of Fundamental Rights of the European Union.[39] These, however, are

issued an order for an illegal exaction from the foreigner. Also, in this case the defence failed and the arbitral tribunal found that the refusal to grant protection amounted to a denial of justice. J Ralston and WTS Doyle, *Venezuelan Arbitrations 1903: including protocols, personnel and rules of commissions, opinions, and summary of awards, with appendix containing Venezuelan Yellow book of 1903, Bowen pamphlet entitled 'Venezuelan protocols,' and 'Preferential question' Hague decision, with history of recent Venezuelan revolutions* (Washington: GPO, 1904) 764.

[35] In this sense there are a large number of authorities in the early half of the 20th century. See, eg Strisower (1927) 1 *Annuaire de l' IDI* 477; A Verdross (1931) 37 *Recueil des Cours* 384; H Kelsen (1932) 42 *Recueil des Cours*, 251; D Anzilotti (1906) 13 *RGDIP* 23. See also the Draft Convention on the Treatment of Foreigners, Art 9, League of Nations Official Documents C 97 M 23 (1930) II, 433.

[36] This was the position taken by the US government in the *Ferrara* case, despite the free access to court clause of the US-Italy Treaty of 1871, Art XXIII. Moore (n 34 above) Vol VI, 674 *et seq*.

[37] Ibid.

[38] Art 14(1) begins with the following statement: 'All persons shall be equal before the courts and tribunals'.

[39] Art II-47 (Right to an effective remedy and to a fair trial) 'Everyone whose rights and freedoms guaranteed by the law of the Union are violated has the right to an effective remedy before a tribunal in compliance with the conditions laid down in this Article. Everyone is entitled to a fair and public hearing within a reasonable time by an independent and impartial tribunal previously established by law. Everyone shall have the possibility of being advised, defended and represented. Legal aid shall be made available to those who lack sufficient resources in so far as such aid is necessary to ensure effective

treaty provisions and cannot be taken as proof that the old principle of *cautio indi-catum solvi* has definitively disappeared. Remnants of the old practice occasionally re-emerge, especially in the law on the treatment of foreign investments. A case in point is provided by the recent *Loewen* litigation[40]concerning a Canadian investor in the United States who, as a condition for appealing and obtaining a stay of an adverse judgment in the state of Mississippi, had been required to post the exorbitant bond of over US$500 million, which the claimant had been unable to pay. It is regrettable that the subsequent claim before a NAFTA Chapter XI tribunal was dismissed for lack of *locus standi* of the claimant, without the arbitral tribunal ever reaching the merits of the case and pronouncing on the compatibility of this type of vexatious bond with the norms of public international law expressly referred to in the North American Free Trade Agreement (NAFTA).[41]

Access to justice as a right of aliens is not limited to the availability of judicial remedies of a civil or administrative nature. It also encompasses the right to see effective criminal prosecution against persons who have committed criminal acts against the alien. Therefore, the territorial state is under a duty to exercise due diligence so as to ensure that its competent organs apprehend, prosecute, and try persons who are responsible for such criminal acts and, at the same time, permit the alien to intervene in the criminal process (*action civile*) in order to obtain compen-sation for loss or damage consequent to the crime. This principle is supported by international practice, both with regard to failure to prosecute,[42] and with regard to intentional or negligent failure to execute the penalty imposed.[43] The ICJ held

---

access to justice.' See also Protocol XII to the Convention for the Protection of Human Rights and Fundamental Freedoms, adopted by the member states of the Council of Europe on 4 November 2000, which introduces the general principle of non-discrimination, and which is also applicable to the principle of access to the courts.

[40] Decision on Hearing of Respondent's Objection to Competence and Jurisdiction of 5 January 2001 (2005), 7 ICSID Reports 421. An electronic text of the decision is available at <http://www. state.gov/documents/organization/3921.pdf>.

[41] According to NAFTA, Art 1130, available at <http://www.mac.doc.gov/NAFTA/naftatext. html> (last visited on 12 April 2006): '[A] Tribunal established under this Subchapter [Art 1125] shall decide the issues in dispute in accordance with this Agreement and applicable rules of inter-national law'.

[42] See eg the *Laura MB Janes Claim*, involving the failure of the Mexican authorities to exercise reasonable diligence in apprehending and prosecuting the murderer of a US citizen in Mexico, reported in the General Claims Commission, US and Mexico, Opinions of Commissioners (1926) 108, as well as a string of mob violence cases in the US involving the killing of Chinese people in Wyoming and the lynching of Italians in New Orleans in 1891 followed with unconscionable inaction by a local authority and clear unwillingness to prosecute the persons responsible for the violent crime. Moore (n 34 above) Vol VI, ss 1025 and 1026. For the contrary view that international law does not recognize as a legally protected right of the alien 'the opportunity to see the criminal punished' but only to recover damages from the offender, see the Sohn and Baxter Draft Convention on the International Responsibility of States for Injuries to Aliens, Art 13 and explanatory note (1961) 55 AJIL, 545, 575.

[43] See the *Mallén* case, General Claims Commission, US and Mexico, Opinions of Commissioners (1927) 429.

Iran responsible for failure to provide a remedy against, and criminal prosecution of, the persons who had materially assaulted the United States Embassy in Teheran and taken the diplomatic personnel hostage.[44] In a radically different situation, the criminal prosecution of the persons responsible of the sinking of the *Rainbow Warrior* was found to be an element of the proper administration of justice, with respect to a criminal act involving the death of an innocent alien, in the arbitral award rendered by the Secretary-General of the United Nations in the dispute between New Zealand and France.[45]

If the right of access to justice includes the opportunity for the alien to see the criminal punished, *a fortiori* such right must entail a corresponding obligation on the part of the territorial state to refrain from adopting positive measures aimed at preventing or shielding the liability of persons or organs who have committed an offence against the foreigner. This is the case when the territorial state adopts an amnesty or similar measure that puts an end to the right of the alien to have judicial relief. These acts, when pre-ordained to relieve the offender of personal liability, constitute a denial of justice within the meaning of international law and entail the responsibility of the territorial state. This principle was widely accepted in the preparatory documents of the Conference on the Codification of International Law of 1930,[46] and it has been recognized in a number of arbitral awards.[47] Today, this principle is further bolstered by the emerging duty to prosecute and punish gross violations of human rights, which tend to extend the prohibition of ad hoc amnesties from the field of the treatment of aliens to the general field of citizens rights and human rights.[48]

F. Individual Access to International Remedies

If, under the customary law on the treatment of aliens, access to justice as an individual right is limited to the domestic remedies of the territorial state, a limited capacity of the individual to access international remedies has developed since the beginning of the twentieth century in relation to several specific areas of international law that deserve a brief examination.

---

[44] *Case Concerning United States Diplomatic and Consular Staff in Teheran (US v Iran)* Judgment, 24 May 1980), ICJ Rep [1980] 3.

[45] 'Ruling Pertaining to the Differences Between France and New Zealand Arising from the Rainbow Warrior Affair' (1987) 81(1) AJIL 325–8.

[46] See Conference on the Codification of International Law (The Hague, 1930) in particular, bases of Discussion Nos 15 and 20.

[47] See the *Cotesworth* and *Powell* cases involving illegal acts of a Colombian judge who was later relieved of his personal responsibility by operation of an act of amnesty. Here the responsibility of the Colombian state was based solely on the positive act of amnesty which foreclosed the exercise of the claimants' right to a judicial remedy. Moores (n 34 above) 2085. For another instance involving an amnesty issued by the President of Panama after a revolution, see the *Montijo* case, ibid 1438.

[48] See C Bakker, 'A Full Stop to Amnesty in Argentina, The *Simòn* Case' (2005) 3 JICJ 1106.

The first area concerns the early establishment of regional or sub-regional organizations endowed with a dispute-settlement machinery, open to individuals. The primary example of such organizations is the Central American Court of Justice, established in 1907 and since then considered in legal literature as the living proof of the possibility for international law to recognize the capacity of the individual to be a party in the international legal process. The Central American Court attributed such capacity to the individual only in a limited sense, ie in relation to claims against any Central American State other than the national state of the claimant. In this respect this Court is part of the development of the law in the field of the international standard on the treatment of aliens, rather than of human rights. Even within these limits, and in spite of the rather thin case law developed in the ten years of its life,[49] the Central American Court represents a remarkable contribution to the modernization of international law from a purely inter-governmental system to a legal order actionable directly by the individual. The setting aside of the requirement that the individual claim ought to be endorsed by the state of nationality or that this state must in any case support the private claim was certainly a revolutionary turn, especially in a region where the idea of sovereignty has always played a pivotal role in international relations. This early precedent also provided a model of regional legal integration that fifty years later would be followed, with more lasting and conspicuous achievement, by the European Communities and the Court of Justice which, under certain conditions, is open to claims by individuals and private parties.

Other early examples of direct access by individuals to international remedial mechanisms are provided by the International Prize Court, contemplated by the Hague Convention XII of 1907, and by the practice of the mixed arbitral tribunals established to adjudicate war compensation claims in the post-First World War treaties. While the International Prize Court is only of historical interest, because the convention establishing it was never ratified, the practice of the war compensation tribunals is of utmost importance for the object of this discussion. Article 304 of the Treaty of Versailles regulated these arbitral tribunals and gave them the competence to adjudicate a variety of claims lodged by citizens of the allied and associated powers against Germany. Such claims included those concerning war damage suffered as a consequence of 'exceptional war measures', such as requisition and other measures affecting the property of claimants, with the exclusion of damage resulting from belligerent activities,[50] and claims arising in connection with disputes over contracts concluded before the entry into force of the treaty. The first of these two categories of claim was reserved for citizens of the allied and associated powers; the second covered claims by German nationals.

---

[49] Only 5 claims were examined by the Court in the 10-year period, and only 1 was decided on the merits. M St Korowicz, 'The Problem of the International Personality of the Individual' (1956) 50 AJIL 553–62.
[50] Treaty of Versailles, Art 297, para 3.

The operation of mixed arbitral tribunals in the post-First World War treaties has contributed significantly to the development of the principle of direct access by individuals to international adjudication machinery. From a quantitative point of view, the Franco-German tribunal alone adjudicated more than 20,000 claims, even though the number was somewhat inflated as a result of France's controversial treatment of the inhabitants of Alsace-Lorraine as French citizens.[51] The very large number of individual claims and the fairly uniform system of processing make these tribunals an early model for the contemporary 'mass tort litigations' and foreshadow later systems of war reparation, such as the United Nations Compensation Commission competent for the adjudication of damage caused by Iraqi aggression against Kuwait in 1990. At the procedural level, the jurisprudence of the mixed arbitral tribunals contributed to the development of criteria to address forum shopping and litispendence, which might be caused by the concurrence of their competence with that of national commissions on war reparations,[52] as well as to the establishment of the *locus standi* of individual and of juridical persons by reference to their nationality.[53]

The importance of the experience of the mixed arbitral tribunal in promoting individual access to international justice cannot obscure some shortcomings and disadvantages of this early experience. One clear disadvantage was the very complex and costly machinery necessary to process a myriad individual claims, which were also amenable to national claims commissions. This stands in contrast to the simpler and more expeditious method adopted in the mixed claims commission established within the framework of the 1921 Berlin Peace Treaty between Germany and the United States (the latter not having ratified the Treaty of Versailles),[54] which did not allow direct individual access, but dealt with categories of claims at a state-to-state level, and managed to process more than 13,500 claims over a period of only two years (1923–25). Another undesirable result of the individual treatment of war compensation claims under the system of mixed arbitral tribunals was the fragmentation of the relative jurisprudence. This is especially evident in relation

---

[51] For these statistics and a comprehensive analysis of the constitution and practice of mixed arbitral tribunals, see A Gattini, *Le riparazioni di Guerra nel diritto internazionale* (2003) 204 *eq seq* and 627 *et seq.*

[52] The criteria applied to these issues were those of *electa una via, recursus ad alteram non datur,* meaning that the jurisdiction of the mixed tribunals was precluded once the national commission had ruled on the same question, and that the international remedy was renounced once the claimant had elected the national commission. For a detailed examination of the case law, see Gattini (n 51 above) 204 *et seq.*

[53] Since access to the mixed arbitral tribunals was limited to nationals of the allied and associated powers, claims arising from 'exceptional war measures' generated a rich jurisprudence on the question of who is a national, who has double nationality, statelessness, and continuity. See Gattini (n 51 above) 210 *et seq.*

[54] For a review of the work of these commissions, see E Borchard, 'The Opinions of the Mixed Claims Commissions, United States and Germany, Part I' (1925) 19 AJIL 133 and Part II of the article in (1926) 20 AJIL 69.

to the treatment of some general legal issues, such as the determination of nationality, the consequences of statelessness, double nationality, and the question of its continuity, with regard to which the case law of the mixed tribunals is not uniform. Also, in this respect the model of the United States-Germany mixed claim commission provides a more systematic treatment of claims, with general principles and guidelines formulated for classes of homogeneous claims and with general decisions establishing criteria for the determination of damage, the valuation of damages, and compensation. In this sense they are an important precedent, which will influence later practice, especially the rich case law of the Iran-United States Tribunal.[55]

Perhaps as a consequence of the above shortcomings, post-Second World War practice relating to war reparations shows a certain regress in the capacity of the individual to address international reparation mechanisms and a return to traditional state-to-state claims for the compensation of war-related damage. This is the case with the Conciliation Commissions established under Article 83 of the Paris Peace Treaty between Italy and the United Nations, which, in spite of their name, were true adjudicatory bodies, formed by an agent of the Italian government and an agent of the relevant United Nations claimant state, to whom, in case of disagreement, a third member would be added.[56] The competence of the Conciliation Commissions was limited to claims arising under Articles 75 and 78 of the Peace Treaty, ie claims concerning restitution and loss or damage to assets, rights, or interests of citizens of the United Nations, and did not cover disputes that might have arisen in connection with Articles 76 and 79 concerning the Italian territorial renunciations and the Italian assets located in the territory of the United Nations. In this system, the claimant state was free to decide whether or not to take up the individual claim before the competent commission and maintained the power to transact or desist regardless of the consent of the interested individual. This traditional feature of the Conciliation Commissions has raised the question of whether the individual had even lost the right of access to *national* remedies as a consequence of the setting up of the international remedy—the Conciliation Commission—or rather maintained the right of access to national courts in parallel or in alternative to the international protection available through the national state. The question has been answered in favour of the maintenance of the individual right of access to national remedies in a series of decisions by the Italian Court of Cassation[57] and on the basis of the double argument that the provisions of the Paris Peace Treaty were directly applicable and that no express provision of the Treaty excluded their direct invocability by private persons before Italian courts. This jurisprudential

---

[55] See section G below.

[56] The third member was to be appointed by agreement between the two governments or, failing such agreement, by a decision of the ambassadors of the four allied powers in Rome, or failing agreement between them, by the Secretary-General of the UN.

[57] See, in particular, Cass I, 14 January 1976, n 107, 'Ministero del Tesoro c. Soc. Mander Bros.' (1997) 3 (with note by F Francioni) IYIL (1977) 349.

orientation of Italian courts has been criticized in the literature as contrary to international practice.[58] But such criticism is misplaced; both because of the absence in the treaty of any specific intent to foreclose domestic remedies in Italy, and because such criticism refers to the power that under international law every state has to deprive its citizens of their right to a national judicial remedy,[59] while in the case law in point Italy was the defendant and not the national state of the claimant, being therefore at liberty to add its own level of judicial protection to that provided under international law. A different question is whether, as a matter of policy, in this situation Italian courts should have a more restrictive interpretation of access to justice for aliens, nationals of the victorious powers, in view of the afflictive nature of the Peace Treaty.[60]

G. Contemporary Developments

Individual access to international remedies has gained much wider recognition in the practice of the last quarter of a century. Leaving aside the human rights aspect of this phenomenon—which will be examined in Part II below—this is especially true in the field of international economic law. Here we can witness the worldwide acceptance of the World Bank Convention establishing the International Centre for the Settlement of Investment Disputes (ICSID), whose jurisdiction now extends also to non-parties under specific arrangements such as the Additional Facility and the NAFTA Chapter 11 investment protection, and the establishment in the early 1990s of the World Bank Inspection Panel, which, although it is not an adjudicatory organ, is capable of providing a flexible *sui generis* mechanism to take into account private interests and the social impact of the Bank's financing projects.

Besides these World Bank institutions, the direct access of individuals and corporations to international mechanisms of dispute settlement is ensured today through the widespread use of international arbitration. The leading institutions in this field have been the International Court of Arbitration in the Hague and the International Chamber of Commerce in Paris, which offer the advantage of institutionally supervised dispute settlement, with the possibility of operating under a uniform set of arbitration rules such as those developed by the United Nations Commission on International Trade Law (UNCITRAL), and with the further advantage that the relative awards may be enforced in a very large number of states

---

[58] See Gattini (n 51 above) 354.

[59] This was the case with the executive orders implementing the Algiers accords in the US after the settlement of the Hostage crisis in 1981. So, in *Dames and More v Regan*, the Supreme Court of the US affirmed the legitimacy of the discontinuance of legal suits and of the presentation of new suits against Iran in US courts because of the removal of such disputes to the arbitral forum created by the establishment of the Iran-US Tribunal. Dames *and* Moore v *Regan*. Judgment of 2 July 1981, 453 US 654 (1981).

[60] In this sense, see Francioni (n 57 above).

under the 1958 New York Convention.[61] Another prominent form of 'institutional-ized' arbitration is the Iran-United States Tribunal, established under the Algiers Accords and competent to adjudicate private claims arising from the events that led to the Iran revolution.[62] In its nearly twenty-five years of operation, the Iran-United States Tribunal has produced a monumental jurisprudence with a significant impact on the development of principles and criteria on the right of individuals and corporations to international justice. In its case law and in its general decisions on points of interpretation of the applicable law, the Tribunal has ruled on important issues such as the *locus standi* of corporations, for the purpose of which, ownership by the claimant of 49.8 per cent of the shares of an entity has been held sufficient to meet the test of nationality.[63] Claims by double nationals, which were rejected under the traditional approach, have been declared admissible on the basis of the criterion of 'dominant and effective nationality'.[64] Similarly, a more favourable and innovative attitude towards effective access to justice for claimants has been shown in respect of pro rata judicial protection of claimants who are owners in non-stock companies, such as partnerships, even when the other partners lack *locus standi* or have decided not to present a claim.[65]

Another innovative model of international processing of private claims is the United Nations Compensation Commission established, together with a Compensation Fund, by Security Council Resolution 692.[66] Although initially the Commission was unable to perform its function because of the obstruction of the Iraqi government in the sale of oil—a percentage of whose proceeds was supposed to feed the Compensation Fund—with the launching of the 'oil for food' programme and the

---

[61] 330 UNTS 38. For commentary, see AJ Van der Berg, *The New York Arbitration Convention of 1958* (1981); A Giardina, 'L'arbitrato internazionale' (1992) *Rivista dell'arbitrato* 21.

[62] This Tribunal consists of 9 judges, of whom 3 are chosen by the US, 3 by Iran, and the other 3 by agreement among the 6 members thus appointed. Failing such agreement, the Secretary-General of the International Court of Arbitration in The Hague has the power to designate an 'appointing authority', which he did on several occasions by designating the President of the Supreme Court of the Netherlands as the authority to fill the disputed posts. The Tribunal operates under UNCITRAL rules and its awards can be satisfied by a Fund established at the Central Bank of the Netherlands and can be enforced in the courts of any state in accordance the domestic law of that state.

[63] *Sedco, Inc v National Iranian Oil Co* 1987, II, 15 Iran-US Claims Tribunal Reports, 23.

[64] *N Esphahanian v Bank Tejarat* 1991, 27 Iran-US Claims Tribunal Reports, 196, referring to the well-known precedents of the *Nottebohm* and *Mergé* cases.

[65] *Housing and Urban Services International, Inc v Islamic Republic of Iran* 22 November 1985, 9 Iran-US Claims Tribunal Reports, 313. Here the Tribunal concluded that 'while international law seems to accept that as a rule a partner may not sue in his own name alone on a cause of action accruing to the partnership, where special reasons or circumstances required it, international tribunals have had little difficulty in disaggregating the interests of partners and in permitting partners to recover their *pro rata* share of partnership claims.'

[66] The Resolution was adopted on 20 May 1991 in order to provide a compensation mechanism for the victims of the Iraqi war.

subsequent elimination of quantitative restrictions on oil sales[67] it was possible to replenish the Fund and proceed with the adjudication and liquidation of claims. Although the Commission is not a judicial or arbitral body in a technical sense,[68] it nevertheless adjudicates claims on the basis of legal rules, the relevant normative acts of the Security Council, and of recognized principles of international law.[69] The most innovative aspect of the Commission is the combination of the modern idea that individual claims remain such at the international level, without the need for their 'transformation' into state claims, and the recognition that for reasons of expediency and cost such claims are to be collected and presented by governments which, by doing so, perform the function of 'agents' of the private claimants. The situation is reversed, as compared to the diplomatic protection model, where the state asserted its own right and the individual was only the indirect beneficiary of that protection.

Besides this conceptual *revirement*, the work of the Compensation Commission has introduced several innovative methods that expand the ambit of individual access to international justice. One such innovation is the opening of the compensation process to individuals and groups who could not rely on a national state to present their claims. This has been to the benefit of many Palestinians, refugees, and displaced persons without a reliable link of nationality. In these cases the relative claims have been processed by the Executive Secretary of the United Nations Compensation Commission in cooperation with the High Commissioner on Refugees, other United Nations agencies, and the International Committee of the Red Cross (ICRC). Flexible rules have also been introduced with respect to the possibility for a state to submit claims on behalf of persons resident in its territory, who may have the nationality of another state,[70] or for private persons to submit their claims directly when they are not able to secure a governmental endorsement.[71] Most radically, the traditional restrictive criteria on access to justice established in the *Barcelona Traction*[72] case have been set aside by Decision 123 of the Governing Council,[73] which permits the lifting of the corporate veil to extend protection to individuals who had an interest in companies in which, because of domestic

---

[67] SC Res 1284 (1999) UN Doc S/RES/1284. For a comprehensive study on the origin and development of the UN Compensation Commission, see M Frigessi di Rattalma, *Nazioni Unite e Danni Derivanti dalla Guerra del Golfo* (1995) and, by the same author, 'Le regime de responsabilité internationale institué par le Conseil d'Administration de la Commission de Compensation des Nations Unies' (1997), 101 *RGDIP* 45.

[68] See the Secretary-General of the United Nations Report to the Security Council of 2 May 1991, which states: 'The Commission is not a court or an arbitral tribunal . . . it is a political organ that performs an essentially fact finding function of examining claims, verifying their validity, evaluating losses, assessing payments and resolving disputed claims.'

[69] The Compensation Commission Rules, Art 31.

[70] UN Compensation Commission, Provisional Rules for Claims Procedure, 1992, Art 5(1)(a).

[71] ibid Arts 5(2) and 5(3) concerning corporations.

[72] ICJ Reports 1970.

[73] Decision S/AC, 26/Dec 123 (2001), 15 March 2001.

nationality requirements, they could not appear as owners. In this situation, a creative system of 'bilateral committees', involving the national state of the relevant corporations and the government or entity filing claims on behalf of individuals, has been set up with the competence to determine the respective rights and payments.[74] The Commission's working methods are remarkable also for having transplanted, at the international level, the experience gained in domestic mass tort litigations. Claims falling within the jurisdiction of the Commission have been classified in six different categories in order to rationalize and expedite the processing of an enormous workload. Categories A, B, and C relate to claims of natural persons having been characterized as urgent. They concern (A) persons forced to quit Iraq or Kuwait as a consequence of the Iraqi aggression in the period from 2 August 1990 to 2 March 1991; (B) physical or moral damage suffered by natural persons in Iraq and Kuwait in the same period; and (C) damage below the threshold of US$100,000.[75] Categories D, E and F concern respectively claims of natural persons exceeding the limits of the first three categories of urgent claims and, in any event, the sum of US$100,000, corporate claims, and governmental claims, including claims by inter-governmental organizations.

By 2005, more than 2.5 million claims had been processed for a total value exceeding US$37 billion. Claims have continued to be processed following the United States-led invasion and occupation of Iraq and most outstanding claims are those submitted by governments, which include claims for damage to natural resources and to the environment.[76]

Perhaps, the most important contribution of the United Nations Compensation Commission to the development of international law[77] can be seen in the recognition of the interest of the international community as a whole in ensuring that one of the consequences of a war of aggression must be the establishment of a mechanism of redress for victims of the conflict. In this sense, the multilateral character

---

[74] See UN Compensation Commission Guidelines for the Work of Bilateral Committees to be formed to Resolve Certain Issues Involving the State of Kuwait and Other States Relating to Overlapping Claims and Stand Alone Claims at the UN Compensation Commission, Decision 123 (n 73 above) Annex I.

[75] Decision of Administrative Council, note 1 *Criteria for Expedited Processing of Urgent Claims* (1991) 30 ILM 1712. The latter category, C, was later subdivided into 8 categories of different types of damage, including personal injury, loss and damage to property, *lucrum cessans* (lost income) and moral damage (mental pain and anguish).

[76] For an important decision on category F claims, see the Panel Report on F 4 Claims of 30 June 2005, Security Council, UNCC, S/AC 26/2005/10. On the issue of compensation for environmental damage, see M Aznar-Gomez, 'Environmental Damage and the 1991 Gulf War: Some Yardsticks Before the UNCC' (2001) 14 LJIL 301.

[77] In literature there are authors who tend to dismiss the idea of such contribution and characterize the Commission as another example of the old system of 'victors' justice'. Bederman, 'The UN Commission and the Tradition of International Claims Settlements' (1994), 27 NYU JILP 1. For a critical view of procedural justice before the Commission, see M Schneider, 'How Fair and Efficient is the UN Compensation System?' (1998) 15 JIA 15.

of the mechanism established by the Compensation Commission stands in sharp contrast to the bilateral nature of the precedents examined in the preceding sections, especially the mixed arbitral tribunals and the conciliation commissions that followed the two World Wars. At the same time, it is a sober reminder that in other contemporary conflicts victims of armed violence have not found (and still do not find) similar mechanisms of redress. This is true for the Balkan conflict, in which the United Nations was more interested in establishing a mechanism of criminal justice to prosecute and try the authors of atrocities,[78] as well as in the current genocidal violence in Darfur.[79]

H. Claims Against the National State of the Individual: From Aliens' Rights to Human Rights

The practice examined so far concerns instances of individual access to justice where the claimant has a nationality different from that of the respondent state. The more radical step of setting up international remedies open to individuals for the adjudication of claims against their own national state is an integral part of the development of the international law of human rights. As such, it will form the object of our examination in part II of this study. However, it is useful, at this point, to clarify that a limited opportunity for individuals to present claims against their national state in an international forum had already emerged before the contemporary law of human rights. Two important precedents are worth signalling. The first concerns the period after the First World War in Central Europe. With the German-Polish Convention on Upper-Silesia, claims

---

[78] As is known, the establishment of the International Criminal Tribunal for Yugoslavia (ICTY) by SCRe 827 of 25 May 1993 did not provide a fund or other mechanism for the compensation of victims of those 'serious violations of humanitarian law', which the Tribunal was supposed to prosecute. Only in the Rules of Procedure and Evidence, Rule 106(B), is the possibility contemplated that the accused found guilty may be sued for damages by the victim, but only in a national court and pursuant to national law. In the ICC Statute some progress has been made in this respect, since Art 75(2) provides that the Court may 'make an order directly against a convicted person specifying appropriate reparation to, or in respect of, victims, including restitution, compensation and rehabilitation'. Rome Statute of the International Criminal Court, 17 July 1998, in (1998) 37 ILM 1002. Unfortunately, even those attempts made by victims of belligerent violence, which prima facie revealed a violation of humanitarian law, have been met with a denial of remedies in domestic law, because of the doctrine of non-justiciability of war operations (see *Marković v Croatia (friendly settlement)*) No 4469/02 (Sect 1) (Eng)—(21 October 2004) and at the international level, before the European Court of Human Rights, because of the alleged extra-territoriality of the *locus commissi delicti*. See *Banković and Ors v Belgium and 16 Other Contracting States* (dec) [GC], No 52207/99, ECHR 2001-XII—(12 December 2001).

[79] A reference to the need for a system of compensation of victims of violence in this region can be found in the Report prepared by A Cassese as Special UN Rapporteur: Report of the International Commission of Inquiry on Darfur to the United Nations Secretary-General, Pursuant to Security Council Resolution 1564 of 18 September 2005, 25 January 2005.

by individuals against the state were permitted under Article 5 for the protection of acquired rights and without distinction based on the nationality of the plaintiff, and under Articles 148 to 152 similar claims were permitted by members of a minority before an ad hoc Mixed Commission.[80] The second early example is the system of minority protection under the League of Nations and ad hoc conventions adopted in the aftermath of the First World War. This system did not involve a full right of individuals to participate in international proceedings, but simply a right to make petitions to the national Minorities Offices, which in turn could trigger a procedure before the Mixed Commission on minorities, and eventually an appeal before the Council of the League of Nations. Despite this limited role of individuals, their capacity to assert rights under the relevant treaties was recognized by the Permanent Court of International Justice in the case concerning the *Jurisdiction of the Courts of Danzig*[81] and, most importantly, paved the way towards the later conceptualization of the right to an effective remedy under international human rights law, as we shall see in the next part of this chapter.

II. ACCESS TO JUSTICE AS A HUMAN RIGHT

A. Introduction

In this part of the chapter the focus will be on whether access to justice has developed into a 'human right' and, if so, what may be the foundation and scope of the corresponding legal obligations in international law, and what mechanisms— national and international—can actually guarantee its enforcement.

In undertaking this task it is necessary, first, to clarify what is meant by the term 'human rights' in the context of customary international law and, then, to see in the light of international practice what is the place of access to justice within the framework of internationally recognized human rights.

At the outset, it is worth noting that the term 'access to justice' is not used as such in the language of most international human rights instruments. The Universal Declaration[82] and the ECHR,[83] for example, speak of 'effective remedy', while the American Convention uses the terms 'prompt recourse' and 'effective recourse'.[84] The Covenant on Civil and Political Rights uses different expressions

---

[80] Geneva Convention on Upper-Silesia, 1922. For the application of Art 5, see the decision of 30 March 1929 in *Steiner and Gross v Poland*, discussed in M St Korowicz, 'International Personality', (n 49 above) 554.

[81] PCIJ Advisory Opinion Series B No 15, 17–21.

[82] Universal Declaration of Human Rights, Art 8.

[83] ECHR Art 13.

[84] Art 25, entitled 'Right to Judicial Protection', American Convention on Human Rights, adopted in San Jose de Costa Rica, 22 November 1969, 1144 UNTS 123.

in different provisions: 'effective remedy';[85] the right 'to take proceedings before a court';[86] and 'to a fair and public hearing'.[87] The Optional Protocol to the Covenant is more descriptive and speaks simply of the individual right to 'submit a written communication to the Committee.'[88] Given this terminological variance, it is not always clear whether reference is made to the right to bring a claim before a competent court, or rather to the right to have a measure or remedy provided in connection with an injury suffered by the claimant. The latter interpretation goes well beyond the mere right of access to justice and implies the right to obtain reparation in one form or another as a consequence of a certain harm suffered in connection with the violation of a right or a legally protected interest. Another question is whether access to justice is an individual right in itself, or is an instrumental guarantee that depends upon the substantive right which is to be vindicated. I shall examine these various questions in the light of judicial practice in the sections below. But, first, a few words are necessary to clarify the meaning of the term 'human rights' for the purpose of the present discussion.

B. The Meaning of 'Human Rights'

In legal language, the term 'human rights' is fairly recent. It dates back to the United Nations Charter and to the development of the concept of inherent 'human dignity' and fundamental rights as universal values entailing international obligations of respect and protection on the part of every state. Before the United Nations, the expression used in constitutional documents and in the writings of legal and political theorists was 'the rights of man' and the 'rights of citizen',[89] or the more expansive expression of 'imprescriptible'[90] and 'unalienable' rights. What was common in this varying terminology was the natural law idea that certain rights pertain to all individuals as human beings, by virtue of their being born free and equal and before they are vested with formal 'legal' rights by the state where they live. As we know, this idea was not born free of contradictions. In the glorious documents of the American revolution, such as the Declaration of Independence of 4 July 1776 and the Bill of Rights attached to the United States Constitution of 1787, the notion of 'human beings' did not include the vast number of black people who had been brought as slaves from Africa; equality was denied to entire

---

[85] International Convenant on Civil and Political Rights, Art2.
[86] ibid Article 9(4).
[87] ibid Article 14(1).
[88] Optional Protocol to the International Covenant on Civil and Political Rights, 1966, Art 2. The Protocol entered into force on 23 March 1976.
[89] See the French *Déclaration des droits de l'homme et du citoyen* of 26 August 1779, which identified such rights as 'Liberty, Property, Safety and Resistance to Oppression'.
[90] Where it is declared that 'the aim of every political association is the preservation of the natural and imprescriptible rights of man' (ibid).

classes of citizens on the basis of race or ethnic origin;[91] in Europe, and other parts of the world, more than half of the human society of the time, that constituted by women, continued to be largely excluded from the 'natural' endowment of the 'rights of man'. Even at a theoretical level, the natural law idea of the 'rights of man' was not free of contradictions and criticism. Fearful that this idea could become the recipe for social disorder and anarchic assertion of individual claims, eighteenth-century conservative philosophers, and even secular progressive thinkers such as Jeremy Bentham, attacked the very foundation of human rights and criticized their enunciation in the French Declaration of 1789,[92] and in the American Declaration of Independence.[93] Opposition to the idea of human rights as natural rights was bound to further harden with the rise of legal positivism in the nineteenth century and the beginning of the twentieth century. The triumph of statalism, on the one hand,[94] and the parallel turning of international legal positivism into 'voluntarism',[95] on the other, left very little margin for the conceptualization of individual rights outside and independently of the strict ambit of state law.

In spite of this historical oscillation and opposition, the idea of human rights as individual claims based on the state of nature, provided a powerful political and moral tool to erode and eventually bring to an end the notion of the divine right of kings; it supported the process of secularization of human society,[96] especially through the supplanting of the religious idea of human 'destiny', with the modern concept of 'progress' as the product of human labour and reason, and with the secular hope in the unlimited perfectibility of the human condition. This process had its very early manifestations in the seminal work of the Italian jurist Cesare

[91] See *The Chinese Exclusion Case* 130 US 581, 32 L Ed 1068, 9 S Ct 623 (US Sup Ct, 1889); *Fujii v California* 217 P 2d 481, 218 P 2d 595 (Cal CA, 1950), 38 Cal 2d 718, 242 P 2d 617 (Cal Sup Ct, 1952).

[92] E Burke, *Reflections on the Revolution in France* (1790), where he characterizes the proclamation of the rights of man as a 'monstrous fiction' of human equality, which, in his colourful and scornful opinion, could only inspire 'false ideas and vain expectations in men destined to travel in the obscure walk of laborious life'. As cited in B Weston, 'Human Rights' *New Encyclopaedia Britannica* (15th edn, (1992), Vol 20, 652.

[93] The scientific approach developed by Bentham to the organization of the human society, based on the search for the maximum utility for the largest number of peoples, led him to dismiss the theory of natural rights in no less scornful terms as 'imaginary rights . . . Natural rights is simple nonsense; natural and imprescriptible rights (an American phrase), rhetorical nonsense, nonsense upon stilts' (ibid).

[94] The expression 'statalism' is used to indicate the theory of law as the command of the sovereign independently of considerations of justice and human dignity. John Austin was a prominent representative of this view, J Austin, *The Province of Jurisprudence Determined* (1832).

[95] With this expression we indicate the doctrine that conceives international law as a system of norms and obligations 'voluntarily' accepted by states in the exercise of their sovereignty and, therefore, not permitting any source of the law outside and above their will.

[96] For a masterful account of the interaction between the process of secularization and the development of a pluralistic society where toleration and individual rights flourish, see O Chadwick, *The Secularisation of the European Mind in the Nineteenth Century* (1975).

Beccaria, *Dei delitti e delle pene*,[97] a treatise which introduced a preventive, rather than repressive, approach to criminal punishment and which resulted in unprecedented criminal reform in Europe and in the abolition of torture and the death penalty in eighteenth-century Tuscany.[98] In the eighteenth century, the predominance of positivism in the general theory of state and law did not prevent the enduring and pervasive effect of the idea of human rights in a variety of forms. It is sufficient to recall here the gradual abolition of slavery, the rise of the women's rights movement and the introduction of universal suffrage, and the early development of social and workers' rights that, in the first part of the twentieth century, would lead to the establishment of the International Labour Organization (ILO) and to the gradual development of the rights of minorities. The legacy of this early impulse to the development of human rights was to emerge with all its importance in 1945 with the United Nations Charter and its affirmation of the 'faith in fundamental human rights, in the dignity and worth of the human person, in the equal rights of men and women...' . The proclamation of human rights at the international level provided for the first time the legal basis for challenging abusive governments, not only upon the abstract 'natural' right of resistance and rebellion against oppressive rulers, as in the French Declaration, but as the basis of positive international standards binding upon all states with regard to the treatment of all people subject to their jurisdiction and under their control. It is the linking of the original idea of natural rights to the nascent international law principle that decent treatment of human beings is a precondition of peace and of a just world order that transforms the purely metaphysical and moral notion of human rights into the positive international law of human rights.

Of course, even after the constitutional moment of the adoption of the United Nations Charter, the meaning, content, and scope of human rights has remained controversial and today we continue to debate whether there can be a universal approach to human rights, whether they depend upon the specific culture and environment to which the affected individuals belong, and whether human rights are individual or collective. Obviously, it would be impossible to address all these theoretical problems within the limits of the present chapter. What is important for the purpose of our discussion is the recognition of the empirical evidence showing that in the sixty years after the adoption of the United Nations Charter, a worldwide system of international protection of human rights has emerged.

---

[97] Published in Livorno, July 1774.

[98] See the *Riforma penale Leopoldina*, in the name of Pietro Leopoldo, Grand Duke of Tuscany, adopted and published in Florence on 30 November 1786, now reprinted with critical text and original translation of the Law into French, German, English, and Latin, in D Zuliani, *La riforma penale di Pietro Leopoldo*, 2 Vols, (1955). An echo of Cesare Beccaria's work can be found also in the Austrian General Code of Crime and Punishment, published in 1797, whose original Italian text is now reprinted in *Codice general Austriaco dei Delitti e delle Pene (1797)* (2005). cf F Venturi, Settecento *Riformatore*, (1990), Vol IV, 757.

After the proclamation of the 1948 Universal Declaration,[99] the content of international human rights has been constantly clarified and precisely defined by ad hoc treaties,[100] the two United Nations Covenants,[101] soft law,[102] customary international law,[103] and a variety of regional instruments, prominent among which are the American and the European conventions on human rights. From the early United Nations Charter conception as a source of international obligations that states owe to one another, human rights have evolved into a source of international obligations that states owe directly to individuals, and sometimes individuals owe to one another, as in the case of grave breaches of human rights that give rise to individual criminal responsibility. More important for the purposes of this chapter is the fact that the network of international instruments for the protection of human rights contain mechanisms of international supervision and implementation, sometimes going as far as to provide direct access to the affected individuals.[104] It would be foolish, today, to dismiss the idea that there is an international standard of human rights protection, which at the same time constitutes a parameter of legitimacy for the action of public authorities and the legal basis of the individual entitlement to be

---

[99] Universal Declaration of Human Rights, GA Res 217 A (III), UN Doc A/810 (1948) 71.

[100] From the early adoption of the 1965 Convention on the Elimination of All Forms of Racial Discrimination (660 UNTS 195), countless treaties have been adopted for the protection of specific categories of human rights, including women's rights (see, in particular, the 1979 Convention on the Elimination of All Forms of Discrimination against Women, GA Res 34/180, 34 UN GAOR Supp (No 46), 193).

[101] 1966 International Covenant on Civil and Political Rights (999 UNTS 171), and 1966 International Covenant on Economic Social and Cultural Rights (993 UNTS 3).

[102] See eg the many declarations adopted by the UN General Assembly on Torture (see, *inter alia*, the Declaration on the Protection of All Persons from Being Subjected to Torture and Other Cruel, Inhuman or Degrading Treatment or Punishment, GA Res 3452 (XXX) of 9 December 1975), as well as the 1993 Vienna Declaration and Programme of Action of the World Conference on Human Rights, Vienna 14–25 June 1993, UN Doc A/CONF.157/23 of 12 July 1993.

[103] It is now generally accepted that customary international law prohibits certain grave violations of human rights by states, such as genocide, torture, slavery, racial discrimination, and the gross and systematic deprivation of the rights and liberty of their citizens. This general obligation has been recognized by the ICJ in the famous dictum of the *Barcelona Traction* judgment ((1970) ICJ Rep 32, para 33) and more recently in the Advisory Opinion of 9 July 2004 on the *Legal Consequences of the Construction of a Wall in the Occupied Palestinian Territory* (2004). ICJ Rep. On the customary law nature of international human rights, see B Simma, 'International Human Rights and General International Law: A Comparative Analysis' in *Collected Courses of the Academy of European Law*, 4 (1993) 153 *et seq*. On the interplay between custom and treaty in human rights adjudication, see F Francioni, 'Customary International Law and the European Convention on Human Rights' (1999) IX IYIL 11. More generally, see American Law Institute, *Restatement of the Law, Third, the International Relations Law of the United States* (1987) Vol 2, section 702, p 161 with comment and Reporter's note.

[104] This is the case, eg, of the Human Rights Committee, established by the 1966 International Covenant on Civil and Political Rights (n 88 above) Art 28. The first Optional Protocol to the Covenant (Optional Protocol to the International Covenant on Civil and Political Rights, GA Res 2200 A (XXI) of 16 December 1966) allows individuals to submit complaints to the Committee.

treated fairly by the state and other actors. This standard exists in positive law, notwithstanding the occasional protestations of some states which want to shield their own violation of human rights from appropriate international review. The continuing vitality of this standard for peace, security, and justice has also been recognized in the context of the current process of United Nations reform. One of the priorities set forth at the September 2005 Summit, was the establishment of a more effective system of human rights monitoring, including the creation of a new Human Rights Council, which was established in 2006 in order to replace the often criticized and discredited Human Rights Commission.[105] The current reform process has led to the formal recognition of the 'responsibility to protect' which would entail the duty to make an active response, including, when necessary, military action,[106] in order to protect the lives of innocent people who are victims of atrocities, such as those being perpetrated now in Darfur.[107]

In the light of more than half a century of international law development in this area, our conclusion is that the meaning of the term 'human rights' for the purpose of this study is to be determined, not in relation to abstract concepts of natural law, but in relation to positive law and more specifically in the light of the complex web of multilateral treaties, of the United Nations' role in consolidating it, of soft law and customary rules that have created a system of international obligations binding upon states in their mutual relations, towards the international community as a whole, and, sometimes, directly upon individuals and private entities. This treaty practice, the jurisprudential development produced by human rights treaty bodies, and the customary law development of the notion of gross violations of human rights as breaches of *erga omnes* obligations under general international law, constitutes the positive law foundation of universal human rights. The universality of the standard is compatible with a broad margin of cultural adaptation in different national legal systems and traditions and does not entail that human rights are understood and implemented in the same way in different parts of the world. What it means is that today the action of the state, and even of other actors,[108]

---

[105] GA Res 60/251, adopted 15 March 2006 with 170 votes in favour, 4 against (US, Israel, the Marshal Islands, and Palau) and three abstentions (Belarus, Iran, and Venezuela).

[106] For a discussion on the impact of human rights on the general prohibition of the use of force, see F Francioni, 'Balancing the Prohibition of Force with the Need to Protect Human Rights: a Methodological Approach' in E Cannizzaro and P Palchetti (eds), *Customary International Law on the Use of force: a methodological Approach* (2005) 269.

[107] See the Outcome Document of the 2005 World Summit, Doc A/RES/60/1 of 24 October 2005 (particularly paras 138 *et seq*); for a comprehensive review of the reform process, see the 'Report on the Conference on the EU, the US and the Reform of the UN Charter', Florence, October 2005, EUI Working Paper, available at <http://www.iue.it/AEL/pdfs/ReformUNCharter.pdf> (last visited on 12 April 2006).

[108] By 'other actors' is meant, in particular, international organizations and business corporations operating at a transnational level. For the former, see the ILC work on the responsibility of international organizations (see, in particular, the 4 reports prepared by the Special Rapporteur Giorgio Gaja to date (26 March 2003) UN Docs A/CN.4/532; (2 April 2004) A/CN.4/541; A/CN.4/553;

can be reviewed in terms of a minimum standard of fair treatment and respect for human dignity, which is the only universally shared standard for the determination of the legitimacy of governmental authority and its exercise of power.

It is against this background that we must understand the meaning of the term human rights; and it is in this context that the question arises of whether the international human rights 'standards' today include also the right of access to justice and the corresponding obligation of states or other empowered institutions to provide justice, in civil and criminal matters, in accordance with international norms of fairness and due process.

C. A Free Standing Right or Procedural Guarantee?

Having clarified the meaning of the expression 'human rights' for the purpose of our discussion, it is now necessary to address the question of whether in the context of human rights law access to justice is a self-standing individual right or, rather, a procedural guarantee that exists only to the extent that there is a substantive right to enforce. This question is relevant not only from a theoretical point of view, but also for practical reasons, since not all human rights are enforceable through judicial means. A fundamental distinction has been made between the classic civil rights and freedoms, which impose 'negative' obligations upon states, and the economic social and cultural rights, which entail 'positive' obligations progressively to implement such rights at a policy, not a judicial, level. This distinction was at the basis of the adoption in 1966 of the two distinct United Nations Covenants, one on civil and political rights, and one on social, economic, and cultural rights. Today it remains relevant because of the inescapable reality that the first category of rights can be fully realized through good governance and non-interference in spheres of human liberty, the second category cannot be meaningfully fulfilled in the absence of resources. As a matter of fact the 'effective remedy' provision of the Covenant on Civil and Political Rights cannot be found in the Covenant on Economic, Social and Cultural Rights and many of its provisions are drafted in the soft language of the progressive implementation of the relative rights. However, this does not mean that in this category of rights a demand for judicial protection may never be admissible. If a state intentionally or negligently obstructs the fulfilment of the rights guaranteed in the covenant—for instance the satisfaction of the right to food—non-compliance mechanisms and remedial processes are necessary. This is the reason why after the adoption of the Covenant on Economic, Social and Cultural Rights a Committee was established, on the model of the Human Rights Committee, but without a corresponding optional protocol, in order to ensure a

and (28 February 2006); A/CN.4/564 . For the latter, see the document adopted in 2003 by the UN Sub-Commission for the protection and promotion of human rights, 'Norms on the Responsibilities of Transnational Corporations and Other Business Enterprises With Regard to Human Rights' (26 August 2003) UN Doc E/CN.4/Sub.2/2003/12 rev 2.

systematic monitoring of state parties' compliance with relative obligations.[109] The Committee on economic and social rights does not receive individual complaints and it is difficult to maintain that a full right of access to justice has developed in its practice. Nevertheless, an important contribution has been made by this Committee, especially in its General Comment 3,[110] to the clarification of those economic and social rights the violation of which requires an effective remedy *in domestic law*. Prominent among such rights are those relating to the equal treatment of men and women,[111] equal pay for equal work,[112] freedom of trade association,[113] protection of working mothers during and after childbirth,[114] the right to education, and freedom of scientific research and creative activity.[115] These rights are closely related to fundamental freedoms and there is no reason for an *a priori* exclusion of their justiciability simply because they are classified as economic, social, or cultural rights.

If a rigid, *a priori* distinction between categories of rights is not justifiable today for the purpose of ascertaining the legal basis and scope of access to justice, it is clear nevertheless that not every legal interest and individual claim can give rise to an individual right of access to justice. A brief look at the relevant provisions in human rights treaties confirms this view.

The Universal Declaration is quite explicit in this respect in so far as its Article 8 recognizes an individual's right to an effective remedy only in relation to 'acts violating the fundamental rights granted him by the constitution and by law'. This language is rather unfortunate since it unwittingly shifts the human right standard from the international level, to which the Declaration belongs, to the national level of the respondent state, which may fall short of such standard. This shortcoming is avoided in the ECHR whose 'effective remedy' provision of Article 13 covers the 'rights and freedoms as set forth in this Convention'. However, in its original 1950 text the ECHR covered only a limited catalogue of human rights. This catalogue has been expanded through the adoption of additional protocols that now cover

---

[109] The Committee on Economic Social and Cultural Rights was established by the Economic and Social Council with Res 1985/17 of 28 May 1985. Later on, in 1994, a proposal to adopt a Protocol to the Covenant on Economic, Social and Cultural Rights, based on the example of the first Protocol to the Covenant on Civil and Political Rights (n 104 above) was advanced by the Chairman, Philip Alston, at the 11th Session of the Committee (see 'Draft Optional Protocol Providing for the Consideration of Communications' (9 November 1994) UN Doc E/C.12/1994/12, but such instrument was never adopted. See eg P Alston and J Crawford (eds), *The Future of UN Human Rights Treaty Monitoring*, (2000).

[110] UN Doc E/1991/23, Annex III.

[111] Covenant on Economic, Social and Cultural Rights, Art 3: 'The State Parties to the present Covenant undertake to ensure the equal right of men and women to the enjoyment of all economic, social and cultural rights set forth in the present Covenant'.

[112] ibid Art 7(a)(i).

[113] ibid Art 8 (concerning trade unions).

[114] ibid Art 10(2).

[115] ibid Art 15(3).

many more rights, including property, the right to participate in free elections, the rights of aliens, and the right to enjoy freedom from discrimination, among others. Yet, economic, social, and cultural rights are still largely outside the scope of the Convention. Besides, the language of Article 13 does not allow the judicial protection of human rights which may be guaranteed under customary international law but not under the Convention.

The Charter of rights of the European Union also contains a specific provision, Article 47, which recognizes the right to an effective remedy and to an impartial court. However, it is consistent with the nature of the Charter as an instrument binding upon the European Union, rather than as a general bill of rights, that this Article creates a right of access to justice only for the situations where the rights and freedoms guaranteed in the Charter have been violated by the European Union's institutions.

A similar but weaker provision can be found in the Covenant on Civil and Political Rights, which requires that every state party 'undertakes'... [t]o ensure that any person whose rights and freedoms herein recognized are violated shall have an effective remedy'.

Interestingly, a broader basis for access to justice characterizes the American Convention on Human Rights. Article 8 of this Convention provides for the right of every person to 'a hearing... by a competent, independent and impartial tribunal' not only for the determination of criminal charges, but also concerning 'rights and obligations of a civil, labor, fiscal, or any other nature'. Moreover, Article 25 extends judicial protection to the fundamental rights recognized by the constitution or laws of the state concerned, besides those recognized by the Convention.

By contrast, no specific provision on access to justice or effective remedy can be found in the African Charter on Human and Peoples' Rights,[116] which simply contemplates a general principle of equal protection (Article 3) and every individual's 'right to have his cause heard' (Article 7), but only in relation to acts violating his fundamental rights, without further specification.

This brief survey of international instruments of general application points to the conclusion that, although access to justice surely constitutes in itself an important interest worthy of legal protection, in the texts of human rights treaties it is rather construed as a procedural guarantee dependant on other substantive rights and freedoms, which are protected by the same treaty and sometimes by *renvoi* to the constitution and the law of state parties. This being the case at a purely normative level, one must recognize that in international judicial practice the picture is less clear cut. Here, the distinction between the cause of action, which must necessarily derive from the substantive legal interest invoked by the claimant, and the right of access to justice often becomes blurred. This happens especially when there is an unreasonable interference with the ability of the claimant to have access to courts, independently of the nature of the right for which judicial protection is sought. By

---

[116] African Charter on Human and Peoples' Rights, 1981 (1982) 21 ILM 58.

the same token, practice shows that the existence of a clear cause of action, such as wrongful harm suffered by the claimant, does not necessarily entail an unconditional right of access to justice, since its exercise may be subject to substantive and procedural restrictions. It is, therefore, necessary to look now at international practice, especially the implementing practice of human rights treaty bodies, to reconstruct the pragmatic approach followed in the determination of the precise scope of this right and the restrictions, substantive and procedural, to which it may be subject. As in part I of this study, we shall distinguish between access to justice in domestic law and access to international proceedings.

D. The Scope of Access to Justice in Domestic Law

There is an abundant practice of human rights treaty bodies with regard to the permissible scope of interference by state law and administrative action with the right of an individual to have access to a court or other domestic effective remedy. This practice reveals, on the one hand, a clear preference for an inclusive scope of the right of access to justice, expanding it also to cases where there is no explicit cause of action, and on the other hand, a careful delimitation of the scope by reference to countervailing objectives and interests pertaining to the public sphere.

1. Expanding the right of access to justice

The first situation to be examined is that in which the claimant is totally deprived of the possibility to access a legal remedy or even prepare for the submission of a complaint because of insurmountable legal or administrative obstacles. The former hypothesis would occur when the potential claimant has been deprived of legal personality or other legal status. In this case a measure which does not in any way affect the substantive right of the claimant, unavoidably results in the deprivation of his or her capacity to institute legal proceedings. This was the case in *Canea Catholic Church v Greece*[117] where the claimant complained about the effect of a law which foreclosed the ability of the church to bring proceedings in Greek courts because of its failure to carry out certain bureaucratic formalities required by the law in order to acquire legal personality. Here the European Court of Human Rights found that the church had long been in existence, it had been recognized as a legal entity in prior practice and case law, and concluded that the deprivation of any means to defend its rights constituted an impermissible interference with the very substance of the right of access to justice. A similar situation arises when domestic law involves an absolute bar on a certain category of persons bringing legal proceedings because of their status.[118]

---

[117] European Court of Human Rights, Judgment of 16 December 1997, (1997) ECHR 100.

[118] See the case of *The Former King of Greece and Ors v Greece*, Judgment by the Grand Chamber of 23 November 2000; see also Judgment of the Grand Chamber on just satisfaction of 28 November 2002. Both judgements are available at <http://www.echr.coe.int/ECHR/EN/Header/Case-Law/HUDOC/HUDOC+database> (last visited on 12 April 2006).

The same conclusion, although in a different context has been reached by the International Tribunal on the Law of the Sea (ITLOS), in the recent *Juno Trader* case.[119] This litigation concerned an application for the prompt release of a foreign vessel seized by the maritime authorities of Guinea-Bissau as a consequence of the operator's failure to pay certain fines imposed as penalties for violation of fisheries regulations. Guinea Bissau, in its capacity as respondent state, had raised a preliminary objection to the jurisdiction of the Tribunal which consisted in the asserted forfeiture of *locus standi* of the claimant—the national state of the vessel—as a consequence of the confiscation of the *Juno Trader* for failure to pay the fines and its reversion to the state of Guinea-Bissau. The logic of the argument was that the vessel had lost the nationality of the claimant state as a consequence of its confiscation and that it had thus become the national property of Guinea-Bissau. The Tribunal rejected this preliminary objection, holding that the fines and the confiscation were subject to challenge in the courts of Guinea-Bissau and that the unilateral denationalization of the vessel could not bar the proceedings before the Tribunal. This is not a case involving the individual right of access to justice, nevertheless it is relevant for our discussion because it reveals a clear tendency to safeguard the right to have access to legal proceedings even when formally such right would be impaired by state legislation or measures modifying the status of the claimant or its property.

Another area in which we can witness an expansion of the right of access to justice beyond the strict letter of the relevant human right treaties is that of discretionary measures that may pose an insurmountable obstacle to the individual's access to legal counsel in order to prepare a defence. One of the most interesting examples in this respect is provided by the European Court of Human Rights in the *Golder* case.[120] As is known, this case concerned a person detained in prison in the United Kingdom. Following some violent disturbances in the prison, Mr Golder had been accused by a warden of having been actively involved, a fact that would negatively impact on his conduct and criminal record. Having decided to challenge the accusation by way of an action in defamation of the accuser, he found that his ability to consult a lawyer with a view to suing the warden was barred by the requirement of a specific authorization from the interior minister. In the proceedings before the European Court, the United Kingdom government argued that the plain meaning of Article 6 of the ECHR was that the 'fair hearing' standard provided therein related to the conduct of the proceedings and that the relative obligation would arise only once the proceedings had been commenced. A textual interpretation of Article 6 would have lent support to the United Kingdom's argument. The Court, however, took a different approach. Relying on the pre-ambular paragraph

---

[119] ITLOS, The *'Juno Trader* case', *Saint Vincent and the Grenadines v Guinea-Bissau* Judgment of 18 December 2004, published 18 March 2005.

[120] *Golder v UK* Judgment of 21 February 1975, (1975) ECHR 1.

of the Convention, which refers to the 'rule of law',[121] and mindful of the need to preserve the heritage of general principles of justice recognized in state parties, the Court resorted to an evolutive and expansive interpretation of Article 6 and read in this article the obligation of state parties to guarantee access to a court. *A fortiori*, this interpretation included access to legal counsel to prepare a defence in order to permit the realization of effective judicial remedies. In this case and in subsequent jurisprudential elaboration, the European Court has also refused to make access to justice contingent upon the discretionary exercise of power by administrative authorities or private persons.[122]

Other aspects of the expansion of the scope of access to justice can be found in the field of criminal law with respect to the right to have a criminal conviction reconsidered in the case of violation of due process or the right to submit an appeal. The former aspect has been highlighted especially by the United Nations Committee in relation to the treatment of persons awaiting execution in capital punishment cases. In *Earl Pratt and Ivan Morgan v Jamaica* the Committee, confirming its view that the victim is entitled to an effective remedy under paragraph 3 of Article 2 of the Covenant, went as far as to state that 'capital punishment should not be imposed in circumstances where there have been violations by the state party of any of its obligations under the Covenant...the victims of the violations of Articles 14, paragraph 3(c) and 7 are entitled to a remedy; the necessary prerequisite in the particular circumstances is the commutation of the sentence'.[123] This right is expressly recognized in some human rights treaties, among which are the Covenant on Civil and Political Rights (Article 14(5)), the ECHR (Protocol 7, Article 2), and the American Convention (Article 8(2)(h)); but it is not expressly contemplated by the African Charter. This notwithstanding, the African Commission on Human Rights has found that the right to appeal is an implied right in the overall guarantee

---

[121] ECHR, last preambular paragraph, which also refers to the 'common heritage of political traditions'.

[122] In the *Golden* case this power was vested with the interior ministry, which could have vetoed the authorization to a prisoner to consult a lawyer. In a subsequent case, the European Court of Human Rights found incompatible with the right of access to justice the granting to the Greek Church of exclusive control over legal actions concerning the property of monasteries endowed with independent legal status. Such exclusive control was found to destroy the possibility of a remedy that the independent monastery might seek against the Church. See *The Holy Monasteries v Greece*, Judgment of 9 December 1994, (1994) ECHR 49. See also *Philis v Greece*, Judgment of 27 August 1991 (Series A No 209), concerning the compulsory transfer of the right to sue to a professional association of engineers, with the consequence of depriving individual members of their right to sue to recover fees for services rendered in their individual capacity.

[123] Views adopted on 6 April 1989, UN Doc A/44/40, Vol II, 222, in relation to Communications 210/1986 and 225/1987. For a comprehensive survey of the UN Committee's jurisprudence with regard to the right to an effective remedy, M Scheinin, 'The Human Rights Committee's Pronouncements on the Right to an Effective Remedy—An Illustration of the Legal Nature of the Committee's Work under the Optional Protocol in N Ando (ed), *Toward Implementing the Universal Human Rights* (2004) 101.

of access to justice, all the more so in cases of capital punishment where irreparable injury may be caused to the individual claimant.[124]

The ICJ has also contributed to the clarification of the role of access to justice as an individual right in the field of criminal law. The well-known *Avena* case[125] involved a large number of Mexican nationals sentenced in the United States to capital punishment without having benefited from the consular assistance required under the Vienna Convention of 1963.[126] The Court rejected the US argument that the failure to observe the Vienna Convention would only entail an obligation on the United States to provide apology and assurance of non-repetition, but not an individual right to further remedy in domestic law.[127] Construing the Vienna Convention in such a way as to give rise to an 'individual right', and not only to a state right, to communicate and contact nationals of the sending state, the Court concluded that the breach of this right by the United States entailed an obligation to provide appropriate domestic remedy in the form of review and reconsideration of the legal proceedings.[128]

Can the right of access to justice also encompass the right of the victims of serious crimes to see the perpetrators prosecuted and punished if found guilty? The answer to this question could be a resolute 'no' if looked at from the narrow viewpoint of criminal law and of its raison d'être as a system designed to preserve the social order and isolate dangerous members of the society, rather than to create individual entitlements. However, from the point of view of international law the distinction between the public sphere of criminal law and the private sphere of individual rights is not so clear cut. First, this distinction is blurred by the increasing inter-penetration between international human rights law and international criminal law, something that has led to the establishment of individual criminal liability and international jurisdictions for the prosecution and punishment of egregious violations of human rights.[129] Secondly, an emerging practice at the state and international level supports the progressive development of a view that

---

[124] See *Akamu, Adega v Nigeria*, (1996) 3 IHRR 132.

[125] *Case concerning Avena and Other Mexican Nationals (Mexico v US)* Judgment of 31 March 2004, available at <http://www.icj-cij.org> (last visited on 12 April 2006).

[126] The relevant provision of the Vienna Convention on Consular Relations is Art 36 concerning 'communication and contact with nationals of the sending State'.

[127] The US position was the result of a strictly 'dualist' approach to the relationship between international law and domestic law and was strongly justified by reference to the so-called 'procedural default' doctrine that precludes the raising of objections to the legality of the criminal process in federal courts, unless those objections were raised in a timely manner at trial before the competent state court. See the Judgment.

[128] See Judgment, para 152.

[129] The Statute of the International Criminal Court (2187 UNTS 90), adopted in Rome on 17 July 1998 and entered into force on 1 July 2002, provides for the prosecution of genocide, crimes against humanity, war crimes, and the crime of aggression, although the latter crime will not be subject to the jurisdiction of the ICC until a provision is adopted in accordance with Arts 121 and 123 defining aggression and setting forth the conditions for its prosecution.

holds that the state's obligation to respect and protect human rights also entails an obligation to investigate, prosecute, and punish their violations, or at least the most egregious violations that amount to international crimes. This view emerges with special force in the jurisprudence of the Inter-American Court of Human Rights,[130] and, more recently, in the case law of the European Court of Human Rights. It is remarkable that the latter has clearly recognized that the idea of effective remedy, at least in cases of grave breaches of human rights, cannot consist in the mere subjection of the accused to civil or administrative proceedings, rather than criminal process. Thus in *Krastanov v Bulgaria*, concerning torture, the Court stated:

> ...if the authorities could confine their reaction to incidents of intentional police ill-treatment to mere payment of compensation, while remaining passive in the prosecution of those responsible, it would be possible in some cases for agents of the state to abuse the rights of those within their control with virtual impunity and the general legal prohibition of torture and inhuman and degrading punishment, despite its fundamental importance, would be ineffective in practice.[131]

But the most compelling evidence that the right to an effective remedy under international law includes a duty of the state concerned to prosecute and punish the person responsible for grave breaches of human rights comes from the recent practice of the highest national courts, which have set aside laws granting amnesty to shield authors of serious human rights violations. In the very recent *Simon* case (2005),[132] the Supreme Court of Argentina held that the amnesty laws adopted in 1986 and 1987,[133] to foreclose prosecution of the atrocities committed during the military dictatorship, were unconstitutional and void. This conclusion was reached on the basis of the recognized precedence of public international law over national law, and on the asserted duty of states to ensure a system of justice that is capable of affording redress to victims of human rights violations. This decision of the Argentine Supreme Court relies on the human rights jurisprudence of the Inter-American Court and provides a forceful and innovative step toward the recognition of a customary law standard in criminal justice

---

[130] See particularly *Velazquez Rodriguez* Judgment of 29 July 1988 (1988) IACHR Series C No 4, para 18; *Barrios Altos* (2001) IACHR Series C No 75, paras 43 *et seq.*

[131] Judgment of 30 September 2004 (2004) European Court of Human Rights 458, para 45. Even more explicitly with respect to the victim's or the next of kin's right to participate in an independent investigation aimed at ascertaining the responsibility for serious injury or death caused to persons in police custody, see *Keenan v UK* Judgment of 3 April 2001 (2001) European Court of Human Rights 242. For an update survey of the case law of the European Court on this matter, see AL Sciacovelli, 'Divieto di tortura e obbligo di inchiesta delle violazioni secondo la Convenzione Europea dei Diritti dell'Uomo e il diritto internazionale generale' in *La Comunita Internazionale* (2005) 269.

[132] *Simon y otros/privación ilegitima de la libertad* Supreme Court, causa No 17,768, 14 June 2005 (see <http://www.derechos.org/nizkor/arg/doc/nulidad.html> (last visited on 12 April 2006) for text in Spanish). For a comment, see C Bakker, 'A Full Stop to Amnesty in Argentina' (2005) 3 JICJ at 1106.

[133] Ley de Punto Final, No 23,492, *Boletin Oficial*, 29 December 1986; Ley de Obediencia Debida, No 23,521, *Boletin Oficial*, 9 June 1987.

that may prevail even over the express will of the legislature, as manifested in the case at hand, in the amnesty laws passed by the Argentinian Parliament.[134]

2. *Restrictions in Judicial Practice*

As for any other individual right, access to justice can be conditioned and limited by the necessity of respecting other rights or countervailing public interests. The examination of the most important limitations, from the point of view of customary international law, will be the object of Part III of this chapter. Here we shall briefly deal with the most common types of procedural and substantive limitations that have been recognized in the judicial practice of human rights treaty bodies.

The most obvious limitation is that deriving from procedural conditions of access to courts, in particular time limits and prescription periods. In this regard the practice of human rights treaty bodies recognizes that states have a wide margin of discretion in laying down procedural requirements for the exercise of the right of access to justice. Thus, a deadline of four weeks for filing an application to be exempted from the cost of legal proceedings was found acceptable under the ECHR, even though the applicant lived abroad and had either to mail the application or submit it to the diplomatic mission of his country.[135] Similarly, time limits have been deemed compatible with access to justice even when their notification was done in the official language to a complainant who was living abroad and did not know that language.[136] As for prescription periods, a six-year limitation, starting from a person's eighteenth birthday, has been found compatible with access to justice by the victim of sex abuse which took place while he was a child.[137] The same conclusion was reached in respect of a three-year statutory period required to commence an action to contest paternity when the time started to run from the birth of the child.[138] In the latter case the applicant had waited over twenty years after the divorce from his wife to raise the issue of paternity.

---

[134] For a comment on these points, see Bakker (n 132 above).

[135] *X v Switzerland* 1980, 20 DR 179. In this case the European Commission found that the applicant would have had sufficient time to mail his application directly to the court and that his deposit of the application with the Embassy of Switzerland did not entail any assurance of a timely forwarding to the competent court. The message we gather from this precedent is that the due diligence required in the observance of the time limit falls upon the individual and not upon the administrative agency to which he or she may have, in good faith, entrusted the application.

[136] See *Bricmont v Belgium* 1986, 48 DR 106, and in connection with Art 14.3(b) and (f) *Harward v Norway* (1994) IIHRL 50.

[137] *Stubbings v UK* Judgment of 22 October 1996 (1996) ECHR 44. In this case the European Court based its decision on the consideration that a limitation period of 6 years was not short, that it aimed at preventing litigation concerning an event too remote in the past, and, further, that in this case alternative remedies, in the form of criminal prosecution, were available and, in fact, the offender had been convicted of sex crimes.

[138] *X v Sweden* (1982) 31 DR 223. In this case, however, the upholding of the Swedish statute of limitation appears to be too harsh, considering that the late action was started only after the applicant

This broad margin of discretion notwithstanding, judicial practice provides evidence that procedural obstacles to access to justice have been subjected to review under the criterion of reasonableness. The Human Rights Committee, for example, has considered the strict six-month limit set by the Czech government in order to commence proceedings for the restitution of property confiscated by prior governments as unreasonably short for potential claimants living outside the country.[139] An important factor in assessing the unreasonableness of the short time limit in this case was that the confiscation of property had been one of the factors that had caused the claimants to leave the country and live abroad.

At the substantive level, restrictions on access to justice must, in principle, be distinguished from the situation where the unavailability of remedies is due to the lack of legal recognition of the right claimed. This has been the case with respect to the denial of action for nuisance caused by the flight of aircraft at a reasonable height. In *Powell and Rayner v United Kingdom* the European Commission held that the applicant could not show any substantive right in respect of the action.[140] Similarly, in *Balmer-schofroth and Ors v Switzerland* the Strasbourg Court denied that Article 6 of the ECHR established a right of access to justice for local residents for the purpose of challenging the extension of a nuclear plant.[141] Instead, one can speak of true restrictions on access to justice when the law of the relevant state provides for a general exclusion, or certain modalities, of suits under certain circumstances or in relation to a certain class of persons. This has occurred in circumstances where it was necessary to process a large mass of claims. In the *Lithgow* case,[142] the European Court of Human Rights upheld the British legislation requiring that all claims related to compensation for the nationalization of an entire sector of the economy be funnelled through a shareholder representative. The orderly processing of the claims, in view of their number and complexity, was considered a legitimate aim of the United Kingdom government. At the same time the restriction was considered to be proportionate to the achievement of such aim. Similarly, in a very different context, the Supreme Court of the United States upheld the legitimacy of the measures implementing the Algiers Accords with respect to the termination of all suits introduced in federal courts by individuals

---

had learned that he was sterile and that he could not have fathered the child at the relevant time. This seems to constitute a new fact that should have provided a new opportunity for obtaining justice, notwithstanding the long lapse of time.

[139] *Adam v Czech Republic* No 586/1994, 23 July 1996.

[140] *Powell and Rayner v UK* Application 9310/81, Report of 19 January 1989, available at <http://www.echr.coe.int/ECHR/EN/Header/Case-Law/HUDOC/HUDOC+database> (last visited on 12 April 2006). A similar conclusion was reached in *Baggs v UK* Application 9310/81, Report of 8 July 1987, ibid. See also *PN v Switzerland*, Application 26245/95, Decision of 11 September 1997; *Glass v UK* Application 28485/95, Decision of 3 December 1997.

[141] ECHR, Series A No 3003-C, 1998.

[142] *Lithgow and Ors v UK* Judgment of 8 July 1986 (1986) ECHR 8.

and companies claiming damages from Iran for loss and harm suffered as a consequence of the 1979 revolution.[143]

Restrictions on access to justice with regard to certain classes or types of persons have also been accepted in the case of 'vexatious' or 'frivolous' litigants who may abuse the right by making repeated and unfounded claims. In this case, the legitimate aim of protecting potential defendants from undue harassment or of preventing the clogging of the judicial system with frivolous claims may justify the requirement of a leave to sue by a senior judge or the imposition of sanctions on frivolous appellants.[144]

More problematic restrictions are those resulting from legislation excluding suits in order to protect a certain category of persons. A prominent example of such restrictions are sovereign and diplomatic immunities, which are dealt with in part III of this chapter. Other categories of persons who are sheltered from legal suits may be servicemen, judges, or workers in a particularly sensitive sector. In the *Ashingdane* case[145] the European Court of Human Rights was called upon to decide on the compatibility with access to justice of national legislation restricting legal proceedings with regard to the treatment of mental patients. The restriction consisted of the requirement for judicial leave following a preliminary assessment that the potential defendant had acted in bad faith or with lack of reasonable due diligence. The Court found this restriction justifiable in the light of the legitimate aim pursued by the law in protecting workers in mental institutions from being unfairly harassed by litigation,[146] and not disproportionate in so far as it left open the possibility for the patient to bring a claim once its merit had been established by the court.

Besides legislation or administrative measures, restrictions on access to justice may result from private action, such as voluntary surrender of the right of action by agreement to resort to arbitration or voluntary settlement precluding further legal action. In these cases the question may arise of whether the voluntary waiver is capable of satisfying a standard of due process and procedural fairness. In the case of arbitration it is arguable that respect of such standard can be ensured by national courts at the stage of the execution of the arbitral award. A more difficult question is whether the surrender of the right to commence or pursue legal proceedings is truly 'voluntary'. In the above-mentioned *Loewen* case, the claimant had settled a suit in a state court of the United States for the sum of US$175 million in order to avoid execution against its assets for the satisfaction of an astronomical

---

[143] *Dames and More v Regan* 453 US 654 (1981). In this case the restriction on the right of action in American courts was found acceptable because of the simultaneous establishment by the Algiers Accords of an international arbitral forum with direct access by the claimants: the Iran-US Tribunal that is examined in the first part of this chapter.

[144] This was the case in *Les Travaux du Midi v France*, 1991, Application 12275/86, Decision of 2 July 1991, available at <http://www.echr.coe.int/ECHR/EN/Header/Case-Law/HUDOC/HUDOC+database> (last visited on 12 April 2006), where the European Commission upheld the French legislation providing for fines on vexatious appellants.

[145] *Ashingdane v UK* Judgment of 28 May 1985 (1985) ECHR 8.

[146] ibid Judgment, para 58.

jury verdict of US$500 million, including US$400 million in punitive damages. Loewen had wanted to appeal against the verdict, but under state law an appeal and the concurrent stay of execution proceedings was contingent upon the payment of a security bond in the amount of 125 per cent of the verdict. It is questionable whether in such circumstances the settlement of the case was truly voluntary and the result of a calculated business decision, or rather the result of time and financial constraints that, in effect, amounted to a denial of justice.[147]

E. Access to International Proceedings

The above examination of human rights treaties and of the relevant judicial practice shows that access to justice is generally recognized as a human right in the context of domestic law and that every state is under an obligation to fulfil such right by making available a system of effective remedies to all persons subject to its jurisdiction and under its control.[148] But does this also entail a right of access to justice in international proceedings? The answer to this question appears to be negative if it is addressed from the point of view of customary international law. The development of human rights standards in the sixty years of international practice that has followed the establishment of the United Nations, has not been accompanied by such a structural transformation of the international legal order as to make it possible for individuals to claim a right of access to international remedial mechanisms on the basis of customary norms of international law. No global institutions exist to guarantee access to justice to individuals from all parts of the world. Thus, the content of the international norm recognizing the right of access justice remains limited to the attribution to every individual of an entitlement to obtain judicial protection by the courts or other remedial bodies in the state where the injury has been caused or to the jurisdiction of which the claimant is subject. At the same time, the international standard works as a parameter of legitimacy for the fair and impartial administration of justice by the state where the individual complaint is lodged. This means that in the event of systematic failure to guarantee effective remedies to victims of human rights violations, a state may be held responsible for gross violations of human rights under customary international law.

The situation, of course, is different if appreciated from the point of view of treaty law. Most human rights treaties establish their own mechanism of supervision and review, and sometimes include direct access by individuals who are

---

[147] See n 40 above. For the sequel of this case before an arbitral tribunal set up under NAFTA Charter 11, see P Acconci, 'The Requirement of Continuous Corporate Nationality and Customary International Rules on Foreign Investments: The *Loewen* Case' (2004), XIV IYIL 225.

[148] I use these expressions in order to highlight that the duty to guarantee respect and protection of human rights extends beyond the formal links of jurisdiction to situations that fall under the effective control of the defendant state following the test adopted by the Strasbourg Court in the *Loizidou* case (*Preliminary Objections*), Series A, Vol 310 (1995).

victims of violations of human rights covered by the relevant treaty. As is known, this is the case with the International Covenant on Civil and Political Rights, which permits individual 'communications' to be addressed to the Committee established under Article 28. However, recognition of the Committee's competence to receive and examine such individual communications is not mandatory; it remains contingent upon the ratification by the state to the jurisdiction of which the claimant is subject of an additional Optional Protocol which has not been ratified by all parties to the Covenant.[149] More progress has been made at the regional level. After the early period of hesitation and distrust concerning the acceptance of the right of individual complaint, the ECHR has rapidly evolved towards a system of direct access by individuals to the international adjudicatory mechanisms, first by the generalized acceptance of the optional clause of Article 25, and then by the elimination of the optional clause and the introduction of a mandatory system of direct individual access to the Strasbourg Court after the adoption of Protocol 11.[150] A different model has been followed by the American Convention and the African Charter. Here the individual access to international remedies follows the bifurcated system of the Commission and the European Court, and it is permitted only before the Commission,[151] while access to the Court in both systems is allowed to state parties and the Commission, and, in the African Charter, to African inter-governmental organizations.[152]

III. LIMITS OF ACCESS TO JUSTICE

A. Introduction

Having concluded that access to justice is a right recognized under general international law does not mean that such right is absolute, for even human rights, with a few exceptions,[153] are subject to restrictions required by the respect of the

---

[149] The Optional Protocol (n 88 above) has been ratified by 104 states, while the Covenant has been ratified by 152; see 'Status of Ratification of the Principal International Human Rights Treaties', available at <http://www.unhchr.ch/pdf/report.pdf> (last visited on 12 April 2006).

[150] See Protocol No 11 to the Convention for the Protection of Human Rights and Fundamental Freedoms, restructuring the control machinery established thereby (CETS No 155) adopted on 11 May 1994 and entered into force on 1 November 1998.

[151] African Chapter (n 9 above) Art 55–59 the American Convention (n 8 above) Art 44.

[152] Protocol to the African Charter on Human and Peoples' Rights on the Establishment of an African Court on Human and Peoples' Rights, Art 5, adopted by the Assembly of Heads of State and Government of the Organization of African Union (now African Union), on 8–10 June 1998, available at <http://www.achpr.org/english/_info/court_en.html> (last visited on 12 April 2006).

[153] Naturally we are referring to the core of non-derogable rights, such as the right to life, not to be tortured, or not to be subject to slavery, and *ex post facto* criminal law, that are recognized in the main international human rights treaties. See ICCPR, Arts (1) and (2), 6, 7, 8, 11, 15, 16, and 18; ECHR, Arts 2, 3, 4 (1), and 7; and the American Convention, Arts 3, 4, 5, 6, 9, 12, 17, 18, 19, 20, and 23.

rights of others or by overriding public interests prescribed by the law. In the case of access to justice, the question of whether and to what extent this right may be suspended or subjected to limitation has acquired great prominence in recent practice. There are many circumstances in which a state may limit or impede access to courts by individuals seeking a remedy. Some of such circumstances may be related to a state emergency, limits of jurisdiction, the political or non-justiciable nature of the dispute, or to special doctrines of the forum, such as the act of state doctrine and *forum non conveniens*, which are followed in a number of common law countries. It would be impossible within the limited space of this chapter to treat all these exceptions. At the same time, it must be recalled that other contributions in this volume will deal with situations of terrorism and armed conflict.[154] Here we will deal only with those exceptions that derive from a source *external* to the domestic law of the forum and are justified by the exercise of rights or the fulfilment of obligations established by *international law*. In particular, we will focus on the following three such exceptions: (1) operation of treaty derogation clauses in time of emergency; (2) immunities; and (3) exclusions required by the need to comply with measures adopted under the United Nations Charter for the maintenance of peace and security.

B. Derogation in Time of Emergency

Human rights treaties permit state parties to adopt measures derogating from the obligations established under such treaties to the extent required by a situation of public emergency or war.[155] At the same time, derogation clauses in human rights treaties contain a list of fundamental human rights provisions which permit no derogation even in a state of exception, such as those prohibiting torture, slavery, or the arbitrary deprivation of life. Access to justice per se is not included in such list, either in Article 15 of the ECHR, or in Article 4 of the United Nations Covenant on Civil and Political Rights. The American Convention, on the other hand, although not including the right to judicial protection (Article 25) among the non-derogable rights listed in Article 27, nevertheless expressly states that 'judicial guarantees essential for the protection of such rights' are not subject to suspension. So, it is clear that, at least at a formal level, the American Convention provides a higher level of guarantee than the Covenant and the ECHR in respect of the right of access to justice in time of emergency, at least to the extent that alleged breaches concern the list of non-derogable rights.

---

[154] See Ní Aoláin, ch 2 below and Ronzitti, ch 3 below.

[155] See UN Covenant on Civil and Political Rights, Art 4; ECHR, Art 15; and the American Convention, Art 27. Emergency has been defined by the European Court of Human Rights as 'a situation of exceptional and imminent danger or crisis affecting the general public, as distinct from particular groups, and constituting a threat to the organized life of the community which composes the state in question', *Lawless v Ireland* Commission Report, 1 ECHR, Series B, 1960–61, para 90.

With the rise of international terrorism after 11 September 2001, and the persistence of armed conflicts and civil strife in many areas of the world, for the sake of security, exceptional measures which tend to restrict civil liberties have been adopted in many countries, including measures affecting privacy, free movement, and property.[156] This raises the question of whether access to justice may be subject to limitations or suspension in times of emergency and public danger.

The answer to this question cannot be an absolute 'yes' or 'no'. On the contrary, it must be based on the criteria of reasonableness and proportionality between the limitation of access to justice and the general interest in the protection of public security. This means that certain restrictions on the actual operation of the judicial system are permissible to the extent that they are strictly necessary to cope with the actual danger posed by the emergency. At the same time, the state invoking a state of emergency cannot free itself of the basic obligation to provide a remedy that is reasonable and effective, even if in diminished form, in the context of the exceptional situation. This position is supported by logic, by the practice of human rights monitoring bodies, and by judicial practice.

In point of logic, it must be noted that all the derogation clauses contained in human rights treaties allow state parties to suspend human rights only on the condition that the derogating measures are not inconsistent with ' their other obligations under international law and do not involve discrimination'.[157] Since the 'other obligations under international law' include international humanitarian law, under which judicial remedies are guaranteed,[158] it would not make sense to provide a lesser guarantee in the context of a war than in a situation of emergency or public danger.

As far as the practice of human rights monitoring bodies is concerned, a General Comment of the Human Rights Committee (HRC) and two advisory opinions of the Inter-American Court confirm this position. In its General Comment 29 of 2001, the HRC stated that, even if access to justice is not included among the non-derogable provisions, 'the state party must comply with the fundamental obligation under article 2, paragraph 3, of the covenant to provide a remedy that is effective'.[159]

In its two advisory opinions on states of emergency and on habeas corpus, the Inter-American Court has followed a similar approach through a robust interpretation of the

---

[156] See eg the US PATRIOT Act, 24 October 2001, HR 3162 RDS, and the Italian Legge No 438 of 15 December 2001 with subsequent legislation adopted after the terrorist attack occurred in London on 7 July 2005, Legge 31 luglio 2005, n 155, published in *Gazzetta Ufficale*, n 177, 1 August 2005. For a comment on the Italian law, see A Saccucci, 'The Italian 2005 Counter-terrorism Legislation in light of International Human Rights Obligations' (2005) XV IYIL 168. For a general overview on these measures and their impact on human rights, see W Benedek and C Yotopoulos-Marangopoulos (eds), *Anti Terrorist Measures and Human Rights* (2004).

[157] This formula is used in ICCPR, Art 4 and ECHR Art 15, as well as in the American Convention, Art 27.

[158] See, for instance, the First Protocol, Art 45, para 2 which concerns judicial protection of prisoners of war.

[159] General Comment 29, States of Emergency (Art 4), UN Doc CCPR/C/21/Rev.1/Add.11 (2001) para 14.

concept of 'judicial guarantees' contained in Article 27 of the American Convention. As a consequence, the Court has held that, in times of crisis, the non-derogable character of rights enumerated in Article 27 must be effectively safeguarded against abuse by the preservation of an essential mechanism of access to justice and due process. In particular:

(1) suspension must be temporary and related to the exercise of rights rather than the suspension of rights;

(2) suspension is subject to a proportionality and reasonableness test, so that it may not go beyond what is strictly necessary according to the exigencies of the situation;

(3) with regard to access to justice, the degree to which suspension of guarantees is permissible depends also upon the right at stake, certain rights being more fundamental than others;

(4) suspension of certain guarantees does not suspend the rule of law; and

(5) amparo and habeas corpus are among the judicial guarantees that are essential to the protection of the rights and freedoms the suspension of which is not permitted under Article 27(2) of the American Convention.[160]

This interpretation is confirmed by recent judicial practice. The European Court of Human Rights has recognized the continuing validity of the obligation to guarantee access to judicial remedies in the context of the fight against terrorism[161] even in the extreme circumstances of an armed conflict such as the one conducted by Russia in Chechnya. In *Isayeva and Ors v Russia*, involving the killing by air attack of civilians in a convoy that had been given 'safe exit' from the city of Grozny, the applicant survivors of the victims complained of a violation of Article 2, right to life, and Article 13, effective remedy. The Court found that, in view of the gravity of the breach of Article 2, Article 13 required (a) effective prosecution of the persons responsible of the attack, (b) full access by the victims to the investigation, and (c) appropriate compensation for loss and damage suffered. Besides, the court indicated the criteria to be used to verify whether the test of 'effective remedies' was satisfied:

(1) the investigation must be public and not left to the initiative of the victims;

(2) the investigating body must be independent;

(3) the inquiry must be carried out in a manner such as to lead to a determination whether the use of deadly force was justified under the circumstances; and

(4) the investigation must be prompt.

---

[160] Inter-American Court of Human Rights, Advisory Opinion in States of Emergency, 9 IACHR (Series A), OEA/ser.L/VI/111.9 Doc 13 (1987) and Opinion on Habeas Corpus in Emergency Situations, 8 IACHR (Series A), OEA/ser L/V/111.17. Doc 13 (1987).

[161] See in particular *Brogan v UK* ECHR, Series A, *Sakik and Ors v Turkey* Judgment of 26 November 1997, and other cases discussed in Ní Aoláin, ch 2 below.

On the basis of these criteria the Court found a violation of Article 13 as well as of Article 2 of the ECHR.[162]

In another case, *Assanidze v Georgia*, involving the prolonged extra-judicial detention of a political leader in the autonomous 'Adjarian Republic', a split region of Georgia, the applicant complained of a violation of his right to liberty, security, and judicial protection. The question here was whether Georgia could effectively implement its law and judicial guarantees in a self-proclaimed autonomous territory largely beyond its control. In a decision of 8 April 2004, a Grand Chamber found that the applicant and the matter complained of fell within the jurisdiction of Georgia in accordance with Article 1 of the ECHR and that there had been a breach of paragraph 1 of Article 5 and of paragraph 1 of Article 6 (right to a fair trial).[163] Similar conclusions were reached in another Grand Chamber decision of 8 July 2004 in the case of *Ilascu and Ors v Moldova and Russia*, involving extra-judicial arrest, torture, and ill-treatment of persons in the split Moldovan republic of 'Transdniestra', where both Russia and Moldova were held responsible for failure to provide judicial protection to the applicants.[164]

This practice of international human rights bodies strikes a correct balance between security exigencies posed by public emergencies, terrorism, or armed conflict and the need to preserve the essence of access to justice in accordance with the rule of law. It is interesting to note how, in the practice of the European Court of Human rights, this balance is sought by linking Article 13 on effective remedies with the relevant substantive provisions whose violation is complained of. The more severe the breach complained of—for example involving Article 2, 3, or 5 on the right to life, torture, and deprivation of personal liberty respectively—the more important it is to preserve the right of the victims or their descendants to have access to remedial measures and to effective investigation and prosecution of the responsible persons.[165]

It is worth noting that the recent practice of the Strasbourg Court goes well beyond the simple finding of a breach of the effective remedy obligation, to indicate what specific measures and initiatives are necessary to ensure an administration of justice that is consonant with the obligations undertaken with the ECHR.[166]

Also the post-September 11 practice of the US courts, in relation to challenges of the detention of captured combatants, enemy aliens, and US citizens suspected of terrorism,

---

[162] Decision of 24 February 2005, available at <http://www.echr.coe.int/ECHR/EN/Header/Case-Law/HUDOC/HUDOC+database> (last visited on 12 April 2006).

[163] ibid Decision of 8 April 2004.

[164] ibid Judgment of 8 July 2004.

[165] This line of jurisprudence can be traced to the Court's decision in *McCann and Ors v UK*, where the killing of suspected terrorists was not in itself held to constitute a violation of ECHR, Art 2, but the UK was found in breach of its obligation to provide access to legal process and effective investigation for those most immediately affected by the event, ie the victims and their descendants.

[166] For a survey of this Practice, see L Caflisch, 'New Practice Regarding the Implementation of the Judgments of the Strasbourg Court' (2005) XV IYIL 3.

points towards the recognition of a fundamental right of access to justice even in the exceptional political and psychological climate of an unprecedented war on terror.[167]

C. Immunities

This category of legal impediments to the effective exercise of access to justice is probably the most problematic since, by definition, such impediments entail exemptions of foreign states and their organs from the operation of judicial remedies in the forum state.

This result has been found increasingly unacceptable in state practice. After the almost universal alignment of judicial practice with the theory of restrictive immunity, based on the distinction between acts *jure imperii* and *jure gestionis*,[168] further restrictions have emerged in the practice of certain states in respect of situations where access to courts was sought by victims of serious violations of human rights, and especially if these violations had been committed in the state of the forum. An early case setting a trend towards a drastic restriction of the traditional immunities was *Letelier v Republic of Chile*[169] in which United States courts found that the assassination by foreign government agents of a former Chilean ambassador and his secretary could not be considered as conduct covered by immunity, since the conduct in question was 'clearly contrary to the precepts of humanity as recognized in both national and international law'.[170] This conclusion, which was confirmed in later cases,[171] was facilitated by the specific 'tort exception' to sovereign immunities recognized in paragraph 5 of section 1605 of the 1976 Foreign Sovereign Immunities Act (FSIA) of the United States, which excludes immunity in cases in which 'damages are sought against a foreign State for personal injury or death, or damage to or loss of property, occurring in the United States and caused by the tortious act or omission of that foreign State or of any official or employee of that foreign State while acting within the scope of his office or employment'. In recent times the tort exception to immunity has somehow also influenced the judicial practice of countries the domestic legislation of which does not include

---

[167] In *Rasul and Ors v Bush* the question was whether district courts had jurisdiction to deal with matters of detention at the extra-territorial naval base of Guantanamo, which the government argued was outside of the reach of the US courts. The Supreme Court found that the basic right of access to justice existed also in such exceptional situation and that aliens detained in Guantanamo were entitled to invoke federal courts authority (542 US 466 (2004) 321 F 3d 1134). In *Hamdi v Rumsfeld* the Court held that although the continuing hostility and the war on terror could justify the detention, nevertheless the 'enemy combatant' status must be open to challenge by the plaintiff by way of access to evidence of the classification in a neutral judicial forum (542 US 507 (2004)).

[168] See the 2004 United Nations Convention on Jurisdictional Immunities of States and Their Properties, available at <http://untreaty.un.org/ilc/texts/instruments/english/conventions/4_1_2004.pdf> (last visited on 13 April 2006); B Conforti, *Diritto internazionale* (2002) 249 *et seq*.

[169] 488 F Supp 665 (DDC 1980).

[170] ibid 673.

[171] See eg *Liu v Republic of China* 642 F Supp 297 (ND Cal 1986).

specific provisions to this effect. In a widely discussed decision of the Italian Supreme Court in the case of *Ferrini v Germany*, the civil action started in Italy by a civilian who had been forcibly deported to Germany during the Nazi occupation of Italy and subjected to inhuman conditions of forced labour in a concentration camp until the end of the conflict, was found admissible notwithstanding the sovereign nature of the defendant, on the basis of the combined argument that the remedy sought concerned a breach of fundamental human rights, amounting to *jus cogens*, and that the tortious act occurred in Italy, the forum state.[172] A similar tendency has been followed by Greek courts in a case also involving atrocities committed by German occupation forces in southern Greece during the Second World War.[173]

This recent practice of the Italian and Greek courts may make a significant contribution to the development of a wider concept of access to justice in cases in which major violations of human rights are at stake. The decisive role played in the cited decisions by the argument that certain human rights violations, such as torture, forced enslavement, and mass killings of civilians, belong to the higher law of *jus cogens*, may have been buttressed by the automatic incorporation of general international law into the constitutions of these countries.[174] The 'constitutionalization' of general norms of international law certainly has the effect of making domestic courts more receptive to the implementation of peremptory norms, but this attitude is not shared all over the world. [175] And, most important,' the practice of international tribunals is still very reluctant to accept an exception to immunity in respect of individual claims for alleged violations of human rights, even if the human rights are so fundamental as to be part of *jus cogens*'. This has become clear in relation to the judgment of the ICJ in the *Arrest Warrant* case (*Congo v Belgium*),[176] where the

---

[172] See *Ferrini c Repubblica Federale di Germania* Italian Corte di Cassazione, Joint Sections, sentenza 6 novembre 2003–11 marzo 2004, n 5044, in (2004) 87 *Rivista di diritto internazionale* 539. On this case, see M Iovane, 'The *Ferrini* Judgement of the Italian Supreme Court' (2004) XIV IYIL 165; A Gianelli, 'Crimini internazionali ed immunità degli stati dalla giurisdizione nella sentenza *Ferrini*' (2004) 87 *Rivista di diritto internazionale* 643; P De Sena and F De Vittor, 'State Immunity and Human Rights: The Italian Supreme Court Decision on the *Ferrini* case' (2005) 16 EJIL, 89.

[173] I am referring to the widely commented upon judgment of the Hellenic Supreme Court (Areios Pagos) in *Prefecture Voiotia v Federal Republic of Germany* No 11/2000 of 4 May 2000. For a summary and comment, see M Gavouneli and I Bantekas, Case Report (2001) 95 AJIL 198.

[174] See the 1947 Italian Constitution art 10, para 1 and the Greek Constitution, art 28(1).

[175] See for instance the statement of a common law scholar with regard to the Australian legal system, who thinks it is 'unlikely that an Australian court would be prepared to recognize an implied exception to immunity for *jus cogens* violations in the Australian [State Immunity] Act', R Garnett, 'The Defence of State Immunity for Acts of Torture', (1997) 97 *Australian Yearbook of International Law* 123. On the relevance of the 'constitutionalization' of human rights norms in the domestic legal order, see F Francioni, 'The Jurisprudence of Human Rights Enforcement: Reflections on the Italian Experience' in B Conforti and F Francioni (eds), *Enforcing International Human Rights in Domestic Courts* (1997) 15, 19.

[176] Decision of 14 February 2002, available at <http://www.icj-cij.org> (last visited on 13 April 2006).

customary law nature of the immunity of a minister of a foreign state was held to be decisive in barring a criminal prosecution for alleged serious violations of human rights and humanitarian law. As far as human rights courts are concerned, a string of cases concerning civil action to obtain compensation for alleged breaches of fundamental rights by foreign states have been brought before the European Court of Human Rights and have all resulted in judgments upholding the principle of jurisdictional immunity of the defendant state from civil suits .[177]

The oscillation of state practice and the incongruence between the jurisprudence of international tribunals, favourable to the maintenance of immunity, and that of some more progressive domestic courts, favourable to the further erosion of immunity in the case of human rights violations, does not permit firm conclusions as to the existence of a human rights exception to immunity under present customary international law. Thus, the solution to the conflict between the traditional norm on immunity and the right of access to justice must be found at the interpretative level.

One radical option would be to resolve the issue through an extensive interpretation of the jurisdictional clauses contained in human rights treaties, such as Article 1 of the ECHR and of the American Convention, and Article 2 of the Covenant on Civil and Political Rights, so as to consider human rights claims against foreign states and their officials as not 'subject to the jurisdiction' of the forum owing to the operation of the international norm on immunity. This approach has been suggested in the literature[178], but it begs the question, since it presupposes that human rights disputes against foreign states and their officials do not lie within the 'jurisdiction' of the state party concerned without rationally explaining why the jurisdictional exemption has to prevail over the competing obligation to ensure respect for human rights and judicial guarantees against their violation.

At the opposite end of the spectrum we can find the approach based on the assumption that the doctrine of immunity is not really part of customary international law, but is primarily the creation of domestic law for international relations purposes, and, as such, it is subject to regulation by domestic norms, save for the immunities governed by treaty. This view has been supported mainly by common law scholars[179] and underlies the contemporary practice of the United States, where the continuous re-definition of the scope of sovereign immunities occurs within the detailed statutory framework of the FSIA of 1976, with little attention paid to its congruence with customary international law developments. This approach is also

---

[177] The most important cases are *McElhinney v Ireland*, *Al-Adsani v UK* (with strong dissent by several members of the Court), and *Fogarty v UK*, treated as a whole by the court, declared admissible on the same grounds, tried by the same Grand Chamber and decided on 21 November 2001. See the Court's website at <http://www.hudoc.echr.coe.int>.

[178] E Voyakis, 'Access to Court v. State Immunity' (2003) 52 ICLQ 297, 309.

[179] I Brownlie, *Principles of Public International Law* (3rd edn, 1979) 333, as well as the 5th edn of 1998.

unsatisfactory. In point of law, it is well established that immunities of states and their officials have their foundation in customary international law. The judgments of the ICJ and of the European Court of Human Rights, mentioned above, provide confirmation of this, if any were needed. In point of policy, it is unwise to locate the issue of immunities entirely within the sphere of domestic law. This may transform a doctrine of fundamental importance for the orderly conduct of international relations into a political tool that governments may use in a discriminatory and arbitrary manner towards other states. This risk appears to be present in the recent reform of the United States immunity statute introduced by the Anti-terrorism and Effective Death Penalty Act of 1996, which, contrary to the original intention of the FSIA to leave the decision on the granting of immunity to an independent determination of the courts, makes immunity contingent upon the designation by the executive of the defendant country as a state sponsoring terrorism or not, a determination that is not free of political considerations.

A more satisfactory approach to reconciling immunities and access to justice is to recognize that both reflect norms of customary international law which need to be reconciled through a pragmatic approach and a careful balancing of the competing interests in the concrete cases. This entails, first of all that immunity should be accorded whenever alternative and effective remedies are open to the claimant in another forum, which can be the state where the injury occurred or an arbitral or other international forum in respect of which the defendant state has waived its immunity.[180] When no viable alternative exists, the choice between immunity and access to courts cannot be made on the basis of an *a priori* mechanical criterion of prevalence *ratione materiae* or *ratione temporis*, which would not make much sense in this context. Rather, it is necessary to ascertain which of the two competing norms, immunity or judicial protection of human rights, under the specific circumstances of the case, would better serve the general interest of the international community and the rule of law in international relations. In this regard, the balancing criteria that currently emerge in international practice are essentially two. The first is the nature of the injury for which judicial protection is sought. As indicated earlier,[181] certain human rights norms, such as those prohibiting torture, genocide, slavery, and arbitrary killing, are never derogable and judicial guarantees must be maintained under all circumstances because they are a component of the non-derogable character of the substantive norm.[182] Therefore, in these circumstances the exercise of jurisdiction is justified even if it entails an encroachment on the immunity rule. The second criterion is the degree of connection of the alleged human rights breach with the forum. As we have seen, the

---

[180] eg the arbitral mechanism available under investment treaties and under regional agreements like NAFTA. This approach is strongly advocated by Conforti, (n 168 above).

[181] See section B on above, 'Derogation in Time of Emergency'.

[182] See judgments of the European Court as well as opinions of the American Court and Human Rights Committee Section B, above.

practice of several states—including the United States, Italy, and Greece—tends to give considerable weight, for the purpose of setting aside immunities, to the fact that the alleged injury occurred in the territory of the forum. This criterion is reasonable in as a much as it is in the *locus commissi delicti* that access to justice can produce useful effects in terms of reparation of the victims, a moral example in redressing injustice, and future deterrence with respect to the local community. Further, this criterion has been accepted, in the form of a tort exception, in Article 11 of the European Convention on State Immunity[183] and in Article 12 of the Convention on Jurisdictional Immunities of States and Their Property[184] with respect to civil actions concerning personal injuries and damage to property. It seems indisputable that these provisions can cover a wide range of possible human rights violations for which state immunity can be set aside.

D. Compliance with United Nations Measures

One of the problematic implications of the increased activity of the Security Council in the adoption of measures under Chapter VII of the Charter and, in particular, the so-called 'smart sanction', which are aimed at specific actors considered to pose a danger for international peace and security, is the difficulty or actual impossibility of finding a judicial remedy against possible errors or abuses that affect the freedom or rights of the targeted subjects. Measures of this kind adopted to help bring peace in the Balkans and, more recently, anti-terrorist measures intended to block financial assets of organizations linked to terrorism have produced a series of disputes where the central issue is the lawfulness of the deprivation of the fundamental right of access to judicial process and review of the United Nations measures or, more precisely, of the specific legislation implementing them in the relevant legal order. Three cases are especially relevant in this respect.

In *Bosphorus v Ireland*[185] a Turkish airline company complained before the European Court of Human Rights that its right of property, guaranteed by Protocol 1, had been violated by Ireland as a consequence of the impoundment and prolonged arrest of an aircraft that the applicant had leased, allegedly in good faith, from a Yugoslav airline (JAT). At the material time, the Security Council had adopted Resolution 820 of 17 April 1993, which had imposed economic sanctions on Yugoslavia with the effect of requiring, *inter alia*, states to arrest all aircraft in their territory in which a controlling interest was held by a person or undertaking of Yugoslavia. Review of the impoundment decision was sought by the applicant before Irish courts but such review was further complicated by the implementation of the United Nations sanctions through Regulation

---

[183] CETS No 74, entered into force on 11 June 1976.

[184] See n 168 above.

[185] European Court of Human Rights, Grand Chamber, Judgment of 30 June 2005. For detailed discussion see C Costello, 'The Bosphorous Ruling of the European Court of Human Rights: Fundamental Rights and Blurred Boundaries in Europe' (2006) 6 HRLR 87–130.

(EC) 990/93, which added a further layer of obligation and no margin of discretion upon Irish authorities. It took recourse by the applicant all the way up to the Supreme Court of Ireland, a preliminary ruling of the EC Court of Justice affirming that the relevant EC Regulation applied to the aircraft in question, the lifting of the sanctions as a consequence of the peace process in Yugoslavia, and the monumental losses suffered by the applicant,[186] before the aircraft was let free. In these tormented circumstances, was there a breach of the judicial guarantee of the applicant's right to the enjoyment of its property? The answer provided by the European Court of Human Rights in its judgment of 30 June 2005—more than twelve years from the facts generating the dispute—appears to be hardly satisfactory. The Court found that Ireland had not breached the provision on the protection of property right contained in Article 1 of Protocol 1, because the impoundment of the aircraft had been justified by the legitimate exigency of complying with mandatory obligations imposed upon Ireland by its participation in an international organization, the European Community, and because the judicial guarantees of fundamental rights provided within the legal system of such organization could be considered 'equivalent' to those provided under the ECHR.

A similar deference towards compliance with international obligation has been shown in two recent cases, *Kadi* and *Yusuf*,[187] brought before the Court of First Instance of the European Community by plaintiffs who had been targeted by EC measures implementing anti-terrorism sanctions adopted by the Security Council against the Taliban government of Afghanistan, Al-Quaeda, and other persons and entities connected to terrorism.[188] The plaintiffs sought judicial relief against the impugned Community Regulations arguing, *inter alia*, that they constituted a breach of the right to enjoy their property and of their right to a fair hearing and to an effective judicial remedy. The Court of First Instance dismissed the claims, using a line of reasoning that can be summarized as follows. First, the Court accepted that the impugned Regulations fell within the scope of its judicial

---

[186] The lease entailed the payment by the applicant of a lump-sum of US$1,000,000 per aircraft and a monthly rental of US$150,000.

[187] Case T-315/01 *Yassim Abdullah Kadi v Council of the European Union and Commission of the European Communities* and Case T-306/01 *Ahmed Ali Yusuf and al Barakaat International Foundation v Council of the European Union and Commission of the European communities*. On 12 December 2006, the Court of First Instance annulled Council's Decision freezing the funds of the Organisation des Modjahedines du Peuple d'Iran, the *Ompi* case, holding that OMPI was deprived of basic guarantees in relation to the disclosure of the reasons justifying the freezing and the rights to a fair hearing and effective access to the Court. OMPI is one of over 100 individuals and entities who have been placed on the terror list under Council Regulation (EC) 2580/2001 of 27 December 2001.

[188] See in particular SC Res 1267 (1999) of 15 October 1999, and SC Res 1333 (2000) of 16 December 2000, and SC Res 1390 (2002) of 16 January 2002. The European secondary legislation implementing these resolutions was Council Regulation (EC) 467/2001 of 6 March 2001, Commission Regulation (EC) 2199/2001 of 12 November 2001, and Council Regulation (EC) 881/2002 of 27 May 2002, repealing Regulation 467/2001.

review. Then, it went on to recognize that obligations under the United Nations Charter and, by extension, those arising from Security Council resolutions prevail over prior or subsequent obligations of the Member States by virtue of the supremacy principle contained in Article 103 of the United Nations Charter.[189] Finally, it concluded that the applicants' right to a fair hearing and to an effective remedy had not been breached: first because there is no right to a prior hearing for persons targeted by Security Council measures under Chapter VII of the Charter; and second, because affected persons could always bring a claim for judicial review based on domestic law in order to have the competent national authorities bring their case to the Security Council's Sanctions Committee for reconsideration.[190] The Court was satisfied that the applicants had been able to bring an action before the Court of First Instance and, taking into account the political context of the measures and the principle of proportionality, reasonable remedial process was available, in the event of errors or abuses, through the diplomatic interposition of the national state before the Sanctions Committee of the Security Council.

These judgments are problematic from the standpoint of the effective implementation of the principle of judicial protection against possible human rights abuses.[191] The *Bosphorus* decision, on its part, in relying on the deferential standard of review represented by the 'compliance with legal obligations flowing from membership . . . of the EC' cuts such a broad exception in the fabric of judicial guarantees for human rights infringements as to make any balancing of private rights against general interests totally impossible or entirely futile. This is clearly inconsistent with prior decisions of the European Court of Human Rights setting forth the principle that, when contracting states transfer parts of their sovereign power to an international organization, the obligations thereby undertaken must be consistent with the provisions of the ECHR.[192] At the same time, the application in *Bosphorus* of the usual 'equivalence' test, to re-affirm that the standard of rights protection in the EC legal order must be presumed to be comparable to that of the Convention, tends to down play the fact that, although fundamental rights are part of Community law, individual access to justice in the Community system remains limited. This is at odds with the principle proclaimed in other judgments that the basic right of individual recourse 'is one of the keystones in the machinery for the enforcement of the rights and freedoms set forth in the Convention'.[193]

---

[189] Judgment, paras 231–234 which refer also to the relevant case law of the ICJ as expressed in the *Nicaragua* case [1986] ICJ Rep para 107, and in the case concerning the *Interpretation of the Montreal Convention* (1992) ICJ Rep, para 39.

[190] *Yusuf* Judgment, paras 315–317.

[191] One commentator has referred to them as 'fundamentally flawed' and as amounting to 'judicial abdication': see P Eeckhout, *Does Europe's Constitution Stop at the Water's Edge? Law and Policy in the EU's External Relations* (2006).

[192] *Matthews v UK* Grand Chamber, Nos 248833/94, ECHR 1999-I.

[193] *Mamatkulov v Turkey*, Grand Chamber, Nos 46827/99 and 46951/99.

The two judgments of the Court of First Instance in the *Kadi* and *Yusuf* cases. pose a similar danger of an unwitting curtailment of the individual right to effective remedy through an acritical reference to the supremacy of Security Council measures via Article 103 of the Charter. Although, the Court of First Instance recognizes through a rather elaborate reasoning, that it has the power to set aside community measures implementing Security Council resolutions when such measures are are contrary to overriding principles of *jus cogens*, in the end it fails to clarify what the parameters of *jus cogens* are in relation to minimum due process and access to justice. Also, in these judgments, now appealed before the European Court of Justice,[194] what is to be criticized is the selective reference to the supremacy of Security Council measures, without considering that an essential part of United Nations law are its principles on the protection of human rights, which are applicable and binding upon United Nations organs besides member states.[195] Certainly, we must be aware of the need to reconcile such protection with the imperative needs of international security and with the legitimate aim pursued by the Security Council in fighting the scourge of terrorism. However, such reconciliation would be better achieved by maintaining the possibility of recourse to a mechanism of review of the measures affecting individual rights and of remedial process capable of making good possible errors or abuses. *Mutates mutandis*, this conclusion is consistent with the position taken by the HRC in the already cited General Comment 29, according to which situations of emergency, including terrorism, do not relieve states from the duty of providing remedies that are effective.[196] Granted, the substantive rights affected by the EC Regulations in the cases at hand were property rights—which are not a matter of *jus cogens* and are subject to a wide range of restriction in the public interest. However, the sweeping United Nations exception carved by the Court of First Instance, like the 'international obligation' exception articulated in the *Bosphorus* decision, opens the door to further erosion of the right of access to justice whenever the breach of human rights, and perhaps even of non-derogable rights, is justified on grounds of compliance with international obligations or Community legislation.

E. Conclusion

As I have tried to demonstrate in the above examination of the practice and sources of international law, access to justice has come a long way towards its recognition as a true enforceable right under international law. Starting from its early emergence as a component of the minimum standard of treatment of aliens, it has gradually

---

[194] See Case C-402/05 P, concerning the appeal brought on 23 November 2005 by Yassim A Kadi, and Case C-415/05 P, concerning the appeal brought on the same date by Yusuf and Al Barakaat International Foundation.

[195] For a favourable comment see, however, the note by C Tomuschat (2006) 43, CML Rev 537.

[196] See n 159 above.

evolved into other areas of international law, notably war reparations and minority rights, to become later entrenched in today's human rights law. It is especially in relation to the judicial practice of international human rights bodies that access to justice emerges as an essential component of every system of human rights protection, which, in principle, must be safeguarded also in times of crisis and emergency. A paradoxical result of this consolidation of the right of access to justice is the increasing workload of courts and the systemic problem of the excessive length of proceedings, which often amounts to a denial of justice. This should remind us that the right of access to courts plays its role and remains fundamental, especially at the level of domestic law, where remedies against human rights violations must be primarily found. At the international level, access to justice remains limited to those treaty systems where breaches of human rights by contracting states fall within the scope of review of a judicial or quasi-judicial body empowered to hear individual complaints. Ideally, however, one should never need such international mechanisms, if domestic remedies were available, just, and effective, the right of access to justice could be satisfied within the domestic law sphere. Like most human rights, access to justice also suffers limitations. Of special interest in contemporary practice are the limitations required by the operation of norms of international law, such as derogation clauses in times of emergency, immunities, and the implementation of United Nations sanctions. The challenge in this context is to strike a fair balance between these countervailing norms and the right of access to courts. In this chapter I have tried to develop legal arguments in favour of a restrictive interpretation of traditional limitations on this right. At the same time, I have advocated a judicial attitude that takes into account the essential role of access to justice as a guarantee of the effective enjoyment of human rights in a society based upon the rule of law and on the availability of effective remedies against the abuse of power.

2

The Individual Right of Access to Justice in Times of Crisis: Emergencies, Armed Conflict, and Terrorism

FIONNUALA NÍ AOLÁIN*

Crises pose very particular challenges to law. This is largely because the legal regulation of crisis—when states are faced with threats, whether internal or external in nature—invariably constrains the full protections which law offers. In times of crisis, justice is a particularly critical concept, in part because the rights and protections of ordinary law are under exceptional stress. More explicitly and practically important, however, is the extent to which access to justice is maintained or restrained in times of crisis. This chapter will examine this broad theme, looking at three key arenas in which these concerns play out.

The demands and compromises of situations of emergency, armed conflict, and terrorism chiefly challenge the reach of law's substantive protections and undermine the procedural mechanisms that make those protections meaningful. Much academic and policy attention has been paid to the substantive legal limitations sought by governments when crisis occurs.[1] Considerably less time has been spent examining the extent to which access to justice is conceptualized as a stand-alone category of response by states in times of crisis. It is evident that the concept of and practices concerning access to justice inhabit a vast legal terrain. This chapter takes a focused view of the term, using it to refer primarily to those procedural legal mechanisms that operate to give persons who are accused of committing violations of human rights or humanitarian law access to due process standards

* Thanks to Adrienne Reilly for research assistance, to Jennifer Johnson for editing on this essay, and to Adam Hanson for research support in the final stages of preparation.

[1] N Questiaux, 'Study of the Implications for Human Rights of Recent Developments Concerning Situations Known as States of Siege or Emergency' UN Doc E/CN.4/Sub.2/1982/15 (1982); SR Chowdhury, *Rule of Law in a State of Emergency: The Paris Minimum Standards of Human Rights Norms in a State of Emergency* (Pinter, 1989); J Fitzpatrick, *Human Rights in Crisis: The International System for Protecting Rights during States of Emergency* (University of Pennsylvania Press, 1994); Jaime Oraá, *Human Rights in States of Emergency in International Law* (Clarendon Press, 1992).

during pre-forum, forum, and post-forum accountability. Reference is also made to include persons who have been the victims of harms by others in a form of legal review or remedy.

This chapter will explore a variety of issues related to access via the prism of international law's response to situations of crisis, with particular reference to the distinctive categories of emergency and armed conflict. Notably, the chapter will assess the extent to which individual access to justice constitutes a linchpin of the interface between international human rights law and the regulation of crisis (whether that be conflict, emergency, or terrorism in form). It will follow with a review of international humanitarian law's approach to individual access, and identify contemporary challenges to and lacunae in that field. In that context, the chapter will particularly focus on two individual subject categories. Primarily the analysis is concerned with the rights of persons who may be the subjects of humanitarian law's application, with a particular emphasis on the due process rights of such individuals. Identifying an extension of access rights in international law generally, the rights of conflict victims to seek access to and enforcement of accountability provisions during and after armed conflicts is also canvassed. By way of conclusion, the chapter will traverse some current territory by examining the problems posed by the legal regulation of terrorism, and the challenges faced by states in the terrorism and law interface. The chapter will explore how these tensions manifest themselves in practical terms as constraints on individual access to justice.

An important caveat is that much of the terrain canvassed by this chapter offers views on the extent to which the applicable legal norms relevant to situations of crisis facilitate access to *law and legal process*. Justice itself is a dense term, and given the multifaceted nature of crisis it is difficult to do more than (at best) ensure access to legal procedures and forums, the quality and outcomes of which can vary considerably from the law and process which might apply in normal times. This is because, as illustrated below, the quality of law may be seriously attenuated by the effects of crisis, and a persistent feature of law's interface with extremity, as manifested in conflict or emergency form, is the struggle to maintain the integrity and depth of legal protections when faced with serious political or economic adversity.

I. EMERGENCIES

Prior to the attacks of 11 September 2001, discussion of emergency powers in general, and counter-terrorism measures in particular, had been relegated to a legal backseat in many democratic states. That stated, it was also evident that a number of states, both democratic and authoritarian, had made frequent recourse to exceptional powers when responding to threats, whether internal or external in nature.

As a matter of definition, there are many types of emergencies. Those that have generally garnered most attention are violent crises and emergencies, such as wars and international armed conflicts, rebellions, and terrorist attacks as distinguished from economic crises and natural disasters.[2] However, it should be acknowledged that emergency powers have been used in times of great economic consternation and in situations of severe natural disasters as frequently, and perhaps even more so, as in the context of violent crises.[3]

A. Derogation

In order to accommodate the exigencies of an emergency, international human rights law offers a specific mechanism, known as derogation, to facilitate state responses to crisis.[4] Derogation refers to the legally mandated right of states to allow the suspension of certain international obligations protecting individual rights in the exceptional circumstances of emergency or war. A state need not enact specific emergency legislation for derogation to follow; ordinary law sufficiently encroaching on rights can activate the treaty requirement for derogation by a state to derogate. The right of derogation is not absolute. Non-derogable rights are those specially protected rights under treaty law that cannot be limited or suspended, notwithstanding the extent of the crisis faced by the state.[5] Both the International Covenant on Civil and Political Rights (ICCPR) and the European Convention on Human Rights (ECHR) limit non-derogable rights to a concise set of substantive provisions. Arguably, the drafters of these documents failed to recognize the significance of procedural rights, specifically those due process rights protecting access to justice in times of crisis.

The one contemporary human rights treaty that formally remedies this deficit is the American Convention on Human Rights. It sets out an expansive number of non-derogable rights provisions.[6] Of particular relevance to this analysis is Article 27,

---

[2] 'Study of the Implications for Human Rights of Recent Developments Concerning Situations Known as States of Siege or Emergency' UN Commission on Human Rights, 35th Session, Agenda Item 10, 8–9, UN Doc E/CN.4/Sub.2/1982/15 (1982); Chowdhury (n 1 above) 15; CL Rossiter, *Constitutional Dictatorship: Crisis Government in Modern Democracies* (Princeton University Press, 1948) 6; AS Klieman, 'Emergency Politics: The Growth of Crisis Government' (1976) 70 Conflict Studies 5.

[3] For discussion of emergency powers in the economic context see eg WE Scheuerman, 'The Economic State of Emergency' (2000) 21 Cardozo Law Review 1869.

[4] European Convention on Human Rights, Art 15; American Convention on Human Rights, Art 27; International Covenant on Civil and Human Rights, Art 4.

[5] eg the European Convention on Human Rights restrictions derogation from Art 2 (the right to life), Art 3 (the right to be free from torture), Art 4, para 1 (the right to be free from slavery), and Art 7 (the application of non-retroactive laws).

[6] Art 27(2) of the Convention does not allow derogation from, Art 3 (Right to Juridical Personality), Art 4 (Right to Life), Art 5 (Right to Humane Treatment), Art 6 (Freedom from Slavery), Art 9 (Freedom from Ex Post Facto Laws), Art 12 (Freedom of Conscience and Religion), Art 17 (Rights of the Family), Art 18 (Right to a Name), Art 19 (Rights of the Child), Art 20 (Right to Nationality), and Art 23 (Right to Participate in Government), or of the judicial guarantees essential for the protection of such rights.

which states that the judicial guarantees essential for the protection of enumerated non-derogable rights cannot be abrogated in times of crisis. This provision is important because it constitutes a robust copper-fasting of the capacity for legal review on the protection of non-derogable rights during a situation of emergency.

B. Definition of an Emergency

Emergency is an opaque concept, capable of multifaceted definition. Pinning down its definitional contours is central to the legal regulation and oversight of crisis both nationally and internationally. International human rights courts have expended some considerable jurisprudential energy in this regard. For example, in *Lawless v Ireland*[7] a nine-member majority in the European Commission of Human Rights ('the Commission') defined a 'public emergency' for the purposes of Article 15 of the ECHR, as 'a situation of exceptional and imminent danger or crisis affecting the general public, as distinct from particular groups, and constituting a threat to the organised life of the community which composes the State in question'.[8] In the subsequent *Greek* case,[9] the majority of the Commission's members identified four characteristics of a 'public emergency' under Article 15: the emergency must be actual or imminent; its effects must involve the whole nation; the continuance of the organized life of the community must be threatened; and the crisis or danger must be exceptional, in that the normal measures or restrictions, permitted by the Convention for the maintenance of public safety, health, and order, are plainly inadequate.[10]

In its General Comment 5/13 on Article 4 of the International Covenant on Civil and Political Rights, allowing certain derogation upon a 'public emergency', the United Nations Human Rights Committee (HRC) indicated that an emergency will justify derogation under that article only if the relevant circumstances are of an exceptional and temporary nature.[11] The principles identified in General Comment 5/13 have recently been revised and extended in the new General Comment 29, again stressing both the temporary and exceptional nature of emergencies.[12] This outlook is echoed in the jurisprudence of both the Inter-American Commission on Human Rights and the Inter-American Court of Human Rights.[13] In its advisory

---

[7] See *Lawless v Ireland* (1960-61) ECHR, Series B, 56 (Commission report) (hereinafter *Lawless* (Commission)); *Lawless* (Court), 3 ECHR, Series A (1960–61).

[8] *Lawless* (Commission) 82, para 90.

[9] 1 ECHR, *The Greek Case*: Report of the Commission (1969).

[10] ibid 81, para 153.

[11] See 'Report of the Human Rights Committee', UN GAOR Human Rights Commission, 36th Session, Annex VII, General Comment 5/13, at 110, UN Doc A/36/40 (1981).

[12] Human Rights Committee, General Comment No 29, States of Emergency (Article 4), CCPR/C/21/Rev.1/Add.11 (31 August 2001).

[13] *Report on the Situation of Human Rights in Argentina*, Inter-American Court of Human Rights, OEA/ser.L/V/II.49, doc 19 corr 1, (1980) 25–7.

opinion on *Habeas Corpus in Emergency Situations*,[14] the Inter-American Court stated that the derogation provision of Article 27 of the American Convention was 'a provision for exceptional situations only.'[15]

Some general observations follow these definitional boundaries. First, international human rights law generally follows a model of legal accommodation with regard to the experience of crisis by states.[16] This means that the regulation of crisis falls within the law, and does not constitute a 'black-hole' where international law's domain does not extend.[17] Secondly, procedural requirements of substance permeate the privilege of derogation, requiring that states take seriously obligations of notification, reporting, necessity, and proportionality when resorting to legal measures which trigger derogation from international human rights law norms. Thirdly, international human rights law's goal lies in protecting individual rights and the dignity of the person. This means that any evaluation of the success of law in the realm of emergency must be measured against the experience of the individual at the micro level. The balance of measurement does not lie in benefits to the state alone in the emergency context.

C. Emergencies and Individual Rights

In examining patterns of state response to crisis, it becomes clear that the encroachment on individual rights is most profound when the state feels itself under threat, whether manifested as internal or external in form. Empirical studies tend to support a number of claims asserted in this chapter.[18] Nonetheless, there is an important caveat that unique micro patterns of state response always present themselves in societies and particular legal systems, in ways that do not always conform to the general trends.

In times of emergency there is a general diminution of rights protections. A number of studies illustrate that violation of non-derogable rights, such as the right to life and the right to be free from torture, experience elevated patterns of abuse and violation during emergency.[19] The fact of crisis, for a variety of institutional

---

[14] *Habeas Corpus in Emergency Situations* Advisory Opinion, (1987) 8 Inter-American Court of Human Rights (series A) OEA/ser.L/V/111.17, doc 13 (1987) 33.

[15] ibid 23.

[16] O Gross and F Ní Aoláin, *Law in Times of Crisis, Emergency Powers in Theory and Practice* (Cambridge University Press, 2006).

[17] F Ní Aoláin, 'The Emergence of Diversity: Differences in Human Rights Jurisprudence' (1995) 19 Ford ILJ 101.

[18] See eg the emergency powers data base held at The Queens University (Belfast) at <http://www.law.qub.ac.uk/humanrts/emergency/emerghome.html>; Questiaux Report (n 1 above).

[19] F Ní Aoláin, *The Politics of Force: Conflict Management and State Violence in Northern Ireland* (Blackstaff Press, 2000) (on the protection of the right to life in situations of emergency); See also Israeli Supreme Court: Legality of the Interrogation Methods Applied by the Israeli General Security Service (6 September 1999) at <http://www.asil.org/ilib/ilib0229.htm>.

and psychological reasons, often creates the political context in which extreme violations are tolerated in ways that would be difficult to defend in non-extreme situations.[20] Substantive liberty rights such as the right to freedom of assembly, association, and expression are first in the derogation firing line, since governments view legitimate dissent as contrary to their capacity to respond and contain the crisis at hand. A compelling similarity across jurisdictions is that constraints on due process rights are a first line response for many states experiencing crisis.[21] Constraints on these rights constitute an identifiable pattern in state derogations from rights protections under international human rights treaties.[22] This also explains why the derogation case law of all international human rights regional systems is mainly concerned with violations of due process rights. Finally, there is an identifiable chill factor for the full enforcement of rights in times of emergency. Part of that chill stems from the dynamics of the language of crisis itself, which highlights fear and undermines belief in the capacity of ordinary law to cope with the threat identified.[23]

All of the patterns identified above contribute to the theme of this chapter, namely they tell us the locales in which individual rights may be most frequently limited, and thus where access protections are most meaningful and most contested. Thus, one obvious conclusion is that it is vital to identify where rights are being limited, because this tells us where the need for remedy and response will be most compelling.

This chapter now explores in some detail the significance of limitations on due process rights in the emergency context. In arguing that due process rights are the guardians of access to justice in times of emergency and otherwise, it follows that the extent to which legal process is diminished or denied is vital to assessing meaningful access to justice in times of crisis. More importantly they play a particularly vital role in times of emergency. Across legal systems and emergency experiences,

---

[20] O Gross, 'Chaos and Rules: Should Responses to Violent Crisis Always be Constitutional?' (2003) 112 YLJ 1011.

[21] Human rights norms which, *inter alia*, support the right of access to justice, eg *ex post facto* law, UN Standard Minimum Rules for the Administration of Juvenile Justice, Code of Conduct for Law Enforcement Officials (GA Res 34/169); Standard Minimum Rules for the Treatment of Prisoners, the UN Body of Principles for the Protection of All Persons under Any Form of Detention or Imprisonment (GA Res 43/173)—obligation to inform detainees of their rights (principle 13), to bring detainees before a judicial or other authority promptly after arrest (principle 11), and to provide access to legal counsel (principle 17); Convention Against Torture, adopted by the UNGA, 10 December 1984, 1465 UNTS 85, Art 15, evidence adduced by means of torture is not admissible; Convention on the Rights of the Child, adopted by the UNGA, 20 November 1989, 1577 UNTS 3, contains several provisions on the rights of fair trial for children. Art 37(d): 'every child deprived of his or her liberty shall have the right to prompt access to legal and other assistance'.

[22] For an overview of derogation notices and status of derogation notices to the International Covenant on Civil and Political Rights, see <http://www.ohchr.org/english/law/>.

[23] See K Roach, *September 11: Consequences for Canada* (McGill-Queen's University Press, 2003).

limitations on due process rights demonstrate the centrality of this set of rights to the exercise of emergency powers, so that a universal aspect of the emergency powers doctrine invariably involves limitation of due process rights. As revealed by the case law analysis below, these include: expanded legal bases for detention as well as extending the length of time persons are kept in state custody; limitations on access to legal counsel; and limitations on access to judicial oversight.

Notably the application of emergency powers (and thus the limitation point for access to justice) is directed at individuals deemed suspect by states experiencing crisis. By contrast, crisis engendered by armed conflict situations has more complex features of application. In situations of international armed conflict, the persons posing the most compelling threat to the state (namely combatants from the other side) have deeply entrenched protections that commonly operate to copper-fasten rights of access to justice. By contrast, in situations of internal armed conflict, access rights applied to the same class of persons (by virtue of a lack of combatant status) are much less secure.

D. International Courts and Individual Protections in Emergencies

This analysis assesses the dynamics of due process limitations, examines how robustly courts have responded to restrictions, and concludes by reflection on what this tells us about the relationship between the use (and abuse) of emergency powers in the access context. A starting point here is to restate that liberty and fair trial rights are derogable under most of the international human rights law regimes. This means that in the internal treaty ranking of rights, these central protections have a lower formal standing than non-derogable rights. If, as suggested here, limitations on liberty and due process rights, and thus by extension access to justice, constitute a key marker of state responses to emergency, then the extent to which international courts and tribunals are prepared to police these limitations firmly, tells us how well the access to justice boundaries are being patrolled by these same bodies.

In this context, note that the United Nations HRC's recent General Comment has outlined that the Committee has a duty to 'conduct a careful analysis under each article of the Covenant based on an objective assessment of the actual situation'.[24] The Committee makes particular reference to limitations on derogable rights, stressing that the status of derogable rights does not mean that these rights can be derogated from 'at will'.[25] Another relevant extension of protection for derogable rights in times of emergency has recently been undertaken by the Committee. It has taken the view that non-derogable rights that also constitute peremptory norms of international law are effectively non-derogable. Moreover, the Committee seems to indicate that derogations from certain rights could never, in their view, be proportionate. Thus the Committee states:

States' parties may in no circumstances invoke article 4 of the Covenant as justification for acting in violation of humanitarian law or peremptory norms of international law,

---

[24] General Comment No 29 (n 12 above) para 6.
[25] ibid.

for instance by taking hostages...through arbitrary deprivations of liberty or by devi-
ating from fundamental *principles of fair trial, including the presumption of innocence*
(emphasis added).[26]

The position taken by the HRC in General Comment 29 has particular significance. A focus on the status of non-derogable rights in the context of Comment
29 means that the HRC has identified the capacity for abuse of these rights in the
emergency context. There is a clear move to bolster certain non-derogable rights
and to inform states that a strict level of scrutiny will be applied to limitations on
these kinds of rights. Moreover, the specific mention of 'fair trial principles', which
inherently include the right of access to fair procedures, means that the Committee
has identified these principles as vital in the emergency context.

This approach has an interesting cross-application to the interpretation of the
Inter-American Court which, in two important advisory opinion decisions, has
found that certain derogable rights under the American Convention are effectively
rendered non-derogable by expansive interpretation of the term 'judicial guarantees' as used in Article 27 of the American Convention.[27] All of these judicial
interventions tell us that notwithstanding the derogable status of due process rights
under most of the international human rights treaties, some of the relevant courts
and tribunals have identified the importance that attach to them in the crisis context, and have positively affirmed the value of looking at any limitations closely.

An extensive case law has developed concerning due process rights in situations
of emergency. The discussion here is focused on a number of selected cases from
the European and Inter-American systems.

E. European Court of Human Rights Jurisprudence

The ECHR was opened for signature in November 1950. Its enforcement structure was
then three pronged, comprising a part-time Court, a full-time Commission, and the overarching political structure of the Council of Europe. Protocol 11 to the ECHR modified
this structure significantly by replacing the Commission with a full-time Court.[28]

1. Brogan v United Kingdom

The case of *Brogan v United Kingdom*[29] provides an example of the European
Court of Human Rights being asked to examine a formal limitation on due process

---

[26] ibid para 11.
[27] See *Judicial Guarantees in States of Emergency* 9 Inter-American Court of Human Rights,
Series A, 40, OEA/ser.L/VI/111.9 doc 13 (1987); *Habeas Corpus in Emergency Situations* 8 Inter-
American Court of Human Rights, Series A, 33, OEA/ser.L/V/111.17. doc 13 (1987).
[28] See <http://www.echr.coe.int/ECHR/EN/Header/The+Court/The+Court/History+of+the+Court/>
(last visited 8 August 2005); A Drzemczewski and J Meyer-Ladewig, 'Principal Characteristics of the New
ECHR Control Mechanism, as Established by Protocol 11' (1994) 15 HRLJ 81 (describing basic features
of reform).
[29] Brogan and Ors v UK (1988) 145-B ECHR, Series A, 16.

rights, in a situation which the state defined as one of crisis in its pleadings. It is also clearly a case about access to justice. The facts concerned the arrest and detention of four persons under section 12 of the Prevention of Terrorism (Temporary Provisions) Act 1984 in Northern Ireland. All four were held in detention centres for periods ranging from four to six days. None was brought before a judicial officer in that period. All were subsequently released without criminal charge. At the heart of this case was a dispute about the right of the four detained persons to have a right of access to judicial remedy to review the merits of their detention.

Importantly, *Brogan* is formally not a derogation case. The United Kingdom had in fact withdrawn a previously submitted notice of derogation in respect of its detention practices in Northern Ireland, though the periods of detention under the emergency powers in force had not changed.

In summary, the Court concluded that a breach of Article 5 had occurred. In reaching this conclusion the Court gave detailed consideration to the requirements of access to justice in general, and in a situation of emergency in particular. Central to its finding was the Court's view on Article 5(1) which provides: 'Everyone has the right to liberty and security of person. No one shall be deprived of his liberty save in the following cases and in accordance with a procedure prescribed by law.' The Court agreed that the arrest and detention of the applicants had been 'lawful'. Its attention then turned to whether Article 5(1)(c) required that the purpose of the arrest or detention ensure that those arrested were brought before a competent legal authority. Substantial evidence had been presented to the Court indicating that there was a pattern in state arrest and detention processes suggesting that the primary purpose of arrests under the Prevention of Terrorism (Temporary Provisions) Act 1984 was to gather information and intelligence rather than to bring criminal charges against persons detained. This question has obvious contemporary resonance in the post-9/11 war on terror, as arrest and detention have come to perform critical roles in the collection of information and evidence against persons other than those in custody. The approach of the Court here is instructive. It refused to second guess the bona fide detention and arrest processes of the state and its agents, stating that 'the Court is not required to examine the impugned legislation *in abstracto*, but must confine itself to the circumstances of the case before it'.[30] The Court went on to conclude that there was no reason to believe that the police investigation was 'not in good faith'. Such a deferential approach evidently poses some problems for the full protection of the right of access to justice in times of emergency, particularly given the patterns of state practice in this arena.

As revealed by practice across jurisdictions,[31] emergency arrest powers reveal themselves as mechanisms of containment, often specifically aimed at securing flows of information and not aimed at producing arrest outcomes. Domestic courts have traditionally found it difficult to challenge and contain police and military

---

[30] ibid para 53.
[31] Oraá (n 1 above) 43; Quextiaux (n 1 above) 4.

practices in this regard. Hence, the importance of international court oversight and awareness of the capacity for the abuse through arrest processes, including the manner in which they can be designed to deliver (in practice) a lack of meaningful access to justice, correlated precisely to the existence of an emergency.

From this point in the *Brogan* case the Court went on to consider the alleged violation of Article 5(3), which requires persons arrested to be brought 'promptly' before a judge or 'other officer authorised by law to exercise judicial power'.[32] Arguably, at least within the European system, this provision is the cornerstone of meaningful access to justice, both in times of crisis and normality. The Court also seems to recognize the pivotal nature of Article 5, and this element of it. It stated:

The Court has regard to the importance of Article 5 in the Convention system: it enshrines a fundamental right, namely the protection of the individual against arbitrary interferences by the state to his right to liberty. Judicial control of interferences by the executive with the individual's right to liberty is an essential feature of the guarantee embodied in Article 5(3), which is intended to minimise the risk of arbitrariness. Judicial control is implied by the rule of law, 'one of the fundamental principles of a democratic society'...[33]

The Court ultimately concluded that the abdication by the government of any resort to judicial oversight when detention was extended from the norm violated the Convention's requirements. The Court was of the view that the procedural requirement of access to judicial monitoring was of a particular significance within the Convention's legal order. Moreover, limitations upon it would 'entail consequences impairing the very essence of the right protected by this provisions'.[34]

Problematically, however, the Court also posited the view that such a breach could be contextualized in relation to the ongoing terrorist campaign in Northern Ireland.[35] Though recognizing that the United Kingdom had withdrawn its notice of derogation, aspects of its reasoning in this context are problematic. This is all the more so in a contemporary reading, where many states have extended their emergency powers as a result of the events of September 11 2001, but have not entered derogation notices based on the measures taken.[36] It is the contextualization used by the Court that is most troublesome. The *Brogan* case constitutes a good example of a Court finding that a democratic government is making a good faith effort to preserve human rights, and de facto granting the state a wider margin of appreciation than those states with lesser reputations for rights enforcement.[37] The judgment contains pervasive

---

[32] Brogan (n 29 above) 131.

[33] ibid para 58 (footnotes omitted).

[34] ibid para 62.

[35] ibid 16.

[36] See C Campbell, 'Wars on Terror and Vicarious Hegemons: The UK, International Law and the Northern Ireland Conflict' (2005) 54 ICLQ 321.

[37] B Mangan 'Protecting Human Rights in National Emergencies: Shortcomings in the European System and a Proposal for Reform' (1998) 10 HRQ 372, 383.

references to the ongoing campaign of terrorist violence in Northern Ireland.[38] The majority states that despite the excluding examination of derogation, account may be taken of other material and concurrent issues: 'This does not, however, preclude proper account being taken of the *background circumstances* of the case.'[39] Again, the resonance of this language post-September 11 2001 is particularly compelling, where nebulous references to the pervasiveness of terrorist threat have fundamentally affected the manner in which states contextualize the extension of anti-terrorist and criminal legislation to combat a variety of behaviours. More particularly, where states have evidenced their willingness to resort to detention without trial, and without access to formal legal review, most notably at Guantanamo Bay, a judicial approach which tends to gloss over the state's limitations on procedural access to review is highly problematic. It thus remains to be seen how the Court will respond to post-9/11 cases, where democratic states like the United Kingdom may make pleadings based on the global and indeterminate war on terror as a basis for the limitations of due process rights without formal resort to derogation.[40]

Following the decision by the Court on the merits (the breach of Article 5 by the state), an important footnote is that the United Kingdom in December 1988 issued a further notice of derogation in respect of Article 5(3).[41] There is a cogent argument that the derogation was issued as a direct response to the judgment rather than to any upsurge in violence or increased threat to the security of the state.[42] The derogation allowed the state to hold persons in detention for longer periods when arrested under the emergency legislation, precisely limiting their right of access to a judicial body. The accommodation made here by the state was thus in response to an external legal decision, rather than to the facts on the ground.

2. Challenges and Pretext—Brannigan and McBride

The matter came then back for review to the European Court of Human Rights in *Brannigan and McBride*, the case which followed *Brogan*, and challenged the

---

[38] Brogan (n 29 above) 21–4, 27, 33.

[39] ibid 27 (emphasis added).

[40] Some indications of the Court's approach, at least on the issues of extra-territorial application of procedural protections can be gauged through an inconsistent line of European Court of Human Rights jurisprudence. The cases include *Bankovic v Belgium and Ors* Application 52207/99; *Ilascu v Moldova and Russia* (2005) 40 EHRR 1030; *Issa v Turkey* (2004) ECHR 31831/96.

[41] See European Commission of Human Rights, Minutes of the Plenary Session, Strasbourg, 16–20 January 1989, DH (89) (Déf), Appendix VI, 10.

[42] Note the statement of Douglas Hogg, at the time Under-Secretary of State for the Home Department, to the House of Commons on 13 December 1988: 'The case of Brogan & Others has rightly exercised Honourable Members' minds. The Committee will recall that my right honourable friend the Home Secretary told the House on 6 December that we shall bring forward our proposal for responding to the judgement in the Brogan case as soon as possible and before the Bill leaves the House. The matter is complex, and whether we opt for derogation or some sort of judicial control, the implications are obviously far reaching.'

bona fides of state implementation of a derogation resulting in limited rights of access to judicial oversight for persons detained under the emergency legislation. A critical analysis of the case reveals that the Court failed to examine the possibility that the United Kingdom's derogation was simply a response to an adverse Court decision.[43] The applicants in the case had specifically contended that the derogation entered by the state was merely a mechanical response to the adverse finding in the *Brogan* case. The Court and the Commission maintained that while the judgment 'triggered off'[44] the derogation, there was no reason to conclude that the derogation was anything other than a 'genuine response'.[45]

In examining the merits of the case the Commission found that, relying on its previously stated position in *Brogan,* the applicants were in an identical position: all were arrested under the same anti-terrorism legislation; the periods of their detention fell short of the stated 'promptness' requirements of the Convention; all did not have an enforceable right under Northern Ireland law to compensation for an Article 5(3) breach; and all had suffered an Article 5(5) breach of the ECHR. The point of contention was whether the potential breaches of Article 5 of the Convention were answered by the United Kingdom's notice of derogation to the Council of Europe submitted on 23 December 1988. The Court, after perfunctory review of the arguments made by the applicants and associated *amicus* briefs which strongly maintained that there was no longer a situation of exceptional crisis warranting a derogation in Northern Ireland,[46] concluded that 'there can be no doubt that such a public emergency existed in Northern Ireland'.[47] It firmly stated that it did not find it necessary to compare the situation when the derogation was withdrawn with the situation when it was reinstated as 'the decision to withdraw a derogation is, in principle, a matter within the discretion of the State'.[48]

The unwillingness of the Court to examine why, prior to the *Brogan* judgment, the state could function adequately without resort to derogation is a clear manifestation of an unwarranted non-interference principle. The Court also clearly failed to engage with the significance of protecting access to justice rights, in a context where the material effects on detained persons were significant, and affected a distinct and identifiable class of persons. Its decision demonstrates timidity and deference on the part of the Court, which parallels the general responses of domestic courts to the review of crisis powers by the state.[49] The case illustrates the danger

---

[43] *Brannigan and McBride v UK* Series A, No 25; (1979) 2 EHRR 25, 37.
[44] ibid 51.
[45] ibid.
[46] ibid paras 41–46 (amicus briefs were submitted by Amnesty International, Liberty, and the government appointed Standing Advisory Commission on Human Rights).
[47] ibid para 47.
[48] ibid.
[49] AM Garro and H Dahl, 'Legal Accountability for Human Rights Violations in Argentina: One Step Forward and Two Steps Backward' (1987) 8 HRLJ 283.

of the burden of proof shifting silently in favour of the state in a way that creates the danger that derogation functions only as an edifice for accountability.

The *Branningan and McBride* decision also illustrates the particularly difficult problem that international courts encounter when they seek to confront permanent emergencies. The International Law Association[50] and other commentators have stressed that one of the 'four basic elements' of an emergency is its provisional and temporary character. [51] The applicants in *Brannigan and McBride* stressed that in situations of permanent emergency it was inconsistent for the national authorities to be allowed a wide margin of appreciation. In short, one can contend the opposite to be desirable, that the longer an emergency persists the narrower the margin of appreciation to the state should be.[52] The longer the emergency persists the more critical it becomes to ensure that there is meaningful access to legal review for persons whose rights have been curtailed by extraordinary law. This is true because permanent emergencies tend to dull the interests of governments and their officials in fully preserving the rights of the individual. There is also a strong correlation between the length of an emergency and its impact on an ever-growing number of citizens. The general experience is that while emergency powers may start out as (and be approved for) use against targeted groups of citizens and others, the longer the emergency persists the wider the application of the powers conferred against a wider net of citizens and non-citizens alike.[53] The *Brannigan* case is testament to the limits of international review of emergency powers in general, and draws our attention to the problems of protection access rights in particular when states assert themselves to be facing a situation of internal crisis.

3. *The Turkish Cases and Eastern European Cases—the Intersection between the Length of an 'Emergency' and Access Rights*

The problems related to emergency oversight, both generally as regards the form and practice of governments who persistently resort to exceptional powers as well as the specific manifestations applied to limitations on the rights of access to justice, are well illustrated when we examine the cases concerning Turkey coming before the European Court of Human Rights. More recent cases from the new Eastern European democracies illustrate some of the same features and trends. The length

---

[50] The International Law Association, at its 61st Conference, held in Paris, 26 August to 1 September 1984, approved by consensus a set of minimum standards governing the declaration and administration of states of emergency that threaten the life of a nation. The standards were the culmination of 6 years of study by a sub-committee of the Association, and 2 additional years of revision by the full committee on the Enforcement of Human Rights Law.

[51] See Chowdhury (n 1 above) 24–9.

[52] O Gross and F Ní Aoláin, 'From Discretion to Scrutiny: Revisiting the Application of the Margin of Appreciation Doctrine in the Context of Article 15 of the European Convention on Human Rights' (2001) 23 HRQ 625.

[53] P Hillyard, *Suspect Community* (Pluto Press, 1993).

of emergency has a definitive link with access to justice concerns. The longer the emergency persists the more harmful the effects on the rule of law generally. When due process rights are at the heart of the state's response to crisis one can identify persistent and damaging effects on the totality of due process rights over time. Moreover there is a genuine danger, revealed by the practice of states, that the longer the emergency the more the general public adjusts to restrictions, thereby making the exception the norm.[54]

In analysing the Turkish cases specifically one can identify both positive and negative dimensions. Positively they increasingly demonstrate that the Court can be fairly robust when it comes to measuring the necessity and proportionality of particular micro measures taken by the state. These augur well for oversight of specific access to justice type protections in emergencies by the European Court of Human Rights. They also show the Court vigorously defining the procedural requirements of derogation and holding some states closely to these standards.

For example, in the case of *Sakik and Ors v Turkey*,[55] concerning the arrest and detention by police of six former members of the National Assembly who were prosecuted in a national security court, the European Court of Human Rights was markedly less deferential to the state's views than it had been in the series of cases emanating from Northern Ireland. The political party to which the applicants belonged was proscribed and dissolved by the Constitutional Court in August 1993. This was on the basis that its members were involved in separatist activity. All of the applicants were accused of committing offences defined in the Turkish Criminal Code as terrorist crimes. All of the applicants were held in police custody for periods ranging from twelve to fourteen days. Previously, in August 1990, Turkey had entered a formal notice of derogation to the Council of Europe.[56] The notice was highly specific both in its geographical scope of application and the rights affected (Article 5).[57] Substantively the Court found that the derogation applied only to the region where a state of emergency had been proclaimed, and did not include the city of Ankara (where the applicants were arrested, detained, and subjected to trial).[58]

---

[54] See, O Gross 'The Normless and Exceptionless Exception: Carl Schmitt's Theory of Emergency Powers and the "Norm-Exception" Dichotomy' (2000) 21 Cardozo Law Review 1825.

[55] *Sakik and Ors v Turkey* Judgment of 26 November 1997, 58 Reports of Judgments and Decisions 2609, 2628, Holding PP 2, 5, 7 (1997-VII).

[56] The applicants had alleged violations of various Convention provisions including Art 5(1), (3), (4), and (5), Art 6(1) and (3), and Art 10.

[57] The notice of derogation also substantially curtailed an earlier derogation by Turkey which had limited the exercise of Arts 5, 6, 8, 10, 11, and 13.

[58] The Court forcefully held that it would be working against the purpose of Art 15, if the territorial scope of the provision were to be extended judicially to a part of the state not explicitly named in the notice of derogation. The Court here is working through and applying spatial distinctions to the exercise of emergency powers, and on some level seeking to make legally meaningful the political and legal distinctions held by the state which maintains that 2 legal regimes can contemporaneously be applied within the territory controlled by the state. In this case the Court held that Art 15 did not apply to the facts of the case.

The *Sakik* case highlights the Court's subtly different approach to the lesser established democracies, one that is not always positive for the overall standards set in derogation review. Of particular interest in this judgment and in the light of procedures put in place by the United States with respect to persons detained in Afghanistan and Iraq, is the view of the Court on the applicability of Article 5(3) of the ECHR to alleged terrorist offenders.[59] This requires that persons detained be brought 'promptly' before a judicial authority, or officer authorized to exercise judicial power. The matter has recently been canvassed unsuccessfully by the British government in relevant domestic litigation where it has asserted that United Nations Security Council Resolution 1546 trumps its own human rights treaty obligations, including those under Article 5 of the ECHR (which would seem to preclude UK military forces from resorting to administrative detention).[60] The Turkish government had argued that the scale and nature of the terrorist threat made it particularly difficult to obtain evidence, thereby making it difficult to proceed with trials in a speedy fashion. While acknowledging that terrorist offences presented meaningful difficulties for the state, the Court trenchantly held that: 'This does not mean, however, that the investigating authorities have *carte blanche* under Article 5 to arrest suspects for questioning, free from effective control by the domestic courts and ultimately, by the Convention supervisory institutions, whenever they choose to assert that terrorism is involved.'[61]

The Court went on to state that the time the applicants were held in police custody (twelve and fourteen days respectively) fell outside the strict constraints of Article 5(3). Moreover and most compelling, was the Court's subsequent statement that even 'supposing that the activities...were linked to terrorism' the Court could not accept that it was necessary to detain them for the time periods in question without judicial intervention. This tells us that with a derogation in place, the state's right to hold a person in detention is limited and subject to a test of proportionality and necessity—the upper time limits of which are being developed by the Court. Again, no post-September 11 2001 cases raising these specific issues have come to the Court and, with the exception of the United Kingdom, no states on this basis have engaged in extended detention practices, but it would seem that a bright line has been drawn on the state's right to detain persons even in times of crisis, and specifically when that crisis is defined as a terrorist threat.

---

[59] Military Order of November 13, 2001: Detention, Treatment, and Trial of Certain Non-Citizens in the War Against Terrorism §4, 3 CFR 918, 919–20 (2001).

[60] *R (On the Application of Al-Jedda) v Secretary of State for Defence*, [2005] HRLR 39, QBD (Admin), 12 August 2005. Note the argument was accepted before the House of Lords decision in March of 2006, *R (Al-Jedda) v Secretary of State for Defence* [2006] EWCA Civ 327, 39. *R (Al Jedda) v Secretary of State for Defence* [2006] 27 HRLR 829, (Ct App Civ Div, 29 March 2006).

[61] *Salik* (n 55 above) para 44.

4. Demir and Ors v Turkey: *Derogation, Effective Oversight Capacity and Access*

The case of *Demir and Ors v Turkey* also illustrates the effective oversight capacity of the European Court of Human Rights combined with a heavy emphasis on thoroughly assessing the necessity of measures taken by the derogating state.[62] The three applicants were all politically active, holding positions in the People's Social Democratic Party. All lived in the province of Sirnak, subject to the state of emergency declared since 1987. All three applicants were arrested in 1993, and were held for between sixteen and twenty-three days.[63] All were subsequently charged and convicted of offences under the Criminal Code and Terrorism Act. At the time of the arrests the only derogation in force was expressly limited to Article 5.

The Court briskly held, with reference to *Brogan v United Kingdom*, that the periods of detention failed to satisfy the requirement of 'promptness' laid down in Article 5(3). This was notwithstanding the government's insistence that the measures were taken to protect the community from terrorism. Without elaboration it noted that where necessary, the authorities facing terrorist threats could 'develop forms of judicial control which are adapted to the circumstances but compatible with the Convention'.[64] This emphasis on judicial control confirms that the European Court has become increasingly diligent in overseeing certain aspects of the access rights of persons detained through the use of emergency powers.

The Court argued that the mere fact that a detention is in conformity with domestic law does not fireproof it from Article 15 review. Nor was it prepared to agree with the government's position that Article 5(3) could not be applied when investigations were ongoing. Instead it asserted that this was precisely when Article 5(3) was enforceable. It further held that subsequent conviction for terrorist offences had no bearing on the question of whether there was a 'situation which necessitated the detention of suspects incommunicado for such lengthy periods'.[65] In short, their terrorism-related convictions did not subsequently justify lengthy periods of prior detention. The Court was also concerned about the lack of safeguards during their detention, especially their lack of access to counsel and the insufficiency of the medical oversight. In conclusion, the Court held that the length of detention was not strictly required by the crisis relied upon by the government.

This general point is confirmed in the case of *Askoy v Turkey*.[66] Here, the Court examined the validity of the Turkish derogation from Article 15 in the context of the applicant's detention and alleged ill-treatment in custody for approximately

---

[62] *Demir and Ors v Turkey* [1998] ECHR 88 (21380/93) (23 September 1998).
[63] The exact length of detention was disputed by the parties. ibid 13.
[64] ibid para 41.
[65] ibid para 53.
[66] *Askoy v Turkey* (1996) 23 EHRR 553, 78.

fourteen days in November 1992.[67] The Court repeated its consistent and problematic assertion that states had a 'wide margin of appreciation' in deciding whether they are facing a public emergency. [68] It did not second-guess the state's call that an emergency was in play, nor seek to tease out the role of the state versus the role of non-state actors (if any) in the circumstances which created the emergency. But, by finding that the state's actions fell outside the acceptable perimeters of the derogation privilege, the judgment stressed again the Court's willingness to hold some states accountable on their practice of emergency powers, and confirmed the importance of access to judicial oversight as a key element of the rule of law in an emergency.

This approach has continued in the case law of the Court following the events of September 11. A small number of cases demonstrate a robust approach by the Court on due process (and by extension access) issues. For example, in *Ocalan v Turkey* the Court found that while the investigation of terrorist offences undoubtedly presented the authorities with special problems, 'this does not mean that the investigating authorities have carte blanche under Article 5 to arrest suspects for questioning, free from effective controls by the domestic courts'.[69] Those controls include access to a lawyer and to judicial oversight of the detention itself. In *Al-Nashif v Bulgaria,* a case concerning deportation and detention, the Court firmly determined that national authorities could not 'do away with' effective control of the lawfulness of detention by choosing to assert that national security and terrorism were involved.[70]

These illustrative cases show some willingness to be robust on critical aspects of rights protection which can be placed under the access to justice umbrella. Nonetheless, given the scope and scale of encroachment on due process rights, particularly during permanent emergencies, such review does not address all the difficult elements that arise in respect of a resort to emergency powers. The European Court of Human Rights generally operates on the assumption of the general necessity for a legally regulated crisis response, but has a limited legal and political vocabulary to challenge the reality of the crisis assertion in the first place.[71] The Court has consistently avoided engagement with the bona fides of state resort to derogation, and perhaps most crucially no systematic jurisprudence

---

[67] There was dispute as to the length of detention time. Based on its fact-finding mission to the region, the Commission concluded that the applicants were held for at least 14 days. ibid para 23.

[68] Though notably the Court stated that it was competent to judge whether the Turkish derogation met the formal requirements of Art 15(3). ibid para 85, 86, 90. It then turned to examine whether the measures taken were 'strictly required' by the exigencies of the situation. Outlining its view that 7 days' detention accompanied by derogation was permissible under the Convention, it went on to state that 14-days' detention was outside that perimeter.

[69] See *Ocalan v Turkey* (46221/99) [2003] ECHR 125 (12 March 2003) para 106; *Filiz and Kalkan v Turkey* (34481/97) [2002] ECHR 504 (20 June 2002) paras 25–26.

[70] See *Al-Nashif v Bulgaria* (50963/99) [2002] ECHR 497 (20 June 2002) 123–4, para 94.

[71] Gross and Ní Aoláin (n 16 above) 247–325.

has been developed to articulate the pertinent and obvious relationship between human rights norms and the applicability of international humanitarian law norms in such contexts.

5. Extending the Scope of Access to Justice in the European Context

A notable feature of recent European human rights law jurisprudence pertaining to states experiencing a situation of emergency has been its approach to the access and oversight issues in the context of Articles 2, 3, and 13 of the ECHR. It is notable that in all the cases discussed here, derogation was not an issue before the Court, either because the rights in question constituted non-derogable rights, or because (as regards Article 13) the state had not entered a derogation on the provision. In this context, access to justice is measured less in terms of meaningful access for the direct victims of the relevant human rights violation (usually because the core violation concerns the right to life), but rather concerns access for extended victims (usually the family members of a deceased individual).

In a series of multi-jurisdictional cases from Northern Ireland, Turkey, and most recently Russia (concerning Chechnya),[72] the Court has 'read-into' the absolute prohibition on the arbitrary taking of life and the prohibition on torture a violation by the state's failure to conduct an adequate and effective investigation. Significantly this includes a core element of procedural access by the relatives of those killed in addition to an investigative process which would be capable of identifying and punishing those responsible for the deaths or injuries. Thus, investigation has become a firm foundation from which to gauge the robustness of access by plaintiffs or victims to legal process. These cases have also frequently found that the lack of an effective remedy (Article 13) constituted a breach of the Convention.

So, for example, *Khashiyev and Akayeva v Russia* involved the execution of five individuals by Russian servicemen soon after the Russian military regained control of Grozny in January 2000. The Court found that Russia had failed to protect the right to life of those concerned and failed to conduct adequate investigations.[73] In the *Isayeva, Yusupova and Bazayeva* case, concerning the aerial bombardment of a civilian refugee convoy fleeing Grozny in October 1999, an Article 2 violation was upheld, and similar findings were made in the *Isayeva* case, where the Court examined the aerial bombardment of a Chechen town alleged to have been infiltrated by separatist fighters.

These cases built on an interesting line of jurisprudence first opened up by the Court in the *McCann and Ors v United Kingdom* decision.[74] The substantive rights

---

[72] See *McCann and Ors v UK*, Series A, No 324 (1996) 21 EHRR 97; *Jordan v UK* Application 24746/94 (2001); *Kaya v Turkey* Judgment of 19 February 1998, 28 EHRR 1; *Khashiyev and Akayeva v Russia* Applications 57942/00 and 57945/00 at <http://www.echr.coe.int>.

[73] ibid paras 13–27 (setting out the factual details surrounding the deaths).

[74] See *McCann and Ors* (n 72 above); *Andronicou and Constantinou v Cyprus*, (1998) 25 EHRR 491; *Gulec v Turkey*, (1999) 28 EHRR 21.

violations were first raised in a context where the state was experiencing an emergency (terrorism contextualized), and where a finding on the merits alone posed significant political costs for the Court. These costs included the political damage of being seen to undermine executive choices in contexts where the perceived stakes were extremely high for the political actors involved. Notably, the Court emphasized the requirement of investigation (stressing the need for victims and next of kin to have meaningful access to such mechanisms), bringing the access to justice theme into slightly different perspective. Here access becomes the practical outworkings of a substantive rights violation, in a context where the facts between the state and applicant are entirely disputed. It becomes the least contentious means to give practical traction to the Court's findings by linking processes of review and oversight (as well as outlining who is entitled to have access to them) to the decisions. In sidestepping the question in the *McCann* case as to whether state use of force was ultimately justified, the Court opened up a new assessment avenue. It required that the measurement of a state's adherence to particular human rights norms was in part established by how well the state's criminal and civil procedures responded when those norms were violated. The 'quality' of the response is, *inter alia*, measured by the inclusion of a right of access to the legal process by those most affected by it, ie direct victims or those representing their interests.

F. The Inter-American Court of Human Rights Jurisprudence

The American Convention was adopted in 1969, and provides for two significant procedural bodies to safeguard the implementation of the rights contained in the Convention. Chapter VII of the Convention outlines the structure of the Inter-American Court of Human Rights, while the role and composition of the Inter-American Court is outlined in Chapter VIII. It is also useful to note that by virtue of the Charter of the Organization of American States (OAS), all member states are bound by the human rights obligations contained in that instrument, which the political and human rights organs of the OAS have recognized are expressed in the American Declaration on the Rights and Duties of Man.[75]

The jurisprudence of the Inter-American Court of Human Rights is markedly sparser than that of the European Court. Nonetheless, the Inter-American Court has been extremely activist in its emergency-related jurisprudence, a product of the hemisphere's long and tragic experiences with dictatorships, authoritarian regimes, and the profound abuse of emergency powers. Arguably the suspect quality of many of the region's democracies, particularly in the early years of the Court's existence, confirms the pattern of more stringent review with problematic democracies. The Court's jurisprudence also affirms the pressure that due process rights experience in times of crisis.

---

[75] Not all states agree with this interpretation of the breadth of their legal obligations under the OAS Statute, specifically the US.

1. Strong Oversight of Limitations on Due Process Rights

Many of these themes are highlighted in the first and most significant case before
the Inter-American Court, namely the advisory opinion in *Judicial Guarantees in
a State of Emergency*.[76] Limitations on due process rights are often the first port of
call for states limiting rights protections in times of crisis. The *Judicial Guarantees*
decision demonstrates the strengths of the Inter-American Court in dealing with
prolonged and problem emergencies. In finding an expansive scope for the non-
derogable character of judicial guarantees, the Court recognized that the exercise
of emergency powers is potentially fraught with abuse and can lead to subversion
of the democratic order.[77] The Court was clearly setting limits on the exercise of
emergency powers, essentially limiting the expansion of state powers in times of
crisis. The Court took a far-reaching view on inter-linking rights in emergency
contexts rather than narrowing its focus on non-derogable rights per se. It examined the extent to which judicial guarantees and remedies could be minimized
during a period of emergency in accordance with Article 27 of the American
Convention.[78] Here the Court concluded that some fundamental guarantees may
never be excluded and that 'judicial guarantees essential for the protection of such
rights' are immune from limitation.[79] It held that the due process guarantees of
Article 8—which protect the right to fair trial, and which include the right to a
hearing by a competent, independent tribunal; the right to be presumed innocent;
the right to notification of pending criminal charges; the right to counsel of choice;
the right to examine witnesses; and the right of appeal to a higher court—could
not be suspended in times of emergency in so far as they are prerequisites for the
necessary functioning of judicial safeguards.

The Court's approach recognizes that the core and the penumbra of derogable
and non-derogable rights are inter-linked and mutually significant. In this conceptualization, access rights have significance beyond that accorded them in the
jurisprudence of other international courts and tribunals. Central to this importance is the commitment to securing the rights of persons who are the subjects of
emergency laws, implicitly acknowledging the vulnerability of the individual in
the crisis context. Clearly, the approach is partly explicable by reference to the
abuse of emergency powers in the region. The *Judicial Guarantees* judgment and
the cases that follow it draw directly from the experience of the hemisphere and
of the individuals who suffered the excesses perpetrated by states in the name of
emergency.[80]

---

[76] *Judicial Guarantees in States of Emergency* at 24. Advisory Opinion OC-9/87, 6 October 1987,
Inter-American Court of Human Rights, Series A No 9 (1987) OEA/ser.L/VI/111.9 doc 13 (1987).

[77] ibid para 36.

[78] ibid para 10.

[79] ibid para 39.

[80] CG Brown, *Chile Since the Coup: Ten Years of Repression* (Americas Watch, 1983); JE
Méndez, *Truth and Partial Justice in Argentina* (Americas Watch, 1987); Lawyers Committee for

2. *Habeas Corpus* as an 'Essential Judicial Guarantee'

The Inter-American Court's approach was subsequently confirmed in the *Habeas Corpus in Emergency Situations* decision.[81] Here the Court was asked to express its views on the question of whether the writ of habeas corpus constituted an 'essential judicial guarantee' that could not be suspended by a state party in a time of emergency. The Court gave detailed consideration to the nature of an emergency situation as well as to the scope of the non-derogable judicial guarantees language contained in Article 27(2) of the American Convention.

The judgment gives strong emphasis to substantive defence of due process rights, with access to justice for persons in the control or custody of the state party being the core irreducible element of these rights. It makes clear that the derogation privilege does not allow for rights to be absolutely suspended in an emergency situation. Rather, only their 'full and effective' exercise could be limited.[82] Even in times of crisis the state operates within the rule of law and cannot operate outside the law to protect the legal and political order.[83] The Court says that the right to derogate, 'does not mean...that the suspension of guarantees implies a temporary suspension of the rule of law, nor does it authorize those in power to act in disregard of the principle of legality by which they are bound at all times'.[84]

As with the *Judicial Guarantees* decision, the Court strongly emphasized the regional experience of emergencies and emergency powers, and forcefully argued that exercise of derogation could only be legally valid when operating in tandem with the 'effective exercise of representative democracy.'[85]

In the *Habeas Corpus* decision the Court explained that the determination as to what judicial remedies were essential would differ depending on the rights that were at stake. The Court then proceeded to characterize the active component of habeas corpus (literally bringing the person before the court) as performing a vital role in ensuring the physical safety and integrity of the person, relevant both to freedom from torture and liberty rights. The Court also found the procedural aspect of habeas corpus necessary to facilitate the verification of whether, in fact, emergency legislative measures authorizing detention were lawful. In such a context, habeas corpus performed a dual oversight function. Following these statements,

Human Rights, *Uruguay: The End of a Nightmare?* (Lawyers Committee for Human Rights, 1984); D Bitel, *The Failed Promise: Human Rights in the Philippines Since the Revolution of 1986* (Geneva: International Commission of Jurists, 1991); Amnesty International, *Nicaragua: The Human Rights Record* (Amnesty International Publications, 1986).

[81] *Habeas Corpus in Emergency Situations*, Advisory Opinion, OC-8/87, Series A, 30 January 1987.

[82] ibid para 18.

[83] ibid para 18, notably here the Court quibbles with the use of the term 'suspension'in the treaty language while effectively limiting its meaning: 'Nevertheless, the Court will use the phrase "suspension of guarantees" that is found in the Convention.'

[84] ibid para 24.

[85] ibid para 20.

the Court held that the writs of habeas corpus and amparo (defined as the right of any individual to procedural protection by means of effective recourse to a court or tribunal) were among the judicial remedies that were essential for the various rights whose derogation was prohibited by Article 27(2) of the American Convention. This ruling is a useful point of reference as we consider the implications of legislation passed by the United States Congress, which while primarily aimed at authorizing the creation of military tribunals has substantial effect on the right of habeas corpus.[86] This is a robust application of international oversight to a state's potential use of emergency powers, confirming the centrality of procedural protections to persons most likely to be suspect or vulnerable to the state's powers in a situation of emergency. It is clear that this judgment was significantly ahead of other enforcement systems in identifying the importance of due process rights, and specifically access concerns to the oversight of a state's emergency powers.

II. ARMED CONFLICT

The right of access to justice in times of armed conflict poses a number of conceptual and practical challenges. Simply put, war always constitutes crisis in extremis, and enforcement of legal rights and remedies presents particular challenges and obstacles in such a context. Foremost among these is the problem of establishing the applicability of the relevant *legal* standards. Specifically, one must identify the form of armed conflict taking place and concretely, whether an international or an internal armed conflict is at hand. These technical thresholds are critical to identifying which protections apply, and specifically what forms of access rights are appropriate, and to what degree in the conflict under scrutiny. As pointed out above, access to justice concerns have a markedly different hue dependent on whether the situation constitutes an international or an internal armed conflict. Notably, many of the tensions that have been identified in respect of access to justice in situations of emergency (ie between individual rights and state prerogatives) are equally observed in situations of internal armed conflict. In fact, there is often a significant legal cross-over between states experiencing a situation of emergency (whether formally proclaimed or not) and states which are in the throes of an internal armed conflict.[87]

A. International Armed Conflicts

If an undisputed international armed conflict is taking place between sovereign entities, the rules and protection of the Hague Regulations and the 1949 Geneva

---

[86] Military Commissions Act of 2006, Pub L No 109–366, § 6, 120 Stat 2600, 2632 (to be codified at 18 USC § 2441).

[87] See, F Ní Aoláin, 'The Relationship between Situations of Emergency and Low Intensity Conflict' (1998) 23 *Israel Yearbook on Human Rights* 97.

Conventions evidently apply.[88] In addition, Protocol I of the Additional Protocols to the Geneva Conventions extends the criteria and status of international armed conflicts to specifically enumerated internal conflicts, deemed 'internationalized', by certain inherent characteristics.[89] Determining these 'privileged' conflicts was a direct corollary to the strong advocacy by newly independant nations for whom 'wars of national liberation', and variations thereof, were a defining feature of state creation and consolidation. Article 1 (4) of the Protocol sets out these favoured conflicts as armed conflicts in which 'people are fighting against colonial domination and alien occupation and against racist regimes in the exercise of their right to self-determination'. For reasons of historical and negotiation specificity, the application of Protocol I is largely irrelevant to most of the internal conflicts experienced today.[90]

1. Rights of Access to Justice in the Context of International Armed Conflicts

This portion of the chapter now briefly assesses the right of access to justice in two ways. The primary focus is with tracing rights of access imputable to combatants and protected persons in situations of international armed conflict. As with all forms of crisis, rights of access tend to be diminished for those who are seen to pose the greatest threat to the state based *either* on the fact of hostilities or resulting from an individual's suspect status. Accordingly, the right of access to justice is most important to these particularly vulnerable individuals when hostile relationships exist between states. The chapter will then briefly examine recent trends which create forums of accountability for violations of human rights and humanitarian law occurring during conflict. These accountability forums create new contexts from which to assess the depth of access rights for victims of conflict.

2. Access Rights for Combatants and Civilians

The Geneva Conventions (GC) broadly establish four categories of protection. Geneva Convention I sets out state obligations with respect to the sick, wounded, and shipwrecked; Geneva Convention II affirms obligations of states on the high seas; Geneva Convention III is concerned with prisoners of war (POWs); and Geneva Convention IV establishes the protections due to civilians in situations of occupation. In all cases the duty rests on the High Contracting Party (state in conflict) to respect the norms outlined, and where breaches are identified to rectify such breaches by process of law. A unique international organization, the International Committee of the Red Cross (ICRC) is exclusively charged to ensure

---

[88] I Detter, *The Law of War* (2nd edn, 2000) 3–26.

[89] Protocol Relating to the Protection of Victims of International Armed Conflicts, opened for signature 12 December 1977, UN Doc A/32/144 (1977) (hereinafter 'Protocol I').

[90] Its scope of application is largely colonial and its material field does not apply to the low-intensity internal armed conflicts that have plagued the international community in recent decades. See, *Human Security Centre Human Security Report 2005* (OUP, 2005).

observance of the norms and plays a critical role of interplay, negotiation, and verification with states in respect of the discharge of such obligations. A particular feature of access rights in the armed conflict context is the overlay of the military environment and the manner in which military exigencies are entered into a judgement of when and whether access to legal process can be ensured.

As a starting point, the right to access to justice is meaningful in respect of various categories of protected persons under international humanitarian law. As an illustration, the most cogent and well known category concerns the rights of POWs. Going as far back as the 1864 Geneva Convention, rudimentary protections for POWs were in evidence,[91] and these were augmented by the Third Hague Convention of 1899, as well as the 1899 and 1907 Hague Regulations.[92] By 1929 a new Convention on Prisoners of War had been adopted, and was substantially extended by the 1949 Geneva Conventions. The Third Geneva Convention sets out an extensive set of prohibited practices governing the rights of persons defined as POWs.

Recent developments in the practice of the United States and its allies involved in military activities in Afghanistan and Iraq, illustrate that the critical issue in respect of protections lies not in the quality of the protections themselves but rather in determining the threshold question as to whether an individual (or group) satisfy the four relevant criteria to establish POW status. These criteria are outlined in the Conventions, as modified by Article 44 of Protocol I in the enumerated conflict situations.[93] It is also clear that where the status of persons as POWs may be at issue, humanitarian law requires that they be treated as POWs until a determination has been made by a competent and independent tribunal. It is from this that one of the most substantial contemporary challenges emerges, namely the application in practice under Articles 96 and 99 to 108 of Geneva Convention III, which prescribe the rights of prisoners of war in judicial proceedings, the provision which essentially creates a fair trial standard.[94] An additional point merits emphasis here, ie that a person who may have committed war crimes does not forfeit their POW status by virtue of those acts. Additionally, Articles 54, 64 to 74, and 117 to 126 of the Fourth Geneva Convention contain provisions relating to the right of fair trial in occupied territories. Protocol I, through its Article 75 provisions, extends fair trial provisions in an international armed conflict to those privileged

---

[91] Detter (n 88 above) 326.

[92] Hague Convention (II) with Respect to the Laws and Customs of war on Land and its Annex: Regulations concerning the Laws and Customs of War on Land, The Hague, 29 July 1899, available at <http://www.icrc.org/ihl.nsf/intro/150>; Convention (IV) Respecting the Laws and Customs of War on Land and its Annex: Regulations Concerning the Laws and Customs of War on Land, the Hague, 18 October 1907, available at <http://www.icrc.org/ihl.nsf/full/195>.

[93] Geneva Convention (GC) I, Art 13; GC II, Art 13; GC III, Art 4; and GC IV, Arts 4, 13, and 27–34.

[94] See S Chernichenko and W Treat, 'The Administration of Justice and the Human Rights of Detainees' E/CN.4/Sub.2/1994/24, para 36.

conflicts, identified above, including to persons arrested for actions related to the conflict. One of the most worrying features of the United States dominated 'war on terror' is both the rhetoric and policy of denying the application of the Geneva Conventions in whole or in part to the conflicts engaged in by the United States. The danger of this approach is that is sets a very dangerous precedent for the protection of both combatants and civilians in times of war, a degree of permission for both states and non-state actors which vacates decades of work on enforcement of and compliance with these norms.

3. Forums of Justice and International Tribunals

An emerging and significant aspect related to the concept of access to justice in times of armed conflict arises from the practice and agreement of states responding to breaches of the laws of war. Of particular interest from an access standpoint is how those who have been victims play a part in that process. Developments in this arena parallel the jurisprudential advancements made by the regional human rights' courts and the United Nations HRC in expanding the notion of procedural rights and widening the scope of a right to remedy to victims under the mantle of human rights treaties.

The historical starting point for these developments lay with the Nuremberg and Tokyo Trials which took place at the end of the Second World War. These constituted the first comprehensive criminalization of acts of violence committed during internal and external war deemed sufficiently abhorrent to warrant international regulation. Nuremberg confirmed the principle that accountability for criminal acts is an individual matter and that it is individuals who will be called to account for behaviour that transgresses accepted norms. From that starting point, access to justice for victims who experienced violations during armed conflict had a rather potted history. Until the creation of the ad hoc tribunals for the Former Yugoslavia (ICTY) and Rwanda (ICTR) the narrative of access to justice for victims of human rights violations in war was illustrative predominantly of the dearth of enforcement and remedy.

The creation of the ICTY Statute and the ICTR Statute gave renewed optimism to those who sought to ensure a more comprehensive and consistent application of the laws of war, and the augmentation of access for those who experienced breaches. Both statues give each tribunal jurisdiction over the grave breaches of the Geneva Conventions (Article 2); Violations of the Laws and Customs of War (Article 3); Genocide (Article 4); and Crimes Against Humanity (Article 5).[95] This accountability has continued to advance in the form of hybrid tribunals, such as the Sierra Leone Tribunal, so that the reach of accountability for violations taking

---

[95] International Criminal Tribunal for the Former Yugoslavia <http://www.icty.org>; International Criminal Tribunal for Rwanda <http://www.ictr.org>.

place in times of conflict continues to consolidate.[96] Moreover, the establishment of the International Criminal Court (ICC) operates as a permanent commitment by states of both process and substantive redress to those who have experienced violations of the gravest kinds.[97] Despite considerable difficulties, and the hostility of the hegemonic state,[98] the Rome statute is a considerable achievement. A number of its substantive components advance and consolidate the law.[99]

Nonetheless, noting the extremity of violations that take place in times of conflict, the creation of these bodies constitutes the most visible outworking of a broad right of access to justice, in that these bodies function as a mechanism where claims of violation (or at least some claims) can be mediated and addressed. For victims of humanitarian and human rights violations, access to justice fundamentally requires a forum in which claims can be adjudicated. For many years, the lack of any such independent forums to address the claims of victims derived from situations of armed conflict functioned as an automatic bar to access. Now, a more nuanced conversation has to take place focused on the quality and depth of that access.

In the context of the ICTY and the ICTR, the numbers of persons tried for crimes committed in times of war are relatively minor by reference to the overall numbers of violations and perpetrators.[100] Thus the matters adjudicated symbolically rather than substantially address the needs of most victims. Given the genuine and practical constraints on unfettered access to international justice we need to recalibrate our understanding of access, in such a manner that meaningful access for some victims and the trials of key perpetrators can operate as a form of symbolic

[96] See, Special Court for Sierra Leone, jointly established by the government of Sierra Leone and the UN <http://www.sc-sl.org/>; M Metin Hakki 'War Crimes and the War in Iraq: Can George W. Bush and Tony Blair be Held Responsible?' (2006) 10 IJHR 3–17.

[97] The aspirations to create such a body can be traced back to the Genocide Convention and the work of the International Law Commission (ILC), mandated through the 1950s to codify the Nuremberg Principles and prepare a draft statute for the ICC. Progress on doing so was clearly stymied by the Cold War, and it was the end of the Cold War, allied with the impetus received from the establishment of the ad hoc Tribunals, which gave renewed energy to those who sought to advance international criminal accountability through formal means. By 1994, the ILC presented the final version of the draft statute of the 6th Committee to the 49th Session of the UN General Assembly, which recommended that a conference of plenipotentiaries be called to enact the statute. Following three years of work and preparatory committee meetings, governments met in Rome in June and July 1998 to conclude arrangements for the ICC. On 18 July 1998 the statute was opened for signature.

[98] M Byers and G Nolte (eds) *United States Hegemony and the Foundations of International Law* (Cambridge University Press, 2003); C Bell, C Campbell, and F Ní Aoláin, 'The Battle for Transitional Justice: Hegemony, Iraq and International Law' in McEvoy, Morrison, and Anthony (eds), *Essays in Honour of Stephen Livingstone* (OUP, 2007) 147.

[99] eg Art 8 augments and amplifies the categories of war crimes. There is an extension of crimes to both internal and international armed conflict (with a notable expansion of the former), and criminalization of common Art 3 and parts of Protocol II is a useful step forward. There is also no doubt that the reach of the Court is stymied by its Statute, by the conditionality linked to activating the jurisdiction of the Court, and by the extent to which the nature and capacity of international justice remains both selective and partial.

[100] For the most recent numbers of indictments, trials, and other proceedings, see n 95 above.

access and retribution for all. Moreover, it also becomes necessary to review the functionality of access for those victims whose cases are considered by the lens of international judicial oversight.

Thus, greater attention needs to be paid to the extent to which these processes are victim centred,[101] particularly when dealing with particularly vulnerable victims. Much work has been done by the ad hoc tribunals with regard to the victims of sexual violence. However, it remains clear that in the context of armed conflict, access remains plagued by the insecurities that accompany the war context—including displaced and insecure populations, an inability to guarantee the safety and security of persons (particularly witnesses), a lack of access to key evidence, and the ongoing tension that continuing and unresolved conflict (or post-conflict situations) will play into trial and accountability processes. As regards procedural access and the International Criminal Court, it is fair to state that much was left unresolved by the terms of the ICC Statute itself. Thus, the Rules of Evidence and Procedure, will define how meaningfully the Statute will work to assist access to the Court for victims and others affected by the crimes that come within its mandate.

By way of conclusion, it is also increasingly acknowledged that the formal ending of hostilities does not diminish rule of law needs, but that these may be more fraught or contested than might be anticipated. Thus, a recent review of peace operations has concluded that 'the signing of human rights conventions by countries emerging from crisis is often taken as a sign of success by international administrations; yet... [a] lack of implementation procedures... prevents ordinary citizens from benefiting from international standards and, most fundamentally from having access to justice'.[102]

4. Rights of Access to Justice in Internal Armed Conflict

It is fair to say that the legal regulation of internal armed conflicts poses greater challenges than that of their international counterparts. Specific to our focus, rights of access to justice have markedly less provision in the governing treaty and customary law applicable to such situations. The nature of such conflicts, because the hostilities generally occur within the state, and are not external to it, means that state encroachments on access rights are likely to be more frequent, pervasive, and cross-cutting than in the context of international armed conflict.

Common Article 3 of the 1949 Geneva Conventions made the first and controversial attempt to incorporate provisions regulating the conduct of parties during

---

[101] F Ní Aoláin, 'Radical Rules: The Effects of Evidential and Procedural Rules on the Regulation of Sexual Violence in War' (1997) 60 Albany Law Review 883.

[102] Para 95, Conflict, Security and Development Group (International Policy Institute, Kings College London), 'A Review of Peace Operations: A Case for Change (Synthesis Report)' (2003), available at <http://ipi.sspp.kcl.ac.uk/rep002/index.html>.

civil/internal strife.[103] It is the sole article of the 1949 Conventions which specifically addresses the problem of non-international armed conflicts. It has been variously described as the 'mini-convention' or the 'convention within a convention', providing minimal rules which parties to an internal armed conflict are 'bound to apply as a minimum'. The opening paragraph to the Article states: 'In the case of armed conflict not of an international character occurring in the territory of one of the High Contracting Parties, each Party to the conflict shall be bound to apply, as a minimum, the following provisions . . .'.

Article 3 contains the lowest threshold of both application and standards. It is intended to provide a minimum basis of protection to persons not participating in hostilities during internal armed conflicts.[104] Protection under the Article is given on the basis of non-discrimination and non-partisanship, many of these principles being derived from the then-embryonic human rights regimes, and indeed, ahead of them.[105] Its protections are to ensure that violence to life and person is prohibited;[106] that outrages against personal dignity, specifically humiliating and degrading treatment, are forbidden;[107] that legal processes enforcing adverse consequences upon persons are carried out by regularly constituted courts affording recognized due process rights;[108] and finally, that all those wounded and sick in conflict be cared for.[109] The obvious and still disputed question is when Article 3 in fact becomes applicable? No easy answers come to this question, largely because state practice is still limited and courts have had few substantive opportunities to assess and affirm application.[110] It is also evident that application is on a 'case-by-case' basis and that political factors will play a determining role in the willingness of states and courts to 'call' application to particular cases.

The next foray into the legal regulation of internal armed conflict came with the 1979 Protocol II to the Geneva Conventions.[111] Protocol II was a compromise document. Neither its proponents nor adversaries were entirely satisfied with it. The traditional view of Protocol II is that it 'develops and supplements Article 3

---

[103] Col Gerald Draper attests to the negotiation difficulties this provoked at the Diplomatic Conference. See GIAD Draper, 'Humanitarian Law and Internal Armed Conflicts' (1983) 13 Georgid Journal of International and Comparative Law 253, 261.

[104] The norms stated in common Art 3 may be viewed as applicable to all conflicts, even those of an international character. See T Meron, '*International Criminalization of Internal Atrocities*' (1995) 89 AJIL 554, 560 (noting the US adherence to this position regarding the application of law to the international conflict in the former Yugoslavia) See also F Ní Aoláin, 'Hamdan and Common Article 3: Did the Supreme Court Get it Right?' Minnesota Law Review 1525 (2007).

[105] See Draper and Int (n 103 above) 253, 269.

[106] Common Art 3, s 3 (1)(a).

[107] ibid s 3(1)(c).

[108] ibid s 3(1)(d).

[109] ibid s 3(2).

[110] *Nicaragua v US* (Merits) (1986) ICJ Rep 14.

[111] Protocol II to the Geneva Conventions of 1979.

common to the Conventions of 1949'.[112] Such a description belies much of the controversy that surrounded its negotiation.[113] Following controversial debates, the agreed document sets a high threshold of application. It was agreed to have the Protocol apply to all non-international armed conflicts which take place in the territory of a party between its armed forces and dissident armed forces. The dissident forces must be under a responsible command. They must be able to exercise sufficient control over a part of the state's territory to carry out sustained and concerted military operations. The dissident force must also be capable of implementing the Protocol.[114]

The language contained in Protocol II specifically articulates a threshold which excludes situations manifesting low intensity violence. Those situations 'of internal disturbances and tensions such as riots, isolated and sporadic acts of violence and other acts of a similar nature' are excluded as outside the supervision of armed conflict law.[115] Generally, these situations fall to be regulated by the domestic law of the relevant state as modified by the use of the derogation privilege. A genuine problem is that given the political difficulties in acknowledging the applicability of Protocol II in conflicts, states frequently use the emergency framework as a means of regulating situations for which it was not designed. Such a mismatch between the form of crisis and the legal standards applied can lead to a gap in coverage or inadequate legal protections for persons caught up in the maelstrom of hostilities not formally recognized by the state. [116]

This chapter acknowledges that the depth of legal protections for persons engaged in hostilities under Protocol II may not be as extensive as those available under international human rights law norms (even as modified by the privilege of derogation). Nonetheless, it is suggested that the formal political and legal status of the conflict matters significantly, as it frames and underwrites the manner in which the state behaves, and forms the basis of external scrutiny to which the state will be subject.

Given the general reluctance of states to concede that an internal armed conflict in fact exists on their sovereign territory, and that international humanitarian law is (to a significant degree) self-activating for state parties, many situations of conflict, particularly internal armed conflict, fail to be formally regulated by international

---

[112] F Kalshoven, *Constraints on the Waging of War* (2nd edn, ICRC, 2001) 132.

[113] See WA Solf and WG Grandison, 'International Humanitarian Law Applicable in Armed Conflict' (1975) 10 JILE 567, 578.

[114] This scope of application is outlined in Protocol II, Art 1.

[115] ibid Art 1(2).

[116] Protocol II's threshold of application is described by the authoritative ICRC commentaries as automatic, 'once the conditions set out in Article 1(1) exist'. Theodor Meron, 'The Geneva Conventions as Customary Law' (1987) 81 AJIL 348. Protocol II, Art 1(1) outlines that the 'material field of application' of the Protocol to all armed conflicts taking place in the territory of the state party 'between its armed forces and dissident armed forces or other organized armed groups which, under responsible command, exercise such control over a part of the territory as to enable them to carry out sustained and concerted military operations and to implement this Protocol'.

humanitarian law. This poses particular problems with respect to ensuring adherence to protections outlined in the existing law. Moreover, it creates sites of resistance for the application of any law, thereby creating a context in which domestic law only applies, and this usually means the activation of extensive emergency-type powers with attenuated protections for individual rights.

The undisputed point is that that common Article 3 of the Four Geneva Conventions and Article 6 of Additional Protocol II contain fair trial guarantees for times of non-international armed conflict, which go a significant way to ensuring rights of access to justice in the relevant conflicts—should they be applied. But, overarching political contexts mean that their application is clearly far more fraught and contested than in the context of international armed conflict. As emphasized above, that contestation is clearly linked to the determination of status (both conflict and individual). These are no easy solutions to the problem of non-application; at best, states must be persuaded that compliance is in their self-interest, allied with a consensus that the political costs of non-compliance are too high.

III. TERRORISM

Terrorism is not a new phenomenon; in fact terrorism has long been experienced in national and international systems, a potent example being the murder of the Austrian Crown Prince that triggered the First World War.[117] The phenomenon poses complex issues of definition and regulation, none more so than addressing the root causes of violence manifested as indiscriminate acts aimed particularly at harming the civilian population. Ensuring access to justice encounters many challenges when a state is confronted with terrorist threats and acts. Here I briefly set out the definitional problems with the terrorism concept; illustrate how access to justice manifests itself as a particular element of state responses to terrorism, and finally, by selective examples, demonstrate how international courts have responded to state limitations on access premised on the threats posed by terrorism.

A. The Elusive Definition of Terrorism

There exists deep disagreement within national and international legal communities concerning the legal definition of terrorism.[118] In this context, the attempt to regulate terrorism through international law is a relatively new enterprise, though as early as 1937 the League of

---

[117] See CA Russell, CA Banker and BH Miller, 'Out-Inventing the Terrorist' in Y Alexander, D Carlton, and P Wilkinson (eds), *Terrorism: Theory and Practice* (Westview Press, 1979) 3; S Harzenski, 'Terrorism, A History: Stage One' (2003)12 JTLP 137. Note that I do not suggest that every act of political assassination constitutes a terrorist act, as there may be multiple causalities for such (illegal) actions.

[118] H-P Gasser, 'Acts of Terror, "Terrorism" and International Humanitarian Law' (2002) 84 IRRC 547, 552–4.

Nations drafted the Convention for the Prevention and Punishment of Terrorism.[119] Upon its creation, the United Nations inherited and sought to advance this work. In parallel, a number of regional international organizations have addressed the manifestations of terrorism at a national and regional level. These include the Council of Europe,[120] the European Union, the Organization for Security and Co-operation in Europe, the African Union, and the Organization of American States.[121] Much of the work by these bodies can be defined as attempts to agree Suppression Conventions as well as cooperative regional action on a multitude of fronts.

Despite ongoing efforts, it is generally agreed that there has been no consensus on an international legal classification.[122] This lack of consensus is most potently illustrated by the lack of an agreed definition of terrorism within the UN General Assembly's Ad Hoc Committee on Terrorism as well as within the working group of the General Assembly's Sixth Committee, in the context of a comprehensive treaty regulating state responses to and responsibility for terrorism.[123] Presently, a Convention in draft controversially seeks to provide a comprehensive definition of terrorism, and is still lacking state agreement.[124] Lack of agreement on a comprehensive definition does not mean that there is no consensus at all between states on what constitutes terrorism. In fact, and definitionally jumpstarted by September 11, the international community has identified certain *acts* of violence that are generally considered to be forms of terrorism.[125]

---

[119] League of Nations, Convention for the Prevention and Punishment of Terrorism, 16 November 1937 (1938) 19 League of Nations Official Journal 23 (never entered into force).

[120] Council of Europe, *The fight against terrorism—Council of Europe standards* (3rd edn, Council of Europe, 2005).

[121] Inter-American Convention Against Terrorism, OAS AG Res 1840, 32nd Session, OAS Doc XXXII-O/02 (3 June 2002), entered into force 10 July 2003; Inter-American Committee Against Terrorism, 'Declaration of San Salvador on Strengthening Cooperation in the Fight Against Terrorism', OEA/Ser.L/X.2.3, adopted 24 January 2003; On 13 June 2002, the EU Council of Ministers adopted a Framework Decision on the European Arrest Warrant. See <http://europa.eu.int/comm/justice_home/fsj/criminal/extradition/fsj_criminal_extradition_en.htm> (last visited 8 August 2005); OSCE Charter on Preventing and Combating Terrorism, Mc(10).Jour/2, 7 December 2002, Annex 1, available at <http://www.osce.org/documents/odihr/2002/12/1488_en.pdf> (last visited 8 August 2005); African Union, 'Declaration of the Second High-Level Intergovernmental Meeting on the Prevention and Combating of Terrorism in Africa', Mtg/HLIG/Conv.Terror/Decl (II) Rev 2.

[122] There is now a regional European agreement on a definition of Terrorism, which speaks to the potential for broader international consensus. Protocol Amending the European Convention on the Suppression of Terrorism, ETS No 190 (15 May 2003). See also SC Resolution 1566 (2004), para 3 broad on agreement def. of terrorism. S/RES/1566 (2004).

[123] See also UN General Assembly Ad Hoc Committee on International Terrorism, 'Observations of States Submitted in Accordance with General Assembly Resolution 3034 (XXVII)', A/AC.160/1 (16 May 1973) and A/AC.160/1/Add.1 (12 June 1973). See also A/AC.160/2 (22 June 1973) (Study by the Secretary-General on the basis of that material).

[124] See eg Report of the Ad Hoc Committee Established by General Assembly Resolution 51/210 of 17 December 1996, Fifth Session (12–23 February 2001), General Assembly Official Records, 56th Session, Supplement No 37, UN Doc A/56/37.

[125] In this ever expanding list are included such acts as the hijacking of civilian aircraft, and taking the lives of hostages, acts the primary purpose of which could be said to be to spread terror among the civilian population both in times of armed conflict and in peacetime.

A clear regulatory problem in this context is that there is an unresolved but evident overlap between the categories of emergency, armed conflict, and terrorism. All refer to situations where the state feels itself either objectively or subjectively to be in crisis. Often states will use the term 'terrorism' to label anti-state violence which threatens the political status quo in any way, or posits the possibility of a change in power. The flexibility of the term, cogently demonstrated by a lack of comprehensive definition, means that its application can be manipulated for political ends, and the loser in this terminology tug-of-war is the rights of individuals. As outlined below and evident in the practice of states post-September 11, limitations on the right of access to justice have been at the forefront of state responses to transnational terrorism. Certain states have also manipulated the events and international responses to the threat of transnational terrorism and limited access rights in a domestic context to ends that are extremely dubious on both substantive and procedural grounds.

B. Where Access and Terrorism Interface

As evidenced by the practice of states following the events of 11 September 2001, and in tune with the theme of this chapter, restrictions on individual access to legal process have constituted a mainstay in the armoury of state responses to terrorist threat. The most controversial of these limitations have been advanced by the United States and include the following: the creation of Special Military Tribunals by Executive Presidential Order allowing those charged with terrorism to be processed by specially created military tribunals;[126] the creation of designated detention sites, most infamously the detention site at Guantanamo Bay Cuba, for questioning and detaining persons suspected of terrorism indefinitely; and denial and restricted access to legal advice for those arrested on charges related to terrorism. Access to justice (defined in terms of procedural access to legal review) becomes a site of contestation in part because states frequently assert that the definitional problems associated with the phenomenon of terrorism, make it (and acts following from the core definition) difficult to process within the confines of normal rules.[127] In particular, the case is sometimes made that because of the potentially catastrophic outcomes that follow from terrorist acts, it becomes incumbent on states to pre-empt such acts by detaining persons or limiting the range of legal rights available to individuals who might be responsible for catastrophe. In this context, access to justice can be seen as working against a higher set of norms, namely the overall safety and security of the body politic. Here, access to justice is poised at the

---

[126] Military Order of 13 November 2001: Detention, Treatment, and Trial of Certain Non-Citizens in the War Against Terrorism §4, 3 CFR 918, 919–20 (2001).

[127] Human Rights First, *Assessing the New Normal: Liberty and Security for the Post-September 11 United States* (2003) available at <http://www.humanrightsfirst.org/us_law/loss/assessing/assessingnewnormal.htm>.

fraught intersection between the state's right to defend itself balanced against the right of the particular individual to legal review and oversight.

A number of states legislated in response to the events of September 11 2001, precisely targeting detention, legal review, and legal access as critical elements needed in their anti-terrorism arsenal.[128] In response there has been a marked increase in the unease articulated by international bodies, human rights organizations, and concerned states about the diminution of individual rights protections. There is increasing disquiet that such measures are ineffective, as they may operate to alienate communities and individuals further, making them more disposed to support violent acts than to oppose them.

National courts have not been entirely silent on the matter. Seised of a number of related cases, the US Supreme Court in its decisions concerning *Rasul v George W Bush, Hamdi v Donald Rumsfeld*, and *Hamdan v Donald Rumsfeld* affirmed the jurisdiction of the US courts to review the legality of executive detention even in situations of emergency.[129] In the *Rasul* case, writing for the majority, Stevens J reached the conclusion that the US courts had jurisdiction based on numerous reasons. This included distinguishing a compelling earlier and contrary decision, *Eisentrager,* on the basis that the nationals concerned in the *Rasul* case were not from countries formally at war with the United States.[130] Moreover, the court found that none of the nationals concerned had been charged with any offence nor could the situation in Guantanamo be equated with that of post-war Germany. Justice Stevens also found that the relevant federal habeas corpus statute did not distinguish on the basis of nationality or citizenship. The only limitation identified was the necessity that the court seised of the application for relief should have territorial jurisdiction. The Court majority was convinced that allowing the writ of habeas corpus to extend to Guantanamo Bay would be consistent with the historical reach of the writ.[131] Finally it was agreed that the detainees had a statutory entitlement to pursue claims under United States federal law, including the Alien Tort Statute.[132] In the *Hamdi* case the Court was assessing the correctness of a classification by the United States government of an American citizen captured in Afghanistan as an 'enemy combatant'. The decision was extremely fractured,[133] a preponderance of the justices agreed that the government

---

[128] EU Network of Independent Experts in Fundamental Rights, *The Balance between Freedom and Security in the Response of the European Union and its Members States to the Terrorist Threats*, 31 March 2003, available online at <http://www.statewatch.org/news/2003/apr/CFR-CDF. Themcomment1.pdf>;# SCR 1373, UN SCOR, 56th Session, 4385th mtg, UN Doc S/RES/1373 (28 September 2001); see also F Ní Aoláin, 'Balancing Human Rights: International Legal Responses to Terrorism in the Wake of September 11' (2003) 33 Israel *Yearbook on Human Rights* 63 79–81.

[129] Case Nos 03-334 and 03-343, 542 US (2004). See T Otty and B Olbourne, 'The US Supreme Court and the "War on Terror": Rasul and Hamdi' (2004) 5 European Human Rights Law Review 558.

[130] 339 US 763 (1950).

[131] *Rasul v Bush* 542 US 466 (2004), Opinion of the Court, 13–14.

[132] ibid 16–17.

[133] The judgment comprises four opinions, none of which attracted a majority of 5 members.

did have the authority to detain Hamdi (five members) but six members agreed this did not negate constitutional due process guaranteeing that detained citizens be given a meaningful opportunity to contest the factual basis of their detention before a neutral decision maker. They concluded that these had been denied to Hamdi. In *Hamdan v Rumsfeld* the United States Supreme Court held that the military tribunals set up to try suspected enemy combatants held at Guantanamo Bay were unconstitutional.[134] In its decision, the Court ruled by a 5 to 3 margin that the tribunal's defects violated both the Geneva Conventions and the Uniform Code of Military Justice. Among the defects identified by the Court were the use of hearsay evidence gleaned from coercive interrogations, a lack of sufficient access to counsel, and an insufficient appeals process.

These cases are clearly the frontline of a sequence now being presented as applications for habeas corpus in United States federal courts. The intervention of the highest Court remains highly significant in an ongoing and contested battle between the state and the courts as to the permissible limits of state restrictions on rights in the stated context of the war on terror. The Supreme Court's response has been robust thus far in affirming the importance of an individual right to liberty and the reach of the rule of law—even to the most extreme crisis.

C. International Courts, Terrorism and Access Issues

International human rights law has developed an extensive jurisprudence responding to limitations on rights resulting from state assertions of terrorist challenges. The most sophisticated manifestation of this institutional response is found by examining the jurisprudence of the European Court of Human Rights. While the European Convention on Human Rights (ECHR) does not contain a definition of terrorism and the European Court of Human Rights has not explicitly developed one in its jurisprudence, its overall approach is found scattered in its terrorism-related case law. Thus, in the *Fox, Campbell and Hartley* case the Court has stated:

...the need, inherent in the Convention system, for a proper balance between the defence of the institutions of democracy in the common interest and the protection of human rights...Accordingly...the Court will...take into account the special nature of terrorist crime and the exigencies of dealing with it, as far as is compatible with the applicable provisions of the Convention in the light of their particular wording and the overall object and purpose.[135]

It is clear across a range of cases dealing with the substantive rights protected by the ECHR that the Court is prepared to take into account a background of terrorism in assessing the counter-terrorism claims of states. However, this background does

---

[134] *Hamdan v Rumsfled, Secretary of Defense and Ors*, decided 29 June 2006.
[135] *Fox, Campbell and Hartley v UK* (1991) 13 EHRR 157, para 28.

not mean that the discretion of states is unlimited. In the *Klass* decision the Court stated that it was aware 'of the danger such [action] poses of undermining or even destroying democracy on the ground of defending it, [and] affirms that the Contracting States may not, in the name of the struggle against espionage and terrorism, adopt whatever measures they deem appropriate.'[136] This general approach of balancing, in the context of terrorism has positive implications for access to justice rights under the Convention. The fact that the Convention's jurisprudence is marked by its emphasis on due process rights, and that protection of procedural propriety constitutes a hallmark of the Court's overall approach to interpretation across a range of rights, also operates positively for the protection of access rights in the context of terrorism.[137] Because of this, restrictions on liberty, and on access to judicial forums or oversight when used to respond to the threat or reality of terrorism tend to receive a higher form of scrutiny in the European system that they might elsewhere.

For example, in its Article 2 jurisprudence, the Court has considered the amount of, and circumstances within, the use of force that can be utilized against terrorist suspects. In *McCann and Ors v United Kingdom* the Court ruled effectively that the existence of a terrorist threat, or the fact that the person killed was a terrorist suspect, does not in and of itself, provide a stronger or different justification for the use of lethal force than would have been the case if the victim were an ordinary criminal.[138]

As noted alone under Article 3, while acknowledging the difficulties of interrogating terrorist suspects, the Court has absolutely prohibited torture or inhuman or degrading treatment or punishment 'irrespective of the victim's conduct'.[139] In the context of Article 5 protections (the right to liberty) as set out above, the Court has examined such matters as preventive detention for terrorist suspects,[140] powers of detention for questioning persons moving within a territory and suspected of terrorism,[141] and bringing suspects arrested under anti-terrorism legislation 'promptly' before a judicial officer.[142] As regards the right to fair trial, the Court (and, again, the Commission) has examined the use of Special Courts,[143] looking at

---

[136] *Klass v Germany* (1978) 28 ECHR, Series A, 5, (1978) 2 EHRR 214, para 48.

[137] C Gearty, 'Democracy and Human Rights in the European Court of Human Rights' (1993) 52 CLJ 69; See S Marks, 'The European Convention on Human Rights and its "Democratic Society"', (1995) 66 British Yearbook of International Law 209.

[138] *McCann and Ors* (n 72 above) para. 159.

[139] *Chahal v UK* (1996) 23 EHRR 413, para 80; F Ní Aoláin, 'The European Convention on Human Rights and Its Prohibition on Torture' in S Levinson (ed), *Torture: A Collection* (OUP, 2004) 213.

[140] *Lawless v Ireland* (Court), 3 ECHR, Series A (1960–61).

[141] *McVeigh and Ors v UK* (1981) 25 European Commission on Human Rights Decisions and Reports, 15.

[142] *Brogan* (n 29 above).

[143] *Incal v Turkey* (1998) 29 EHRR 448, (1998-IV) ECHR 1547.

whether trials involving persons charged with terrorist offences should be public,[144] and examined the right to silence and the privilege against self-incrimination for all defendants.[145] Here, while there is still clear evidence of accommodating the uniqueness of the terrorist context as articulated by states, the Court has been robust in its conclusions on the incompatibility of such measures as military trials for terrorist defendants.[146] With respect to the right to silence, the Court has highlighted the right of access to legal advice and counsel as a key element of a fair procedure where a defendant may incriminate herself by silence.[147]

IV. CONCLUSION

In time of crisis, justice is a particularly critical concept, in part because the rights and protections of the ordinary law are under particular stress in such times. As this chapter has explained, most explicitly and practically important is the extent to which access to justice is maintained or restrained in times of crisis. In examining this broad theme, I have looked at three key arenas, namely situations of emergency, armed conflict, and terrorism. What is evident across all three contexts, is that access to justice when defined as the ability to have the mediating capacity of legal form regulate state responses—as well as the capacity of legal forums to review the actions of state and non-state actors—invariably becomes a pressure point where state responses coalesce. Thus, access to justice constitutes a barometer of a state's response to emergency, conflict, and terrorism. The defence of access rights, and litigation related to them, can be seen as a litmus test of a society's ability to respond to extremity, and a place where the resistant quality of law is tested and defended.

That resistant quality has been demonstrated by the regional human rights courts, essentially demonstrating that the response of states to crisis can be adjudicated by courts. At a basic level, this provides a bulwark to the argument that crisis in general, but terrorism in particular, is a non-justiciable category or at least a category where the courts should tread lightly. The case law examined in this chapter broadly illustrates the position that states remain willing to be subject to review, domestically and internationally, for their legal responses to crisis of various kinds. In this review process as the 'war on terror' proceeds with no end in sight, it is important to remain mindful that as crisis entrenches and normalizes, individual rights become increasingly vulnerable. Specifically, contemporary history teaches

---

[144] *Ocalan v Turkey* (n 69 above).

[145] *John Murray v UK* (1996) 22 EHRR 29.

[146] See also the decision of the UN Human Rights Committee in *Kavanagh v Ireland*, Communication No 1114/2002/Rev 1, UN Doc CCPR/C/76/D/1114/2002/Rev 1.

[147] *Magee v UK* (2000) ECHR 215, (2001) 31 EHRR 822; *Heaney and McGuinness v Ireland* (2000) ECHR 675, (2001) 33 EHRR 12.

us that rights of access to justice are a barometer of the experiences of individuals in times of crisis and a solid marker on the compliance of states to their international law obligations. Thus, keeping a close eye on the health of their enforcement is a solid point of assessing the ability of legal norms and restraints to remain meaningful throughout the duration of wars, emergency, and terrorist episodes.

3

Access to Justice and Compensation for Violations of the Law of War

NATALINO RONZITTI

I. INTRODUCTION

A. The Interplay between the Protection of Human Rights and International Humanitarian Law

This chapter addresses access to justice by individuals in order to obtain compensation for violations of the law of war. The law of war is a term which is no longer employed the way it used to be.[1] Nowadays international humanitarian law (IHL), encompassing both Hague law and Geneva law, has become a more popular term. This is why the term IHL is employed here. IHL has points of contact and differences with international human rights (IHR). It is important to point them out since, as we shall see, the two disciplines cannot be kept completely separate and IHR can be used in some circumstances as a basis for obtaining compensation for violations of IHL. IHL and IHR have similarities from the point of view of the values protected. The most prominent values are human life and property.

The right to life is protected by two kinds of international law norms: human rights law and humanitarian law. It is useful, therefore, to recall the main features of the two bodies of law, since they influence the mode of protection of this basic right. The right to life is a right protected both in time of peace and in time of armed conflict, even though the mode of protection is not the same. It is one of the basic human rights protected by human rights instruments, both at the universal

---

[1] The subject is now being studied by the International Law Association, which has established a Committee on Compensation for Victims of War. A background Report was prepared by Rainer Hofmann and Franck Riemann in 2004. An interim report was drafted for the ILA Toronto Conference and 2 papers are attached, respectively by R Hofmann, 'Do Victims of Violations of International Humanitarian Law Have an Individual Right to Reparation?' and S Furuya, 'State Immunity: An Impediment to Compensation Litigation, Assessment of Current International Law'. For details and access to the relevant documentation see the Compensation for Victims of War Committee at <http://www.ila-hq.org/html/layout_committee.htm>.

and regional level. As far as the universal level is concerned, it is sufficient to recall Article 3 of the 1948 Universal Declaration of Human Rights and Article 6 of the 1966 United Nations Covenant on Civil and Political Rights. As for regional instruments, the right to life is protected by Article 2 of the European Convention on Human Rights (ECHR); Article 4 of the American Convention on Human Rights; and Article 4 of the African Charter on Human Rights and Peoples' Rights.

In time of armed conflict, it is obvious that life is at risk. However, several norms address the right to life, even though indirectly. The following principles can be extracted from relevant conventions:

(1) persons in the power of the enemy cannot be murdered;
(2) it is prohibited to use weapons causing superfluous injury or unnecessary suffering;
(3) during attacks the principle of distinction should be abided by, in order not to hit the civilian population;
(4) starvation as a method of warfare is prohibited; and
(5) reprisals against protected persons (prisoners of war, civilian population) are forbidden.

Property, too, is a value protected by both IHL and IHR.

The Hague Convention No IV of 1907 and the Regulations appended to it, as well as the subsequent codification, dictate the following principles:

(1) prohibition of wanton destruction of property;
(2) prohibition of targeting civilian objects; and
(3) protection of cultural property.

Under IHR law, property is protected by the Universal Declaration of Human Rights. Article 17 states that property should be respected and cannot be arbitrarily confiscated. However, there is no direct protection of property under the 1966 Covenant on Economic and Social Rights, while it is afforded by additional Protocol I to the ECHR and by the Organization for security and co-operation in Europe (OSCE) Human Dimension. Other regional instruments, for instance, the American Convention on Human Rights, mention the right to property.

Humanitarian law and human rights have points of divergence and convergence[2]. The codification of humanitarian law goes back to the end of the nineteenth century with the 1868 St Petersburg Declaration and the 1899 Hague Conventions. The codification of human rights is more recent. Provisions of the United Nations Charter apart, the first comprehensive instrument is the 1948 Universal Declaration of Human Rights.

---

[2] See generally L Doswald-Beck and S Vité, 'International Humanitarian Law and International Human Rights' (1993), 293 IRRC 94; J-M Henckaerts and L Doswald-Beck (eds), *Customary International Humanitarian Law* (2005) Vol I: Rules, 299–306.

While humanitarian law is described in terms of duties by which states should abide (obligations of *non facere*), IHR is described in terms of rights of individuals, even though the duty corresponding to the right is incumbent on the state.

Another distinguishing feature is related to the sphere of application: indeed, humanitarian law is universal and no regional application is foreseen, while IHR is both universal, as proven by the United Nations Covenants on Human Rights, and regional, as proven by the ECHR and other regional conventions.

A very important element of distinction is related to derogation clauses. States are not allowed to derogate from duties imposed by humanitarian law; on the contrary, IHR allows derogation in two ways: rights attributed to individuals can usually be derogated, since the provision embodying a given right contains the attribution of the right in the first paragraph and its exception in the subsequent paragraph or paragraphs. For instance, while Article 19 of the United Nations Covenant on Civil and Political Rights attributes the right of freedom of expression, the third paragraph allows for a derogation. Moreover, human rights instruments contain a general clause authorizing a suspension of the rights guaranteed, with the exception of a few fundamental rights which can never be suspended. Note also that the provisions establishing the mechanisms of compliance under IHR may be suspended, while this is not true for humanitarian law (for instance, the functions performed by the Protecting Powers or by the International Committee of the Red Cross (ICRC)).

The machinery for monitoring compliance is also completely different. Humanitarian law is grounded in two pillars: the system of Protecting Powers, which has proved not to be very effective, and the functions entrusted to the ICRC. The individual has no remedy before an international body. IHR, on the other hand, relies on three kinds of remedies: a reporting system; interstate complaints; and individual complaints. Thus, an individual has *locus standi* before an international body.

For a long time, the United Nations did not show any interest in humanitarian law. There were two reasons for this: *jus ad bellum* had been abolished by the United Nations Charter and the United Nations was not supposed to be involved in a body of law which regulates a phenomenon (war) outlawed by the Charter; and while war is a negation of human rights, peace is the condition for human rights enjoyment. This situation of hostility changed with the 1968 Tehran Declaration, adopted by the International Conference on Human Rights. The Declaration stated that 'even during the period of armed conflict, humanitarian principles must prevail'. After that, the General Assembly dealt 'with respect for human rights in armed conflict'. General Assembly Resolution 2444-XXIII, entitled 'Respect for Human Rights in Armed Conflict', endorsed the Tehran resolution and paved the way for the study by the UN Secretary-General on 'Respect for Human Rights in Armed Conflict' (1973).

Modern instruments of humanitarian law, such as Article 75 of the 1977 Protocol I, additional to the Geneva Conventions, contain a catalogue of human rights and this is a point of contact between IHL and IHR law.

The relationship between humanitarian law and IHR has rightly been pointed out by AH Robertson: 'humanitarian law is a species of IHR or, to put it in another way, IHR is the genus, while humanitarian law is the species'.[3] This, as we shall see, has been affirmed by the International Court of Justice (ICJ) Advisory Opinion on the Threat or Use of Nuclear Weapons (1996)[4] and restated by the Advisory Opinion on A Wall in Palestine (2004).[5] This finding entails practical consequences: if humanitarian law is *lex specialis*, it follows that IHR should be applied whenever humanitarian law does not regulate matters. Indeed lacunae in humanitarian law should be filled by recourse to the Martens clause. However, given the *lex generalis-lex specialis* relationship between IHR and humanitarian law, the present author wonders whether it would be possible to fill humanitarian law lacunae through recourse to the principles of IHR. There are obvious limits. For instance, human rights machinery is not supposed to be employed for enforcing IHL, with specific regard to individual complaints. This is more a problem of *de lege ferenda* rather than of *de lege lata*.

The close connection between IHR Law and IHL from the perspective of access to justice is at the foundation of Resolution 2005/35, adopted in 2005 by the Commission for Human Rights.[6] The resolution, as we shall see later, sets out basic principles and guidelines for a remedy and reparation for victims of both violations of human rights and serious violations of IHL.

B. Right to Life and Belligerency: the United Nations Covenant on Civil and Political Rights and The ECHR

As noted above, the right to life is protected by both the 1966 United Nations Covenant on Civil and Political Rights and the ECHR. Article 6 of the United Nations Covenant stipulates: 'Every human being has the inherent right to life. This right shall be protected by law. No one shall be arbitrarily deprived of his life'. The ECHR protects the right to life in Article 2. While exceptions are established, for instance, in the case of self-defence against illegal violence, no derogations are allowed. Article 15 establishes that in time of war or other public emergency, derogations are admitted in the sense that a number of rights may be suspended. Derogation from Article 2 is not allowed unless death is the consequence of a lawful act of war. Articles 2 and 15 should be read together in order to give a correct interpretation of the content of the right to life.

---

[3] AH Robertson, 'Humanitarian Law and Human Rights', *Studies and Essays in Honour of Jean Pictet* (1984) 797.

[4] See n 7 below.

[5] See n 9 below

[6] 'Basic principles and guidelines on the right to a remedy and reparation for victims of gross violations of international human rights law and serious violations of international humanitarian law' UN Doc E/CN.4/2005/L.48, 13 April 2005.

The first question to be examined is whether human rights treaties apply in time of war or armed conflict. The effect of war on treaties is a classic topic and, in principle, legal writers distinguish between three categories of treaties:

(1) treaties which apply in wartime (for instance, humanitarian law treaties);
(2) treaties for which war is a ground for extinction (for instance, treaties of alliance); and
(3) treaties which are suspended in wartime (treaties of commerce).

The doctrine of the effect of war on treaties was elaborated before the birth of human rights treaties, and the three categories quoted above do not cover human rights treaties. Their fate, in wartime, was clarified by the 1996 ICJ Advisory Opinion on Nuclear Weapons.[7] During the proceedings, it was argued that the use of nuclear weapons was contrary to Article 6 of the Covenant on Human Rights. It was contended that 'the Covenant was directed to the protection of human rights in peacetime, but that questions relating to unlawful loss of life in hostilities were governed by the law applicable in armed conflict'.[8]

This line of reasoning was rejected by the Court, which held the Covenant applicable also in wartime. In paragraph 25 of its Opinion, the Court stated:

The Court observes that the protection of the International Covenant on Civil and Political Rights does not cease in time of war, except by operation of Article 4 of the Covenant whereby certain provisions may be derogated from in time of national emergency. Respect for the right to life is not, however, such a provision. In principle, the right not arbitrarily to be deprived of one's life applies also in hostilities. The test of what is an arbitrary deprivation of life, however, is to be determined by the applicable *lex specialis*, namely, the law applicable in armed conflict, which is designed to regulate the conduct of hostilities. Thus whether a particular loss of life, through the use of a certain weapon in warfare, is to be considered an arbitrary deprivation of life contrary to Article 6 of the Covenant can only be decided by reference to the law applicable in armed conflict and not deduced from the terms of the Covenant itself.

The important findings made by the Court are worth pointing out:

(1) IHR law does apply in time of war;
(2) the relationship between IHR and humanitarian law is *lex generalis-lex specialis*;
(3) in time of emergency, states are entitled to derogate from the Covenant's articles invoking the exception clause; however:
   (a) Article 6 of the Covenant is not subject to any derogation;

---

[7] *Legality of the Threat or Use of Nuclear Weapons* (1996) ICJ Rep 226. The effect of war on treaties is now the object of study by the International Law Commission. The Secretary-General has delivered a Memorandum, entitled 'The effect of armed conflict on treaties: an examination of practice and doctrine', which takes into account also the effect of war on treaties protecting human rights (A/CN.4/550, 1 February 2005, para 32). The subject has been dealt with by the Special Rapporteur: see I Brownlie, 'First report on the effect of armed conflicts on treaties', ILC, 57th Session, Geneva, 2 May–3 June and 4 July–5 August 2005, paras 84–87, UN Doc A/CN.4/552, 21 April 2005.

[8] ibid 239, para 24.

    (b) Article 6 states when deprivation of life is not arbitrary, for instance in the imposition of the death penalty as a consequence of a court decision;

    (c) in time of armed conflict, the word 'arbitrary' should be interpreted in the light of humanitarian law: thus death as a consequence of a lawful act of belligerency is not an arbitrary deprivation of life (for instance, killing the enemy in the battlefield is lawful, while killing a prisoner of war is unlawful and constitutes a war crime).

The same line of reasoning is valid, *mutates mutandis*, for the ECHR. The right to life is protected under Article 2. Exceptions are listed in paragraph 2 of the same provision. As far as belligerency is concerned, the relevant provision is paragraph 2 of Article 15, which does not allow for any derogation from Article 2, except in the case of 'death resulting from lawful acts of war'. In order to bring humanitarian law into force, it is not necessary to set the procedure under paragraph 1 of Article 15 in motion. The exception 'lawful acts of war' should be added to those listed in paragraph 2 of Article 2.

Other human rights instruments follow the pattern of the Covenant, as far as protection of life and its exception are concerned. For instance, Article 4 of the 1969 American Convention on Human Rights states that: 'No one shall be arbitrarily deprived of his life'. Likewise, Article 4 of the 1981 African Charter of the Human and Peoples' Rights protects the right to life with a wording similar to that of Article 6 of the Covenant. The exception is constituted by the adverb 'arbitrarily'.

The ICJ findings on the application of IHR law have been restated in the Opinion on A Wall in Palestine, which affirms that 'the Court considers that the protection offered by human rights conventions does not cease in case of armed conflict, save through the effect of provisions for derogation of the kind to be found in Article 4 of the International Covenant on Civil and Political Rights'.[9]

C. How Violations of IHL may be Remedied

The International Law Commission (ILC) draft Articles on State Responsibility[10] enumerate the following ways to remedy violations of an international obligation:

* Cessation
* Assurances and guarantees of non-repetition

---

[9] *Legal Consequences of the Construction of A Wall in the Occupied Palestinian Territory*, 9 July 2004, para 106, reproduced in (2004) 43 ILM 1009. The Court further stated: 'As regards the relationship between international humanitarian law and human rights law, there are thus 3 possible situations: some rights may be exclusively matters of international law; others may be exclusively matters of human rights law; yet others may be matters of both these branches of international law. In order to answer the question put to it, the Court will have to take into consideration both these branches of international law, namely human rights law and, as *lex specialis*, international humanitarian law'. The special relationship between IHL and human rights law has been confirmed by the ICJ in the *Case Concerning Armed Activities on the Territory of the Congo (Democratic Republic of the Congo v Uganda)*, 19 December 2005, para 216.

[10] Official Records of the General Assembly, 56th Session, Supplement No 10 (A/56/10) 43.

- Reparation, which may take the form of restitution, compensation, or satisfaction.

Human Rights Resolution 2005/35[11] spelt out these obligations in connection with violations of IHL, stating that:

— cessation should be the first move: the wrongdoer should immediately terminate any violations, for instance in the case of genocide;

— assurances and guarantees of non-repetition can be achieved through civilian control of military force, independence of the judiciary. In our opinion, putting appropriate rules of engagement into place is also a useful way to assure and guarantee non-repetition;

— restitution: 'Restore the victim to the original situation', for instance, 'return to one's place of residence...return of property';

— compensation 'should be provided for any economically assessable damage';

— satisfaction means punishment of those responsible and 'full and public disclosure of the truth'.

The above remedies are tailored to the international responsibility of states. When an entity or an individual is sued by the victim before a domestic (or an international) court, compensation is usually sought. Punishment of the responsible individual is an obligation of the nation state or may be carried out by an international criminal tribunal.

Here the focus is on compensation. It is not the object of this chapter to calculate the amount of compensation. Guidance in this regard is offered by paragraph 20 of Human Rights Commission Resolution 2005/35, which sets out suitable criteria:

Compensation should be provided for any economically assessable damage, as appropriate and proportional to the gravity of the violation and the circumstances of each case, resulting from gross violations of international human rights and serious violations of international humanitarian law, such as:

(a) Physical or mental harm;
(b) Loss of opportunities, including employment, education and social benefits;
(c) Material damages and loss of earnings, including loss of earning potential;
(d) Moral damages;
(e) Costs required for legal or expert assistance, medicine and medical services, and psychological and social services.

Article 36(2) of the ILC Draft Articles on State Responsibility states : 'The compensation shall cover any financially assessable damage including loss of profit in so far as it is established'. The ILC Commentary spells out this obligation, saying that compensation should cover material damage, loss of profit, and non-material damage (for instance moral damage to individuals). Punitive damages are not granted.[12]

---

[11] See n 4 above.
[12] UN Doc A/56/10, 258–63.

D. Who is Obliged to Redress the Violation of IHL?

States and individuals are the subjects obliged to redress the violation of IHL:

(1) States: the obligation to redress the tort committed is due to another subject of international law (as a rule, the state of which the injured individual is a national). In very limited instances, states may be sued before an
international tribunal (for example before the European Court of Human
Rights). The proposition by which the obligation is due to the individual
is only theoretical, and not yet endorsed by the ILC (even though Article
33(2) contains a saving clause, which states: 'This Part is without prejudice to any right, arising from the international responsibility of a State,
which may accrue directly to any person or entity other than a State.')[13]
This provision will be commented upon later.

(2) Individuals:
   (a) may have indirect access to an inter-state claim through the institution
   of diplomatic protection;
   (b) may sue the responsible state in its own domestic legal order or in the
   domestic order of another state;
   (c) may have access to an international tribunal such as the European Court
   of Human Rights.

The International Criminal Court (ICC), when rendering a judgment, may
allocate monetary compensation for the individual or individuals damaged.
The major hurdles for an individual are: state immunity, if a foreign state is
sued; non-justiciability of political questions if the national state of the individual is sued; and functional immunity, if an individual organ of the wrongful
state, is sued.

E. States and Individuals as Entities Capable of Violating
Rules on Armed Conflict

Only states can violate *jus ad bellum*. The individual may be held responsible when
aggression is committed, since aggression is also an international crime, as stated
by Article 5 of the ICC Statute.

Individuals may commit a violation of *jus in bello* amounting to an international
crime (crime of war). The individual bears responsibility. The state is also responsible when a crime is committed by an individual, since the act is imputed to the
state. The state is responsible for each violation of law of war committed by its
belligerent organs.

---

[13] On this point, see recently R Pisillo Mazzeschi, 'The Marginal Role of the Individual in the
ILC Articles on State Responsibility' (2004) XIV IYIL 39.

The ILC has not endorsed the notion of crime of state, even though Chapter III of the 2001 Draft Articles on State Responsibility deals with 'serious breaches of obligations under peremptory norms of general international law'. However, even if one maintains the terminology crimes of states for the sake of argument, not every individual war crime is also a crime of state. Having said this, one has to point out that an individual war crime carries state responsibility, even though it is not a crime of state (or a serious violation of international law). This is proven both by Article 3 of the Hague Convention IV of 1907 and by Protocol I, additional to Geneva Conventions, which will be considered later.

F. *Jus ad bellum and jus in bello*

As a rule, complaints by individuals have been brought for violations of *jus in bello*. However, Dutch and German tribunals have been requested by individuals to render a judgment also on questions of *jus ad bellum*.

Violations of *jus ad bellum* can be relevant at the domestic level, for putting an end to hostilities. Claims have been introduced before Dutch tribunals for terminating the Kosovo war and before German tribunals for terminating both the Kosovo and Iraqi wars. The crime of aggression was invoked. However, these claims were rejected and the German Chief Federal prosecutor decided not to investigate for crimes of aggression.[14]

At the international level, violations of *jus ad bellum* can be relevant for claiming damages even though claims for damages are usually filed in connection with violations of *jus in bello*. The United Nations Compensation Commission (UNCC) was established under UNSCR 687 (1991) and 692 (1991) to process claims against Iraq, because of violation of *jus in bello* and *jus ad bellum*. However, only states can bring claims to the attention of the UNCC. The same is true for the Eritrea-Ethiopia Claim Commission instituted under the peace treaty concluded between the two countries on 12 December 2000.[15] In other words, a state may be responsible not only for violations of the law of war, but also for violations of *jus ad bellum*. Violations of *jus ad bellum* relate to state to state relations and it is difficult for an individual to claim compensation for such violations. The case law is scarce and domestic tribunals have, as a rule, rejected this kind of claim.

---

[14] The Hague Tribunal and the Court of Appeal of Amsterdam (23 November 2000) dismissed the claims as non-justiceable: see, respectively, NMP Steijnen, 'The First Experiences with Legal Action against NATO War Crimes before Domestic Courts in the Netherlands' (April–June 2000), 51 Review of International Affairs 45 and E Sciso, *L'intervento in Kosovo. Aspetti internazionalistici e interni* (2001) 437, where the judgment *Danikovic v Kingdom of the Netherlands* is reproduced and translated into English. For the German judicial practice, see M Bothe and A Fischer-Lescano, 'The Dimension of Constitutional and Statutory Limits on the Use of Force' in M Bothe, ME O'Connell, and N Ronzitti, *Redefining Sovereignty. The Use of Force after the Cold War* (2005) 195, 207.

[15] For a brief account of the Eritrea-Ethiopia Claims Commission, See Ch G Weeramantry, Note (2005) 99, AJIL 465.

II. CURRENT OBSTACLES TO VICTIMS OBTAINING COMPENSATION

Mention was made in the previous section of how difficult it is for a victim to obtain compensation. The major hurdles include the following.

A. Immunity of States and International Organizations from Civil Jurisdiction in Foreign States

The distinction between absolute and relative immunity from civil jurisdiction in foreign countries is a well settled principle of international law. Since military activities are by definition a manifestation of a state's sovereignty, they fall squarely within the principle of absolute immunity, namely having to do with combat activities.

The law of state immunity has been the subject of two conventions, the 1972 Basle Convention, within the Council of Europe, and the 2005 United Nations Convention on the Jurisdictional Immunities of States and Their Property. Both conventions follow the method of lists. They affirm the principle of state immunity (Article 15 of the CE Convention and Article 5 of the United Nations Convention). Article 5 is paradigmatic: 'A state enjoys immunity, in respect of itself and its property, from the jurisdiction of the courts of another state subject to the provision of the present Convention'. The list enumerates the instances in which a state may be submitted to the jurisdiction of another state, for example in case of commercial transactions or contracts of employment with local manpower. Military activities are excluded from the jurisdiction of foreign states. This principle is expressly stipulated in Article 31 of the CE Convention and is also affirmed, albeit implicitly, by the United Nations Convention.[16]

For our purposes, the immunity of international organizations from jurisdiction is also important. The United Nations, NATO and, more recently, the European Union dispatch troops abroad. Other regional organizations, such as the Economic Community of West African States, also do so. The immunity of international organizations from the jurisdiction of foreign states is a moot point.[17] However, several scholars affirm that such organizations enjoy immunity from jurisdiction like states, since a specific norm of general international law does exist or the rule of state immunity applies by analogy to international organizations.

How can the rule on sovereign immunity be removed? In three ways: the tort exception; the *jus cogens* argument; and the terrorism exception.

---

[16] G Hafner and L Lange, 'La Convention des Nations Unies sur les Immunités Juridictionnelles des Etats et de leurs biens' (2004) 50 *AFDI* 45, 75.

[17] A Reinisch and U Weber, 'In the Shadow of Waite and Kennedy. The Jurisdictional Immunity of International Organizations, the Individual's Right of Access to the Courts and Administrative Tribunals as Alternative Means of Dispute Settlement' (2004) 1 International Organizations Law Review 59.

(1) The tort exception is established both in Article 11 of the CE Convention and in Article 12 of the UN Convention. A number of conditions are required to nullify the rule on sovereign immunity. First, the damage should occur in the forum state; secondly, the author of the damage should have been present in the territory of the forum State when the damage occurred. The action should be aimed at recovering pecuniary compensation for death or injury or damage or loss of property. As stated before, Article 31 of the CE Convention states that the Convention cannot prejudice actions of armed forces wstationed in foreign territory. Such a clause is not contained in the UN Convention even though scholars believe that it is implied.

In the *Distomo* case, the Greek Supreme Court (Areios Pagos) decided, in November 2000, that Germany could not invoke immunity from jurisdiction for atrocities committed during the occupation of Greece at the time of the second World War.[18] The Greek Special Supreme Court reversed the Areios Pagos decision in 2002.[19] It stated that the Basle Convention was not applicable, since Greece was not a state party, and that it is not declaratory of customary international law. Nor was the tort exception retained by the European Court of Human Rights in the judgment *McElhinney v Ireland*.[20] McElhinney was fired upon by a British policeman when passing the border with Northern Ireland. The Supreme Court of Ireland (1985) stated that the United Kingdom was entitled to immunity from jurisdiction. The Irish judgment was confirmed by the CE Convention.

(2) According to a doctrinal construction, *jus cogens* norms are hierarchically superior to the other provisions of international law. If a state infringes a *jus cogens* norm, it implicitly forfeits its right to immunity from jurisdiction. The *jus cogens* exception was recognized, together with other lines of reasoning, by the Court of Cassation of Italy in the *Ferrini* case. Mr Ferrini was deported to Germany during the occupation of Italy by Germany and the Court said that Germany was not entitled to sovereign immunity, since Germany violated fundamental principles of international law.[21]

It is worth noting that the drafters of the 2005 United Nations Convention knew the *jus cogens* exception argument. However, it was not taken into account in completing the list of exceptions to sovereign immunity.[22]

---

[18] *Prefecture of Voiotia v Federal Republic of Germany*, 4 May 2000, reproduced in (2001) 95 AJIL 198.

[19] Panezi, 'Sovereign Immunity and Violation of Ius Cogens Norms' (2003) 58 *Revue hellénique de droit international* 199.

[20] *Mc Elhinney v Ireland* [GC], No 31253/96, 21 November 2001, ECHR 2001-XI.

[21] *Ferrini c Repubblica federale di Germania* (Cass Sez Un no 5044/04) 11 March 2004, reproduced in (2004) 87 *Rivista di diritto internazionale* 539.

[22] Haffner and Lange (n 16 above) 67.

(3) The terrorism exception is a principle contained in United States legislation. It constitutes a derogation to the 1976 Federal Sovereign Immunities Act (FSIA). States sponsoring terrorism are not entitled to sovereign immunity for civil actions. This exception is contained in the 1996 Antiterrorism and Effective Death Penalty Act and is valid against those states that the United States Department of State has qualified as states sponsoring terrorism.[23]

B. Immunity of State Property

Let us pose the problem in this way: supposing the plaintiff has successfully sued a foreign state, can he enforce a judgment for damages against the property of the respondent state? The 2005 United Nations Convention lists categories of property which are not subject to measures of constraint, such as property of a military nature, property of the central bank, etc (Article 21). In the *Distomo* case, the plaintiff tried to seize the Goethe Institute and the German Archaeological Institute in Athens.[24] The Distomo case was brought before the European Court of Human Rights.[25] The European Court denied that Greece had violated Article 6 of the CE Convention and stated that there is no rule of customary international law allowing denial of the rule of non-attachment of state property subject to sovereign immunity in case of commission of war crimes and crimes against humanity.

In the United States, the 1996 Antiterrorism and Effective Death Penalty Act allows for the execution of a judgment against state-owned property used for commercial purposes. A subsequent amendment to the FSIA, enacted in 2002, makes it possible to execute a judgment against diplomatic or consular property of a state sponsoring terrorism. However, the United States President may suspend enforcement of the judgment.[26]

C. Enforcing Judgments on Damages in Foreign States

Within the European Union, enforcement of foreign judgments is facilitated by the 1968 Brussels Convention on Jurisdictional Competence and Recognition of Judgments on Civil and Commercial Matters. This Convention has been superseded by Regulation (EC) 44/2001, which entered into force on 1 March 2002. The Regulation applies only in civil and commercial matters. Judgments allocating a sum of money for damages fall, in principle, within the civil sphere. However, if the judgment is a consequence of a controversy connected with acts *jure imperii* of the administration, the Regulation does not apply. There is no explicit provision on this point. It is a matter of interpretation. The case law confirms this interpretation.

[23] SR Ratner and JS Abrams, *Accountability for Human Rights Atrocities in International Law* (2nd edn, 2001) 244 *et seq.*

[24] See Panezi (n 19 above).

[25] *Kalogeropoulou and Ors v Greece and Germany* (dec) No 59021/00, 12 December 2002, ECHR 2002-X.

[26] Murphy, 'Contemporary Practice of the United States' (2000) 94 AJIL 117, (2001) 96 AJIL 128, (2003) 97 AJIL 187.

The Federal Court of Germany did not recognize a Greek judgment in the *Distomo* affair, whereby Germany was condemned to pay reparation to civilians killed during the German occupation of Greece. The German Court held that an action aimed at recovering damages for conduct which is an exercise of sovereign power cannot be considered either civil or commercial.[27]

The *Ferrini* judgment[28] is not connected with the recognition of foreign judgments. However, the claimant relied on the 1968 Brussels Convention to substantiate the international competence of the Italian judge. The Court of Cassation held that the Convention cannot be applied to acts committed by the public administration when it exercises its sovereign powers.

Regulation (EC) 44/2001 admits the exception of *ordre public* as a cause for not recognizing foreign judgments (Article 34, paragraph 1). The question is whether the non-recognition of sovereign immunity by the foreign judge substantiates a cause of *ordre public*. If the Regulation does not apply, the possibility of recognizing a foreign judgment depends on the bilateral treaties in force between the forum state and the state where the judgment should be recognized. The German Federal supreme Court denied recognition of the Greek judgment since it was considered inconsistent with German *ordre public*: therefore the German-Greek bilateral Convention on Recognition of Foreign Judgments did not apply. The German Court found the Greek judgment inconsistent with *ordre public* for the following reasons: the Greek Court denied the sovereign immunity of Germany for an act *jure imperii* and retroactively applied a norm of *jus cogens* (the Greek Court said that the *jus cogens* rule on crimes of war overrules the norm on sovereign immunity).

The enforcement of money judgments is a sensitive point. Resolution 2005/35 issued by the Human Rights Commission recommends: 'states shall, with respect to claims by victims, enforce domestic judgments for reparation against individuals or entities liable for the harm suffered and endeavour to enforce valid foreign legal judgments for reparation in accordance with domestic law and international legal obligations. To that end, states should provide under their domestic laws effective mechanisms for the enforcement of reparation judgments'. This recommendation has two caveats: first, enforcement should be given only to 'valid' foreign judgments; secondly, enforcement should be granted in accordance with domestic and international law.

D. Immunity of State Officials

The problem is as follows: A wrongful act is imputed to both the state and the state official. The state official does not enjoy functional immunity since a war crime has been committed. Can the state official be sued to recover damages?

---

[27] Bundesgerichtshof, Judgment of 26 June 2003, reproduced in (2003) 56 *Neue Juristische Wochenschrift* (2003) 3488: R Hofmann, 'Do Victims of Violations of International Humanitarian Law Have an Individual Right to Reparation?', Report prepared for the ILA Toronto Conference, (n 1 above) 14–15.

[28] Ferrini (n 21 above).

Problems of immunity are usually raised in connection with criminal jurisdiction, while civil jurisdiction comes into consideration here. Whether a civil action can be established in the framework of criminal proceedings (for instance in Italy: 'parte civile') depends on the domestic legal order concerned. The issue of universal jurisdiction has been assessed in connection with Belgian law. A civil action can be started in relation to criminal jurisdiction, whether or not the claimant is a citizen of the forum state. If an international crime is committed, there is no immunity from criminal proceedings. It is possible that in the case of action against the state to which the wrongful act is imputed, the state in question is immune from jurisdiction, while the individual is not. This is in particular true for common law countries.

Re Karadzic and *Re Priebke* may be quoted here. Under both the Alien Torts Claim and the Torture Victims Protection Act, the Serbian leader Karadzic was found responsible for the atrocities perpetrated by Serbian militias and condemned by a United States Tribunal to pay compensation to victims.[29] In *Re Priebke* the Rome Military Tribunal found that the massacre of the 'Fosse Ardeatine', where scores of hostages were killed in retaliation for an action by Italian partisans against German soldiers, was a violation of the law of war. It sentenced Priebke and the other person convicted to several years' imprisonment, and at the same time awarded the families of the victims compensation to be qualified later.[30]

A complication arises in those cases in which the crime has been committed by high ranking officials such as heads of state, heads of government or members of government. In the *Arrest Warrant* affair, the ICJ held that heads of state, heads of government, or incumbent ministers cannot be subject to criminal proceedings.[31] This rule is valid only for domestic tribunals and does not apply to international tribunals such as the ICC. The rule stated by the ICJ is connected to personal immunity and not functional immunity. Upon termination of the mandate, the head of state or government and minister may be submitted to criminal jurisdiction. If we compare state immunity with individual immunity, we find an inconsistency: the state has immunity from jurisdiction while the individual does not.[32]

A point to be discussed is whether criminal jurisdiction can be severed from civil jurisdiction. Can an individual be immune from criminal jurisdiction and not from civil jurisdiction? Can civil responsibility be established independently of criminal responsibility? As I noted, this was possible in the United States for the *Karadzic* case.

---

[29] JF Murphy, 'Contemporary Practice of the United States Relating to International Law: Award Damages Against Bosnian Serb Leader Radovan Karadzic' (2001) 95 AJIL 143.

[30] *Cassazione penale* (1998) 668 *et seq.*

[31] *Arrest Warrant of 11 April 2000 (Democratic Republic of the Congo v Belgium)*, ICJ Reports (2002), reproduced in (2002) 41 ILM 536.

[32] Bianchi, 'L'immunité des Etats et les violations graves des droits de l'homme: la fonction de l'interprétation du droit international' (2004) 108, *Revue générale de droit international public* 82.

E. The Political Question Doctrine

This doctrine usually leads to denial of jurisdiction, even if the action is brought against the forum state. The doctrine in question has, as a consequence, the denial of jurisdiction since the act is not justiceable. This happened, for instance, in Italy with the *Markovic* case, an action brought by the relatives of victims of the NATO bombing of Belgrade (1999) against the Italian government. The Court of Cassation (5 June 2002) stated that the Rome Tribunal, before which the action was brought, lacked jurisdiction, since the bombardment was an 'act of government', ie a political act which could not fall within the competence of the ordinary or administrative jurisdiction.[33] The Federal Supreme Court of Germany in the *Distomo* case (26 June 2003) stated that 'at least in 1944 international humanitarian law did not provide for a basis of individual complaints to reparation'.[34] Landgericht Bonn (10 December 2003) held that German law on public liability could not be applied to compensate the victims of the bombing of the Varvarin bridge during the Kosovo War and that humanitarian law could not provide compensation for individual claims. The Court decision was appealed before the Oberlandesgericht Colognes, which confirmed the Bonn judgment, stating that IHL cannot be a ground for compensation under the German domestic legal order, leaving the door open, however, for application of the German law on compensation for wrongful acts of the government, to be applied in time of peace as well as in time of armed conflict.[35]

F. The Inter-State Character of IHL

As noted in the introduction, while human rights provisions seem to attribute rights to individuals, the provisions of IHL attribute rights and duties to states. Usually they address the high contracting parties and the high contracting powers. Even the provisions of Protocol II, additional to the Geneva Conventions, address the parties to the conflict: the constituted government and insurgents. The only provisions which seem to attribute duties to individuals are those related to crimes of war. But this is a controversial point. Such provisions could also be construed according to a different interpretation: states are obliged to implement the provisions on crimes of war within their own domestic legal orders. Consequently, duties for individuals derive from the domestic legal order and not from international law.

---

[33] *Presidenza Consiglio Ministri c Markovic e altri* (Cass Sez Un, No 8517) 5 June 2002, reproduced in (2002) 12 *Italian Yearbook of International Law* 292.

[34] See n 27 above.

[35] See J Wetzel,'Das Berufungsurteil im Fall der Brücke von Varvarin: Ein Schritt weiter für die Staatshaftung bei Verstößen gegen das humanitäre Völkerrecht' 295D *Bofaxe* (02.09.2005), available at <http://www.ruhr-uni-bochum.de/ifhv/publications/bofaxe/x295D.pdf>.

G. The Non-Self-Executing Nature of IHL

Even though IHL has an inter-state character and does not give rights and duties
to individuals, a provision of IHL, once implemented in the domestic legal order,
can have a self-executing nature. This means that the provision in question grants
rights (and duties) to individuals. Even if it is not possible to construe an individual
right to compensation within the international legal order, such a right could con-
ceivably be construed within the domestic legal order.

The issue of the self-executing nature of IHL came into consideration with
Article 3 of the 1907 Hague Convention on the law of war on land and Article 91
of Protocol I. This issue was central in the proceedings against Japan for damages
committed during the second World War.

Few doctrinal opinions share the view that the above provisions are of a self-
executing nature. Frits Kalshoven has argued that Article 3 of the Hague Convention
IV, unlike Article 91 of Protocol I, confers rights on individuals.[36] This view is
open to criticism. I agree that Article 3 of the Hague Convention IV and Article
91 of the 1977 Protocol have a different scope: the first addresses violations of the
Regulations appended to the 1907 Convention, while the second addresses violations of both the Geneva Conventions and Protocol I. However, nowhere in the
travaux préparatoires is it said that compensation is due to the individual. Kalshoven
gives both a broad and a narrow interpretation of Article 3. He says that it creates
rights for individuals and at the same time that it addresses only civilian populations, both neutral and of the enemy. Kalshoven's view is supported by Christoper
Greenwood, who delivered an opinion for the case of Philippine comfort women.[37]
He says that both conventional and international law confer rights on individuals,
including a right to compensation. Greenwood follows through on this line of
reasoning: since the law of war imposes duties on individuals, it should also confer
rights. Otherwise there would be an asymmetry. This interpretation is also open
to criticism. In no place in the drafting history of the Hague Convention IV or
of Protocol I does it say that rights are conferred upon the individual. Kalshoven
is obliged to refer to the 'implied' history of negotiation, which is unconvincing,
also taking the function of the *travaux préparatoires* into account, which are only a
supplementary means of interpretation and should be employed only if the textual
interpretation leaves the meaning ambiguous or obscure. Greenwood's argument
is based on the assumption that the law of war imposes duties on individuals and
therefore should also impose rights. This is inconsistent with a dualistic vision of
international law. Duties are not conferred on individuals by the international
legal order, it is the domestic legal order that is obliged to implement an obligation

---

[36] F Kalshoven, 'State Responsibility for Warlike Acts of the Armed Forces' (1991) ICLQ 40,
835–6.

[37] Greenwood's opinion has been reprinted in H Fujita, I Suzuki, and K Nagano (eds), *War and
the Rights of Individuals. Renaissance of Individual Compensation* (1999) 59–71.

stemming from international law. Greenwood is obliged to admit that claims for reparation may be submitted by states (on behalf of individuals through diplomatic protection) and individuals alike.

The case law is almost entirely against Kalshoven's view: all claims brought before Japanese and United States tribunals by Philippine and Korean comfort women have been rejected on the assumption that the law of war norms are not self-executing.[38] The UNCC, dealing with claims against Iraq for the Kuwait invasion, is competent only for state claims.

The sole case in which compensation has been awarded for an individual claim is that of the *Shimonoseki* judgment (1998). However, it was grounded in an argument of domestic law: there is a constitutional obligation in Japan to pass compensatory legislation. The 1998 judgment was, however, overruled in 2001 by the Hiroshima High Court.[39]

Note that Article 3 of Hague Convention IV and Article 91 of Protocol I apply only to international armed conflicts. There are no such provisions in Protocol II related to internal conflicts.

H. The ILC Draft Articles on State Responsibility and the Individual

The ILC Draft has an inter-state approach to the question of international responsibility. The violation of an international norm by a state entails responsibility towards another state and not towards an individual. There are two openings in the ILC Draft: paragraph 2 of Article 33 and paragraph 2(b) of Article 48.

Paragraph 2 of Article 33 is a mere saving clause. The provision specifies that the obligations of the responsible state are owed to another state, several states, or the international community as a whole. Afterwards, Article 33 affirms that '*This Part is without prejudice to any right, arising from the international responsibility of a State, which may accrue directly to any person or entity other than a State*' (emphasis added). The saving clause implies that obligations of reparation are owed directly to individuals, which they can enforce without the state as intermediary. This is spelt out in the ILC's commentary to Article 33 . The ILC assumes that a state has primary obligations to a non-state entity like an individual. Violation of such a primary obligation entails a state responsibility towards the individual (secondary obligation). The individual, in certain cases, may file a complaint before an international body (tertiary obligation).[40] In other words, there is a right to reparation at the international level. However, paragraph 2 of Article 33 of the ILC Draft is

---

[38] The Japanese case law is particularly rich. See H Fujita, 'Post-War Compensation Litigation from the Viewpoint of International Law' in H Fujita *et al* (n 37 above) 9 ; M Igarashi, 'Post-War Compensation Cases, Japanese Courts and International Law' (2000), 43 *Japanese Annual of International Law* 45; HB Shin, 'Compensation for Victims of Wartime Atrocities. Recent Developments in Japan's Case Law' (2005), 3 JICJ 187.

[39] HB Shin (n 38 above) 194–5.

[40] Pisillo Mazzeshi (n 13 above) 46–8.

a mere saving clause (in a document that is just a draft by a non-state body that has not been formally endorsed but only put to the attention of states for their consideration).

Paragraph 2(b) of Article 48 deals with the obligations owed to the international community as a whole. In this case, a state other than the injured state may invoke the performance of the obligation of reparation in the interest of the injured state or in the interest of the 'beneficiaries' of the obligation breached. This is true, for instance, in the case of genocide. However Article 48 presupposes state intervention for individuals to be compensated for the wrongful act.[41]

I. Peace Settlements and Reparations for Law of War Violations

Peace settlements often affirm that the vanquished state renounces per se, as do its citizens, any reparation or claim against the victor for the damages incurred in wartime. Sometimes the peace treaty states that both former warring parties renounce any claim. This means that the victor state and its citizens are also barred from filing a complaint against the vanquished state. Such a clause was stipulated, for instance, in the 1951 San Francisco Treaty with Japan. Waiver of any claim was deemed necessary for Japan's reconstruction. A number of claims have been raised to challenge this kind of treaty provision. The claims are twofold:

(1) claims brought by the citizens of the vanquished state against their own government, since it renounced exercise of the right to the diplomatic protection of its citizens; and

(2) claims by citizens of the victor state against the vanquished.

The wording of point (1) forms the content of the famous Shimoda claim for damages stemming from the atomic bombing of Nagasaki and Hiroshima.[42] The claim was rejected on the assumption that the exercise of diplomatic protection is a right of the state and not a right of citizens. Other claims were filed against Japan on the ground that renunciation of the exercise of diplomatic protection was a kind of expropriation without compensation and infringed the constitutional rights of citizens. This kind of claim was also rejected.

Claims by citizens of the victor state against the vanquished were also rejected by courts, since it was assumed that the claim was barred by clauses inserted in peace treaties. The plaintiff argued that the renunciation clause covered claims which might be filed by the state as well as the exercise of diplomatic protection. It could not cover claims which would be filed by the citizens. An additional argument was drawn from the common clause inserted in the Geneva Conventions (51/52/131/148), according to which: 'No High Contracting Party shall be allowed to absolve itself or by another High Contracting Party in respect

---

[41] See UN Doc A/56/10, 232.
[42] (1964) 8 *The Japanese Annual of International Law* 212–50.

of breaches referred to in the preceding Article'. The article in question is the one that regulates grave breaches to the Geneva Conventions. The clause common to the Geneva Conventions is not very useful for circumventing the waiver contained in peace treaties. First, the common clause is connected with criminal proceedings. Secondly, it is difficult to construe the common clause as *jus cogens superveniens* terminating a previous contrary agreement; or as a *jus cogens* rule invalidating a contrary treaty. And, thirdly, a subsequent treaty can always derogate a prior treaty, unless a *jus cogens* rule comes into question.[43]

J. Statutory Limitation under Domestic Law

Prescription is an obstacle for obtaining compensation. This depends on each legal order and on the statute of limitations under civil law. Common law countries do not have a statute of limitation even for trivial violations and the judge can always allocate a sum of money for the victim.

In Japan, claims for damages due to unlawful acts become void if they are brought within three years of the plaintiff becoming cognizant of the damage. Claims in any case become void twenty years after the wrongful act. Shin tells us that several Chinese claims against private companies that concurred in perpetrating war crimes were rejected by Japanese tribunals because of prescription.[44] Thus statutory limitation seems more a problem of civil law than of common law.

A line of reasoning from a *de lege ferenda* viewpoint seems to be the following: since there is no prescription for war crimes, there should be no prescription for compensation (the parallelism between criminal law and civil law was affirmed by the Swiss Federal Court in the *Spring* case, 2000. The Court held that the statute of limitations under criminal law is also applicable to rights under civil law. It affirmed this position to dismiss the plaint of the claimant who asked for compensation since he had been handed over to German troops by Swiss border guards in 1943).[45] The rule on non-applicability of statutory limitations for war crime punishment is set down in the United Nations Convention on the Non-Applicability of Statutory Limitations to War Crimes and Crimes Against Humanity (1968), the European Convention on the Non-Applicability of Statutory Limitations to Crimes Against Humanity and War Crimes (1974), and Article 29 of the ICC Statute. Therefore it should be paralleled by a rule on non-applicability of statutory limitations to

---

[43] The argument that the 1951 Peace Treaty with Japan and subsequent treaties entered into with the states of nationality of claimants barred any claim against Japan was recently endorsed by the DC Circuit, in the US, that dismissed the claim for damages submitted against Japan in the US by 15 women from China and other Far Eastern countries. The political question was also raised in order to reject the claim: Crook, 'Contemporary Practice of the United States Relating to International Law' (2005) 99 AJIL 902–4.

[44] HB Shin (n 38 above) 197–200.

[45] See, Henckaerts and Doswald-Beck (eds) (n 2 above) Vol II, part 2, 3566.

compensation rights.[46] This assumption is reinforced by Article 75 of the ICC Statute, which confers a right to compensation on victims of international crimes, under the jurisdiction of the ICC, which are not subject to prescription. Obviously, if a right to compensation is grounded in international law, there is no prescription. As Greenwood reminds us, the ICJ considered a claim brought by Nauru against Australia relating to events which occurred in the period 1946 to 1967.[47]

The non-application of statutory limitation for civil claims has also been advocated by Human Rights Resolution 2005/35 of the Commission on Human Rights. Under international law, there is usually no statutory limitation. However, it may happen that a treaty sets out a statute of limitation for submitting a claim for war reparations. This is more likely to happen in connection with a claim submitted to a claim commission than in connection with an action brought before a domestic court.[48] Emmanuel Roucounas quotes a 1996 judgment of the German Constitutional Court in the field of reparation. Sometimes protocols are concluded giving individuals the right to claim compensation (for example Germany-US), although the state may submit the claim to a time limit.

III. INTERNATIONAL RESPONSIBILITY

There are two kinds of armed conflict: international and non-international. It is worth differentiating.

In the case of international armed conflict, if a violation of IHL occurs, ordinary state responsibility comes into consideration. A differentiation may be made between violations which do not amount to a crime of war and violations that constitute a war crime. In the latter case, the violation may constitute a 'serious breach of an obligation under a peremptory norm of general international law', according to Article 40 of the ILC Draft. In all these cases, the responsible state is obliged to make reparation. The obligation is due to another state, for instance the national state of the individual who suffered the violation. In the case of a war crime, the perpetrator of the crime should be prosecuted.

Should a non-international armed conflict occur, the state might be responsible for violation of common Article 3 of the Geneva Conventions. Article 3 is now considered a provision of customary international law. Should a state be a party to Protocol II, it may commit a violation of the provisions contained therein. It is a moot point whether Protocol II is in all or in part declaratory of customary

---

[46] contra P D'Argent, 'Des règlements collectives aux règlements individuels (collectivisés)?' (2003) 5 *International Law FORUM, du droit international* 10, 24.

[47] C Greenwood (n 37 above) 69.

[48] See E Roucounas, 'Time Limitation for Claims and Actions under International Law' in E Yakpo and T Boumedra (eds), *Liber Amicorum Mohammed Bedjaoui* (1999) 223, 235–6. See also Roucounas, 'Facteurs privés et droit international public' (2002) 299 *Recueil des cours* 9, 386–7.

international law. This question has now been addressed by the ICRC study on customary IHL, quoted above. How should responsibility for violation of the law of internal conflicts be construed? No party (read international entity) can claim a right corresponding to the obligation violated, unless the international entity is the insurgent party. However, the norm violated might be construed as a norm embodying *erga omnes* obligations. In this case, it might be: (a) an *erga omnes partes* obligation (if a breach of a conventional norm), or (b) an *erga omnes* obligation, ie towards the international community as a whole, of a breach of customary international law.

Can violation of a provision of law regulating internal armed conflict amount to a crime of war entailing responsibility for individuals? Before the creation of the International Criminal Tribunal for the Former Yugoslavia (ICTY), this was a moot point. It is no longer, after the creation of the two ad hoc tribunals and the establishment of the ICC, whose Statute, under paragraph 2(c) and (e) of Article 8, qualifies serious violations of the law of armed conflict as crimes of war. This is important, since the ICC can establish compensation for the victims. In the case of non-international armed conflict, reparation is sought from the constituted government. Is it possible to seek reparation from insurgents? The ICRC customary international law commentary answers in the positive.[49] However, it is difficult to construe an international obligation for insurgents, unless they overthrow the constituted government and become the lawful government of the country.

Collateral damages are lawful acts causing harm to individuals and civilian objects. Causing collateral damage is not a violation of IHL, provided there is proportionality between the military advantage anticipated and the incidental loss of civilian life and damages to civilian objects. If a rule of IHL is violated, the wrongdoer is obliged to make reparation. If the damaged caused is truly collateral, no violation of IHL is committed. Collateral damages fall within the category of lawful acts causing harm. Should collateral damages be qualified as a circumstance precluding wrongfulness? If yes, Article 27(b) of the ILC Draft on State responsibility states that: 'The invocation of a circumstance precluding wrongfulness... is without prejudice to the question of compensation for any material loss caused by the act in question'. The ILC left the door open. In other instances, the exercise of lawful activities causing harm is expressly regulated, for instance within the framework of the law of the sea in connection with piracy, the slave trade and trafficking of illegal immigrants, or maritime nuclear terrorism. Other instances of lawful activities causing harm are connected with hazardous activities, such as satellite navigation or transfrontier pollution. War is by definition a hazardous activity. In principle, when international law calls for the payment of compensation for a lawful activity producing harm, a treaty law rule regulates the matter. In the absence of a provision requiring payment of compensation, there is no obligation to do so for collateral damages. This line of reasoning is strengthened by Article 3

---

[49] Henckaerts and Doswald-Beck (eds) (n 2 above) 149.

of the Hague Convention IV and by Article 91 of Protocol I, which address only compensation for *violation* of IHL.

As for the consequences of violation of IHL, the matter is regulated by Article 3 of the Hague Convention IV of 1907 on war on land. There is no such clause in the Geneva Conventions. The lacuna was filled by Article 91 of Protocol I, which addresses both violations of the Geneva Conventions and of Protocol I. Article 91 is formulated almost in the same way as Article 3 of the Hague Convention.

Both provisions address violation of the law of war, stating that:

(1) the violating party is liable to pay compensation; and
(2) each party is responsible for all acts committed by persons forming part of its armed forces.

Both provisions qualify the obligation to pay compensation, stating 'if the case demands'. This does not imply a limitation of responsibility. It only means that compensation shall be given if other forms of reparation are not possible (for instance *restitutio in integrum*). Article 3 of the Hague Convention and Article 91 of Protocol I are declaratory of customary international law. The most interesting question is to see whether they are self-executing, a problem which we shall examine later. The two provisions state that a party is responsible for acts committed by its armed forces. As for Protocol I, this is a consequence of the principle affirmed in Article I, according to which a party is obliged to respect and to ensure respect for the Protocol in all circumstances.

In the event of a violation of IHL attributable to an international organization, who is responsible? The member States? The International Organisation? Or both? The issue is now under review by the ILC, which has started its work on the responsibility of international organizations, to parallel that of states. There is also some practice in connection with the United Nations and the regional organizations which carry out peacekeeping and peace-enforcement operations, such as NATO or the European Union.[50]

The most simple solution would be: the international organization has legal personality and consequently bears international responsibility if the wrongful conduct is attributed to it. However, this solution has been criticized as being too simple and based on a private law analogy. It has been borrowed from the company law of domestic legal orders.[51]

International practice varies. The United Nations has accepted responsibility for its operations in the Congo (1960). On the contrary, NATO has not accepted any

---

[50] See generally Klein, 'Les organisations internationales dans les conflits armés: la question de la responsabilité internationale' in M Benchikh (ed), *Les organisations internationales et les conflits armés* (2001) 167.

[51] T Stein, 'Kosovo and International Community. The Attribution of Possible International Wrongful Acts: Responsibility of NATO or of Its Members States?' in C Tomuschat (ed), *Kosovo and the International Community. A Legal Assessment* (2002) 181, 192.

responsibility for hostilities carried out against the Federal Republic of Yugoslavia (FRY) NATO not only denied any violation of *jus ad bellum* for its air campaign against the FRY, but also did not admit any responsibility for warlike acts of dubious legality, such as the bombing of the Radio-Television Station in Belgrade, the destruction of the Varvarin bridge, or the bombing of the Djakovica convoy. Likewise, NATO denied any responsibility for the jettison areas and the explosive devices cleared from the Adriatic continental shelf upon the initiative of a naval squadron made up of several NATO countries, which was deemed a sort of exercise and not a duty imposed by international law.[52]

Obviously NATO, as an international organisation, cannot have any *locus standi* before the ICJ. Proceedings were instituted before the world court by the former Yugoslavia against NATO's member states and their joint and several responsibility was asserted. The same happened for the European Court of Human Rights. Proceedings were instituted by individuals, heirs of those hit by the bombing, against NATO member states party to the ECHR. Legal actions were set out against Germany and Italy, in their respective legal orders, accusing the two states of aiding NATO air operations. Again the plaintiffs did not raise NATO's responsibility.

In military matters, the responsibility for violation of the law of war is further complicated by the fact that the international organization is not party to any instrument of IHL. Moreover, not all member states are party to the same conventions and this raises the question of the legal interoperability of the coalition forces. For instance, at the time of intervention against the former Yugoslavia, France and the United States, of all the NATO participating states, were not party to Protocol I. The United Nations has remedied the legal impossibility of becoming party to the Geneva Conventions and Additional Protocol, firstly by enacting proper rules of engagement obliging military personnel to respect the spirit and principles of IHL and thereafter establishing a Bulletin reaffirming the main rules of IHL.[53] In military matters, the issue of imputability of the wrongful act is particularly important since the international organization has no military personnel of its own, in that they are seconded by member states.

The other question is that of acts performed under authorization from the international organization or in order to carry out a resolution, for instance a resolution calling on states to inspect ships suspected of violating an embargo or establishing a no-fly zone.

As for organs or agents placed at the disposal of an international organization, the ILC Draft on the responsibility of international organizations (Article 5) singles out control as the criterion to be applied.[54] If the organization exercises effective control

---

[52] For the relevant practice see M Mancini, 'Air operations against the Federal Republic of Yugoslavia (1999)' in N Ronzitti and G Venturini (eds), *The Law of Air Warfare—Contemporary Issues* (2006) 273.

[53] UN Doc ST/SBG/1999/13 (6 August 1999).

[54] Report of the International Law Commission, 56th Session (3 May–4 June and 5 July–6 August 2004), UN Doc A/59/10, 109.

over the conduct of the organ or agent, the act performed by the organ is attributable to the international organization, which consequently is fully responsible. It should be pointed out that an organ fully seconded entails the sole responsibility of the international organization. However, in military matters states usually retain a degree of control over contingents assigned to the organization. An agreement may be stipulated between the contributing states and the organization, apportioning responsibility between the two entities. Obviously the agreement is *res inter alios acta* for the third state. The ILC Report quotes a number of precedents in which the United Nations accepted responsibility for the national contingents forming part of the United Nations Operations in the Congo and the United Nations Peacekeeping Force in Cyprus.[55] This was done on the premiss that the United Nations had exclusive command and control over the force. Subsequent practice, however, shows that states want to retain a degree of control over their national contingents, as happened in Somalia with United Nations Operation in Somalia II (ONUSOM II). In this case, it is not possible to arrive at a unitary conclusion. As admitted by the Secretary-General of the UN, the criterion of effective control is decisive in the case of joint operations. If a norm of humanitarian law is violated, who gave the order and controlled the operation must be established. If a United Nations soldier is doing something wrong, independently of any order given (for instance sexual abuse), it is important to ascertain the disciplinary command (whether it is attributed to the United Nations or the national state).

Recent practice shows several instances of use of force authorized by the United Nations, since the United Nations Forces under Charter Articles 43 and 45 have never been implemented. The criterion adopted by the ILC is that of the interest of the organization. If states are acting for their own interest, the organization is not responsible; on the contrary, it is if the authorisation is given in the pursuance of the interest of the organization. The 'interest' criterion is questionable, for the organisation is in some respect always involved. The state is supposed to carry out an operation, since there is an authorization. Otherwise it would not have acted. The Secretary-General of the UN relied on the more sound criterion of command and control for excluding United Nations responsibility at the time of Operation Turquoise (1994).

For a binding resolution (for instance imposing sanctions), the ILC proposes that the organization be responsible, unless member states have been given the choice to select a mode of implementation which does not violate the international obligation. It is assumed that the resolution is lawful. This is true, as a matter of principle, for United Nations resolutions, because under Article 103 United Nations obligations prevail over any other treaty or customary rule (unless *jus cogens* is involved). The ILC Draft cannot be accepted for the other international organizations. If a binding resolution (for instance an EEC regulation) is contrary to international law, the responsibility of the international organization is also involved.

Scholarly opinion is not always in keeping with the ILC findings. For instance Ian Brownlie affirms that the existence or non-existence of a legal personality is

---

[55] Report of the International Law Commission (n 54 above) 110–14.

irrelevant for the international responsibility of states and international organizations.[56] Quoting the Institut de Droit International (1995), he states that 'a State cannot avoid responsibility by creating an international organisation'. The ILC Draft presupposes the existence of responsibility of the international organization, since Article. 3 reads that 'every internationally wrongful act of an international organization entails the international responsibility of the international organization'. Imputability of the act is thus the decisive criterion. If it is assumed that the organization is 'the corporate veil' of states, the concept of concurrent and subsidiary liability seems more appropriate. According to the former, states, at their choice, are allowed to have a claim against the international organization or member states; according to the latter, if the organization defaults, states are allowed to have a claim against member states.

IV. INTERNATIONAL CRIMINAL TRIBUNALS

Compensation for victims of violations of the law of war may be granted by international tribunals, once the responsibility of the individuals having committed the war crimes has been ascertained. International criminal tribunals deal with the responsibility of individuals and not of the states for which individuals have acted. Here, the proceedings for recovering damages before the ICC, the two ad hoc international tribunals, and the hybrid tribunals are considered.

A. The International Criminal Court

The ICC has only complementary jurisdiction vis-à-vis national tribunals. It has jurisdiction over war crimes, in particular (under Article 8 of the Statute) when committed as a part of a plan or policy; and as part of a large-scale commission of such crimes.

The head of ICC jurisdiction constitutes—in a certain way—a limitation to compensation, since the ICC does not judge isolated crimes but, in principle, only those committed on a large scale.

Article 75 of the ICC Statute deals with reparations. The Court may award reparation to the victim upon request or on its own motion, but only in exceptional circumstances in this latter case. The Court is empowered to adjudicate claims against individuals, but not against the state to which the individual belongs, even though the State bears international responsibility.

Reparation may consist of:

(1) restitution, for instance restoration of property;
(2) compensation, ie a sum of money for any economically assessable damage;

---

[56] I Brownlie, 'The Responsibility of States for the Acts of International Organizations' in M Ragazzi (ed), *Essays in Memory of Oscar Schachter, International Responsibility Today* (2005) 355, 357.

(3) rehabilitation, which 'should include medical and psychological care as well as legal and social services'.

The three kinds of reparation are listed in Article 75, while the examples given are drawn from the Human Rights Resolution 2005/35 on Basic Principles for Remedying Gross Violations of Human Rights.[57] According to Article 75, the Court should establish principles relating to reparations. This proposition is rather obscure, since the Court has not been endowed with the power to change the Statute. These principles have not yet been drafted and the Court is working on them.[58]

Article's 75 content has been spelt out by the ICC Rules of Procedure and Evidence. While Article 94 deals with requests for reparation by the victim, Article 95 deals with the case in which the Court proceeds on its own motion.

Article 97 of the Rules of Procedure and Evidence specifies how reparation is given. Reparation may be awarded on an individual basis or on a collective basis or both. Reparation on a collective basis means that a sum is awarded for all victims, should reparation take the form of compensation. Reparation on a collective basis may be awarded through the Trust Fund, as explained below. The ICC makes an order which is pronounced against the convicted person or executed through the Trust Fund, allowing the victim to recover compensation. The Court may order interim measures (for instance freezing property of the convicted person). The decision of the Court should be implemented in the domestic order of the relevant state party and enforced under Article 109 of the ICC Statute. The enforcement procedure is that of the state party. This rule is customary for such kinds of proceedings (the same, for instance, happens with the EEC Tribunal).

The Trust Fund is disciplined by Article 79 of the Statute. The Fund was established by a decision of the Assembly of States Parties and is made up of the fines and forfeitures ordered by the Court. The Trust Fund has already been set up and its governing board named.

Paragraph 6 of Article 75 contains a saving clause. It is stated that 'nothing in this Article [75] shall be interpreted as prejudicing the rights of victims under national or international law'. This clause is also difficult to intepret and should be clarified with respect to the Court's case law. It could mean that the victim can avail him or herself of a court's judgment before a domestic tribunal. Is it the same for an international tribunal? Can the victim seek compensation before an international tribunal availing him or herself of the Court judgment? A couple of problems come into consideration. The first is raised by the exhaustion of local remedies. Are proceedings before the ICC considered equivalent to the exhaustion of local remedies? The second is raised by the issue of complementarity. Supposing that the national tribunal delivers a judgment establishing a penalty for the guilty without awarding any compensation (or only a nominal compensation), can the

---

[57] See text following n 11 above.
[58] The ICC website was visited in January 2006.

ICC be activated under the principle of complementarity to obtain full compensation? What about the principle of complementarity between the ICC, on the one hand, and ad hoc international tribunals and hybrid tribunals, on the other? This issue is not resolved by the ICC Statute.

As concerns access to justice, the ICC raises the following issues:

(1) The individual cannot start a criminal proceeding (only a state party, the Security Council or the Prosecutor are entitled to trigger the Court's jurisdiction).

(2) The ICC is competent for war crimes committed on a large scale. Isolated crimes are not within the ICC's reach.

(3) Under Article 94 of the Rules of Procedure and Evidence a victim may request reparation under Article 75. This means that criminal proceedings are triggered by a state party, the Prosecutor or the Security Council, but once the proceedings are initiated, the victim has some power.

B. The International Criminal Tribunal for the Former Yugoslavia

The Statute of the ICTY does not contain any specific rule on compensation. It has only one provision—Article 24(5)—that states that the Trial Chamber can order restitution of property, in addition to a penalty for the guilty. Restitution is regulated by Article 105 of the Rules of Procedure and Evidence. The request is formulated either by the Prosecutor or the Tribunal, on its own motion, orders the restitution. The victim is not a party to the proceedings (unlike the ICC procedure, where the victim as well as the convicted person may be invited by the Court to make observations).

Compensation is possible only through indirect means. Article 106 of the Rules of Procedure, under the title 'Compensation to victims', states that the Registrar transmits the guilty judgment to the competent national authorities. The victim may bring an action to a national court. The provision states that the claim can also be brought before an 'other competent body'. What does this mean? Rule 106 of the Rules of Procedure and Evidence states that, for the purpose of obtaining reparation, the Tribunal's judgment shall be considered 'final and binding'. In other words, Article 106 does not give a right to compensation. This can be obtained only through national tribunals. A different problem is whether Article 106 is ultra vires, since the Statute does not establish any compensation procedure. These questions cannot be answered here.[59]

The same considerations as for ICTY apply, *mutates mutandis*, to the International Criminal Tribunal for Rwanda (ICTR). Paragraph 3 of Article 23 of the ICTR statute is drafted in the same way as paragraph 3 of Article 24 of the ICTY statute. There is also a provision of the Rules of Procedures and Evidence—Article 106— drafted like the corresponding provision of the ICTY.

---

[59] See generally A Cassese, *International Criminal Law* (2003) 429.

C. Internationalized and Hybrid Criminal Tribunals

Internationalized or hybrid criminal tribunals[60] are those courts of law established under an agreement between the United Nations and a specific state or under a resolution by the international authority mandated by the United Nations to administer a country. The Special Court of Sierra Leone and the Tribunal for Cambodia are examples of the former, while the Special Panels for Serious Crimes in Dili (Timor Leste) and National Courts in Kosovo are examples of the latter. The basic instruments contain provisions on compensations, confiscation, and restitution of property and pecuniary penalties.

Paragraph 3 of Article 19 of the Special Court for Sierra Leone statute states that 'in addition to imprisonment, the Trial Chamber may order the forfeiture of the property, proceeds and any assets acquired unlawfully or by criminal conduct, and their return to their rightful owner or to the State of Sierra Leone'. Paragraphs 2 and 3 of Article 39 of the Law on the Establishment of Extraordinary Chambers in the Courts of Cambodia for the Prosecution of Crimes Committed During the Period of Democratic Kampuchea says that 'in addition to imprisonment, the Extraordinary Chamber of the trial court may order the confiscation of personal property, money, and real property acquired unlawfully or by criminal conduct'. Strangely enough, the individual does not come into consideration, since the Cambodian Law goes on to affirm that 'the confiscated property shall be returned to the State'. For Timor Leste, paragraph 1 of section 10 of Regulation No 2000/15 on the Establishment of Panels with Exclusive Jurisdiction over Serious Criminal Offences establishes that a Panel may impose a fine of up to US$500,000 and the forfeiture of proceeds, property, and assets derived from the crime, in addition to imprisonment for a specified number of years. The same Regulation, under section 25, provides for the possible constitution of a Trust Fund for the benefit of the victims of crimes. The Trust Fund should be endowed through fines collected, property confiscated, and foreign donations.

The Trust Fund is an appropriate mechanism for providing victims with reparation when it is impossible to recover damages from those responsible for serious crimes. The Trust Fund could be a useful tool for those situations in which it is materially impossible to find a responsible entity for crimes.

V. THE EXTRA-TERRITORIALITY OF HUMAN RIGHTS CONVENTIONS: THE CASE OF DISPATCHING TROOPS ABROAD

As we have seen, human rights law is *lex generalis* vis-à-vis humanitarian law, which is *lex specialis*. Hence IHR law also applies in time of war unless derogated by humanitarian law. The importance of relying on IHR is evidenced by the fact that

---

[60] See generally C Romano, A Nollkaemper, and JK Kleffner (eds), *Internationalized Criminal Courts and Tribunals: Sierra Leone, East Timor, Kosovo and Cambodia* (2004).

the individual has no *locus standi* before an international tribunal under humanitarian law, while such a right is conferred under IHR. It is now undisputed that human rights treaties apply in time of war or armed conflict. The problem is whether they also apply beyond a state party's territory. If yes, the individual damaged may stand before an international tribunal and may use IHR law to challenge the lawfulness of acts performed abroad by the responsible state. This requires an examination of the territorial reach of human rights treaties.

A. The 1966 Covenants and the Convention on the Rights of the Child

The issue was clarified by the ICJ in its 2004 opinion. Article 2 of the Covenant on Civil and Political Rights obliges the contracting parties to apply the Covenant to individuals present in their territory and subject to their jurisdiction. Article 2 takes into account the requirements of the territory and jurisdiction, and it seems that both should be present to determine the sphere of applicability of the Covenant. Article 1 of the Optional Protocol, on the other hand, adopts jurisdiction as the sole connecting criterion. Consequently, several authors say that the two requirements—ie territory and jurisdiction—should not be read together, but separately.[61] Each of them is attributive of competence to the Human Rights Committee (HRC). The broad interpretation of Article 2 has been supported by the jurisprudence of the HRC. The case law of the HRC includes the cases of Uruguayan citizens captured abroad (Brazil and Argentina) by Uruguayan agents (1981).[62]

As for Guantanamo, the United States is party to the 1966 Covenant, but not to the Optional Protocol. No case law may consequently be quoted. IHR law was not considered by the US Court in the Guantanamo cases. The Covenant on Civil and Political Rights is held not to be self-executing.[63] The ICJ, in its 2004 Advisory Opinion on A Wall in Palestine, stated that the Covenant 'is applicable in respect of acts done by a State in the exercise of its jurisdiction outside its own territory'.[64] In its General Comment No 31 to Article 2 of the 1966 Covenant, the HRC stated that a state party should ensure application of the Covenant by its peacekeeping forces operating abroad.[65]

---

[61] L Condorelli and P De Sena, 'The Relevance of the Obligations Flowing from the UN Covenant on Civil and Political Rights to US Courts Dealing with Guantanamo Detainees' (2004) 2 JICJ 107.

[62] *Lopez Burgos v Uruguay* Communication No R.12/52, UN Doc Suppl No 40 (A/36/40), 176; *Lilian Celiberti de Casariego v Uruguay* Communication No 13/56, UN Doc Suppl 40 (A/36/40) (1981) 185.

[63] See the criticism by Condorelli and De Sena (n 61 above) 119.

[64] See n 9 above, para 111. See also ibid *Case Concerning Armed Activities on the Territory of Congo*, etc, para 216.

[65] CCPR/C/21/Rev.1/Add. 13, 26 May 2004, para 10. For a contrary view see MJ Dennis, 'Application of Human Rights Treaties Extraterritorially in Times of Armed Conflict and Military Occupation' (2005) 99 AJIL 124–7.

Both the HRC and the Belgian government affirmed that the Covenant should be applied in Somalia (ONUSOM II).[66] In the Committee conclusion of 27August 2001 it was stated that the Srebrenica events should be covered by the Covenant (Dutch contingent).[67]

For its territorial reach, the Convention on the Right of the Child of 20 November 1989 adopts the criterion of jurisdiction (Article 2) and thus applies outside state territory.

The Covenant on Economic and Social Rights has no clause for determining its territorial application. However the ICJ, in its Opinion on A Wall in Palestine, gave an extensive application, taking into account that the rights guaranteed are essentially territorial—and that it was thus not necessary to define their scope—and that Article 14 of the Covenant addresses metropolitan territory as well territories under the jurisdiction of the state party.[68]

B. The Case Law of the ECHR on the Territorial Scope of the Convention

According to Article 1 of the ECHR, the Convention applies to everyone within the jurisdiction of the high contracting party. Five major cases have clarified the territorial scope of the Convention: The *Loizidou* case (Merit, 1991); the *Bankovic* case, 2001 (Grand Chamber); *Ilascu and Ors v Moldova and the Russia Federation*, 2004 (Grand Chamber); *Issa and Ors v Turkey,* 2004; and *Behrami v France* (not yet decided).

The *Loizidou* and *Ilascu* cases were connected with the extra-territorial application of the ECHR outside the territory of the defendant state, but in a territory of a state party to the ECHR. The other three were in connection with the application of the European Convention in the territory of a state not party to the Convention.

1. *The* Loizidou *Case*[69]

After Turkey's intervention in Northern Cyprus in 1974, a new state was established, the Turkish Republic of Northern Cyprus. Turkey maintained its troops in Northern Cyprus. The Turkish state of Cyprus is not an effective independent entity and cannot become a party to the ECHR. Cyprus is a party but it does not control the territory of Northern Cyprus which, on the contrary, is under the effective control of Turkey.

---

[66] UN Doc CCPR/CO/79/Add. 99, 19 November 1998. *Concluding Observations of the Human Rights Committee*: Belgium, 19/11/98.

[67] UN Doc CCPR/CO/72/NET, 27 August 2001. *Concluding Observations of the Human Rights Committee*: Netherlands, 27/08/2001.

[68] See n 9 above para 112. See also ibid. *Case Concerning Armed Activities on the Territory of Congo*, etc, para 216.

[69] *Loizidou v Turkey (Merits)* Judgment of 18 December 1996, ECHR 1996-VI, 2216.

Since the rights of Loizidou were violated under the ECHR, Loizidou brought a claim against Turkey. The Court had to determine whether the violation was attributable to Turkey and whether the Convention applied. The Court stated that the 'concept of "jurisdiction" under Article 1 is not restricted to the national territory of the contracting States'. Accordingly, their responsibility can be invoked as a result of acts and omissions of their authorities which cause effects outside their own territory. Note that according to the Court, Northern Cyprus is a territory under Turkey's military control and therefore the Turkish Cypriot administration is under the control of Turkey. Moreover, the Turkish Cypriot part of the island is a territory where the ECHR applies since Cyprus is a state party.

2. *The* Bankovic *Case*[70]

During the Kosovo conflict, NATO bombed the Radio-Television Station in Belgrade on 23 April 1999. The heirs of the victims lodged a complaint before the ECHR, alleging, *inter alia,* the violation of Article 2 of the Convention (right to life). The acts were performed outside the territory of state parties to the ECHR. Article 1 of the Convention obliges the parties to secure the rights protected within their jurisdiction. The issue was a typical question of admissibility. Given the importance of the affair for the interpretation of the Convention, the issue was brought before the Grand Chamber. The application was rejected and declared inadmissible.

The applicants submitted the following arguments:

- The striking States had control of Yuogoslav territory during the bombing.
- Article 15 on the suspension of the Convention in time of war would be meaningless unless there were extra-territorial application. In effect, war often takes place outside the territory of state parties.
- If the bombing governments were not accountable, the individual would be deprived of any remedy.
- The control of air space by NATO was equal, *mutates mutandis*, to the control of Turkish troops in Northern Cyprus (*Loizidou* case).
- The act (ie the bombing) was decided on the territory of the member states.

The Court argued in the following way to reject the application:

(1) According to its ordinary meaning, jurisdiction is essentially territorial. Other kinds of jurisdiction are limited and exceptional, for instance invitation or acquiescence by the territorial state, occupation of foreign territory.

---

[70] *Bankovic and Ors v Belgium and Ors* (dec) [GC], No 52207/99, 12 December 2001, ECHR 2001-XII. For this case, I draw from my article 'Compensation for Violations of the Law of War and Individual Claims' (2002) XII IYIL 39, 43–6.

(2) Member states did not make a derogation pursuant to Article 15 when they intervened in the Gulf (against Iraq), Bosnia-Herzegovina, or the former Yugoslavia. This means that they did not feel obliged to abide by the Convention when they operated outside their territory.

(3) The latter interpretation is confirmed by the *travaux préparatoires*. The Expert Inter-governmental Committee replaced the words 'all persons residing within their territories' with the words 'with their jurisdiction' to cover all persons present in the territory, but not resident there in legal terms.

(4) The case law of the Court demonstrates that only in exceptional cases has extra-territorial jurisdiction been recognized: extradition or expulsion, in connection with Article 3, bearing in mind that the person to be extradited to a third country was present in the territory of the member state; effective control of the territory, as in the *Loizidou* case, was through the presence of the army.

(5) Normal cases of extra-territorial jurisdiction are connected with actions of diplomatic or consular agents abroad, or activities on aircraft or vessels of member states on the high seas in and the superadjacent air space.

(6) The 'jurisdiction' does not extend to any act performed outside the territory, even though this act brings consequences damaging to an individual. Article 1 of the ECHR cannot be read in the same manner as Article 1 common to the Geneva Conventions, according to which the high contracting parties undertake to respect and to ensure respect for the Conventions in all circumstances.

The finding by the ECHR has been subject to criticism:

(a) In a number of decisions, the Court applied the criterion of imputability of the activity carried out by the member state. Even though the activity was performed abroad, the imputability brought the act within the jurisdiction of the respondent state.

(b) The activity performed by the respondent states originated in their territory (the Aviano base). Consequently, the bombing was an extra-territorial effect of an activity started in the territory of a member state.

3. Ilescu and Ors v Moldova and Russia Federation[71]

After the secession of the province of Transdniestria from Moldova (1991), the Russian army helped the breakaway province. The Court, after having said that the applicants were partly under the jurisdiction of Moldova, within the limited powers that Moldova still exercised in Transdniestria, stated that they were also under Russian jurisdiction because of the support given by the Russian army to the seceded province.

[71] *Ilaşcu and Ors v Moldova and Russia* [GC], No 48787/99, 8 July 2004.

4. Issa and Ors v Turkey[72]

In 1995, Turkey entered Northern Iraq in order to take measures against Kurdish rebels who entered Turkey from the Iraqi sanctuaries. A number of Kurds were killed.

The Court declined jurisdiction because there was no factual evidence that the Turkish troops were responsible for the killing. One may, however, speculate that the Court would have affirmed its jurisdiction if there had been sufficient evidence that the death of the relatives of the applicants was a consequence of Turkish military operations. This was so even though the military operation in Iraq (unlike the military presence in Cyprus) was of limited duration (six weeks) and did not imply the occupation or stable control of Iraqi territory.

5. Berhami v France[73]

In 2000, two children of the Berhami family were hit by a cluster bomb: one was wounded; the other died. The area of Kosovo where this happened was under the control of the French contingent of NATO's Kosovo Force (KFOR). The applicant accused the French army of not having marked the dangerous area and of having violated Article 2 of the ECHR. The French government, in rejecting the claim, relied on *Bankovic*. Moreover, it said that the French contingent was part of KFOR and thus was an organ of the troops dispatched by NATO. A remedy was established in Kosovo to deal with applications for wrongful acts of KFOR and the UN Mission in Kosovo (UNMIK). The observations of the United Kingdom, which intervened under paragraph 2 of Article 36 of the ECHR, are of the utmost importance. The United Kingdom relied on *Bankovic* and said that the concept of jurisdiction is entirely distinct from that of state responsibility or liability. It further observed that the rights secured by the ECHR are indivisible and cannot be severed in order to tailor a particular right to a particular circumstance. Nobody, in effect, can reasonably pretend that all rights protected by the Convention apply in a territory under occupation or in a situation short of occupation. Moreover, the Convention did not apply to the Kosovo territory since the former Yugoslavia was not party to the ECHR and thus the *Behrami* case is completely different from that of Loizidou.

The *Behrami* case has not yet been decided.

VI. HOW THE VICTIM CAN OBTAIN COMPENSATION

In the foregoing, the numerous obstacles the victim has to face to obtain compensation have been indicated. In this section, examples of mechanisms that allow the victim to obtain compensation will be addressed. These mechanisms are not

---

[72] *Issa and Ors v Turkey* No 31821/96, 16 November 2004.
[73] *Behrami v France* Application 71412/01.

always in tune with victims' claims and the odds of being able to exert them with success is often very low.

A. The Practice of Mixed Arbitral Tribunals

After the end of the first World War, the Peace Treaties of 1919–20 instituted mixed arbitral tribunals to deal with claims for violations of the law of war. Individuals were allowed to file a complaint directly to those tribunals. One can quote, as an example, the decisions taken for damages incurred in the aerial bombardment of Salonicca and Bucharest by German Zeppelins. The plaintiffs claimed violation of Articles 25 and 26 of the Regulations appended to the Hague Convention IV of 1907, dealing with bombardment and assault, which forbid bombardment of undefended localities and the obligation to give a warning before attack. The two arbitral awards, after having stated that the two provisions were applicable to air warfare, obliged Germany to compensate the claimants.[74]

B. Claim Commissions

Usually claim commissions (or equivalent panels) do not have a judicial nature. Claim commissions, for instance, are used for claims against the United Nations for damages incurred during peacekeeping missions.[75] The commission is usually composed of three members, appointed respectively by the Secretary-General of the UN, the government of the host state, and the two parties on common understanding (if agreement is not reached, the ICJ President nominates). Individuals may file a complaint before a claim commission. As a rule, a ceiling applies (US$50,000) and compensation for non-pecuniary loss is excluded unless serious violations of human rights and/or humanitarian law are involved. It is not clear which law should be applied. Wickremasinge and Verdirame[76] rightly observe that, because of United Nations immunity from local courts, a claim cannot be brought to a domestic tribunal. If the claimant cannot obtain any compensation, his government can always intervene in diplomatic protection.

For damages incurred in Kosovo and attributable to KFOR and UNMIK, UNMIK Regulation No 2000–47 of 18 August 2000 states that claims for damages may be brought to the attention of claim commissions established by KFOR and UNMIK. However, these claim commissions are not competent for damages caused by 'operative necessity', ie by military operations.

---

[74] *Coenca Brothers v Germany*, 1927; *Kiriadolou v Germany*, 1930, *Annual Digest*, 1927–1928, Case No 389; ibid 1929–1930, Case No 301.

[75] C Wickremasinge and G Verdirame, 'Responsibility and Liability for Violations of Human Rights in the Course of UN Field Operations' in C Scott (ed), *Torture as Tort: Comparative Perspectives on the Development of Transnational Human Rights Litigation* (2001) 465, 482 *et seq*.

[76] Wickremasinge and Verdirame (n 75 above).

The claim commission established under the peace treaty between Eritrea and Ethiopia on 12 December 2000 is of a different nature.[77] In this case, individuals cannot present a claim directly. Claims may be filed by the two states on behalf of their nationals for violations of IHL. The Commission applies the relevant rules of international law and cannot decide *ex aequo et bono*. The award of the Commission is final and binding.

C. Compensation Commissions

The establishment of a compensation commission has been proposed, for instance, in order to make proper reparation by the Commission of Inquiry created by the Secretary-General of the UN for genocide in Darfur. The basis, according to the Commission Report, is an obligation stemming from customary international law. It states that 'whenever a gross breach of human rights is committed which also amounts to an international crime, customary international law not only provides for the criminal liability of individuals who have committed that breach, but also imposes an obligation on states of which the perpetrators are nationals, or of which they acted as *de jure or de facto* organs, to make reparation (including compensation) for the damage made'.[78] The statement on the customary international law obligation is important and contributes to the development of international law in this field.

The United Nations Compensation Commission (UNCC) established under Security Council Resolution 687 (of 1991) for damages incurred in Kuwait at the time of the Iraq occupation, is the best known example of a compensation commission.[79] This commission generally evaluates claims for violations of *jus ad bellum* rather than *jus in bello*. Moreover, claims cannot be filed by individuals, but only by states, acting on behalf of individuals.

D. Individual Civil Responsibility

Criminal responsibility for violations of the law of war is usually established in all legal orders and is now an obligation stemming from international law. Civil responsibility is a consequence of criminal responsibility. In civil law countries the victim may act to recover damages as *parte civile*. The obstacle, here, is represented by the immunity of the responsible agent. One can affirm that a civil action should parallel a criminal action: if the victim is not immune from criminal jurisdiction,

---

[77] See generally 'Arbitrating Responsibility for Violations of IHL: The Eritrea-Ethiopia Claims Commission', Bofaxe No 263E, 12.12.2003 <http://www.ruhr-uni-bochum.de/ifhv/publications/bofaxe/x263E. pdf>.

[78] UN Doc S/2005/60, Report of the International Commission of Inquiry on Darfur to the United Nations Secretary General, Geneva, 25 January 2005, para 598, at 151–2.

[79] See generally M Frigessi di Rattalma and T Treves, *The United Nations Compensation Commission. A Handbook* (1999).

he cannot be immune from civil jurisdiction. The ICJ, in the affair of *Congo v Belgium*, recognized the immunity of jurisdiction from domestic tribunals only for heads of state and other incumbent members of government (they are not, however, immune from international criminal jurisdiction, such as that of the ICC or the two ad hoc criminal tribunals, as we have seen).[80]

What about civil responsibility? Can it be severed from criminal responsibility? For example: an individual is immune from criminal proceedings, can he or she be sued under civil action? This is possible in the United States under the Alien Tort Claim Act (ATCA). For instance, Karadzic was sued with an action in tort for having committed war crimes.

E. Universal Civil Jurisdiction

The best known example is that of the United States and ATCA.[81] The Act allows a foreign individual to sue another foreign subject (individual or state) in the United States for acts committed abroad: thus an action in tort. The connecting criterion with the US legal order is very tenuous: it is sufficient for the defendant to be present in US territory occasionally. ATCA was established in 1789 and was resurrected in connection with the Filartiga affair (1980) in which two Paraguayans sued a Paraguyan policemen for acts of torture committed in Paraguay. ATCA was employed to establish jurisdiction against Karadzic, temporarily present in the United States, for crimes of war committed in Bosnia Herzegovina. ATCA is often difficult to employ as a remedy, since it can be challenged in various ways: for instance because the defendant enjoys immunity from jurisdiction, or the doctrine of act of state applies, or there is a more suitable forum to which the claim may be brought under the doctrine of *forum non conveniens*. Supposing that the plaintiff is successful in suing for violation of law of war under ATCA, another major hurdle is enforcement of the judgment abroad where the assets of the respondent are located. The international competence of the US judge may be challenged and the judgment not recognized.

F. State Responsibility under Domestic Law: Suing the Responsible State within Its Own Legal Order

A state committing a violation of the law of war is also committing a violation of its own legal order. Therefore a foreign claimant can sue the state within its own legal order, ie the legal order of the wrongful state. In principle, the foreign nationality of the victim should not be an obstacle. In the *Behrami* case[82] before

---

[80] See n 31 above, para 61.
[81] See generally KL Boyd, 'Universal Jurisdiction and Structural Reasonableness' (2004) 40 Tex ILJ 1. For a continental view see I Moulier, 'Observations sur l'alien tort claim act et ses implications internationals' (2003) 69 *AFDI* 129.
[82] *Behrami* (n 73 above).

the ECHR France said that, according to French administrative law, the state is responsible for the acts of its agents that cause damages. A complaint may be filed before the Paris Administrative Tribunal or the Conseil d'Etat. However, this mode of recovering damages runs counter to the doctrine of political acts as well as that of non-justiciability of acts of government. As has been pointed out, in the *Markovic* case the Italian Court of Cassation held that the claim for damages caused by the bombardment of Belgrade was non-justiciable.[83] The same conclusion was reached by the Bonn Tribunal in Germany and the finding was confirmed by the Cologne Court of Appeal.[84]

G. Complaint by the Victim before an International Tribunal

International tribunals dealing with the criminal aspects of violations of IHL are only criminal tribunals.[85] They can award reparation to the victim in addition to inflicting punishment on the culprit. However, the proceedings are not set in motion by the individual. Since there is no international tribunal with competence over violations of the law of war which may be set in motion by an individual, the only existing possibility is to file a complaint before a human rights tribunal, such as the European Court of Human Rights. In this case, the violation which comes into consideration is a violation of a provision relating to human rights. Nevertheless, this violation may well constitute a violation of the law of war. The classic example is the right to life or a violation of the provisions, forbidding degrading and inhuman treatment. Under these provisions, infringements occurring during an internal conflict may also be sanctioned. The problem with human rights tribunals is that they are not numerous, do not have worldwide competence (like the ICC), and their statutes sometimes contain an optional clause for hearing individual claims. The 1966 United Nations Covenant on Civil and Political Rights is endowed with an optional Protocol for hearing individual complaints. Moreover, the HRC does not deliver binding decisions.

The United States is not party to the 1966 Inter-American Convention on Human Rights. Thus, decisions taken by the Inter-American Commission on Human Rights, when the United States is involved, are grounded on the 1948 American Declaration on Human Rights which the United States does not consider obligatory. The Inter-American Court on Human Rights can issue a 'Decision on Reparation', under Article 63.1 of the American Convention on Human Rights.

---

[83] Markovic (n 33 above).

[84] See n 35 above.

[85] The commission of an international crime usually entails not only individual responsibility but also state responsibility. This is why the alleged violation of international law may be the object of an international dispute like *Bosnia-Herzegovina v Serbia and Montenegro* for violation of the 1948 Convention on genocide, pending before the ICJ since 1993. Bosnia-Herzegovina demands that the Court declare that Serbia Montenegro violated the Genocide Convention and must pay appropriate reparation.

Note that the United States has declared that the provisions of the 1966 Covenant on Civil and Political Rights are not self-executing and are thus not applied, in principle, by United States Courts.[86]

H. Diplomatic Protection

Diplomatic protection is a classic mode of recovering damages through the action of the state. The state, of which an individual who suffered the tort is a national, can intervene on behalf of the individual against the state that caused the damage.

The requirements of an action in diplomatic protection are that the individual should have the nationality of the claimant state and that domestic remedies should be exhausted before starting an action in diplomatic protection. The two requirements limit the possibility of relying on diplomatic protection for recovering damages, since the individual may have changed nationality and trying all local remedies is time-consuming and expensive. Moreover, under international law, the national state has no obligation to exercise diplomatic protection on behalf of its citizens. The right to submit a claim may be forfeited by the government, as happened with the San Francisco Treaty with Japan and the Shimoda affair.[87] Note that there are instances in which it is very hard to discover the national state of an individual and the individual's nationality may be legally fictitious. For instance, who is entitled to espouse the claim of a victim in a Kosovo-like situation?

VII. CONCLUSION: *DE LEGE FERENDA* CONSIDERATIONS

As we have seen, the chances of a victim being compensated for violations of the law of war are very meagre. The traditional modes for recovering damages are not satisfactory and are fraught with obstacles. Thus there is a need to explore new methods.

According to the Report of the Darfur Commission of Inquiry, there is an obligation to pay compensation to individuals for war damages caused by violation of the of law of war.[88] This is an obligation of the responsible state towards the individual. In my opinion it is not yet customary international law. As a corollary of such a substantive obligation, there should be a right for the individual to address an international tribunal to enforce his or her right.[89] Such a tribunal does not yet

---

[86] Condorelli and De Sena (n 61 above) 119–20.

[87] See n 42 above.

[88] Report of the International Commission of Inquiry on Darfur to the Secretary-General of the UN (n 78 above) 150–2, paras 594–600.

[89] Even if one admits that an individual right to compensation does not exist, such a right would not be enforceable by the individual but only by the national state on behalf of the individual: see the forthcoming interim report of the ILA Toronto Conference and the Draft prepared by R Hofmann (n 1 above) 13.

exist for IHL. It does exist within the framework of IHR. However, there is a broad difference. While under IHR an individual brings a complaint against her or his own state, under IHL the individual brings a complaint against the hostile state, unless a violation of the law of non-international armed conflict is involved.[90]

Universal civil jurisdiction should parallel universal criminal jurisdiction. However, the former should be accompanied by a proper mechanism for enforcing civil judgments awarding compensation.

An action for recovering damages may be brought against the State, against the individual, or both:

- In action against the state, is the principle of non-sovereign immunity in the case of war crimes emerging? Can one make a parallel with individuals whose immunity is denied in case of war crimes?
- Action against an individual entails the problem of recovering compensation, even when the court has ordered compensation. Often the responsible individual lacks funds for compensation, especially in the case of mass killing. Article 75 of the ICC statute was right in establishing a Trust Fund.

Is it best to leave things as they now stand and live with a fragmented system, waiting for customary international law to change while trying to exploit the few openings in the system? In this connection, the following points should be taken into account:

(1) the erosion of the rule of State sovereign immunity;
(2) the system of universal civil jurisdiction (the ATCA model should be expanded);
(3) international criminal jurisdiction should leave room for reparation on the model of Article 75 of the ICC statute; and
(4) the possibility of applying IHR and related mechanisms to violations of the law of war which are at the same time violations of human rights.

As a corollary of a domestic judgment granting compensation to the victim, the right to access to justice should also contemplate the implementation of the judgment. The European Court of Human Rights stated that the implementation of a judgment is an integral part of a fair trial under Article 6 of the ECHR. This right 'would be illusory if a contracting state domestic legal system allowed a final, binding judicial decision to remain inoperative to the detriment of one party'. Article 6(1) of the Convention should protect not only the right to access to justice, but also the right to implement a judicial decision.[91]

---

[90] R Provost, *International Human Rights and Humanitarian Law* (2002) 55–6.
[91] Concurring Opinion of Judge Pellonpää in *Al-Adsani v UK* [GC], No 35763/97, 21 November 2001, ECHR 2001-XI, 107. This opinion is contradicted by subsequent decisions, in particular *Kalogeropoulos and Ors v Greece and Germany* (n 25 above).

Unlike IHR law, there is no access for individuals to an international remedy for IHL violations. A revolutionary proposal might be to establish mechanisms under IHL paralleling those existing under IHR law. For instance, the negotiation of a Protocol Additional to the Geneva Conventions and to the two Additional Protocols establishing a Compensation Commission.[92] The Protocol should be based on the model of the ECHR but should be universal.

[92] In this connection, a proposal has been already made by the Hague Agenda for Peace and Justice for the 21st Century: Draft Additional Protocol to the Geneva Conventions Establishing an Individual Complaints Procedure for Violations of Humanitarian Law, <httpl/:www.haguepeace.org>.

4

Access to Justice before International Human Rights Bodies: Reflections on the Practice of the UN Human Rights Committee and the European Court of Human Rights

MARTIN SCHEININ

I. TWO HUMAN RIGHTS TREATIES—TWO SUPERVISORY BODIES

The supervisory bodies under the International Covenant on Civil and Political Rights (ICCPR)[1] and the European Convention on Human Rights (ECHR),[2] ie the Human Rights Committee (HRC) and the European Court of Human Rights, respectively, possess important similarities. Both have the same interpretive function in respect of the treaty in question. Hence, both participate in the establishment of the law through institutionalized practices of interpretation. However, there are, of course, also important differences in the functions of the two bodies. While the European Court of Human Rights is a fully judicial organ, the HRC operates in respect of individual complaints as a quasi-judicial body and in respect of periodic reports by states more as a body for administrative review. Only the European Court conducts, selectively, oral hearings when dealing with complaints, and only the European Court provides legal aid for the complainants. While it is not appropriate to characterize the final Views by the HRC as mere 'recommendations',[3] there is nevertheless a difference in the legal nature of the determinations by the two

---

[1] 999 UNTS 171.

[2] References to the ECHR are to its current text, as amended by Protocol No 11, European Treaty Series 155.

[3] See, M Scheinin,: 'The Human Rights Committee's Pronouncements on the Right to an Effective Remedy: An Illustration of the Legal Nature of the Committee's Work under the Optional Protocol' in N Ando (ed), *Towards Implementing Universal Human Rights: Festschrift for the Twenty-Fifth Anniversary of the Human Rights Committee* (Martinus Nijhoff Publishers, 2004) 101–15.

bodies in that the *judgments* of the European Court enjoy legally binding force by virtue of the European Convention,[4] whereas HRC Views represent authoritative interpretations as to the substance of the legally binding *treaty* obligations. Hence, it is evident that the European Court has clear advantages as compared to the HRC in the issue of effective access to justice on the level of international adjudication. From the perspective of the complainant, the decisive difference is often that the European Court will hand out a legally binding order to pay just satisfaction to the complainant in most cases of a human rights violation, whereas even a successful case before the HRC may still result in a situation where the complainant must initiate new proceedings on the domestic level in order to be compensated. Sometimes such efforts fail and for the victim of the human rights violation, the real benefit of a successful case is a public and reasoned opinion by an international panel of experts declaring that there indeed was a human rights violation.

However, the HRC also has some comparative advantages. One of them is that the other, non-judicial functions of the HRC may indirectly serve effective access to justice. This is particularly true for the mandatory monitoring mechanism of periodic implementation reports by state parties.[5] The reporting procedure allows for systematic and comprehensive periodic review that has the capacity to address both negative and positive state obligations and does not suffer from the somewhat coincidental nature of complaints-driven jurisprudence. In the long run, however, the outcomes from the reporting procedure enrich the understanding of the scope and substance of the treaty provisions and may provide a point of departure for dealing with novel issues under the complaints procedure when the opportunity arises.

Another comparative advantage of the HRC lies in the fact that the European Court of Human Rights has become a victim of its own success, in the sense that the exponential growth in the number of complaints has resulted in serious delays in the consideration of complaints; a need for a strict interpretation of the admissibility requirements; and proposals that would enable the Court to dismiss even meritorious cases on a discretionary basis when they do not have broader significance.[6] The relatively small number of complaints under the Optional Protocol to the ICCPR—a symptom of the procedure not being widely perceived of as providing effective access to justice—has resulted in a more liberal approach to the interpretation of formal admissibility requirements.[7]

---

   [4] ECHR, Art 46.
   [5] See ICCPR, Art 40.
   [6] See, European Court of Human Rights, Survey of Activities 2005, according to which during the year 41,510 applications were lodged, 27,612 applications declared inadmissible or struck off the list, 1,036 applications declared admissible, and 1,105 judgments delivered by the Court <http://www.echr. coe.int/NR/rdonlyres/4753F3E8-3AD0-42C5-B294-0F2A68507FC0/0/SurveyofActivities2005.pdf>.
   [7] By 7 April 2006, the HRC had concluded its consideration in 1,172 cases, out of which 433 (37%) had been declared inadmissible, 202 (17%) discontinued, and 537 (46%) decided on the merits. In 420 cases (36%) 1 or more violations of the ICCPR had been found. On the same date, there were 291 living registered cases. Source: <http://www.ohchr.org/english/bodies/hrc/stat2.htm>.

Any pronouncement by an international monitoring body to the effect that there has been a human rights violation in a particular case serves as a device for access to justice on the international level. A public, reasoned, and authoritative decision, based on the interpretation and application of the treaty obligations of the state in question, often provides a form of redress to the affected individual. However, it is clear that the mechanism of the European Court provides strong comparative advantages beyond this dimension of a remedy. The Court is competent to issue binding orders as to just satisfaction for any human rights violation established by the Court, and the Committee of Ministers of the Council of Europe supervises the execution of these orders.[8] In contrast, although the ICCPR provides for an individual right to an effective remedy whenever there has been a violation, the HRC usually does not quantify the remedy it calls for, and following up the implementation of the Views by the Committee, including pronouncements on the remedy, is by and large left to the HRC itself.[9]

The establishment of a new inter-governmental body, the Human Rights Council, to replace the United Nations Commission on Human Rights, has the potential to strengthen the role of political support for the implementation of the findings by the HRC and other treaty bodies. According to the pertinent General Assembly resolution, the functions of the Council will include the duty to:

(e) Undertake a universal periodic review, based on objective and reliable information, of the fulfilment by each State of its human rights obligations and commitments in a manner which ensures universality of coverage and equal treatment with respect to all States; the review shall be a cooperative mechanism, based on an interactive dialogue, with the full involvement of the country concerned and with consideration given to its capacity-building needs; such a mechanism shall complement and not duplicate the work of treaty bodies; the Council shall develop the modalities and necessary time allocation for the universal periodic review mechanism within one year after the holding of its first session;[10]

At best, the idea of the Council complementing and not duplicating the work of the treaty bodies will mean that similarly to the Committee of Ministers within the Council of Europe framework, the main political body in human rights issues will have the task of overseeing the implementation of the treaty-based findings by the independent expert bodies. At worst, the Council's peer review mechanism will be utilized to second-guess and question the findings and interpretations by the treaty bodies.

---

[8] See ECHR, Art 46, para 2 and Rules adopted by the Committee of Ministers for the application of Art 46, para 2, of the European Convention on Human Rights (2001), available at <http://www.coe.int/T/E/Human_rights/execution/02_Documents/>.

[9] See, Rules of Procedure of the Human Rights Committee (CCPR/C/3/Rev.8), rules 71 (follow-up on concluding observations adopted in the reporting procedure) and 101 (follow-up on Views under the Optional Protocol).

[10] GA Res A/RES/60/251 (15 March 2006) para 5(e).

II. THE REQUIREMENT OF EXHAUSTING DOMESTIC REMEDIES

In October 2005 the HRC, the treaty body that monitors states' compliance with the ICCPR, decided the case of *KL v Peru*.[11] The case involves a novel human rights issue, at least in the context of the ICCPR, and touches upon many crucial questions as to access by individual victims of human rights violations to domestic courts and international bodies.

The *KL* case originates from Peru, a country with very restrictive abortion laws that on various occasions have been criticized by international human rights bodies for their adverse impact on the human rights of women.[12] The HRC had clearly stated that the Peruvian abortion laws were 'incompatible with articles 3, 6 and 7 of the Covenant'.[13] Nevertheless, in 2001 the restrictive abortion laws were still in place.

KL was 17 years old when she became pregnant in 2001. Some three months later it was discovered that the foetus was anencephalic, this condition causing a risk to the health and even life of the woman, and being in all cases fatal to the foetus. Nevertheless, KL was refused abortion with the explanation that therapeutic abortion was permitted only when the termination of the pregnancy was the only way of saving the life of the pregnant woman or avoiding serious and permanent damage to her health. In January 2002, KL gave birth to an anencephalic baby girl, who survived for four days, during which time the mother had to breastfeed her. Unavoidably, the baby died. KL suffered deep depression and an inflammation.

For a discussion on access to justice as a human right the most interesting dimension of the case relates to the questions whether KL had on the domestic level any effective avenues to claim her reproductive rights in order to have her pregnancy terminated, and whether such remedies had to be exhausted before a prospect for international remedies before human rights treaty bodies could open. These two inter-related questions are dealt with in a single paragraph in the Views by the HRC:

5.2 The Committee notes that, according to the author, the same matter has not been submitted under any other procedure of international investigation. The Committee also takes note of her arguments to the effect that in Peru there is no administrative remedy which would enable a pregnancy to be terminated on therapeutic grounds, nor any judicial remedy functioning with the speed and efficiency required to enable a woman to require the authorities to guarantee her right to a lawful abortion within the limited period, by

---

[11] *KL v Peru* Communication No 1153/2003, HRC Views of 24 October 2005.
[12] See concluding observations by the Human Rights Committee, CCPR/C/79/Add.72, para 15 (1996) and CCPR/CO/70/PER, para 20 (2000); concluding observations by the Committee on the Elimination of Discrimination Against Women A/53/38/Rev.1, para 339 (1998).
[13] CCPR/CO/70/PER, para 20.

virtue of the special circumstances obtaining in such cases. The Committee recalls its jurisprudence to the effect that a remedy which had no chance of being successful could not count as such and did not need to be exhausted for the purposes of the Optional Protocol. In the absence of a reply from the State party, due weight must be given to the author's allegations. Consequently, the Committee considers that the requirements of article 5, paragraph 2 (a) and (b), have been met.

The outcome of the *KL* case—recognizing the complainant's access to justice on the international level—was largely dependent on the decision by the state party, Peru, not to respond to the complaint. Had Peru reacted and invoked the requirement of exhausting domestic remedies before making use of an international procedure, the outcome would have depended on the HRC's closer assessment of the availability and effectiveness of the judicial or other remedies that Peru would have invoked. The result of that kind of an assessment is often hard to predict and one may get the impression that it represents more an art than a science. The practical application of the requirement of domestic remedies is one of the most unpredictable issues in international human rights litigation. In the *KL* case the position of the complainant was accepted by default when the state party failed to cooperate.

For comparison, reference can be made to the case of *Galina Vedeneyeva v the Russian Federation*, declared inadmissible by the HRC in March 2005.[14] The son of the complainant, Mr Konstantin Vedeneyev, was arrested in April 1994 but never tried. He was allegedly tortured and kept in pre-trial detention in an overcrowded cell with 100 other inmates. In those circumstances, he contracted tuberculosis, and in January 1995 he died of tuberculosis of the lungs and of pneumonia.

The mother filed complaints before various authorities and in March 1996 received a letter by the director of the pre-trial detention centre where her son had died, stating that the circumstances of her son's death had been investigated. According to the director, no violations of rules relating to conditions of detention or the provision of medical assistance to detainees had been identified.

Before the HRC, the Russian Federation chose a different strategy to that of Peru. The state party argued that after the response to her first round of complaints the mother should have taken the case to the General Procurator of the Russian Federation, and further to the Supreme Court. Although the mother responded that she did not consider these as effective remedies in the case, the HRC ruled the case as inadmissible due to non-exhaustion of domestic remedies:

7.3 The Committee has noted the State party's submission that the author did not exhaust available domestic remedies, as she did not take her complaints about the alleged mistreatment of her son to the General Procurator of the Russian Federation and subsequently to the Supreme Court. Whilst the author contends that these bodies would not provide an effective remedy in the present case, no explanation has been provided by her in support

---

[14] *Galina Vedeneyeva v the Russian Federation* Communication No 918/2000, HRC inadmissibility decision of 29 March 2005.

of this contention. The Committee considers that, whilst the author of a communication does not bear the sole burden of proof for a contention that a particular domestic remedy is ineffective, an author must at least present a prima facie argument in support of such a proposition, and substantiate his or her reasons for believing that the remedy in question is or would be ineffective. In the present case, the author has not done this.

The obvious difference between the cases of *Vedeneyev* and *KL* is in the litigation strategy of the state party. Where Peru chose to ignore the complaint, effectively waiving its right to invoke the requirement of exhausting domestic remedies, the Russian Federation launched an offensive, and insisted before the Committee that specific domestic remedies existed and were available and effective. In the assessment of the HRC, the mother had not done her share in arguing the ineffectiveness of domestic remedies and the word of the state party weighed more.

This outcome of the Committee's assessment of the requirement of exhausting domestic remedies can be criticized as being formalistic, or unreasonable in respect of the respective situations of the two parties of the case. The inadmissibility can also be criticized as incoherent with earlier jurisprudence concerning cases brought by detainees or their relatives about conditions of detention.[15] Although European Court of Human Rights practice—simply due to the huge number of cases—is quite restrictive in respect of the admissibility conditions, including the requirement of exhausting domestic remedies, the notion of 'administrative practice' as a valid excuse to the requirement of exhaustion appears to be an area where the HRC could learn a lesson. For instance, in the case of *Akdivar v Turkey* the European Court formulated its position as follows:

...there is...no obligation to have recourse to remedies which are inadequate or ineffective. In addition, according to the 'generally recognised rules of international law' there may be special circumstances which absolve the applicant from the obligation to exhaust the domestic remedies at his disposal...The rule is also inapplicable where an administrative practice consisting of a repetition of acts incompatible with the Convention and official tolerance by the State authorities has been shown to exist, and is of such a nature as to make proceedings futile or ineffective...[16]

Reading the *Vedeneyev* decision, one is tempted to say that the HRC simply got it wrong, that the remedies invoked by the state party were plainly ineffective to provide an effective remedy for the human rights violation that had already taken place. One would have good grounds to say that even when the state party invokes the requirement of exhausting domestic remedies the Committee must independently

---

[15] In the case of *Lantsova v the Russian Federation* Communication No 763/1997, the HRC found a violation of the right to life when the son of the complainant had died of pneumonia in pre-trial custody in overcrowded and unhygienic conditions. However, in that case the Russian Federation chose not to contest the admissibility of the communication but, instead, sought to defend itself on the merits.

[16] *Akdivar v Turkey*, ECHR Judgment of 30 August 1996, para 67. See, also P Leach, *Taking a Case to the European Court of Human Rights* (2nd edn., OUP, 2005) 145–6.

assess the effectiveness of those remedies and have the courage to rule against the state party. Mrs Vedeneyeva *did* contest the effectiveness of the remedies that were invoked by the state party. Much like the *KL* case, it could be seen as obvious that the remedies mentioned by the Russian Federation could not have prevented the alleged human rights violation—after all, the son of Mrs Vedeneyeva was already dead at the time she unsuccessfully invoked the remedies that were known to her. No further proceedings before the General Procurator or the Supreme Court could have brought back her son or provided an 'effective' remedy for the loss of his life.

There is, however, another important difference between the two cases. While the case concerning the late Mr Vedeneyev was initiated and argued by his mother, without the assistance of a lawyer, KL was assisted by qualified lawyers acting through three non-governmental organizations (NGOs), Estudio para la Defensa y los Derechos de la Mujer (DEMUS), Comité de América Latina y el Caribe para la Defensa de los Derechos de la Mujer (CLADEM), and the Center for Reproductive Law and Policy. It is submitted here that this factor of effective representation might have been even more important for the outcome of the two cases than the immediately visible difference in the choice of litigation strategy by the state party.

And although the *KL* case deserves to be celebrated as a landmark case in respect of women's access to justice on the international level to claim their reproductive rights, it suffers from a disturbing internal contradiction. The notion of an effective remedy does not only appear in paragraph 2(b) of Article 5 of the Optional Protocol to the ICCPR that establishes the requirement of exhausting domestic remedies before taking a case to the HRC. Also paragraph 3(c) of Article 2 employs the same notion when affirming that whenever there has been a violation of the Covenant, the victim of that violation shall have a right to an effective remedy. In the *KL* case the Committee, rightly, stated that no domestic court or other body could have provided KL with an effective remedy that would have enabled her to terminate her pregnancy in time. But in its own views, after establishing that there was a violation of Articles 7, 17, and 24 of the Covenant, the Committee calls for 'compensation' as an effective remedy to KL.

Granting compensation would probably have been an option also to Peruvian courts and authorities after KL delivered and lost her baby. And compensation for the suffering caused by the death of her son was probably available to Mrs Vedeneyeva through the remedies invoked by the Russian Federation. If one reads the HRC's Views in the *KL* case as indicating that compensation would as such be an effective remedy for the human rights violation suffered by KL, then there seems to be no coherent explanation for the Committee concluding that effective domestic remedies would have existed in the *Vedeneyev* case but that they did not exist in *KL*. Of course, one may explain this apparent paradox by taking the position that compensation through national remedies is one thing, and a finding of a human rights violation by an international body, coupled with an order to the state to pay compensation, is quite a different thing.

III. ISSUES OF STANDING BEFORE THE HRC AND THE EUROPEAN COURT OF HUMAN RIGHTS

For an assessment of the effectiveness of access to justice at the international level through complaint procedures under human rights treaties, the basic question is who can bring a case to these bodies. Setting aside the issue of inter-state complaints,[17] and focusing instead on 'individual' complaints and the legal issue of who is entitled to complain, we are addressing the question of who has *standing* to initiate such a case. The range of hypothetically available options includes individuals, groups of individuals, peoples, NGOs, other juridical persons, and even entities of a public law nature. From an access to justice perspective equally important as the question of formal standing is the practical effectiveness of access, for instance by children, persons with disabilities, and indigenous peoples.

Both the ECHR and the ICCPR mechanisms for complaints include as one of the admissibility conditions the requirement that the complainant is a *victim* of an alleged human rights violation.[18] Hence, abstract complaints of an *actio populuris* nature, or pursuing a case on behalf of someone else in the absence of authorization, is not permitted. However, international bodies may be quite flexible as to the form of authorization.[19] For instance, a relative may act on behalf of a disappeared person[20] or a person otherwise in a vulnerable position,[21] and a non-custodial parent on behalf of a child also without a power of attorney. In the latter situation the European Court of Human Rights appears to be more restrictive than the HRC,[22] and even before the HRC documenting the opinion of the child may be crucial for substantiating the complaint submitted without a power of attorney on her behalf.[23] The exclusion of *actio populuris* complaints also means that NGOs cannot act on behalf of individuals without an authorization from them—or in some cases from their family.

---

[17] See ECHR, Art 33 and ICCPR, Art 41.

[18] See ECHR, Art 34 and Optional Protocol to the ICCPR, Art 1.

[19] See M Nowak, *UN Covenant on Civil and Political Rights: CCPR Commentary* (2nd edn,NP. Engel, 2005) 835–6.

[20] See *Basilio Laureano Atachahua, acting on behalf of his granddaughter, Ana Rosario Celis Laureano v Peru* Communication No 540/1993, HRC Views of 25 March 1996.

[21] See Leach (n 16 above) 119 and the cases referred to there.

[22] ibid 119–20 and of the cases *Hokkanen v Finland* ECHR Judgment of 23 September 1994 (standing of non-custodial parent rejected) and *Scozzari and Giunta v Italy* ECHR Judgment of 13 July 2000 (standing of non-custodial parent accepted).

[23] See *Deborah Joy Laing v Australia* Communication No 901/1999, HRC inadmissibility decision of 9 July 2004, para 7.3: '…Notwithstanding the consistent practice of the Committee that a custodial, or, for that matter, non-custodial, parent is entitled to represent his or her child under the Optional Protocol procedure without explicit authorization, the Committee points out that it is always for the author to substantiate that any claims made on behalf of a child represent the best interest of the child…'

The exclusion of *actio popularis* is closely related to the question of standing by groups, minorities, or peoples.[24] Article 34 of the ECHR explicitly recognizes that 'groups of individuals' have standing, hence largely settling the matter so that bigger or larger groups of persons may submit a joint complaint provided all members of the group have given authorization to counsel or other representative. Under Article 1 of the Optional Protocol to the ICCPR the matter is a bit more complicated, as that provision only mentions 'individuals' (in the plural) as complainants and as the CCPR nevertheless has substantive clauses on minority rights (Article 27) and even the right of all peoples to self-determination (Article 1). The legal issues that arise were resolved in *Chief Bernard Ominayak and the Lubicon Lake Band v Canada*[25] where the HRC established the following position:

(1) As the Optional Protocol only gives standing to 'individuals' to submit complaints to the HRC and as the right to self-determination is in Article 1 of the ICCPR proclaimed as a collective right of 'peoples', that right cannot become the subject matter of an individual complaint. In other words, the HRC took the view that there cannot be individual victims of a violation of the right of self-determination.[26] In its later case law, the HRC has somewhat modified this approach by affirming that Article 1 of the ICCPR may nevertheless be taken into account when interpreting, under the Optional Protocol, other provisions of the ICCPR.[27]

(2) Despite the procedural approach taken in respect to the right of peoples, the HRC affirmed that smaller or larger groups of individuals may jointly submit a communication, including under Article 27 of the ICCPR, that proclaims certain rights to 'persons belonging to...minorities'.[28]

(3) The HRC affirmed that a community leader, acting on behalf of his community, may have standing to represent all members of the community without separate written authorization from the individuals concerned.[29]

Prima facie, the ECHR is more liberal in respect of standing in that Article 34 explicitly provides for applications 'from any person, non-governmental organization or group of individuals claiming to be the victim of a violation'. While the victim requirement is identical to the Optional Protocol to the ICCPR, otherwise the characterization of various categories of complainants is broader than just 'individuals' as in the ICCPR system.

---

[24] Nowak (n 19 above) 829–30.

[25] *Chief Bernard Ominayak and the Lubicon Lake Band v Canada* Communication No 167/1984, HRC Views of 26 March 1990.

[26] ibid para 13.3.

[27] See *Apirana Mahuika and Ors v New Zealand* Communication No 547/1993, HRC Views of 27 October 2000, para 9.2.

[28] *Ominayak*, (n 25 above) para 13.4.

[29] ibid paras 2.2 and 14.

The category of 'non-governmental organizations' does not merely refer to national laws that may define a specific category of registered associations but generally to registered or non-registered associations, trade unions, professional associations, political parties, companies (also when dissolved), trusts, religious organizations, etc. Together with the reference to 'a group of individuals', the notion of NGOs may also cover, for instance, a group of journalists[30] or shareholders, or an indigenous village[31] collectively. The crucial criterion defining standing in respect of such juridical persons or groups of persons without distinct juridical personhood is that the complainant must be a victim of an alleged violation of the ECHR. There are some ECHR rights that due to their material content are easily applicable also in respect of juridical persons or other groups of individuals, such as the right to a fair trial (Article 6 of the ECHR) or the right to peaceful enjoyment of possessions (Article 1 of Protocol 1). However, there are also rights that only can be invoked by natural persons, such as the right not to be subjected to degrading treatment or punishment (Article 3 of the ECHR).[32]

In some cases it will be important to determine whether an entity is distinct from the state itself, so that it can qualify as a group of individuals or an NGO bringing a case against a state that is a party to the ECHR. This borderline was addressed in the case of *The Holy Monasteries v Greece* where the European Court of Human Rights held that the monasteries in question were distinct from the respondent state:

...the Court notes at the outset that the applicant monasteries do not exercise governmental powers. Section 39(1) of the Charter of the Greek Church describes the monasteries as ascetic religious institutions.... Their objectives—essentially ecclesiastical and spiritual ones, but also cultural and social ones in some cases—are not such as to enable them to be classed with governmental organisations established for public-administration purposes. From the classification as public-law entities it may be inferred only that the legislature—on account of the special links between the monasteries and the State—wished to afford them the same legal protection vis-à-vis third parties as was accorded to other public-law entities. Furthermore, the monastery councils' only power consists in making rules concerning the organisation and furtherance of spiritual life and the internal administration of each monastery...[33]

In respect of minors and mentally incapacitated persons it is important that their *de jure* and *de facto* access to international human rights bodies is not necessarily determined by domestic laws which due to their restrictive nature may be at the heart of the claimed human rights violation.[34] Against this principle, *Nielsen v Denmark*, concerning the placement of a twelve-year-old child in psychiatric treatment

---

[30] *Sunday Times v UK* ECHR Judgment of 26 April 1979.
[31] *Muonio Saami Village v Sweden* ECHR Admissibility decision of 15 February 2000.
[32] Leach (n 16 above) 115.
[33] Case of *The Holy Monasteries v Greece*, ECHR Judgment of 9 December 1994, para 49.
[34] Leach (n 16 above) 118–19.

appears problematic, as the European Court held that the treatment in question was not a deprivation of liberty as it was based on a request by the mother in her reasonable exercise of custodial authority. Hence, although the application submitted by the child was admissible, the Court on the merits held that Article 5 of the ECHR was not applicable.[35]

In *Herczegfalvy v Austria*, which originated from a handwritten letter sent by a psychiatric patient to the European Commission of Human Rights, written on brown paper bags,[36] the European Court of Human Rights ultimately established a violation of Article 8 of the ECHR because of undue interference with the applicant's correspondence.[37] This highlights the close connection there is between *de jure* standing before, and *de facto* access to, the Court.

The requirement of the complainant being personally a victim of an alleged human rights violation may in the context of a case be interpreted somewhat liberally but without opening the door for abstract *actio popularis*. This may occur by referring to the complainant as a 'potential victim', although it is not at all clear whether this notion is actually needed. Consenting adults wishing to engage in criminalized homosexual practices,[38] women of child-bearing age subject to restrictive abortion laws,[39] possible targets of secret surveillance of telephone conversations,[40] or foreigners subject to a real risk of torture as a consequence of a deportation decision[41] could all be referred to as potential victims. However, that concept is unnecessary if the right to respect for private life (Article 8 of the ECHR, Article 17 of the ICCPR) or the notion of inhuman treatment (Article 3 of the ECHR, Article 7 of the ICCPR) is interpreted to be engaged already at the stage where the person now is.

Conditional or selective acceptance of the right of international complaint tends to be incompatible with the object and purpose of a human rights treaty. As human rights belong to all individuals irrespective of their origin, status, or characteristics, it would run counter to the idea of human rights if states were able to pick and choose who has the right to complain and who does not. In *Loizidou v Turkey* the European Court of Human Rights came to the conclusion that certain

---

[35] *Nielsen v Denmark* ECHR Judgment of 28 November 1988, para 73.

[36] In the report by the European Commission of Human Rights (Application 10533/83, 10 March 1988), the following description appears: 'It appears that writing material was withheld from the applicant also at later dates. Thus a letter to the Commission of 27 November 1978 was written on brown paper bags and the applicant stated that he had been refused other paper and had also complained of this to the Ministry. Most of the applicant's subsequent letters to the Commission were according to him smuggled out under circumvention of the prison rules because he did not get sufficient writing material or permission to write.'

[37] *Herczegfalvy v Austria* ECHR Judgment of 31 August 1992.

[38] *Dudgeon v UK* ECHR Judgment of 23 September 1981; *Toonen v Australia* Communication 488/1992, HRC Views of 31 March 1994.

[39] *Open Door Counselling and Ors v Ireland* ECHR Judgment of 29 October 1992.

[40] *Klass and Ors v Germany* ECHR Judgment of 6 September 1978.

[41] *Chahal v UK* ECHR Judgment of 15 November 1996.

territorial and other exceptions declared by Turkey when accepting the—then optional—jurisdiction of the Commission and Court were 'invalid', taking into consideration the character of the Convention, the ordinary meaning of the relevant jurisdictional provisions in their context, and in the light of their object and purpose and the practice of contracting parties.[42] Hence, Turkey's acceptance of the right of complaint was treated as valid but the unilateral qualifications to the right as invalid.

The HRC took the same approach of severability in *Rawle Kennedy v Trinidad and Tobago* where the state party had denounced the Optional Protocol and then reacceded to it with a reservation excluding persons sentenced to death from the scope of the right of international petition. The HRC treated the reaccession as valid but held that the reservation was without effect:

6.7 The present reservation, which was entered after the publication of General Comment No. 24, does not purport to exclude the competence of the Committee under the Optional Protocol with regard to any specific provision of the Covenant, but rather to the entire Covenant for one particular group of complainants, namely prisoners under sentence of death. This does not, however, make it compatible with the object and purpose of the Optional Protocol. On the contrary, the Committee cannot accept a reservation which singles out a certain group of individuals for lesser procedural protection than that which is enjoyed by the rest of the population. In the view of the Committee, this constitutes a discrimination which runs counter to some of the basic principles embodied in the Covenant and its Protocols, and for this reason the reservation cannot be deemed compatible with the object and purpose of the Optional Protocol. The consequence is that the Committee is not precluded from considering the present communication under the Optional Protocol.[43]

In securing access to justice on the international level, the European Court of Human Rights has been quite strict in dismissing also other kinds of hindrances to the effective exercise of the international right of petition. In *Kurt v Turkey* it was held to be in breach of the right of individual complaint that the authorities had taken steps to institute criminal proceedings against the applicant's lawyer, even though they were not followed up.[44] In *Petra v Romania*, concerning hindrances to correspondence between a prisoner and the supervisory organs of the ECHR, the Court found a violation of the right of individual complaint and stated:

43. The Court recalls that it is of the utmost importance for the effective operation of the system of individual petition instituted by article 25 that applicants or potential applicants should be able to communicate freely with the Commission without being subjected to any form of pressure from the authorities to withdraw or modify their complaints.
The expression 'any form of pressure' must be taken to cover not only direct coercion and flagrant acts of intimidation of applicants or potential applicants or their families or

---

[42] *Loizidou v Turkey* ECHR Judgment on the preliminary objections, 23 February 1995, para 89.
[43] *Rawle Kennedy v Trinidad and Tobago* Communication 845/1999, HRC admissibility decision of 2 November 1999. Four HRC members dissented.
[44] *Kurt v Turkey* ECHR Judgment of 25 May 1998, para 165.

legal representatives but also other improper indirect acts or contacts designed to dissuade or discourage them from pursuing a Convention remedy...[45]

IV. SECURING EFFECTIVE ACCESS THROUGH INTERIM MEASURES OF PROTECTION

One dimension of the effectiveness of access to justice on the international level relates to the existence and effect of interim measures of protection while a case is pending before an international body. Here the main rule is that human rights courts and treaty bodies have at their disposal a possibility to request interim measures but that such competence is not provided in the human rights treaty itself but in secondary instruments—such as Rules of Procedure—issued by the monitoring body itself.[46] As to the two treaties discussed here, the relevant rules are in Rule 92 of the HRC Rules of Procedure[47] and in Rule 39 of the European Court of Human Rights Rules of Court.[48]

As a consequence of the absence of specific treaty provisions on interim measures of protection, it may be argued that the state parties to a human rights treaty do not have a legal obligation to comply with a request for interim measures of protection. Indeed, in *Cruz Varas v Sweden* the European Court in 1991 took the view that a request by the then existing European Commission of Human Rights not to deport an individual while his application was being considered, was not legally binding on the state and that Sweden did not violate the ECHR by deporting the applicant in disregard of the Commission's request for interim measures.[49]

---

[45] *Petra v Romania* ECHR Judgment of 23 September 1998.

[46] An exception to this rule can be found in the Optional Protocol to the Convention on the Elimination of Discrimination against Women (GA Res A/54/4 of 6 October 1999) which has, in Art 5, a provision on the powers of the CEDAW to request interim measures of protection.

[47] 'The Committee may, prior to forwarding its Views on the communication to the State party concerned, inform that State of its Views as to whether interim measures may be desirable to avoid irreparable damage to the victim of the alleged violation. In doing so, the Committee shall inform the State party concerned that such expression of its Views on interim measures does not imply a determination on the merits of the communication.'

[48] Rule 39, Para 1: 'The Chamber or, where appropriate, its President may, at the request of a party or of any other person concerned, or of its own motion, indicate to the parties any interim measure which it considers should be adopted in the interests of the parties or of the proper conduct of the proceedings before it.'

[49] *Cruz Varas v Sweden* ECHR Judgment 20 March 1991. Before the European Court of Human Rights, the issue of non-compliance with the Commission's request for interim measures of protection was argued as a violation of the right of individual complaint. The European Court held that their request had no legally binding authority as such and that the issue of violating the right of individual complaint was to be addressed through the duty to implement the ECHR in good faith: '102. Accordingly, the Court considers that the power to order binding interim measures cannot be inferred from either Article 25 §1 *in fine*, or from other sources. It lies within the appreciation of

In 2000, however, the HRC for the first time addressed the issue of the legal consequences of a state party's non-compliance with a request for interim measures of protection. In *Dante Piandiong and Ors v The Philippines* the Committee concluded that by ratifying the Optional Protocol on the procedure for individual communications a state undertakes to cooperate with the Committee in good faith so as to permit and enable it to consider the communication and that a state party commits a 'grave breach' of its obligations under the Optional Protocol if it acts to prevent or frustrate consideration by the Committee of a communication. Specifically, a state party breaches its obligations under the Protocol if it, having been notified of the communication, proceeds to execute the alleged victim.[50] It is to be noted that the HRC builds its argument on a state's general duty to comply with its treaty obligations in good faith,[51] and not on the relevant provision in its own Rules of Procedure.

Less than a year after the HRC decided the *Piandiong* case, the International Court of Justice (ICJ) addressed the legal nature of its own requests for interim measures, in the *LaGrand* case (*Germany v United States of America*) that concerned capital punishment in respect of two German nationals in the United States.[52] Unlike the situation under most human rights treaties, the power of the ICJ to request interim measures was provided by Article 41 of the ICJ's Statute and not merely a subsidiary instrument. Despite the fairly cautious wording of the actual provision,[53] the Court confirmed that its request was legally binding.[54]

What is to be taken as a promising sign of interaction between various international judicial and quasi-judicial bodies, is that after the *Piandiong* and *LaGrand* cases the European Court of Human Rights has now changed its own approach. In *Mamatkulov and Askarov v Turkey*, relating to the extradition of two individuals by Turkey to Uzbekistan and decided in the final instance by a Grand Chamber, the European Court cited these and other decisions by international bodies, including

the Contracting Parties to decide whether it is expedient to remedy this situation by adopting a new provision notwithstanding the wide practice of good faith compliance.'

[50] *Dante Piandiong and Ors v The Philippines* Communication 869/1999, HRC Views of 19 October 2000.

[51] See, Vienna Convention on the Law of Treaties (1155 UNTS 331) Art 26: 'Every treaty in force is binding upon the parties to it and must be performed by them in good faith.'

[52] *LaGrand* case (*Germany v United States of America*), Judgment of 27 June 2001, General List No 104.

[53] The Statute of the International Court of Justice, Art 41(1) reads: 'The Court shall have the power to indicate, if it considers that circumstances so require, any provisional measures which ought to be taken to preserve the respective rights of either party.'

[54] '...It follows from the object and purpose of the Statute, as well as from the terms of Article 41 when read in their context, that the power to indicate provisional measures entails that such measures should be binding, inasmuch as the power in question is based on the necessity, when the circumstances call for it, to safeguard, and to avoid prejudice to, the rights of the parties as determined by the final judgment of the Court. The contention that provisional measures indicated under Article 41 might not be binding would be contrary to the object and purpose of that Article...' (para 102).

the United Nations Committee against Torture and the Inter-American Court of Human Rights, and essentially echoed the HRC approach when concluding:

128. The Court reiterates that by virtue of Article 34 of the Convention Contracting States undertake to refrain from any act or omission that may hinder the effective exercise of an individual applicant's right of application. A failure by a Contracting State to comply with interim measures is to be regarded as preventing the Court from effectively examining the applicant's complaint and as hindering the effective exercise of his or her right and, accordingly, as a violation of Article 34 of the Convention.

129. Having regard to the material before it, the Court concludes that, by failing to comply with the interim measures indicated under Rule 39 of the Rules of Court, Turkey is in breach of its obligations under Article 34 of the Convention.[55]

V. AVAILABILITY OF LEGAL AID

In its final judgments establishing a violation of the ECHR, the European Court of Human Rights orders the respondent state to pay, besides just satisfaction for the human rights violation, also legal costs. It also has a scheme for legal aid from Council of Europe sources in pending cases. Both arrangements are important for effective access to justice on the international level. Nevertheless, they come into play only in a small minority of all registered applications. Legal costs are ordered only where a violation of the ECHR is established and even legal aid is available only after an application has been either communicated to the government or declared admissible, ie only after certain important steps of screening incoming applications.[56]

One of the most evident shortcomings of the complaint procedures before the HRC, and of the United Nations human rights system in general, is that there is no arrangement for legal aid to applicants that submit cases to the HRC or the other treaty bodies. As there are not even plans for introducing a legal aid scheme within the United Nations, the most viable option for improving the situation appears to be the creation of some sort of a coalition by NGOs that would provide legal aid for victims of human rights violations who want to take a case before a United Nations human rights treaty body. So far, many NGOs have provided legal assistance on an ad hoc basis or when using individual test cases as a part of their litigation strategy. However, they have not pooled together their resources in order to form a legal assistance scheme to which individuals could turn on their own initiative.

As to awarding legal costs, the HRC has, in some of its fairly recent Views establishing a violation, made a move towards ordering the state party in question

---

[55] *Mamatkulov and Askarov v Turkey* ECHR Grand Chamber Judgment of 4 February 2005.

[56] Rules of the Court, Rule 91. See, also, Rules 92–96 and LJ Clemens, N Mole, and A Simmons, *European Human Rights: Taking a Case under the Convention* (2nd edn, Sweet & Maxwell, 1999) 99–101; Leach, (n 16 above) 26–7, 49–51.

to pay for the legal costs of the applicant. The first case in that category was *Laptsevich v Belarus*, decided in 2000, where the HRC expressed the remedy called for as follows: 'Under article 2, paragraph 3(a), of the Covenant, the State party is under an obligation to provide Mr. Laptsevich with an effective remedy, including compensation amounting to a sum not less than the present value of the fine and any legal costs paid by the author. The State party is also under an obligation to take measures to prevent similar violations in the future.'[57]

To date, this 'Laptsevich formula' has not become a standard element in those HRC Views that establish a violation of the ICCPR. Rather, the HRC requests only on a discretionary basis the respondent state to compensate the legal costs of the victim of a human rights violation. From the perspective of effective access to justice this is to be regretted.

VI. REFORM OF THE EUROPEAN COURT OF HUMAN RIGHTS: IS ACCESS TO THE COURT UNDER THREAT?

Currently the trend in the ECHR system is not necessarily towards the broadening of *de facto* access to the European Court of Human Rights. Rather, the Court has become a victim of its own success in the sense that it is flooded by incoming applications. The number of pending registered cases has reached 84,000,[58] which is a level totally out of proportion when compared with the ability of the Court to deliver judgments. The possible entry into force of Protocol No 14 to the ECHR[59] will introduce certain new screening mechanisms but is widely seen as insufficient in respect of the real need to improve the Court's capacity to address the huge backlog of applications.[60] In the long term, improving effective access to justice on the domestic level is probably the only sustainable avenue towards solutions that are compatible with human rights but that at the same time are capable of reducing the backlog of cases before the Court.

Much of the inter-governmental discussion on 'saving' the European Court through measures that would introduce new filtering devices or even make the

---

[57] *Vladimir Petrovich Laptsevich v Belarus* Communication 780/1997, HRC Views of 20 March 2000, para 10.

[58] According to statistics provided by the Court, there were 84,150 pending cases on 1 March 2006. <http://www.echr.coe.int/NR/rdonlyres/4A8D6AD6-D533-4632-B911-F65FCC575C78/0/stats2006.pdf>.

[59] Council of Europe Treaty Series No 194 (not yet in force).

[60] In the Warsaw Declaration of May 2005 the Council of Europe Member States committed themselves to the rapid ratification of Protocol No 14 and to further steps to increase the ability of the European Court of Human Rights to deal with its caseload, *inter alia*, by establishing a group of wise persons to make new proposals. See, in particular para 2 of the Declaration, available at <http://www.coe.int/t/dcr/summit/20050517_decl_varsovie_en.asp>.

Court operate on the basis of discretionary jurisdiction, rather than being based on an individual right of access to the Court. Hence, that discussion has included a risk of seriously weakening access to justice at the European level. In relation to such a prospect, the final text of Protocol No 14 represents a carefully worded compromise that does not abandon the principle of direct access to the European Court. Article 35 of the ECHR will be amended to include a new paragraph 3(b) according to which an application would be declared inadmissible if the Court considers that 'the applicant has not suffered a significant disadvantage, unless respect for human rights as defined in the Convention and the Protocols thereto requires an examination of the application on the merits and provided that no case may be rejected on this ground which has not been duly considered by a domestic tribunal'.

Subsequent to the adoption of Protocol No 14 and while awaiting its entry into force,[61] it has become evident that the planned amendments to the ECHR will not be sufficient to cope with the European Court's case load. From an access to justice perspective, and thinking also more generally about the criterion of 'respect for human rights', it is promising that parallel to preparing for the entry into force of Protocol No 14, measures other than further treaty amendments that would restrict access to the European Court are being considered.

In a report by Lord Woolf, delivered in December 2005,[62] *inter alia*, the following recommendations are made in order to reduce the backlog of the European Court of Human Rights:

— Instead of proposing further amendments to the Convention, the Rules of the Court would be amended to define more clearly that only completed application forms need to be registered in the first place as pending applications.
— Satellite Offices of the Court's Registry should be established in key high case count countries. Currently, applications from four countries represent more than 50% of all pending cases.[63] Such Satellite Offices would provide applicants with information, and carry out the initial processing of applications so that those that proceed to Strasbourg are ready for allocation to a decision-making structure. The Court and its satellite offices should encourage greater use of national Ombudsmen and other methods of alternative dispute resolution.
— The Court should make more use of pilot cases that would guide resolving a whole class of applications without a need to deliver an ECtHR judgment in each one of them. The Court should also improve its work on compensation, and publish

---

[61] As of 13 May 2007, 46 states had ratified the Protocol and only 1 required ratification, that of the Russian Federation, was missing. See at <http://conventions.coe.int/Treaty/Commun/ChercheSig. asp?NT=194&CM=7&DF= 5/16/2007&CL=ENG>.

[62] The Right Honourable The Lord Woolf *et al Review of the Working Methods of the European Court of Human Rights*, December 2005, available at <http://www.echr.coe.int/ECHR/Resources/ Home/LORDWOOLFREVIEWONWORKINGMETHODS.pdf>.

[63] These four countries are Russia (17%), Turkey (13%), Romania (12%), and Poland (11%). See, Chart 3 in the Lord Woolf report, ibid.

guidelines as to rates of compensation. This will assist and encourage member states to resolve cases domestically.

— The Court should through various internal measures, elaborated in some detail in the report, improve its capacity to handle applications in a speedy and efficient manner.

These and other proposals made in the report demonstrate that a more efficient European Court could improve, rather than endanger, effective access to justice. Of particular importance among the recommendations in this respect is the improved use of pilot cases. Here, the Lord Woolf report builds upon the example of *Broniowski v Poland*[64] in which the Court in a friendly settlement confirmed that there was a violation of the right to property (Article 1 of Protocol 1) not only for the claimant, but for a whole class of individuals. The Court addressed the issue what measures were required at the national level in respect of a whole class of applications, which then were adjourned, 'pending the implementation of the relevant general measures'.[65] In particular, before approving a friendly settlement in the individual case, the Court emphasized the pilot case nature of the application in relation to resolving the grievances experienced by a whole class of individuals:

37. In these circumstances, in determining whether it can strike the present application out of its list pursuant to Articles 39 and 37 § 1(b) of the Convention on the ground that the matter has been resolved and that respect for human rights as defined in the Convention and its Protocols does not require its further examination, it is appropriate for the Court to have regard not only to the applicant's individual situation but also to measures aimed at resolving the underlying general defect in the Polish legal order identified in the principal judgment as the source of the violation found.

From the perspective of effective access to justice, this kind of an approach by international supervisory bodies is commendable.

---

[64] *Broniowski v Poland* Judgment (Friendly Settlement) of 28 September 2005.

[65] For a discussion of the pilot case of *Broniowski v Poland*, see the Lord Woolf report (n 62 above) 39.

5

Access to Environmental Justice

CATHERINE REDGWELL

In order to contribute to the protection of the right of every person of present and future generations to live in an environment adequate to his or her health and well-being, each Party shall guarantee the rights of access to information, public participation in decision-making, and access to justice in environmental matters in accordance with the provisions of this Convention.

> Article 1 of the 1998 Aarhus Convention on Access to
> Information, Public Participation in Decision-making and
> Access to Justice in Environmental Matters.

I. INTRODUCTION

Access to environmental justice by non-state actors grafts onto three major post-war developments in international law: (1) the recognition of universal human rights, both civil and political, and social, economic, and cultural; (2) the rise of environmental awareness in the 1960s which led to the flourishing of domestic, regional, and international environmental law; and (3) changes in governance, both nationally and internationally, with an enhanced role for non-state actors in decision-making procedures.[1] Access to environmental justice is thus located at the interstices of procedural human rights, environmental law, and good governance. It maps onto concepts already recognized in international human rights law.

This is clearly evident in the Economic Commission for Europe's (ECE's) 1998 Convention on Access to Information, Public Participation in Decision-making and Access to Justice in Environmental Matters (the 'Aarhus Convention'), which is the first international instrument to address procedural human rights in an

---

[1] For developments internationally see S Charnovitz, 'Two Centuries of Participation: NGOs and International Governance' (1996–7) 18 Mich JIL 184; J Ebbesson, 'The Notion of Public Participation in International Environmental Law' (1997) 8 *International Yearbook of International Environmental Law* 51; K Raustiala, 'The "Participatory Revolution" in International Environmental Law' (1997) 21 Harv Env LR 537; and Part VI, 'Actors and Institutions', in D Bodansky, J Brunnee and E Hey (eds), *Oxford Handbook of International Environmental Law* (2007).

environmental context and sets a 'benchmark for environmental democracy'.[2] As its title suggests, it establishes international minimum standards[3] in respect of its three pillars: (1) access to environmental information; (2) public participation in environmental decision-making; and (3) access to environmental justice. We see the direct intersection of environmental and human rights in Article 9 (access to justice) which 'looks very much like an application of [the right to a fair hearing provisions of] Article 6(1) of the European Convention on Human Rights (ECHR) and of the decisions in *Lopez-Ostra* and *Guerra*' adapted to the particular characteristics of environmental problems.[4]

Unlike the ECHR, however, the Aarhus Convention does not create a supranational forum, but rather is concerned with states' implementation of their treaty obligations at the national (and, for the European Union, at the regional) level. The Convention is considered in detail in part IV below. Although open to the members of the ECE, which include the United States, Canada, and former republics of the Soviet Union in Asia, it is not a global instrument.[5] This remains a gap in the international law framework for access to environmental justice, despite discussion of public participation and good governance at both the United Nations Conference on Environment and Development (UNCED) (1992) and at the World Summit on Sustainable Development (WSSD) (2002).[6] Given the general absence

---

[2] 'Human Rights and the Environment: The role of the Aarhus Convention', Submission by the UN Economic Commission for Europe provided as input to the report being prepared by the Office of the High Commissioner for Human Rights pursuant to Res E/CN.4/RES/2003/71, December 2003, para 5.

[3] Art 3(5) provides explicitly for upward derogation: 'The provisions of this Convention shall not affect the right of a Party to maintain or introduce measures providing for broader access to information, more extensive public participation in decision-making and wider access to justice in environmental matters than required by this Convention.' Art 3(6) provides, by way of mirror image, a safeguard in that nothing in the Convention shall require derogation from existing rights in respect of the three pillars.

[4] P Birnie and AE Boyle, *International Law and the Environment* (2nd edn, 2002) 263. On ECHR, Art 6, see further A Grotian, *Article 6 of the European Convention on Human Rights: the right to a fair trial* (1994) and, generally, C Ovey and R White, *Jacobs and White: The European Convention on Human Rights* (4th edn, 2006). The right to a fair trial is also found in other regional and international instruments, eg Article 10 of the Universal Declaration of Human Rights, Art 10; the 1966 ICCPR, Art 14 (for further commentary on which see S Joseph, J Schultz, and M Castan, *The International Covenant on Civil and Political Rights: Cases, Materials and Commentary* (2nd edn, 2004)); and the 1969 American Convention on Human Rights, Art 8.

[5] See further discussion of the geographical scope of the Convention in part IV below.

[6] eg the WSSD Plan of Implementation, para 119, like the Rio Declaration, Principle 10, emphasizes the need for information, participation, and access to justice in decisions affecting the environment. See further discussion by J Ebbesson, 'Public Participation' in D Bodansky, J Brunnee, and E Hey (eds), *Oxford Handbook of International Environmental Law* (2007) 685. Principle 10 is further reinforced by the 'Type II Partnership Agreements' established at the WSSD in 2002 as a mechanism for cooperation among governments, civil society, and international organizations. Partnership for Principle 10 (PP10) focuses explicitly on the three pillars of Principle 10 and of the Aarhus Convention, see further <www.pp10.org>.

of access to justice provisions in international environmental agreements, access to justice in environmental matters is most likely to be achieved through the right to a fair trial and other provisions of human rights instruments and in greater integration between human rights and environmental law.[7]

It should also be borne in mind that most existing international dispute settlement forums focus on inter-state complaints (ICJ, ITLOS, WTO, etc).[8] At best, non-state actors may have the opportunity to submit an *amicus curiae* brief, as was controversially permitted for the first time by the WTO Appellate Body in an environmental case before it in 1998.[9] There is scope for arbitration—for example at the Permanent Court of Arbitration[10]—where non-state actors might proceed against a state or another private party, but this may only occur with the consent

[7] A point also noted by Ebbesson (n 6 above) 701. Such integration is reflected in ongoing cooperation between the Council of Europe and the UN Commission on Human Rights, for example. There is close cooperation between the ECE and the Council of Europe, including on access to justice. See the 'Resolutions and Recommendations adopted by the Committee of Ministers of the Council of Europe which are relevant to the implementation of Article 9 of the Aarhus Convention' at <http://www.unece.org/env/pp/a.to.j.htm>. Links between access to justice in the context of environmental rights and access to justice in the context of social and human rights have also been noted in the work of the Task Force on Access to Justice under the Aarhus Convention, particularly in the light of the 'Report on Access to Social Rights in Europe' adopted by the European Committee for Social Cohesion in May 2002. See Report on the Second Meeting of the Task Force on Environmental Justice, MP.PP/WG.1/2004, 3, 8 January 2004, para 45, available at <http://www.unece.org/env/pp/a.to.j.htm>.

[8] Of these, only the ICJ has plenary jurisdiction over disputes between states involving any question of international law; it does not, however, enjoy compulsory jurisdiction, in contrast to the WTO Dispute Settlement Body, which has compulsory jurisdiction but only over disputes arising under the covered agreements (eg GATT).

[9] *US—Import Prohibition of Certain Shrimps and Shrimp Products*, Report of the Appellate Body of 12 October 1998, Doc WT/DS58/AB/R, para 110. This approach was confirmed in *US—Imposition of Countervailing Duties on Certain Hot-Rolled Lead and Bismuth Carbon Steel Products Originating in the United Kingdom*, Report of the Appellate Body of 10 May 2000, Doc WT/DS138/8, para 30. Of course such briefs are not treated on the same basis as submissions by the parties: see further M Matsushita, TJ Schoenbaum and PC Mavroidis, *The World Trade Organization: Law, Practice and Policy* (2003) 36. An *amicus* brief was also accepted for the first time in international arbitral proceedings under NAFTA in *Methanex v US* where the Tribunal ruled that it was empowered under Art 15(1) of the UNCITRAL rules governing the proceedings to accept *amicus* written submissions, in this case from the International Institute of Sustainable Development: see Decision of the Tribunal on Petitions from Third Persons to Intervene as 'Amici Curiae', 15 January 2001, at <http://www.iisd.org/pdf/methanex_tribunal_first_amicus_decision.pdf>. For a review of the practice of other judicial bodies, including the ICJ, see further D Shelton, 'The Participation of Non-Governmental Organizations in International Judicial Proceedings' (1994) 88 AJIL 611.

[10] The Permanent Court of Arbitration has developed Optional Rules for Arbitration (2001) and Conciliation (2002) of Disputes Relating to Natural Resources and/or the Environment. The Rules are available to states, international organizations, and private parties and are intended to fill a lacuna in environmental dispute resolution. The 2005 Annual Report notes, in the context of environmental dispute resolution, a number of cases with 'environmental components' administered in 2005: 4 involving the 1982 UN Convention on the Law of the Sea; 1 relating to OSPAR (Ireland-UK); 1 dispute regarding the use and modernization of the 'IJzeren Rijn' on the territory of the Netherlands

of the state or corporation and such environmental claims are rare in practice.[11] This gap remains under the Aarhus Convention, which is concerned with access to justice not at the inter-state level, but within state parties. It does not provide a forum or venue for environmental complaints. This is true even when the non-compliance procedure mechanism under the Aarhus Convention is taken into account.[12] The Convention is thus philosophically closer to the access to justice which non-state actors have enjoyed to enforce international human rights norms before the domestic courts of states under existing human rights instruments.

II. ENVIRONMENT AND HUMAN RIGHTS

A. Substantive Human Right to a Clean/Healthy/Satisfactory Environment

The Aarhus Convention is a reflection of the procedural dimension to the intersection between environment and human rights. Under general human rights law there is only limited express recognition of a *substantive* right to environment, as an addition to the panoply of other human rights recognized in international human rights instruments, and thus far only at the regional level.[13] Such recognition is found in Article 24 of the African Charter on Human and Peoples' Rights ('All peoples shall have the right to a generally satisfactory environment favourable to their development') and Article 11 of the 1988 Protocol of San Salvador to the 1969 American Convention on Human Rights ('Everyone shall have the right to live in a healthy environment and to have access to public services'). Indeed, Article 24

(Belgium-The Netherlands); and 'several disputes involving private parties' (para 44). For the full text of the 2005 Annual Report and of the Environmental Rules see <http://www.pca-cpa.org>.

[11] National response to the absence of supranational enforcement of international and domestic environmental law by individuals and NGOs is found in the establishment in 1994 of the International Court of Arbitration and Conciliation as a civil association under Mexican law, see <htpp://www.environmentalcourt.org/>.

[12] Established by Decision I/7 at the first meeting of the Conference of the Parties, it allows for communications by, *inter alia*, members of the public regarding state implementation of the Convention: see further part IV below and, generally, V Koester (the current chairperson of the Aarhus Compliance Committee), 'Review of Compliance under the Aarhus Convention: A Rather Unique Compliance Mechanism' (2005) 2 Journal for European Environmental and Planning Law 31. The Convention also has a dispute settlement clause, Art 16, which provides for the submission of disputes to the ICJ or arbitration in accordance with Annex II of the Convention, if expressly accepted by the parties to any dispute thereunder.

[13] See generally AE Boyle and D Anderson (eds), *Human Rights Approaches to Environmental Protection* (1996); CAR Robb (ed), *International Environmental Law Reports Vol. 3: Human Rights and Environment* (2001); D Shelton, 'Environmental Rights' in P Alston (ed), *Peoples' Rights* (2001) 185 and 'Human Rights, Environmental Rights, and the Right to Environment' (1991) 28 Stan JIL 106; and J Merrills, 'Environmental Rights' in D Bodansky, J Brunnee, and E Hey (eds), *Oxford Handbook of International Environmental Law* (2007). See also P Eleftheriadis, 'The Future of Environmental Rights in the European Union' in P Alston (ed), *The EU and Human Rights* (1999).

of the African Charter combines recognition of the substantive right with recognition of an *actio popularis*, thus reducing the obstacle of standing to enforce the substantive right. But this is a rare example, and the recognition of a direct 'right' to a clean and healthy environment remains both relatively rare and controversial. John Merrills, for example, questions whether the recognition of new rights such as the right to a healthy/clean/satisfactory environment is needed when account is taken of what is already in place. He notes that 'the violation of the collective right to a "general satisfactory environment" found by the African Commission on Human and Peoples' Rights in *The Social and Economic Rights Action Centre and the Centre for Economic and Social Rights v Nigeria* was accompanied by so many other individual and collective rights as to add relatively little to the decision'.[14]

Recognition of indirect environmental rights is more prevalent, ie through existing rights such as the right to private, home, and family life (for example *Lopez-Ostra v Spain*[15] and *Fadeyeva v Russia*[16] concerning Article 8 of the ECHR),[17] or the right to life and to the preservation of health and well-being (*Yanomami* case[18] considering Articles I, VIII, and XI of the 1948 American Declaration of the Rights of Man). International and regional human rights bodies thus offer the prospect of direct access by non-state actors to challenge violations of international law for the protection of human health and the environment lacking in environmental forums.[19] While the focus of such instruments is national, for instance the application of international rules and standards to the domestic arena, it is not exclusively so, since instruments

[14] *The Social and Economic Rights Action Centre and the Centre for Economic and Social Rights v Nigeria* (2003) 10, IHRR 282, discussed by Merrills (n 13 above) 669. See also AE Boyle, 'The Role of International Human Rights Law in the Protection of the Environment' in Boyle and Anderson (eds) (n 13 above) 43.

[15] European Court of Human Rights, Case 41/1993, 9 December 1994. In paragraph 51 of its judgment the Court acknowledged that 'severe environmental pollution may affect individuals' well-being and prevent them from enjoying their homes in such a way as to affect their private and family life adversely, without, however, seriously endangering their health'. Accordingly, the state has a duty to protect the right to respect for home and private and family life under Art 8 through regulation. The fact that Art 8 gives rise to a positive obligation to act, and not merely a negative claim of non-interference in private and family life, was confirmed in *Guerra v Italy* (116/1996/735/932), 19 February 1998, para 58.

[16] European Court of Human Rights, Case 55723/00, 9 June 2005.

[17] See generally DG San Jose, *Environmental Protection and the European Convention on Human Rights*, Human Rights Files No 21 (2005); and R Desgagne, 'Integrating Environmental Values into the European Convention on Human Rights' (1995) 89 AJIL 263.

[18] Inter-American Commission on Human Rights, Case 7615, IACHR 24, OEA/Ser.L/V/11.66, doc 10, rev 1 (1985). The case is also notable for its emphasis upon preventive measures, where violations of the Convention are irreversible, as in the taking of life or the destruction of a unique natural resource.

[19] See generally Boyle and Anderson (eds), (n 13 above); Merrills (n 13 above); and Robb (ed) (n 13 above). Access to information, public participation in environmental decision-making, and some issues of access to justice also arise directly or tangentially in the cases reported in CAR Robb (ed) ibid, *Vol. 4: International Environmental Law in National Courts* (2004).

such as the ECHR also create a supranational forum for the bringing of claims against states for infringement of the rights recognized thereunder.

B. Access to Justice as a Procedural Human Right

In classical legal theory, procedural rights feature as central to the principle of the rule of law. The link between procedural human rights and the rule of law is acknowledged in a number of treaty instruments, including the 1992 Treaty on European Union, which notes 'respect for human rights and fundamental freedoms and the rule of law'. There is less agreement on modalities, ie the content of the access to justice concept/right. Access to judicial forums is clearly one element, and the quality of such forums. But access to the court room is only one element of access to justice. As Harlow observes: 'It would be wrong to let discussion of the rule of law stop short at the level either of principle or of procedure without any consideration of social inequality.'[20] Establishing a right to a legal remedy for the violation of human rights is also an element of access to justice. Examples include Article 8 of the Universal Declaration of Human Rights, Article 13 of the ECHR, Article 2(3) of the International Covenant on Civil and Political Rights, and Article 47 of the EU Charter of Fundamental Rights.

But does the right to a legal remedy have a distinctive environmental dimension? One attempt to add such a dimension commenced in 1989, when non-governmental organizations (NGOs) successfully prevailed upon the United Nations Sub-Commission on the Prevention of Discrimination and Protection of Minorities to examine the intersection of human rights and the environment. In 1994, a Draft Declaration of Principles on Human Rights and the Environment was annexed to the Report of the Special Rapporteur, which sets out a number of substantive and procedural rights.[21] Of particular relevance for present purposes is Part III, addressed to procedural human rights, principle 20 of which states: 'All persons have the right to effective remedies and redress in administrative or judicial proceedings for environmental harm or the threat of such harm.'[22] This builds on both the recognition in key human rights instruments of the right to a

---

[20] C Harlow, 'Access to Justice as a Human Right: The European Convention and the European Union' in P Alston (ed), *The EU and Human Rights* (1999) 189.

[21] '*Human Rights and the Environment. Final Report of the Special Rapporteur*', E/CN.4/Sub.2/1994/9 (1994). For article-by-article commentary, see N Popovic, 'In pursuit of environmental human rights: Commentary on the Draft Declaration of Principles on Human Rights and the Environment' (1996) 27 Col HRLR 487.

[22] The Draft Declaration also explicitly recognizes a right to environmental information (Principle 15) and to public participation (Principle 18). These rights—to information, participation, and to an effective remedy—find their mirror image in duties set forth in Principle 22. As under the Aarhus Convention, these rights are explicitly linked with the duty effectively to implement a substantive right, here 'the right to a secure, healthy and ecologically sound environment'. For similar linkage under the Aarhus Convention, Art 1 see further part IV below.

legal remedy cited above and upon the environmental principles of liability and compensation for environmental harm found in various soft law instruments. For example, the 1982 World Charter for Nature, embodied in a General Assembly resolution,[23] provides that: 'All persons, in accordance with their national legislation, shall have the opportunity to participate, individually or with others, in the formulation of decisions of direct concern to their environment, and shall have access to means of redress when their environment has suffered damage or degradation.' Other soft law examples include Principle 22 of the 1972 Stockholm Declaration on the Human Environment and Principle 13 of the 1992 Rio Declaration on Environment and Development. Indeed, in his commentary to the Draft Declaration, Popovic suggests that 'It is a staple of international environmental instruments that the contracting parties recognize their obligation to provide means by which injured parties may exercise their right to a remedy' citing, *inter alia*, Articles 207 to 212 of the 1982 Law of the Sea Convention (national laws to prevent, reduce, and control marine pollution) and the oil pollution liability and compensation instruments.[24]

III. OBSTACLES TO ACCESS TO ENVIRONMENTAL JUSTICE

The existence of these international instruments, hard and soft, is testament to the processes indicated at the outset: the intersection of environment and human rights and increasing focus on global governance issues. But it is also an attempt to ensure the effective enforcement of environmental law in domestic forums and thus to address the enforcement deficit in environmental law. Effective implementation and enforcement of international environmental law in particular is heavily dependent on domestic legislative and judicial measures.[25] Access to justice provisions may also assist in surmounting obstacles such as the non-transposition into domestic law of international treaty obligations which are of a non-self-executing character.[26] In supplying a buttressing procedural right, the failure to provide access

---

[23] UN GA Res 37/7 (1982).

[24] Popovic (n 21 above) 563. The convergence of the right to a remedy and the duty to protect the environment is also noted in the *Study Concerning the Right to Restitution, Compensation and Rehabilitation for Victims of Gross Violations of Human Rights and Fundamental Freedoms*, Final Report submitted by Mr. Theo van Boven, Special Rapporteur, UN Sub-Commission on Prevention of Discrimination and Protection of Minorities, UN Doc E/CN.4/Sub.2/1993/8, 2 July 1993, 9, discussed ibid.

[25] See further M Anderson and P Galizzi (eds), *International Environmental Law in National Courts* (2002) and C Redgwell, 'National Implementation' in D Bodansky, Brunnee, and Hey (eds) (n 1 above).

[26] This is a particular problem in some jurisdictions, such as the US, which has explicitly declared ICCPR, Arts 1–27, including the remedy provisions, non-self executing. For critique see C Redgwell, 'US reservations to human rights treaties: all for one and none for all?' in M Byers and G Nolte (eds), *United States Hegemony and the Foundations of International Law* (2003).

to justice (including effective remedies) is without more a breach of the procedural right guaranteed by treaty.[27]

The negotiation of the Aarhus Convention, and its subsequent implementation, has been informed by a number of studies on access to justice which have sought to identify legal and non-legal barriers to access to justice in domestic law in particular.[28] The Aarhus Convention Implementation Guide (2000)[29] identifies three key barriers to environmental justice: (1) restrictive rules on standing; (2) the absence, or limited availability, of injunctive relief; and (3) weak or no enforcement. Nicolas De Sadeer, Gerhard Roller, and Miriam Dross, in their original 2002 study for the European Commission[30] assessing access to justice in environmental matters in eight Member States, group different inhibiting conditions for access to justice under six headings: (1) venue for action (where NGOs can bring claims); (2) standing; (3) the scope of review (for example procedural or substantive); (4) interim relief; (5) costs; and (6) length of proceedings. A 2004 report by the United Kingdom-based Environmental Justice Project identified four obstacles: (1) costs; (2) lack of judicial understanding of environmental issues; (3) limited scope for judicial review; and (4) remedies (specifically, inability to obtain injunctive relief).[31] The purpose here is not to reproduce the extensive national and transnational legal and empirical research on barriers to access to justice, but rather to identify key recurring themes in access to justice against which the contribution of Article 9 may be judged. Restrictive rules on standing and lack of available remedies have been two highly recurrent themes.

In respect of standing, there is no level—national, regional, or international—where this issue does not loom large for environmental litigants. A recent survey of international environmental law in national courts concludes that 'restrictive

---

[27] See discussion of Principle 20 of the Draft Declaration of Principles on Human Rights and the Environment by Popovic (n 21 above) 561–2.

[28] In addition to the studies cited immediately below, see also Regional Environmental Centre for Central and Eastern Europe, *Handbook on Access to Justice under the Aarhus Convention* (2003), including 19 brief national case studies, available at <http://www.rec.org/REC/Programs/EnvironmentalLaw/PDF/accesstojustice.pdf> and J Verschuuren *et al*, *Complaint Procedures and Access to Justice for citizens and NGOs in the field of the environment within the European Union* (2000), available at <http://www.europa.eu.int/comm/environment/impel/access_to_justice.htm>; and J Ebbeson (ed), *Access to Justice in Environmental Matters in the EU* (2002). Further links are available on the Aarhus clearing house mechanism site at <http://www.aarhusclearinghouse.unece.org/index.cfm>.

[29] Full text is available at <http://www.uneceorg/env/pp/acig.htm> at 135–49.

[30] N de Sadeleer, G Roller, and M Dross, *Access to Justice in Environmental Matters* (2002), ENV. A.3/ETU/2002/0030 available at <http://ec.europa.eu/comm/environment/aarhus/index.htm> published also as a book, N De Sadeleer, G Roller, and M Dross (eds), *Access to Justice in Environmental Matters: Empirical Findings and Appraisal* (2005), and summarized by eg M Dross, 'Access to Justice in the EU Member States' (2005) 2 Journal for European Environmental and Planning Law 22.

[31] Entitled *Environmental Justice* and available at <http://lawzone.thelawyer.com/cgi-bin/item.cgi?id=109230>. The UK Department for Environment, Food and Rural Affairs (Defra), responding to the Aarhus Convention and Principle 10 of the Rio Declaration, has aggregated research on the environmental justice theme, available at <http://www.defra.gov.uk/environment/enforcement/justice>.

standing rules are likely the most significant barrier to the implementation of international environmental law by domestic courts'.[32] Where permitted, public interest intervention in cases before domestic courts can be an effective method for introducing international law and policy arguments. A recent survey of six major environmental cases before the Supreme Court of Canada concludes that in four of these cases such issues were considered only because of the arguments of the public interest interveners.[33] The principle of intergenerational equity was famously relied upon by the Philippines Supreme Court to confer standing on minors wishing to oppose the grant of timber licences in one of the last remaining areas of untouched forest in the Philippines. *Re Minors Oposa* finds an echo in progressive decisions of the Indian Supreme Court,[34] yet these cases remain on the whole exceptional. Many European jurisdictions do not readily acknowledge the standing of plaintiffs to claim on behalf of the environment, a domestic echo of the international judicial reluctance to develop *actio popularis*.[35] Nonetheless, there have been some progressive developments, including the recognition of the standing of NGOs, such as the Sierra Club and Greenpeace, to challenge private and public action detrimental to the environment at the national and regional levels.[36]

Linked to the problem of standing is remedies, especially where plaintiffs seek to bring an *actio popularis*. A standard criticism of the application of private law remedies to environmental problems is the essentially retrospective nature of private law, which focuses on remedying harm caused to a legally recognized interest.

---

[32] D Bodansky and J Brunnee, 'Introduction: The Role of National Courts in the Field of International Environmental Law', in M Anderson and P Galizzi (eds) (n 25 above).

[33] J DeMarco and M Campbell, 'The Supreme Court of Canada's Progressive Use of International Environmental Law and Policy in Interpreting Domestic Legislation' (2004) 13 Review of European Community and International Environmental Law 320.

[34] See further M Anderson, 'International Environmental Law in Indian Courts,' in Anderson and Galizzi (eds) (n 25 above). For recent critical analysis of the 'Green Bench' of the Indian Supreme Court, see Rajamani, 'Public Interest Environmental Litigation in India' forthcoming in the Journal of Environmental Law.

[35] The *locus classicus* on standing for the national environment is C Stone, 'Should Trees have Standing?' published in the course of proceedings in *Sierra Club v Morton* (1972) 45 Southern California Law Review 450. Other judicial techniques include recourse to public trust and related doctrines: see generally C Redgwell, *Intergenerational Trusts and Environmental Protection* (1998).

[36] Contrast *R v HMIP, ex p Greenpeace* [1994] 2 CMLR 548 (where Otton J stated at 570–1 that he has 'not the slightest reservation that Greenpeace is an entirely responsible and respected body with a genuine concern for the environment.... It seems to me that if I were to deny standing to Greenpeace those they represent might not have an effective way to bring issues before the court. There would have to be an application either by an individual employee of BNFL or a near neighbour. In this case it is unlikely that either would be able to command the expertise which is at the disposal of Greenpeace') with Case C-321/95P *Stichting Greenpeace Council (Greenpeace International) and Ors v Commission* [1998] ECR I-1651 (position of non-privileged applications under Community law with Art 173(4) restrictively applied). See discussion in PGG Davies, 'Public Participation, the Aarhus Convention, and the European Community' in D Zillman, A Lucas, and G Pring (eds), *Human Rights in Natural Resources Development: Public Participation in the Sustainable Development of Mining and Energy Resources* (2002) 176.

Anticipatory action using private law remedies is still relatively rare, a circumstance which poses particular problems in connection with the intertemporality of the precautionary principle. As was observed by a United States court in the pollution context: 'Environmental injury, by its nature, can seldom be adequately remedied by money damages and is often permanent or at least of long duration, i.e. irreparable. If such injury is sufficiently likely, therefore, the balance of harms will usually favour the issuance of an injunction to protect the environment.'[37] Generally speaking, there is no harmonization of remedies under international law, save for the few examples of liability and compensation regimes established principally in connection with hazardous activities (for example nuclear, hazardous waste, and maritime transport of petroleum).

Many of these obstacles to environmental justice are addressed in the one international instrument to have been concluded addressed to access to justice issues, the Aarhus Convention, to which we now turn.

IV. THE AARHUS CONVENTION: A COMPREHENSIVE SOLUTION?[38]

A. The Convention

The Convention entered into force on 30 October 2001 and as of mid-2007 there were forty-one parties, including recently the EC, Germany, and Greece.[39] The

---

[37] *Amoco Production Co v Gambell* 480 US 531, 545 (1987).

[38] See <http://www.unece.org/env/pp> for the text of the Convention and its current status. In 2003 the Kiev Protocol on Pollutant Release and Transfer Registers was adopted but has not yet entered into force. Since its provisions are chiefly concerned with access to public information, it is not considered further here. Non-binding and voluntary 'Guidelines on Access to Information, Public Participation and Access to Justice with respect to Genetically Modified Organisms' were also adopted at Kiev (Decision I/4, ECE/MP.PP/2003/3), para 32 of which invites parties which decide to implement the guidelines through a legally binding mechanism to consider whether they should also provide for access to justice in accordance with Art 9 of the Convention, including where appropriate GMO activities within the Guidelines but which may not be subject to Art 9. In 2005, at the second Meeting of the Parties, an amendment to the Convention was adopted which will insert a new Art 6*bis* with consequential amendments to Art 6(11) and to Annex I (see Decision II/1, ECE/MP.PP/2005/2/Add.2). The amendment will enter into force when the conditions set forth in Art 14 of the Convention are satisfied. These require an 'opt-in' for amendments to the treaty text (Art 14(4)) but an 'opt-out' of amendments to the annex within 12 months of their communication which are otherwise considered to bind all parties unless more than one-third of the Parties have expressly signalled their lack of approval within the stipulated time period (Art 14(6)).

[39] EC ratification of the Convention was preceded by a debate on the extent to which a new directive on access to justice was a prerequisite for such a step. In the event, a proposed directive on access to justice was not part of the initial ratification package, though a proposed regulation on the application of the Covention to EC institutions and bodies did form part of the package

fact that the European Community has ratified the Convention does not mean that all of its twenty-seven Member States automatically become parties. Each must ratify separately, with only one state yet to do so, Ireland.[40] Although members of the Economic Commission for Europe, Canada and the United States have neither signed nor ratified the Convention, participation in which is presently confined to the wider European region, with participants stretching from Portugal to Kazakhstan. However, its capacity to influence beyond the ECE region is contained both in its participation provisions and in its substantive obligations. Widened participation is possible under Article 19(3), which provides that any member of the United Nations may accede to the Convention with the approval of the Meeting of the Parties. Pursuant to Article 3(7), parties have the express obligation to promote the application of the principles of the Convention in international environmental decision-making processes and within the framework of international organizations in relation to environmental matters.[41]

This capacity for the Aarhus Convention as a regional instrument to influence wider international developments is enhanced by its roots in international soft law instruments. It is a 'hard' or binding reflection of non-binding provisions at the international level. Specifically, the three pillars of the Aarhus Convention have

which focuses on the first two pillars. Ratification of the Convention took place on 17 February 2005. The main instruments to align Community legislation with the provisions of pillars I (access to information) and II (public participation) of the Aarhus Convention are Directive (EC) 2003/4 of 28 January 2003 on public access to environmental information (repealing Council Directive (EEC) 90/313), and Directive (EC) 2003/35 of 26 May 2003 providing for public participation in respect of the drawing up of certain plans and programmes relating to the environment and amending with regard to public participation and access to justice Council Directives (EEC) 85/337 and (EC) 96/61. With respect to pillar III on access to justice, as indicated above the Commission has adopted a Proposal for a directive to address the access to justice requirements of the Convention, which is also aimed at improving the enforcement of environmental law (COM(2003)624 final). This passed its first reading in the European Parliament in 2004 and was discussed in Council in 2005 but has seen little progress since. Shortcomings in the enforcement of environmental law are pointed out, *inter alia*, in the 6th Community Environment Action Programme where it was recognized that better access to courts for NGOs and individuals would have a beneficial effect on the implementation of Community law. On 28 September 2006, the 'Aarhus Regulation' (Regulation 1367/2006/EC) entered into force, which extends the application of all three pillars of the Convention not only to the institutions, but also to the bodies, offices or agencies established by, or on the basis of, the EC Treaty. For text, and current status, see <http://ec.europa.eu/comm/environment/aarhus/index.htm>.

[40] Ireland has signed the Convention, which gives rise under the Vienna Convention on the Law of Treaties Art 18 (and customary international law) to the obligation not to act inconsistently with the object and purpose of the Convention.

[41] At the second meeting of the Conference of the Parties in 2005, the Almaty Guidelines on Promoting the Principles of the Aarhus Convention in International Forums were adopted: Decision II/4, ECE/MP.PP/2005/2/Add.5, 20 June 2005, available at <http://www.unece.org/env/pp/a.to.j.htm>. A Task Force on Public Participation on International Forums has also been created to consult with international forums on the implementation of the Almaty Guidelines during 2006 and 2007.

their origin in Principle 10 of the 1992 Rio Declaration on Environment and Development which provides:

Environmental issues are best handled with the participation of all concerned citizens, at the relevant level. At the national level, each individual shall have appropriate *access to information* concerning the environment that is held by public authorities, including information on hazardous materials and activities in their communities, and the opportunity to *participate in decision-making processes*. States shall facilitate and encourage public awareness and participation by making information widely available. *Effective access to judicial and administrative proceedings*, including redress and remedy, shall be provided (emphasis added).

This is a soft law declaration, which does not give rise directly to binding obligations upon states, nor may it be invoked as a direct source of procedural rights by litigants before national courts. Nonetheless it has had a catalytic effect on the development of 'hard law'—binding obligations—under the auspices of the ECE.[42] In 1995, ECE ministers adopted the non-binding Sofia Guidelines on Access to Environmental Information and Public Participation in Environmental Decision-Making, which recall Principle 10 of the Rio Declaration and set forth in twenty-six paragraphs the guidelines relating to what were to become the three pillars of the Aarhus Convention.[43] The Guidelines are an example of 'soft-soft' law[44] in the sense both that their form is non-binding and their content is expressed in permissive language. Thus, for example, the access to justice provisions provide that 'The public should have access to administrative and judicial proceedings, as appropriate. Suitable legal guarantees should ensure that proceedings are fair, open, transparent and equitable. It is desirable that proceedings are not prohibitively expensive' (paragraph 25) and 'It is desirable that standing should be given a wide interpretation in proceedings involving environmental issues' (paragraph 26). Yet hard law soon followed, with treaty negotiations for the Aarhus Convention taking place from 1996 to 1998 with a high level of NGO involvement, especially by environmental citizens' organizations (ECOs), the chief beneficiaries of the Convention. The resulting treaty text is considered by Patricia Birnie and Alan Boyle to constitute 'the most significant and comprehensive multilateral scheme giving effect to Rio Principle 10'.[45] Indeed, the first two paragraphs of the preamble to the Aarhus Convention recall Principle 1 of the 1972 Stockholm Declaration on the Human Environment, and Article 10 of the Rio Declaration, respectively.

[42] As Ebbesson stresses (n 6 above) 'Principle 10 of the Rio Declaration does not reflect a general principle of international law. However, by suggesting a level of consensus regarding the desirable direction of policy formulation, it has framed legal discourse and induced legal development, in particular at the regional level.' The Aarhus Convention is at the forefront of these developments.

[43] The full text of the Guidelines, which run to 31 paragraphs with the provisions on implementation thereof, is available at <http://www.ece.org>.

[44] See D Shelton, 'Law, Non-Law and the Problem of "Soft Law" ' in D Shelton (ed), *Commitment and Compliance: The Role of Non-Binding Norms in the International Legal System* (2000).

[45] Birnie and Boyle (n 4 above) 262.

Both the Preamble (seventh indent) and Article 1 underscore the explicitly rights-based approach of the Convention.[46] Article 1 highlights the instrumentality of the *procedural* rights to be guaranteed by States parties 'in order to contribute to the protection of the right of every person of present and future generations to live in an environment adequate to his or her health and well-being'.[47] As Jonas Ebbeson describes it: 'International law thus becomes a vehicle to improve the effectiveness of national as well as international environmental laws.'[48]

This linkage between substantive and procedural rights in the Convention has caused some disquiet. This is evidenced in the UK declaration in respect of the preamble, seventh indent, and Article 1 to the Aarhus Convention. The preamble recognizes 'that every person has the right to live in an environment adequate to his or her health and well-being, and the duty, both individually and in association with others, to protect and improve the environment for the benefit of present and future generations'. Article 1 views the three pillars of the Convention as buttressing this right. The United Kingdom objected to this potentially implicit recognition of a substantive right to environment and made a declaration on signature, confirmed on ratification,[49] that these references merely 'express an aspiration which motivated the negotiation of this Convention and which is shared fully by the United Kingdom'. The only legal rights each party undertakes to guarantee under the Article 1 are the procedural rights of the three pillars (access to information, public participation in decision-making, and access to justice in environmental matters) in accordance with the provisions of the Convention. This declaration has been reiterated in the context of the work of the Convention's Task Force on Access to Justice in relation to relevant provisions of the Convention regarding the third pillar. Here the United Kingdom delegation recalled its declaration, with the consequence that it considered that access to justice under Article 1 was already available through Articles 4 and 6.[50]

---

[46] *Human Rights and the Environment: The role of the Aarhus Convention* Submission by the UN Economic Commission for Europe provided as input to the report being prepared by the Office of the High Commissioner for Human Rights pursuant to Res E/CN.4/RES/2003/71, December 2003, para 14.

[47] It continues: 'each Party shall guarantee the rights of access to information, public partici-pation in decision-making, and access to justice in environmental matters in accordance with the provisions of this Convention'.

[48] Ebbeson (n 1 above).

[49] For the text of all declarations and reservations, see <http://www.unece.org/env/pp/ctreaty.htm>. The Aarhus Convention is silent on reservations, which under the 1969 Vienna Convention on the Law of Treaties, Art 19 considered reflective of customary international law, means that a reservation may be made so long as it is not incompatible with the object and purpose of the treaty. Although classification is by effect—to exclude or modify the application of the Convention to the reserving state—rather than title, only 1 state has made an expressly titled 'reservation' to the Convention, while 7 states and the EU have made declarations (though not confirmed on ratification by Denmark or Germany). The expressly reserving state is Sweden, with respect to Article 9.1 and 9.2, considered further below.

[50] Report of Second Meeting of the Task Force on Access to Justice, MP.PP/WG.1/2004/3, 8 January 2004, para 47, available at <http://www.unece.org/env/pp/a.to.j.htm>.

B. The Third Pillar: Access to Justice

Access to justice is the third pillar of the Aarhus Convention, which is set forth in Article 9:[51]

ACCESS TO JUSTICE

1. Each Party shall, within the framework of its national legislation, ensure that any person who considers that his or her request for information under article 4 has been ignored, wrongfully refused, whether in part or in full, inadequately answered, or otherwise not dealt with in accordance with the provisions of that article, has access to a review procedure before a court of law or another independent and impartial body established by law.

In the circumstances where a Party provides for such a review by a court of law, it shall ensure that such a person also has access to an expeditious procedure established by law that is free of charge or inexpensive for reconsideration by a public authority or review by an independent and impartial body other than a court of law.

Final decisions under this paragraph 1 shall be binding on the public authority holding the information. Reasons shall be stated in writing, at least where access to information is refused under this paragraph.[52]

2. Each Party shall, within the framework of its national legislation, ensure that members of the public concerned
    (a) Having a sufficient interest
    or, alternatively,
    (b) Maintaining impairment of a right, where the administrative procedural law of a Party requires this as a precondition,

have access to a review procedure before a court of law and/or another independent and impartial body established by law, to challenge the substantive and procedural legality of any decision, act or omission subject to the provisions of article 6 and, where so provided for under national law and without prejudice to paragraph 3 below, of other relevant provisions of this Convention.

What constitutes a sufficient interest and impairment of a right shall be determined in accordance with the requirements of national law and consistently with the objective of giving the public concerned wide access to justice within the scope of this Convention. To this end, the interest of any non-governmental organization meeting the requirements referred to in article 2, paragraph 5, shall be deemed sufficient for the purpose of subparagraph (a) above. Such organizations shall also be deemed to have rights capable of being impaired for the purpose of subparagraph (b) above.

The provisions of this paragraph 2 shall not exclude the possibility of a preliminary review procedure before an administrative authority and shall not affect the requirement

---

[51] For very detailed analysis of Art 9, see the Implementation Guide (n 29 above).

[52] Sweden made a reservation to Art 9(1) excluding from judicial review decisions taken by Parliament, the government, and ministers on issues involving the release of official documents: see status of ratification at <http://www.unece.org/env/pp/ctreaty.htm>.

of exhaustion of administrative review procedures prior to recourse to judicial review procedures, where such a requirement exists under national law.[53]

3. In addition and without prejudice to the review procedures referred to in paragraphs 1 and 2 above, each Party shall ensure that, where they meet the criteria, if any, laid down in its national law, members of the public have access to administrative or judicial procedures to challenge acts and omissions by private persons and public authorities which contravene provisions of its national law relating to the environment.

4. In addition and without prejudice to paragraph 1 above, the procedures referred to in paragraphs 1, 2 and 3 above shall provide adequate and effective remedies, including injunctive relief as appropriate, and be fair, equitable, timely and not prohibitively expensive. Decisions under this article shall be given or recorded in writing. Decisions of courts, and whenever possible of other bodies, shall be publicly accessible.

5. In order to further the effectiveness of the provisions of this article, each Party shall ensure that information is provided to the public on access to administrative and judicial review procedures and shall consider the establishment of appropriate assistance mechanisms to remove or reduce financial and other barriers to access to justice.

It is important to consider *what* might be sought through access to justice: for example remedying of environmental harm, improvement of quality of life, recognition of violation of a procedural right such as public participation in environmental decision-making or access to environmental information, or enforcement of a substantive right to a particular quality of environment. The focus of Article 9 is twofold. First, it buttresses the other two pillars, ensuring access to justice for violation of the procedural rights of access to information (Article 4) and public participation in environmental decision-making (Article 6) provisions of the Convention. The public 'enforces' the Convention through domestic law. As Sionaidh Douglas-Scott has observed in the EU context: 'Rights to information and to participate in environmental decision-making would be rendered nugatory if individuals or environmental interest groups did not also have the right to challenge certain measures.'[54] This might be referred to as 'internal review', ensuring that the access to information and public participation provisions within the Convention are rendered effective through legal enforcement in domestic law.

---

[53] Finland made a declaration in respect of Art 9(2) to the effect that it does not apply to decisions in principle by government which are then endorsed—or rejected—by Parliament, so long as Art 9(2) is applicable at a subsequent decision-making stage of the activity: see status of ratification at <http://www.unece.org/env/pp/ctreaty.htm>. Sweden made a reservation in respect of Art 9(2) exempting from judicial review by environmental organizations decisions on local plans requiring environmental impact assessments, and decisions regarding the issuing of permits that are taken by the government at first instance (eg permissions under the Natural Gas Act) and after appeal under the Swedish Environmental Code, Ch 18. At the same time it indicated this to be a temporary measure, with the 'ambition that Sweden will shortly comply with Article 9.2 in its entirety' (ibid).

[54] S Douglas-Scott, 'Environmental Rights in the European Union—Participatory Democracy or Democratic Deficit?' in AE Boyle and M Anderson (eds), *Human Rights Approaches to Environmental Protection* (1996) 120.

Secondly, Article 9(3) employs access to justice to provide for the horizontal and vertical enforcement of domestic[55] environmental law by the public against both private persons and public authorities. This is a form of 'external review' in so far as the access to justice provisions of the Convention are used to permit challenge of 'acts and omissions' contravening national environmental law through administrative or judicial procedures. Paragraphs 1 and 2 are directly related to the internal provisions of the Convention while paragraph 3 reinforces external domestic standards. The latter can form a useful private supplement to regulatory enforcement of domestic environmental law by the State, and allow challenge of regulatory inaction. The complementarity of state and public enforcement action is underscored in the preamble (thirteenth indent), which recognizes 'the importance of the respective roles that individual citizens, non-governmental organizations and the private sector can play in environmental protection'. This has the potential significantly to strengthen the effective enforcement of domestic environmental law—often embracing regional and international standards—in domestic forums. This is of particular importance in the light of the absence of supranational forums for the direct enforcement of international environmental law in particular. International environmental law relies upon domestic implementation and enforcement for its effectiveness. Thus, in both its internal and external dimensions, the Convention is designed to address an 'enforcement deficit' in environmental law. Recent research has demonstrated that public interest litigation by NGOs has a high success rate and fulfils an important function in enforcing national and EU environmental law.[56]

In Article 9(1) the standing requirement for information requests review (Article 4) is 'any person' who has requested information. This is consistent both with Article 4 itself, and with the scope of 'the public' in the definition clause, Article 2, which defines 'the public' as 'one or more natural or legal persons, and, in accordance with national legislation or practice, their associations, organizations or groups'. For substantive or procedural review of public participation (Article 6), the standing provision is more restrictive. It has two limbs: (1) 'the public concerned'; and (2) 'having a sufficient interest'. The former is defined in Article 2 as 'the public affected or likely to be affected by, or having an interest in, the environmental decision-making; for the purposes of this definition, non-governmental organizations promoting environmental protection and meeting any requirements under national law shall be deemed to have an interest'. For NGOs in particular, the reference to 'any requirements of national law' may introduce further restrictions, such as legal personality within the state concerned. This is both a geographical restriction—the NGO must have some legal connection with the state concerned—and a temporal one, in that ad hoc citizens' coalitions may not satisfy a requirement of formal constitution within

---

[55] Indirect enforcement of international and regional standards may occur where the national law in question is designed to implement EC or international obligations.

[56] de Sadeleer *et al* (n 30 above) 33.

the jurisdiction. The latter restriction is reflected in the national laws of Member States.[57] It would also prevent transboundary complaints without some form of 'establishment' in the state in respect of which review of acts or omissions is sought.[58] Also problematic is the requirement under the Convention that the NGO 'promote' environmental protection. In the draft EU directive on access to justice, this has been expressed as '*the* objective to protect the environment' which could prevent NGOs of mixed objectives from satisfying such requirement.[59]

More innovative in Article 9(2) is the treatment of the requirement of 'sufficient interest'. The test itself strikes a middle ground between an expansive view of standing—an *actio popularis* for example, which is not common in European states—and a restrictive view which would require the demonstration of a subjective right. Such middle ground thus resonates with general state practice, including the 'direct and individual concern' test of Article 230(4) EC. Where Article 9(2) is innovative is in its treatment of NGOs. If an NGO surmounts the first hurdle of 'the public concerned' as defined under Article 2(5) discussed above, then Article 9(2) deems that NGO to have sufficient interest (or, where the administrative procedural law of a state party to the convention requires this as a precondition for standing, deems such organizations to have rights capable of being impaired). Other persons will still need to satisfy the requirements of national law, but with the proviso that any such requirements must be consistent 'with the objective of giving the public concerned wide access to justice within the scope of the Convention'. As Jonas Ebbeson observes, the standing criteria of the Aarhus Convention seek to balance a range of complex interests at stake in environmental decision-making, and 'deviates from international human rights law by relaxing the distinction between public and private matters'.[60]

Standing under Article 9(3) is even more restrictive. The price paid for the right to challenge violations of national laws relating to the environment or omissions by public authorities, divorced from any linkage with either of the first two pillars of the Convention, is that parties have greater flexibility in implementation. It is left to national law to decide whether redress is administrative or judicial and to determine standing requirements to challenge acts or omissions in connection with national environmental law. The innovations in standing in the Convention are thus restricted to the enforcement of the procedural rights of access to information and public participation embedded in the Convention (internal review) and do not apply *ipso facto* to the review of national environmental law. This does not mean that there are no constraints on implementation. In particular, the general

---

[57] ibid 35.

[58] This would be consistent with the general provision of Art 3(9) which requires *within the scope of the relevant provisions of the Convention* that the rights under each pillar are enjoyed 'without discrimination as to citizenship, nationality or domicile and, in the case of a legal person, without discrimination as to where it has its registered seat or an effective centre of its activities'.

[59] see n 40 above.

[60] Ebbeson (n 6 above) 701.

treaty law obligation to implement in good faith, expressed in the maxim *pacta sunt servanda* found in Article 26 of the 1969 Vienna Convention on the Law of Treaties and in customary law, will apply. In addition, there is soft law, such as the non-binding Sofia Guidelines, which exhort states to promote a broad notion of standing in proceedings on environmental issues.

The Task Force on Access to Justice has considered the development of guidelines or the identification of best practice to assist with implementation of Article 9(3), but the diversity in national practice—and a lack of political will—has led to little progress on this issue. The inability of the European Union to agree a directive on access to environmental justice further underscores this difficulty. A majority of Member States remain unconvinced of the need for a directive on access to justice.[61] The harmonization of provisions on access to justice, including aspects of remedies, is clearly a complex task given the diversity of legal systems and traditions represented by the Member States of the European Union. Of course, since all of the Member States save for Ireland are parties themselves to the Aarhus Convention, they have an independent treaty obligation to implement, *inter alia*, the access to justice provisions.

A further difficulty with Article 9(3) is the absence of a treaty definition of 'national law relating to the environment', leaving it open to parties to define this in their implementing measures.[62] The Task Force on Access to Justice has considered this issue, but with mixed views expressed therein on whether the broad definition of 'environmental information'[63] contained in Article 2(3) of the Convention might assist. Agreement does exist that 'national law relating to the environment' is wider than specific 'environmental legislation' and 'includes any provisions of national law whether statutory or regulatory whose enforcement has an effect on the state of the elements of the environment or on factors and activities or measures affecting or likely to affect these elements'.[64]

---

[61] Report of the First Meeting of the Task Force on Access to Justice, ECE/MP.PP/WG.1/2006/4, 15 March 2006, para 11 (report by the expert of the European Commission on the Aarhus 'package').

[62] National implementation reports are available at <http://www.unece.org/env/pp/reports%20 implementation.htm>.

[63] Art 2(3) defines 'environmental information' as 'any information ... on:
   (a) The state of elements of the environment, such as air, atmosphere, water, soil, land, landscape and natural sites, biological diversity and its components, including genetically modified organisms, and the interaction among these elements;
   (b) Factors, such as substances, energy, noise and radiation, and activities or measures, including administrative measures, environmental agreements, policies, legislation, plans and programmes, affecting or likely to affect the elements of the environment within the scope of subparagraph (a) above, and cost-benefit and other economic analyses and assumptions used in environmental decision-making;
   (c) The state of human health and safety, conditions of human life, cultural sites and built structures, inasmuch as they are or may be affected by the state of the elements of the environment or, through these elements, by the factors, activities or measures referred to in subparagraph (b) above.

[64] Report of First Meeting, para 28.

In addition to addressing access to justice to challenge impairment of the procedural rights recognized under the Convention, and violations of national environmental law, Article 9 also addresses remedies, and the removal or reduction of financial and other barriers to access to justice. Paragraph 4 stipulates that access to justice procedures must be fair, equitable, timely and not prohibitively expensive. Remedies must be adequate and effective, including injunctive relief 'as appropriate'. The latter is of particular importance in environmental cases where the absence of injunctive relief may lead to irreversible environmental harm.[65] It is an essential adjunct to the precautionary and preventive principles. The difficulty in practice is one of balance, in weighing up the potential costs to the project developer of temporary or permanent[66] suspension of the activity against the environmental impact, with the risk not only that courts are more traditionally familiar with the former but that prohibitively high cross-undertakings in damages will be required of complainants.[67] Nor does the minimum requirement in Article 9(4) that procedures are not 'prohibitively expensive' go so far as relieving NGOs from a costs burden where representing the general public interest.[68]

Finally, Article 9(5) exhorts Parties 'to consider the establishment of appropriate assistance mechanisms to remove or reduce financial and other barriers to access to justice'. This covers matters such as provision of legal aid, cost of litigation (for example witness and counsel fees), costs awards (a factor in Denmark, the United Kingdom, Germany, and the Netherlands in civil cases) and the requirement for a cross-undertaking in damages where injunctive relief is sought.

Reducing legal complexity is the 'other side of the coin of legal assistance' in the currency of access to justice. One mechanism for reducing the financial and other barriers to access to justice is to establish specialist environmental courts, with streamlined procedures, liberal rules on standing, and tailor-made remedies. The question of the establishment of national environmental courts has arisen from time to time during discussions in the Task Force on Access to Justice, especially in the context of paragraph 9(4) fair and equitable procedures.[69] The cost of such institutions, and the possibility of ensuring environmental expertise through the

---

[65] 'Environmental injury, by its nature, can seldom be adequately remedied by money damages and is often permanent or at least of long duration, i.e. irreparable. If such injury is sufficiently likely, therefore, the balance of harms will usually favour the issuance of an injunction to protect the environment.' *Amoco Production Co v Gambell* 480 US 531, 545 (1987).

[66] It should also be noted that permanent suspension of the undertaking, including eg the revocation of permits, may give rise to constructive takings or indirect expropriation arguments, such as occurred in *Southern Pacific Properties (Middle East) Ltd v Arab Republic of Egypt* (1993) 32 ILM 933 (ICSID arbitration arising from the revocation of planning permission) or *Metalclad v Mexico* (2001) 40 ILM 35 (municipal denial of a construction permit under NAFTA).

[67] See the Report on the First Meeting of the Task Force on Access to Justice, MP.PP/ WG.1/2003/3, 26 June 2003, para 30, available at <http://www.unece.og/env/pp/a.to.j.htm>.

[68] This is 1 of the recommendations of the de Sadeer *et al* report (n 30 above) 40.

[69] See the Report on the First Meeting of the Task Force on Access to Justice (n 67 above) para 22.

training of specialized judges in general courts, were both observed but no rec-ommendation on the establishment of such tribunals was made. Discussion of the possibility of establishing an international environmental tribunal foundered given the Task Force's focus on national implementation of the access to justice provi-sions.[70] What has been highlighted is the need for appropriate training for judges in environmental cases as a means of addressing one of the non-legal obstacles to access to justice. This is a theme which has also been taken up at the international level through the United Nations Environment Programme (UNEP). The Global Judges Symposium held in South Africa prior to the 2002 WSSD produced the 'Johannesburg Principles on the Role of Law and Sustainable Development'.[71] Capacity-building should extend beyond the judiciary to civil servants, public prosecutors and public-interest lawyers, and should include knowledge not only of national, but also international, environmental law.[72] Capacity-building has also played a role in responding to non-compliance by Parties with their Article 9 obligations, considered further below.

C. Subsequent Developments

The first Meeting of the Parties to the Aarhus Convention in 2002 decided to establish a task force on access to justice to support the implementation of the third pillar of the Convention by, *inter alia*, examining good practices, sharing experience with implementation of Article 9(3) to (5) of the Convention, and assessing the impact of certain barriers in access to justice, such as costs and delay (Decision I/5). It met three times between the first and second meetings of the par-ties.[73] Questionnaires were circulated to delegations, focal points and stakeholders (including NGOs and members of the judiciary) on criteria for standing under Article 9(3) and on non-legal obstacles to access to justice under Article 9(5). Building on the work of the Task Force, Decision II/2 on promoting effective access to justice was adopted at the second Meeting of the Parties in Kazakhstan in 2005. It focuses on the need, especially for countries in transition, to improve training in environmental law and related disciplines (science, technology) for the judiciary, other legal professionals, and civil servants. Cooperation, for example with UNEP, is underscored. This was relatively uncontroversial in the work of the Task Force. However, in terms of support for the implementation of Article 9, very little of substance results from Decision II/2, reflecting the lack of consensus within the Task Force which was ultimately reflected in a number of experts lodg-ing scrutiny reservations with respect to Chapters III to V of the draft decision

---

[70] ibid para 33.
[71] See Carnwath LJ, 'Judicial Protection of the Environment: At Home and Abroad' 2004 16 Journal of Environmental Law 315.
[72] Report on the Second Meeting of the Task Force on Environmental Justice, MP.PP/WG.1/2004, 3, 8 January 2004, para 36, available at <http://www.unece.org/env/pp/a.to.j.htm>.
[73] Reports of the Meetings are available at <http://www.unece.org/env/pp/a.to.j.htm>.

pertaining to implementation of Article 9(3), (4), and (5), and to further activities in respect of these provisions. Thus, in respect of standing, the first two paragraphs of Decision II/2 relating to implementation of Article 9 stress that 'it is for each Party to determine the criteria, if any, which must be met by members of the public in order to have access to administrative or judicial procedures within the scope of that paragraph' while noting that 'the Convention puts no obligation on Parties to establish criteria for standing'.[74] No harmonization of provisions on standing where they exist, even at the level of good practice, has emerged. On remedies, little concrete is found in Decision II/2 apart from matters such as general encouragement to share good practice on interim and permanent injunctive relief and on the effective contribution of remedies to the Convention's objectives.[75] Alternative dispute resolution, as one vehicle for addressing non-legal obstacles to access to justice, is recommended 'for exploration'. In addition to the capacity-building provisions already noted, encouragement is also given for greater dissemination of, and public accessibility to, judicial and other decisions, and an invitation to participate in the international World Conservation Union (IUCN)-UNEP Judicial Portal.[76]

As required by Article 15, a review of compliance arrangements took place at the first meeting of the parties in 2003. Although not legally obliged to do so given the very weak working of Article 15, the Parties decided to establish a Compliance Committee building on the work of a Task Force and a Working Group on Compliance and Rules of Procedure.[77] This decision created an innovative procedure[78] which, unusually when compared with other multilateral environmental agreements employing compliance mechanisms,[79] allows for submissions by members of the public, including NGOs. Its eight members operate on a facilitative basis as required by Article 15 ('non-confrontational, non-judicial and consultative'), to identify instances of non-compliance and to facilitate a return to compliance. It comprises independent experts—individuals serving in their personal capacity, not government representatives—who are nominated by parties, signatories, and NGOs. In keeping with the spirit of the Convention, submissions regarding compliance may be communicated from members of the public (subject to opt-out, but no party has done so) or from other parties regarding their own or another party's compliance, or by the Secretariat. The Committee has no independent decision-making powers, but rather makes recommendations to the Meeting of the Parties

---

[74] Decision II/4 Promoting Effective Access to Justice, ECE/MP.PP/2005/2/Add.3, 8 June 2004, paras 14 and 15, available at <http://www.unece.org/env/pp/a.to.j.htm>.

[75] ibid paras 18–20.

[76] See further <http://http://www.iucn.org/themes/law/dev09.html>.

[77] Decision I/7 on review of compliance (ECE/MP.PP/2/Add. 8) available at <http://www.unece. org/env/pp/a.to.j.htm>.

[78] Veit Koester notes that other multilateral environmental agreements have drawn on the Aarhus Convention compliance model, including the 2000 Cartagena Protocol on Biosafety (n 12 above) 44.

[79] See generally M Fitzmaurice and C Redgwell, 'Environmental Non-Compliance Procedures and International Law' (2000) XXXI Netherlands Yearbook of International Law 35.

(although, with the consent of the party concerned, certain interim measures may be recommended).[80] A proposal by the Task Force that the Committee could propose measures of redress for the satisfaction of the public concerned was rejected. This may have been because this would have transformed the non-compliance procedure into an individual complaints procedure, *de facto* permitting seeking redress before Convention institutions for state breaches of their treaty obligations (forum creation) rather than a facilitative vehicle for influencing parties' return to compliance with their treaty obligations.[81]

The first 'batch' of communications was considered by the Compliance Committee between the first and second meetings of the parties. It met on seven occasions between 2003 and 2005 and received twelve submissions, one from a party with regard to compliance by another party, and eleven communications from the public. Three of the latter fell at the admissibility stage. Three of the remaining nine complaints argued violation, *inter alia*, of provisions of Article 9,[82] but in only one instance was non-compliance upheld by the Committee in connection with Article 9(1). This was a communication made by the Kazakh NGO 'Green Salvation'[83] concerning Kazakhstan's compliance with Articles 4, 6, and 9. A request for information to Kazatoprom National Atomic Company about the import and disposal of radioactive waste was ignored. Recourse to the courts followed, which, given the restrictive rules on standing, failed in the view of 'Green Salvation' to satisfy the requirements of Article 9(1). The Compliance Committee found a violation, *inter alia,* of Article 9(1) in consequence of the 'lengthy review procedure and denial of standing to the non-governmental organization in a law suit on access to environmental information' and recommended a range of facilitative measures to ensure compliance, ranging from requesting of Kazakhstan a strategy with a time schedule for compliance, training of public officials and, from

---

[80] The range of responses the Meeting of the Parties may consider is listed in para 37 of the compliance procedures (see n 77 above) and in this respect does not depart from the general pattern of non-compliance procedures under multilateral environmental agreements.

[81] Koester (n 12 above) 34.

[82] Communications ACCC/C/2004/01 and ACCC/C/2004/02 were made by the Kazakh NGO 'Green Salvation'. The first communication related to information on the import and disposal of radioactive waste and is discussed further in the text below. The second communication argued violation of Art 6, paras 2–4 and 6–8, and Art 9, paras 3 and 4, in the case of a high-voltage power line through a residential area of Almaty. Non-compliance with some provisions of the Convention was found in both instances. Communication ACCC/C/2004/04 was lodged by the Hungarian NGO 'Clean Air Action Group' alleging violation of Art 6 and Art 9, paras 2–4, in connection with the introduction of a new Act, the Public Interest and the Development of the Expressway Network. In this instance Hungary was not found to be in non-compliance with its Convention obligations. See further the Report of the Compliance Committee to the Second Meeting of the Parties, ECE/MP.PP/2005/13, 11 March 2005, available at <http://www.unece.org/env/pp/a.to.j.htm>.

[83] Anonymous communications from members of the public are not permitted: see para 20(a) of the Annex to Decision I/7 (n 77 above).

other institutions, advice and assistance for Kazakhstan.[84] Save for the request for assistance, these measures were endorsed by the Meeting of the Parties.[85]

V. CONCLUSION

Access to justice is not only a fundamental element in the rule of law, but an essential component in the effective enforcement of environmental law. One of the contributions of the Aarhus Convention is to address the enforcement deficit in environmental law through the recognition of the procedural right of access to justice, including for domestic enforcement of environmental law. It is further evidence of the synergies between two dynamic areas of international law, protection of human rights and of the environment, as well as of the current global emphasis upon good governance. It is important to recognize both the strengths and the weaknesses of the Convention. Its strength is undoubtedly the procedural buttressing of a right to a satisfactory environment through the procedural rights of access to information, public participation, and access to justice. The unprecedented role for environmental NGOs in particular in the negotiation of the treaty text, and in its implementation, both at the national level in the innovative provisions on standing enhancing the opportunity for NGO enforcement both of the Convention provisions and of national environmental laws, and as active participants in the selection of the Compliance Committee members, and in making complaints thereunder, is welcome recognition of the role which non-state actors play in national and international legal systems. Weaknesses lie in the continuing inability to achieve consensus even on good practice under Article 9(3), and the further work to be done in the harmonization of remedies. The inability of the European Union to conclude a directive on access to justice is a reflection of the legal diversity which continues to persist on issues of standing, remedies, and costs, in particular. It is not the fact of diversity, but that standing restrictions, inadequate remedies, and the risk of substantial costs awards continue to pose a major obstacle to access to environmental justice in many jurisdictions, which underscores the work yet to be done.

[84] Report of the Compliance Committee, 'Findings and Recommendations with respect to Compliance by Specific Parties (Kazakhstan (1))' ECE/MP.PP/2005/13/Add.1.

[85] Decision II/5a Compliance by Kazakhstan with its Obligations under the Aarhus Convention, ECE/MP.PP/2005/2/Add.7, 13 June 2005.

6

Access to Justice in European Comparative Law

EVA STORSKRUBB AND JACQUES ZILLER

I. INTRODUCTION

Access to Justice in Europe should ideally be analysed commencing with a bottom-up depiction and comparative analysis. However, for the purposes of a short chapter with its inherent limits, we propose initially to review the constitutional provisions of the EU Member States, since these incorporations in constitutional texts are easier to identify and can be used as a tool and stepping stone into the practical reality of access to justice. Therefore, after a review of the constitutional provisions, some of the most pressing issues with regard to implementation and enforcement of the access to justice ideal will be analysed. The aim of this chapter is to assume a European comparative approach and to deal with access to justice on two levels: the national level of the Member States and the supranational level of the European Union.[1] Though, naturally, the European Convention on Human Rights (ECHR) will form the backdrop to these two dimensions of access to justice or fair trial.

Comparative law is adopted because it is a particularly apt tool for identifying the panoply of problems or issues which form the core of the access to justice debate. Every emanation of access to justice is, of course, idiosyncratic in the strict legal technical and practical political sense. Hence, the problems and lacunae are in their detail diverse. Comparative law allows us to adopt an overarching vision and identify a broad range of common issues and trends. Using comparative law to identify issues and solutions does not necessarily imply that a model or optimal structure for all systems could be established, since access to justice is always embedded in a historical, cultural, and socio-economic context or system. There is scope to learn between systems and also to identify similarities. In the

---

[1] All 25 Member States of the EU formed part of the inquiry and research for this article. However, it was naturally impossible to review all states equally in the text or gain in-depth knowledge of them all. Therefore, the chapter only uses examples which are taken randomly from different jurisdictions based on relevance to the specific matter being discussed and the knowledge of the authors. Developments in national and European Law have been included up until February 2006.

European context a comparative approach is imperative when one embarks upon an evaluation of the need for harmonization or a uniform application of Community norms. Furthermore, in the European context a comparative approach in the sense of dealing with both the national and the supranational level is also most relevant. Such a broad focus will lead to a less in-depth analysis of the issues; however, the aim is rather to have an overarching view and to establish the connections between the issues at the different levels, thereby creating fertile topics for further research.

II. THE CONSTITUTIONAL PROVISIONS

A. Access to Justice as Incorporated in National Constitutions

1. *Background*

The development of access to justice as an explicit concept in national constitutions is a recent trend. In the more recent constitutional texts of the twenty-five Member States of the European Union one can therefore sometimes find the words 'access to justice' but also specific statements regarding legal aid, the right to request the use of a particular language, or the right to precise remedies. To a large extent, this development can academically and in the context of the legal community be ascribed to the work of Mauro Cappelletti and his colleagues, who in the 1970s and 1980s assembled and exchanged detailed comparisons on 'access to justice', identifying a modern access to justice trend in society and depicting a model of three waves of development.[2] This scholarship, which is widely disseminated, can hardly be ignored by current jurists.

Behind this trend identified by Cappelletti lies a historical development which has several practical and theoretical strands. After the Second World War in Europe new national constitutions initially commenced to uphold what might be called the forerunner notion to access to justice, namely the 'right to a natural judge', as stated in the German Basic Law of 1949. This is an elegant way to stipulate that courts, and their judges, should be established by law, by an Act of Parliament, inherently expressing the presumption that being established by law they are also independent and impartial. The idea of courts or judges being established by law is, of course, one of the elements of the rule of law concept. Therefore, historically, access to justice can be seen as part of or emerging from the rule of law ideal. From a United Kingdom perspective, AV Dicey includes the condition that courts have to be independent from power in his rule of law definition.[3] The German or Prussian 'Rechtsstaat' theory and ideology is strongly based on the law and

---

[2] M Cappelletti and B Garth, 'Access to Justice and the Welfare State an Introduction' in M Cappelletti (ed), *Access to Justice and the Welfare State* (1981) 2–6.

[3] AV Dicey, *Introduction to the Study of the Law of the Constitution* (1885).

professional lawyers, for example judges and courts, as the underpinning guarantee of law.[4] In contrast, within the French tradition, due to the particular *Ancien Régime* state of affairs in which the judges themselves were seen as an obstacle to justice, the idea of independent courts is given less emphasis. Instead the law as the expression of public will is the most important element.[5]

Looking beyond the rule of law ideal at earlier dispersed events in Europe can give us an indication of the varied forces behind the emerging access to justice notion. Without being able to provide a complete set, the following are suggestions which might contribute a few pieces of the puzzle. Criminal law and procedure has been a field which has attracted ideological and theoretical attention. During the enlightenment, Italian jurists, and in particular Beccaria, developed a fair system of criminal justice starting with the law of evidence.[6] A different but hugely important development in the civil procedural field took place around the eve of the twentieth century, exemplified by the Austrian Civil Procedure Code of 1895 developed by Franz Klein, pioneering a new ideological and theoretical vision for civil procedure. According to the vision, both the procedural rules and the judges as leading and steering the proceedings were intended to assist the litigants and thereby provide fair proceedings.[7] The idea of case management by judges and a social notion of the procedural rules have today increasingly gained ground and are evident in several of the current and recent twentieth century civil procedural reforms in European countries.[8]

Socio-economic factors also form pieces of the puzzle. A relatively recent historical political theme which cannot be overlooked and which is intertwined with the access to justice notion is the welfare state ideal. The welfare state has impacted very much on the realm and volume of litigation but also on the structure of the judicial systems, *inter alia*, by mooting specialized courts, procedures, or judicial compositions for such issues as employment or social matters.[9] The welfare state ideal also raises the spectre of state responsibility for providing support and funding for less fortunate litigants. These developments inevitably colour the perception of access to justice. Another more socio-economic question which has arisen in the modern era of regulated professions is the role of the legal profession. Its regulation and status within the legal system can have great practical consequences on access to justice, either as a source of fostering access to justice initiatives or perhaps even

---

[4] J Ziller, 'The Continental System of Administrative Legality' in G Peters and J Pierre (eds), *Handbook of Public Administration* (2003) 260–8.

[5] R Carré de Malberg, *La loi, expression de la volonté générale* (1931, reprint 1984).

[6] C Beccaria, *On Crimes and Punishment* (1764).

[7] M Cappelletti, 'Social and Political Aspects of Civil Procedure—Reforms and Trends in Western and Eastern Europe' (1970–1971) Mich LR 854–8.

[8] AAS Zuckerman, 'Justice in Crisis: Comparative Dimensions of Civil Procedure' in AA S Zuckerman (ed), *Civil Justice in Crisis, Comparative Perspectives of Civil Procedure* (1999) 3, 47. C Van Rhee, 'Introduction' in C van Rhee (ed), *European Traditions in Civil Procedure* (2005) 3, 21.

[9] Cappelletti and Garth (n 2 above) 20–3.

as an inhibitor on access where, *inter alia*, there is an obligation to employ counsel or where there is a professional monopoly.[10]

Finally, particularly evident is the fundamental rights ideology or doctrine, developed after the Second World War in Europe, precipitating a constitution-alization, socialization, and internationalization of the protection of procedural guarantees.[11] The Strasbourg Court and the ECHR have been a non-negligible source of influence and cross-fertilization for national developments, in particular developing the idea and content of procedural guarantees and the notion of fair trial. These disparate elements have all contributed to the concept of access to just-ice and in varying degrees have fed into each national constitutional provision on access to justice. Therefore, even if these are not constitutionally entrenched and acknowledged, their contribution should be borne in mind.

2. *Three Broad Categories of Constitutional Provisions*

The first type of constitutional provision can be considered an early model formulation and is a forerunner to an explicit inclusion of the notion 'access to justice'. The category includes national constitutional provisions which guarantee a right to 'one's natural judge'. Such a right can in its classic formulation be found in, *inter alia*, the constitu-tions of Germany (Article 101), Austria (Article 83), Belgium (Article 13 of Chapter II), Luxembourg (Article 13), the Czech Republic (Article 38), and Spain (Article 24).

The most well-known of these is Article 101 of the German Basic Law of 1949: '(1) Extraordinary courts shall not be allowed. No one may be removed from the jurisdiction of his natural judge.' The right to a judge actually means that the right to a court established by law, ie by an Act of Parliament. This stipulation of legal-ity clearly shows a wish to protection against, and an aversion to, extraordinary or ad hoc courts. A particular current example is provided by the critique against the extraordinary court at the United States military base of Guantanamo.[12] The stipulation also shows clearly that the ideal is that of a fully fledged court, rather than a 'tribunal' in the English legal sense, which often entails laypersons or profes-sionals other than judges either being included in the adjudicating panel or even constituting its exclusive members.

However, with the volumes of litigation in the modern state, it is admittedly unrealistic that all litigation could or should be brought to court. The interesting question therefore is what are the limits to the constitutional guarantee of the right to a judge? Can one interpret these constitutional provisions of 'judge' or 'court' as

---

[10] M Cappelletti, *The Judicial Process in Comparative Perspective* (1989) 239 *et seq*. See also Zuckerman (n 8 above) 44 *et seq*, who gives a discouraging account of lawyers' vested interests.

[11] Cappelletti (n 10 above) 262–7.

[12] See for instance Select Committee on Constitutional Affairs Minutes of Evidence, 2.12.2003, Rt Hon Lord Hope of Craighead, available at <http://www.publications.parliament.uk/pa/cm200304/cmselect/cmconst/48/3120203.htm>.

encompassing non-professional judges or non-court institutions? It is undoubtedly difficult to advocate a liberal interpretation of the constitutional provision and it would be interesting to establish the position of national constitutional courts.

Article 21 of the Finnish Constitution of 1 March 2000 is much more recent than the German Basic Law, and shows an awareness of this question and gives more detail: 'Everyone has the right to have his or her case dealt with appropriately and without undue delay by a legally competent court in law or other authority as well as to have a decision pertaining to his or her rights or obligations reviewed by a court of law or other independent organ for the administration of justice.'

The second type of access to justice provision or category includes national constitutional provisions which are often more recent and which either explicitly include the concept of 'access to justice' or give more specific content than the bare mention of the right to a judge.

As an example, Article 24 of the Italian Constitution of 1947 includes several specific elements of access to justice:

(1) Everyone may bring cases before a court of law in order to protect their rights under civil and administrative proceedings.
(2) Defence is an inviolable right at every stage and instance of legal proceedings.
(3) The poor are entitled by law to proper means for action or defence in all courts.
(4) The law defines the conditions and forms for reparation in the case of judicial error.

Note in particular the mention of legal aid and reparation in case of judicial error. The latter is rarely included specifically in the constitutional provision relevant to our comparison.

Other examples of very detailed specifications can be found in Articles 30, 31, 109, and 117 of the Constitution of Lithuania of 1999, or Articles 36 to 38 of the Czech Republic's Constitution of 1993. Both of these protect an individual's right to the use of a comprehensible language. In the words of Article 37(4) of the Constitution of the Czech Republic: 'Whoever states that he or she does not speak the language in which proceedings are conducted is entitled to the services of an interpreter.'

An example of a combination of the two broad categories identified thus far is provided by the constitution of the Netherlands of 1983, which succinctly includes an elegantly phrased right to one's natural judge and a clear right to legal aid:

Article 17

No one may be prevented against his will from being heard by the courts to which he is entitled to apply under the law.

Article 18

(1) Everyone may be legally represented in legal and administrative proceedings.
(2) Rules concerning the granting of legal aid to persons of limited means shall be laid down by Act of Parliament.

Finally, we can for our purposes identify a third category of constitutional provision on access to justice which includes scarcely worded or perhaps even non-existent provisions. In this category we find Article 66 of the French Constitution of 1958, which 'only' enunciates that civil and criminal courts shall protect individual liberty. Similarly, the most ancient of the relevant constitutional provisions, the United Kingdom Habeas Corpus Act 1697, derives the right to a judge from the protection of liberty. These kinds of 'scarce' provisions do not imply that access to justice is not constitutionally protected in these countries. However, in order to determine the exact position of those seeking access to justice it is necessary to have knowledge of further sources of law.

3. Does Form Matter?

With regard to the national constitutional provisions, apart from the background history and ideological underpinnings, the bare transparent clauses themselves should be read and analysed in the broader context of the relevant national legal system. In order to avoid comparative pitfalls one should ideally be aware and have knowledge of: (1) general national constitutional principles (complemented by EU and ECHR principles); (2) additional relevant statutory law; (3) the case law of constitutional or other relevant courts; and (4) legal literature.[13]

Furthermore there are significant consequences which derive from the 'form' of the constitutional provision and its ancillary legal technical context. The following should by default be considered by the prudent comparative jurist:

(1) The strength of the principle of *Gesetzesvorbehalt* or *réserve de loi*, according to which the nucleus of a right cannot be regulated by delegated legislation, and which is expressed by paragraph (2) of Article 101 of the German Constitution: 'Courts for particular fields may be established only by law.' In other words, government does not have the right to propose and parliament does not have the right to accept that legislation be delegated. Therefore, the core value is that courts are established by parliamentary law offering protection against institutions with judicial power being established without the guarantees of a public debate enshrined in parliamentary procedure. However, in practical terms the strength of this principle and its protective reach *de facto* depend on each particular national set of rules regarding constitutional review of parliamentary law.

(2) The existence of potential exceptions to the constitutional protection and in particular whether these are clearly expressed in the constitution, for instance Article 45 of the Constitution of Poland of 1997: '(2) Exceptions to the public nature of hearings may be made for reasons of morality,

---

[13] In addition, translation issues might compound the comparative difficulties, as might a problem in understanding the focus and style of the legal literature or case law.

State security, public order or protection of the private life of a party, or other important private interest. Judgments shall be announced publicly.' The constitutions which foresee or enunciate exceptions are more transparent and hence more protective, since the exception can only be modified by constitutional amendment. In comparison, where exceptions are not explicitly mentioned in the text of the constitution their scope will depend on, among other things, constitutional interpretation which might be less transparent.

(3) The avenues of constitutional review are imperative to an understanding of the practical implications of an access to justice protection espoused constitutionally. The exact procedure, including important questions of standing, and the means of judicial interpretation prevalent in the relevant legal system are significant. In addition, the legal cultural constitutional tradition is a factor to take into account, for example direct ECHR review. It should be borne in mind that not all democratic countries have a system of constitutional review of acts of parliament. The United Kingdom's doctrine of parliamentary sovereignty impedes such a system, which would in any event be difficult to set up due to the fact that the country lacks a written constitution. In the Netherlands, after a long debate in academia and political circles during the 1970s, it was decided not to set up such a system, which was considered as infringing upon democratic principles. However, in the Netherlands, courts have given precedence to the ECHR whenever a statute conflicts with the rights it protects, and in the United Kingdom the Human Rights Act 1998 has also led courts to check the conformity of statutes with the ECHR.

(4) All constitutional incorporations of access to justice do not distinguish between criminal, civil and administrative procedural divergences and the particular issues related thereto. However, evidently the access to justice issues will be different for each of these types of proceeding. In particular criminal procedure has an inherently idiosyncratic nature residing in the fact that it pitches the state against the individual as litigants and in the fact that it results in sanctions including potential deprivation of liberty.

Finally, in addition to these observations of a more technical nature, comparative law has to be based upon the understanding that access to justice in its practical emanation has, at least since the development of the welfare state ideal, surpassed the idea of the lawful judge as the nexus of the concept. Today, access to justice is being played out in other forums too. Statistically, cases are to a large extent also being resolved by public administration or in private bodies. The question is thus whether, and to what extent, the guarantees of access to justice have to reach beyond the right to one's natural judge.

B. The Emanation of Access to Justice in EU Primary Law

It is pertinent first to turn our attention to the Charter of Fundamental Rights of the European Union[14] (hereinafter 'the Charter') included in Chapter II of the Treaty establishing a Constitution for Europe[15] (hereinafter 'the Constitutional Treaty') as the most recent constitutional emanation of access to justice. At present we have a politically unclear scenario in the European Union, since the negative national referenda in France and the Netherlands will have implications for the ratification of the Constitutional Treaty which was foreseen for November 2006.[16] However, the signature of the Treaty in Rome on 29 October 2004 by the twenty-five Member States of the EU has a legal consequence: they have agreed to the wording of the Articles of the Charter as being representative of the contents of the rights it endeavours to protect.

The provision is either Article II-46 of the Charter or Article II-107 of the Constitutional Treaty:

Right to an effective remedy and to a fair trial

Everyone whose rights and freedoms guaranteed by the law of the Union are violated has the right to an effective remedy before a tribunal in compliance with the conditions laid down in this Article.

Everyone is entitled to a fair and public hearing within a reasonable time by an independent and impartial tribunal previously established by law. Everyone shall have the possibility of being advised, defended and represented.

Legal aid shall be made available to those who lack sufficient resources in so far as such aid is necessary to ensure effective access to justice.

Starting with the title, it is noteworthy that regardless of 'access to justice' not being mentioned as a concept, the Article is *de facto* a formulation of the right to access to justice. In addition, the initial word 'everyone' is very significant, since it is broader than citizenship of the Union.

Another word to note is 'tribunal', which in English is problematic. Strictly legally this word does not necessarily entail or mean a court in English, in comparison, for example, to the French *tribunal*, the German *Gericht*, and the Italian *giudice* (judge), which indeed do specifically denote a court.

Furthermore, it is noteworthy that the Article commences with the idea of a remedy because, as elaborated earlier from a comparative constitutional perspective, the starting point is more often the judge with different connotations and consequences. Following upon this it is significant to note that the Charter includes

---

[14] [2000] OJ C364/1.

[15] [2004] OJ C310/1.

[16] See B De Witte, 'The Process of Ratification and the Crisis Options: A Legal Perspective' in D Curtin, AE Kellermann, and S Blockmans (eds), *The EU Constitution: The Best Way Forward?* (2005) 21, for a legal analysis of the options available if ratification of the Treaty is not completed in all Member States.

the 'possibility of being advised, defended and represented'. This particular modern aspect of access to justice already resonates in specific EU secondary law regarding legal aid. Legal aid is indeed explicitly mentioned in the final part of the Article.

Additionally, in the legal aid context at the very end of the Article we suddenly find the notion or concept of access to justice. As noted in the presentation of national constitutions, it is striking in comparative law that there are different ways to incorporate it constitutionally. Today the overarching notion and theme is that of access to justice in which, as aptly depicted in the supranational EU Charter and Constitutional Treaty, the emphasis is on obstacles to achieving redress, whether these obstacles are of a personal or generic nature, due to economic or cultural reasons, or perhaps resulting from the complexities of the procedural rules. This is a more recent perception, which goes beyond the idea that it is enough to guarantee that there is a judge for everyone.

Ostensibly, however, this particular incorporation of Article II-107 is strictly limited in application, since it only applies to the European institutions and to the Member State national authorities or judges when the latter are applying European law, ie when they are applying directives and regulations (European laws and framework laws in the Constitutional Treaty).[17] However, it is often forgotten that it will additionally apply to national authorities or judges when these are dealing with directly applicable Treaty rights. In conjunction with the fact that the access to justice substantive guarantees are broad, the Article definitely has the potency to contribute in practical terms to access to justice both on the EU and Member State levels and is *de facto* not limited.

Furthermore, we must not forget its grounding in and background stemming from a particular strand of case law of the European Court of Justice (ECJ). This case law already elaborates administrative or procedural guarantees that should be available whenever there is a question concerning directly applicable Treaty rights. Thus, when, for example, the EC right to free movement or non-discrimination on grounds of nationality arises in a matter, the national authority or judge must justify and give reasons for its decision and there must be an available remedy to challenge that decision.[18]

Another source of primary or constitutional European law which is relevant for the concept of access to justice is Article I-29 of the Constitutional Treaty, and specifically its paragraph dealing with national courts: 'Member States shall

---

[17] See the so-called horizontal clauses, Articles 51 and 52 of the Charter, Arts 51 and 52 and the Constitutional Treaty, Arts II-111 and II-112. Note that the wording has changed between these 2 documents. On the debate regarding the delimitation of the scope of application of the Charter and of the Constitutional Treaty, *Chapter II*, see, *inter alia*, A Arnull, 'Protecting Fundamental Rights in Europe's New Constitutional Order', in T Tridimas and P Nebbia (eds), *European Union Law for the Twenty-First Century—Rethinking the New Legal Order* (2004); P Craig, 'The Community Rights and the Charter'(2002) 14(1) European Review of Public Law 195; and G De Búrca, 'Fundamental Rights and Citizenship' in B De Witte (ed), *Ten Reflections on the Constitutional Treaty for Europe* (2003).

[18] See sources in n 19 below.

provide remedies sufficient to ensure effective legal protection in the fields covered by Union law.' This Article also constitutes an emanation of a particular strand of case law of the ECJ, which has been developed since the 1970s, namely the doctrine of 'effective judicial protection'. This successively developed case law, which has already led to significant developments in the Member States and contributed to access to justice on the national level, thus receives constitutional recognition. This strand of case law also stipulates that when EC law rights are at issue or applicable in a national case, there has to be a national remedy for the litigants to realize these rights.[19]

As a practical example we can take the Netherlands and job applications to the civil service. Until the early 1980s, unsuccessful applicants who wanted to appeal against the decision of rejection had no remedy at all. Their status as applicants denied them standing in the specialized courts dealing with civil service matters but their claims as pertaining to civil service related matters also fell outside the material scope of the judicial review procedure.[20] Only when cases regarding discrimination started coming to the attention of the National Ombudsman, after the creation of this institution in 1981,[21] did this discrepancy become evident. When viewed in the light of the access to justice notion, it is illuminating to note that the case demonstrates one category of litigants, natural persons applying for a job, for which the practical consequences of the constitutional right actually was and can be of great consequence. Finally, as a result of the *Heylens* judgment rendered in 1987, EC law obliged Member States to establish a court remedy whenever the application of the Treaty was at stake—which implied '*inter alia*' checking whether there was no discrimination on grounds of nationality in the access to a number of civil service positions.[22] Since Article I -29 permeates the whole realm of EC law, with its current broad substantive range of matters including among others employment, competition, and above all internal market law—which is based on the 'four freedoms' of circulation of goods, services, persons, and capital—it is highly significant to access to justice.

---

[19] The first cases were Case 33/76, *Rewe-Zentralfinanz eG and Rewe-Zentral AG v Lanswitschaftskammer für das Saarland* [1976] ECR 1989 and Case 45/76, *Comet v Produktschap voor Siegewassen* [1976] ECR 2043. See also P Craig and G De Bùrca, *EU Law—Text, Cases and Materials* (3rd edn, 2002) ch 6. For a more detailed and recent monograph see M Dougan, *National Remedies Before the Court of Justice, Issues of Harmonisation and Differentiation* (2004). Among the wealth of articles, see, *inter alia*, M Hoskins, 'Tilting the Balance: Supremacy and National Procedural Rules' (1996) 21(5) ELR 365,S Prechal, 'EC Requirements for an Effective Remedy' in J Lonbay and A Biondi (eds), *Remedies for Breach of EC Law* (1997) 3, and C Smith, 'Remedies for Breaches of EU Law in National Courts: Legal Variation and Selection', in P Craig and G De Búrca (eds), *The Evolution of EU Law* (1999) 287.

[20] Wet administratieve rechtspraak overheidsbeschikkingen (Wet AROB), 1975.

[21] Wet Nationale ombudsman van 4 februari 1981.

[22] Case 222/86 *Union nationale des entraîneurs et cadres techniques professionnels du football (Unectef) v Georges Heylens and Ors* [1987] ECR 4097.

In addition, Article III-269 of the Constitutional Treaty establishes the specific legal basis or attributed competence for the European Union in the policy area of 'judicial cooperation in civil matters'. This policy area in its current form, Article 65 of the EC Treaty, has already contributed to developing practically and substantively access to justice in the European Union. One example is the aforementioned Directive on Legal Aid.[23] However, for our comparison regarding the expression of access to justice on the constitutional or primary law level, it is significant that the Constitutional Treaty has added subparagraph (e): 'access to justice' among the aims that the policy area is intended to ensure. This provision is very interesting because it falls within Chapter III of the Constitutional Treaty and, as such, it represents a granting of competence to harmonize 'access to justice', which is a broad and vague notion. The inter-governmental conference changed this provision, the original Treaty establishing a Constitution for Europe elaborated by the Convention had suggested the wording 'a high level of access to justice'. The legal and political difference between 'access to justice' and 'high level access to justice' is unclear.

III. NATIONAL AND SUPRANATIONAL THEMES OF ACCESS TO JUSTICE

Having identified the trend towards ever more detailed espousal of the access to justice concept in national constitutions and the more recent resurgence of the concept on the supranational level of the European Union, the aim is forthwith to unveil the reality behind these proclamations and consider the complexities involved in the implementation of the access to justice ideal. First we shall deal with the decentralized level of the national legal system.

A. National Complexities Uncovered

Again, some of the complexities that have arisen on the national level are of a more ancient origin than on the supranational level and give us an inkling of some of the recurring themes. One commentator has observed that access to justice is an extremely broad concept and therefore chooses to use a tripartite division.[24] The first category is 'access to legal justice', which encompasses the enforcement of rights and the hurdles within the legal recourse mechanisms. These questions of an essentially procedural nature will be dealt with below in the following subsection. The second category is 'access to the machinery of justice of the welfare state'. The modern welfare state has brought very specific questions to the fore. A few particular substantive types of dispute will in this subsection be used to highlight

---

[23] Council Directive 2003/8, [2003] OJ L26/41 and corrigendum [2003]OJ L32/15.
[24] A Tunc, 'The Quest for Justice', in M Cappelletti (ed), *Access to Justice and the Welfare State* (1981) 315 *et seq.*

the issues. The final category is access to 'Justice with a capital J'. Which can be expressed in German as *Gerechtigkeit* rather than *Justiz*, ie we are here not only dealing with the law administered and enforced by the courts but with a broader view of the realization of fairness and equity in society. This category falls outside the realm of this chapter; however, it is fascinating to note the separate meta-physical and sociological analyses that can all feed into our understanding of the multifaceted notion of access to justice.

1. Asymmetries and Caseloads in the Welfare State

Without identifying the particular manner and period in which the development took place in various states, one can as a generalization note that the emergence of the welfare state led to social regulations and institutions in all industrialized countries. Furthermore, what might be called economic regulation spawning a number of diverse fields such as competition, product standards, and environmental protection emerged.[25] This completely new legal landscape put its own pressures on the legal systems and raised new access to justice issues.[26] Before moving on to these issues, two general points should be made.

First, one special strand of welfare state access to justice, which has been mentioned as a particular constitutional emanation and which cannot be overlooked, is the recognition of the right to legal aid and the creation of legal aid systems. However, these systems were, like the welfare state itself, to a certain extent the prisoners of their own success and became financially unsustainable in several countries.[27] Today, the issue of creating an adequate and balanced legal aid system is still an issue which many countries grapple with and has also been recognized in the European Union. Furthermore, the Council of Europe has recently published a detailed empirical study for its Member States.[28] In general, the report shows that if public funding for courts and legal aid per inhabitant is scaled as a percentage of the gross average salary there are no differences between East and West. In most countries the public expenditure is between 0.1 and 0.3 per cent of the average gross salary. In relation to legal aid only, however, the study does show

[25] Note that welfare state issues do not substantially relate to criminal law or questions of access to justice in a criminal procedural context. However, 'the rest', eg both civil law (in its broad sense including commercial law) and administrative law, has been significantly affected by welfare state development. Disregarding divergences in national legal definitions and court structures, one can generally say that both civil and administrative procedures have been put under pressure as a result of the emergence of the welfare state.

[26] See Tunc (n 24 above) 331–8, for an exposé of this development.

[27] See K Yuille, 'No One's Perfect (Not Even Close): Reevaluating Access to Justice in the United States and Western Europe' (2004) 42(3) Col JTL 863, 864–93 as well as Zuckerman (n 8 above) 36–42, 45 *et seq*.

[28] European Commission for the Efficiency of Justice (CEPEJ), 'European Judicial Systems 2002—Facts and figures on the basis of a survey in 40 Council of Europe Member States' (2005) 19–27. The report is published but is also available online at <http://www.coe.int/cepej>.

substantial differences in budget, in the allocation of funds, and in the level of citizens covered, for example the amount granted per case varies between €34 and €2433. Secondly, one should note that the general question of the justiciability of these 'new' social rights is still debated and controversial, as has been recently evidenced in the Convention on the Future of Europe in relation to the social rights enumerated in the Charter of Fundamental Rights.[29]

Notwithstanding, and progressing from these two general points, observing four substantive dispute groups, employment, consumer, environment, and traffic accident litigation respectively, two typical features of welfare state litigation surface which we shall elaborate upon. These are, first the imbalances of power or asymmetries of means between the litigants of a dispute, and secondly the sheer volume of litigation, including the phenomenon of huge clusters of similar and sometimes low value claims.

In the field of employment law and social law the same access to justice concerns and developments are evident in many countries. The increased regulation and diversity of regulatory sources make the realization of rights complex and dependant on substantive legal information and knowledge. This creates one facet of the clear and significant differences in power between the litigating parties. The employer has, in general, more resources and funding and is less affected than the employee by the length of proceedings. Thus, special features developed in social and labour law to counter the asymmetries. In the field of employment a common solution has been the creation of special courts, for example *conseils de prud'hommes* in France. However, since these offer facilitated access the ever increasing caseload is straining the system, thereby causing new concerns of overloading and slowness of the system. In the field of social law, a common trend has been to concentrate the handling of claims out of court and into an administrative procedure. However, this has in turn sometimes caused cumbersome bureaucracies with lengthy procedures. Furthermore, these fields have also raised the questions of representation and diffuse interests, for example can trade unions represent the employees, as one method of responding to the concerns.

Chronologically, substantive consumer protection and consumer access to justice issues developed later than those in the field of employment. However, the same issue of asymmetries exists. In addition, consumer law is a field which highlights aptly the issue of small claims. Litigants are deterred, since the cost of bringing proceedings is disproportionate to the potential damages awarded as a remedy. The lengthy timeframe of proceedings is also naturally not particularly suitable to redress for small monetary claims. Furthermore, the producers or sellers as counterpart are not deterred by the sanction itself because it is so low. The generic issue of small claims has also been raised in the context of the European Union, the European Commission noting in its Green Paper that the complexity of the national legal systems, including the delay and costs of proceedings, is a

---

[29] See in particular Title IV, 'Solidarity', Articles II-87 to II-98.

particularly virulent problem in the case of small claims, where because the values are relatively speaking small the individual parties might be discouraged from exercising their rights. Therefore many of the Member States have specific small claims procedures, and many of those which do not nevertheless provide simplified alternatives to the ordinary procedure.[30] The European Commission has also recently launched a legislative proposal for small claims.[31]

The specific solutions for small consumer claim disputes vary among legal cultures. The obvious example is class actions or multi-party actions, which are intended to assemble a group of claimants and thereby create procedural synergy. However, the palette of solutions is broader, including representation by consumer associations and the development of specialized alternative dispute resolution (ADR) mechanisms. The quest to resolve access to justice for consumers on the national level can be mirrored and seen in parallel to the Community pursuit of achieving access to justice for consumers. In 1995, the Commission launched an in-depth study, 'Cost of Legal Barriers to Consumers in the Internal Market', after which a legislative proposal resulted in Directive (EC) 98/27 on injunctions for the protection of consumer interests, which regulates collective consumer interests or grievances.[32] The Commission further adopted an Action Plan for the regulation of individual consumer disputes,[33] which has resulted in a Communication regarding dispute prevention and in a Recommendation on principles for the out-of-court resolution of disputes.[34] In addition, even though the consumers themselves or consumer interests do not have standing, the development of public authority monitoring of standards and competition practices can be seen as avenues to redress the asymmetries.

The field of law in which questions of standing have been in particular focus is environmental law, due to the diffuse interests inherent in most claims. The issue is by no means yet resolved despite international efforts in the Aarhus Convention.[35] However, here the question of giving standing, not just representation rights, to associations is imperative because the affected parties may or may not want to litigate, and may not even know that they are affected, whereas there still is a strong

[30] Green Paper COM(2002)746, 49, 51–58. See also the study commissioned by the Commission: E Serverin, *Les procedures judiciaires applicable aux demandes de faible importance* (2001). In 1981, the Council of Europe had already highlighted the need for simplified procedures in small claims cases, Recommendation R(81)7 at 8,25 *et seq.*

[31] COM(2005)87. See also G Haibach, 'The Commission Proposal for a Regulation Establishing a European Small Claims Procedure—An Analysis' (2005) 13(4) European Review of Private Law 255.

[32] [1998] OJ L166/51.

[33] COM (1996) 13.

[34] COM (1998) 198, and [1998] OJ L115/31. See also M Tenreiro, 'L'accès du consommateur à la justice: une perspective européenne' in G Barret (ed), *Creating A European Judicial Space, Prospects for Improving Judicial Cooperation in Civil Matters in the European Union* (2001) 111 *et seq* for an exposé of this development.

[35] UNECE Convention on Access to Information, Public Participation in Decision-Making and Access to Justice in Environmental Matters (The Aarhus Convention) of June 1998.

public interest. A different type of substantive group is that of traffic accident-related tort litigation. Quantitatively, in many countries this group constitutes one of the largest caseloads pending in the lower courts. Here the question is mainly one of the systems dealing or coping with the volume of litigation. One solution has been to regulate the matter into the public domain, for example to deal with it as an administrative or criminal matter. Another ancillary structure which has affected the caseload is the development of the insurance market and insurance law. Therefore, in some countries the insurance companies handle such disputes, which changes the character of the system completely.

In conclusion, total asymmetries of power and volumes of small claims both throw new challenges of creating access to justice upon national procedural systems and on the legal systems as a whole. We see these tendencies in the aforementioned varied types of disputes as well as in other fields which are experiencing exponential growth in many countries, such as family law for societal reasons and tenancy disputes for market deregulation reasons.[36] The pressure forces the systems to find solutions but these are rarely easy and can cause or feed into new concerns. Solutions include representation by associations and flexible, less cumbersome, and simplified procedural rules for specific cases. These reforms have affected the make-up of the procedural rules. Other reforms have impacted upon the court structure or judicial architecture and include the setting up of specialized courts, de-judicialization, or diverting the caseload to other forums and an increase in the number of lay judges.

2. Procedural Impediments to the Realization of Rights and the Wheel of Reform

As a preceding matter to procedural rules and systems and the impediments these might introduce, as well as to the wave-like or wheel-like motion of the reform of procedural systems, one cannot in the modern world ignore the very practical issue of legal information. With regard to knowledge or information, it is crucial for citizens to be aware of the legal system and their rights in order to be able to protect them.[37] The question of transparency and availability of information has become more topical, and the solutions more difficult to find, due to the ever increasing complexity and volume of legal rules and procedures. The measures adopted on the national level to assist the information deficit are varied. There is, to our knowledge, no country in which legal education is provided in primary and secondary school, although in Finland or France, for example, legal knowledge is an optional extra subject in secondary school.

However, it is more common to have measures within the court structure or legal profession which of course are the first avenues of enquiry to which one

---

[36] See C Schmid *et al*, *Tenancy Law and Procedure in the European Union*, available at <http://www.iue.it/LAW/ResearchTeaching/EuropeanPrivateLaw/tenancyLaw.shtml>.

[37] See Tunc, (n 24 above) 320.

would expect citizens to turn. In Austria, for example, every month the courts are obliged to provide one day of 'open court' for citizens with legal enquiries. In other countries, for instance in the Netherlands, professional lawyers set up legal advice centres or clinics, being state sponsored or private initiatives, and devote a part of their time to giving general pre-litigation advice to citizens. These mechanisms could all be developed further, and with the advent of the internet, states are of course in varied degree providing information via this medium. The European Union is also aware of this problem and has created the European Judicial Network, which on its website gives detailed updated information regarding the legal systems of each of the Member States, as well as the cross-border cooperation mechanisms for eighteen different procedural topics, such as bringing a claim, service of documents, legal aid, and ADR.[38]

A central theme with regard to procedural rules creating impediments to access to justice is that of the costs of litigation. First of all, this might only be conceived of as a question of legal aid, an institution which we noted previously emerged in the context of the welfare state. We also previously noted that no system has been able to support legal aid schemes in their broadest emanation where the entire legal service, regardless of outcome or and without an upper limit, is delivered at the same level of remuneration as for privately funded litigation.

It is well known that costs are at least traditionally conceived of as higher in common law jurisdictions. Therefore, the new scheme introduced in England and Wales in parallel with the new Civil Procedure Rules (CPR) in 1999 is particularly interesting.[39] The provision of legal aid has been severely curtailed and instead an option of conditional fee agreements has been introduced. Thereby a victorious party will, under such an agreement, pay the ordinary fees of his lawyers and a success fee which can be no more than 10 per cent of the ordinary fee. These costs will normally be covered by the losing party according to the normal indemnity rule. If the party loses, he will not pay his lawyer at all.[40] There are naturally a lot of concerns raised vis-à-vis the system, since it puts lawyers in a conflict of interest with their clients and with the court, it might favour the access of strong claims above weak ones, and it might increase the overall cost of litigation with the added elements of the success fee and the potential legal expenses insurance.[41]

---

[38] Council Decision 2001/470 of 28 May 2001,[2001] OJ L174/25. See <http://ec.europa.eu/comm/justice_home/ejn/index_en.htm>.

[39] Civil Procedure Rules, in force 26 April 1999, enacted by SI 1998/3132, but with many subsequent amendments. See website of the Department for Constitutional Affairs for the most up-to-date version of the CPR, at <http://www.justice.gov.uk/civil/procrules_fin/index.htm>.

[40] N Andrews, 'The New English Civil Procedure Rules (1998)' in CH van Rhee (ed), *European Traditions in Civil Procedure* (2005) 161, 176 *et seq.*

[41] ibid 177 *et seq.* Note also that there have been some practical difficulties in implementation at the beginning of the regime and a lot of uncertainty about whether the success fee and the insurance premium—before and/or after the event—would be considered reasonable. The UK government has

A general issue which the conditional fee system highlights is the very high expenses of lawyers, which might hamper access for both poor and rich litigants. It is therefore hardly surprising that in several jurisdictions the legal profession has been seen to resist reform and defeat proposals which have threatened its economic interests. Fixed litigation costs and competition in the legal market have, on the other hand, been seen as successfully contributing to lower costs.[42] However, one commentator notes wisely that the solution to the problem of access to justice for poor or middle-income litigants is not only about costs. The costs issue is in part indivisible from the provision of reasonable legal services as a whole. Only systems which manage to find a sensible balance between the three dimensions of justice—'truth, time and cost'—can also manage to achieve financial access.[43]

Another central theme of assisting access to justice is that of the role of the judge in civil proceedings. Across the civil law/common law divide—which is partly relevant in matters of procedure, albeit erroneously overemphasized in this and other fields of law—and embracing jurisdictions, is a general trend or convergence in civil procedural reform towards so-called case management and an increased facilitative role for judges in proceedings.[44] Naturally, this has implications for the transparency of the proceedings and the sense of the litigants that they are kept informed. A particularly interesting example is again provided by the CPR in England and Wales, which as stated above entered into force in 1999, and which demonstrate on the domestic level a change of perspective and a recognition of the importance of case management. The Rules can be seen as a compromise between the liberal and social conceptions of civil litigation.[45] The 'Overriding Objective', CPR Part 1.1, spells out the policy goals of the new ethos and emphasizes proportionality:

(a) ensuring that parties are on equal footing;
(b) saving expense;
(c) dealing with the case in ways which are proportionate—
    (i) to the amount of money involved;
    (ii) to the importance of the case;
    (iii) to the complexity of the issues; and
    (iv) to the financial position of each party;
(d) ensuring that it is dealt with expeditiously and fairly;
(e) allotting to it an appropriate share of the court's resources, while taking into account the need to allot resources to other cases.

---

conducted a consultation into the functioning of the system in order to simplify it, and clarifying case law is emerging, eg *Callery v Gray (Nos 1 and 2)* [2002] 1WLR 2000.

   [42] Andrews (n 40 above) 179 *et seq*. Zuckerman (n 8 above) 44 *et seq*.

   [43] Zuckerman (n 8 above) 46 *et seq*.

   [44] N Trocker and V Varano, 'Concluding Remarks' in N Trocker and V Varano (eds), *The Reforms of Civil Procedure in Comparative Perspective* (2005) 243, 247–252.

   [45] van Rhee (n 8 above) 21 *et seq*.

Naturally, the implementation of a new ethos has to be underpinned by a change in attitude of all actors on the legal scene, above all the judges. A government assessment of the reform and its initial implementation suggested that case management conferences had been instrumental in making litigation less complex and had been a success.[46] However, it has also been noted that strict case management can be difficult, in particular the weighing of the global effects of individual cases in the context of process obligations. Judges are still influenced by the desire to do justice on the merits and therefore there is a risk that full holistic efficiency will not be achieved until a duty-based litigation culture among litigants and their counsel is also imposed.[47]

Apart from the themes of costs and case-management the CPR in their minutiae, for example rules about framing the claim, amending pleadings, presenting written, oral and expert evidence, and possibilities of appeal, will all affect access to justice. Using the same example as before, the CPR in England and Wales show some interesting features in order to attempt to create efficient procedures. Bearing in mind the still valid maxim 'justice delayed is justice denied', all modern civil procedures aim for speed and low costs in order to combat delay and achieve access to justice. One of the significant novelties of the CPR includes the restructuring of the procedure at first instance into three 'tracks': small claims, fast-track, and multi-track, with specific rules for each of these. The underlying goal is to be proportionate and allocate the right procedures and resources to each case.[48] On each track the court or the Rules directly set a timetable which governs the preparation for trial and the trial date, in contrast to the previous party control of the timetable.[49] The Rules also include novelties in relation to the rules on evidence, including documentary disclosure, witness statements, and expert evidence. The overriding theme for each form of evidence is that of curbing excessive overloading of evidence and curbing costs whilst still giving the parties the opportunity to present all relevant evidence. As an example, single joint experts were introduced in the CPR because the previous system of party-appointed experts was considered expensive and lacking objectivity. The result has been positive, even fostering a less adversarial culture and achieving earlier settlements.[50]

---

[46] *Civil Justice Reform Evaluation: Further Findings* (2002) paras 5.7–5.13, available on the website of the Department of Constitutional Affairs at <http://www.justice.gov.uk/civil/procrules_fin/consult.htm>.

[47] A Zuckerman, 'Procedural Reform in England' in N Trocker and V Varano (eds), *The Reforms of Civil Procedure in Comparative Perspective* (2005) 143, at 148 and 159.

[48] CPR Part 26. Small claims are those not exceeding £5,000, fast-track claims are between £5,000 and £15,000, whereas multi-claims are the ones that exceed £15,000. However, these presumptions can be rebutted, eg the legal complexity of a low value claim can result in its allocation to another track.

[49] Andrews (n 40 above) 167. See also CPR Parts 27, 28, and 29 for timetable rules of each separate track.

[50] ibid. 170, 173. See also *Civil Justice Reform Evaluation: Further Findings* (n 46 above) paras 4.21–4.29, and CPR Part 35.

Thus, even at a brief glance it is possible to identify several issues of national procedural rules, coupled with their implementation and practice, which significantly affect access to justice. It is also apparent that modern procedural reforms are challenging entrenched legal cultures and grappling with the dual and sometimes contradictory aims of introducing speed and efficiency whilst ensuring high standards of fair trial.

B. Persistent Lacuna and New Cooperation Models at the European Level

The national complexities uncovered illustrate how difficult it is to implement access to justice and that there are recurring themes of information deficit, costs, and procedural impediments including standing. Similarly on the EU level, the problem does not lie in the constitutional incorporation of access to justice and in the articles presented above, but in the practical implementation for individual litigants. The most pressing question which has gained importance incrementally is related to standing and the right of constitutional review before the ECJ, which will be highlighted in the first subsection below. This lacuna in the European supranational system demonstrates that in order to ascertain the true meaning of a constitutionally protected right to access, the review mechanisms should be investigated. If this issue could be called 'the dark side' of access to justice in the European Union, a 'bright side' will also be presented in the second subsection. In a similar way to attempts at national level, there are new forms of cooperation evolving in order to simplify and expedite procedures with the aim of achieving access to justice for such groups as transfrontier, small, or undisputed claims in Europe.

1. Access to the European Court of Justice

The issue of the constitutional review of European secondary legislation, for example the review of the constitutional legality of directives, regulations, or decisions, comprises such important questions as whether the institutions have followed the correct legislative procedures and whether there is attributed competence in the Treaties for legislation in the particular field. Specifically, we are dealing with the question of review when individuals are involved in disputes concerning rights emanating from EC secondary law or want to challenge the legality of such law.[51] The question is whether the structure of review offers adequate access to justice. The system of review before the ECJ has been characterized as a double system of legality review, because individuals have the opportunity to challenge EU law through both the preliminary ruling mechanism under Article 234 of the Treaty, and through the review mechanism, under Article 230 of the Treaty.

---

[51] We are not concerned with the availability of review for the Member States and institutions of the EU as is established in Art 230(1) of the current Treaty. However, this avenue can of course *in casu* benefit individuals who are affected.

With regard to the first of these mechanisms, from the perspective of access to justice for the individual party it has certain apparent limitations even though this is the common and more successful route. A referral to the ECJ from the national court asking for a preliminary ruling on validity can only be seen as a route of incident control. In practice, the mechanism is often dependent on the litigants requesting the national court to do so, and on the discretion of the national judge as to whether to make the referral or not.[52] Furthermore, according to the express prohibition in the *Foto-Frost* doctrine of the ECJ, in contrast to some national systems, if there is no preliminary referral to the constitutional court, the lower court cannot itself, pronounce acts of Community law illegal.[53]

In addition, one should be aware that this first mechanism is not open to all litigants because where no national implementation measure exists there might not be any national cause of action to render them capable of bringing a claim in the national court. It is even more of a cause for concern that the affected individual might have to break the law in order to be himself brought to justice and thereby, in his defence, challenge the legality of the European legislation.[54] The gaps in the access to justice of this mechanism should be therefore be filled by the more traditional form of redress under the second mechanism in Article 230, ie individual claims of legality review before the ECJ.

However, legality review under Article 230 also displays some limitations which are of concern from an access to justice perspective. First, paragraph 5 stipulates a relatively strict time limit for bringing proceedings, ie within two months of publication of the measure or of the knowledge of the plaintiff of its existence. Secondly, paragraph 4 stipulates strict criteria for standing for so-called 'non-privileged applicants': 'Any natural or legal person may, under the same conditions, institute proceedings against a decision addressed to that person or against a decision which, although in the form of a regulation or a decision addressed to another person, is of direct and individual concern to the former.'

It has become clear, through the restrictive application of Article 230 by the ECJ, that it is difficult for private litigants to fulfil the criteria of 'direct and individual concern'.[55] In particular, the test of individual concern elaborated by the

---

[52] According to the well established *CILFIT* doctrine of the ECJ, only courts of the last instance are obliged to refer questions, and only when these are relevant to the outcome of the case or unclear, ie have not previously been ruled upon by the ECJ. See Case 238/81 *Srl CILFIT and Lanificio di Gavardo SpA v Ministry of Health* [1982] ECR 3415.

[53] Case 314/85 *Foto-Frost v Hauptzollamt Lübeck-Ost* [1987] ECR 4199.

[54] See Advocate General Jacobs in Case 50/00 *Unión de Pequeños Agricultures v Council of the European Union* [2002] ECR I-6677, in particular paras 36–44 where he poses the question: 'Is the assumption correct that the preliminary ruling procedure provides full and effective judicial protection against general Community measures?' and concludes in para 49 that 'proceedings ... under the fourth paragraph of Article 230 EC are clearly more appropriate where a case concerns exclusively the validity of a Community measure.'

[55] The leading case is Case 25/62, *Plaumann & Co v Commission* [1963] ECR 95.

Court means that even economic operators must show that they have attributes or characteristics which distinguish them from others in order to have *locus standi* for legality review. This is, in practice, often very difficult or impossible.[56] Furthermore, as evidenced in the *Greenpeace* case, the ECJ was also not prepared to consider an association as fulfilling the condition of individuality.[57] Even though the limitations in Article 230(4) can be explained by the historically very different standing rules for legality review in the original six European Member States, they have together with the ECJ case law been lamented and criticized by commentators.[58]

The obvious solution to this gap in access to justice before the ECJ is an amendment to the current Treaty. Despite the forceful critique, this has not been accomplished by any Treaty revision so far.[59] However, Article III-365 of the Constitutional Treaty does include a change, which would be significant, if or when it enters into force, because it addresses one of the above points. Under this provision, an individual litigant would additionally have standing when 'a regulatory act which is of direct concern to him or her does not entail implementing measures'.

In the meantime, this amendment not yet being in force, litigants have tried another route to resolve the lack of standing and have applied to the European Court of Human Rights in Strasbourg. These cases demonstrate the particular significance of the lacuna when Community measures of secondary law might be challenged in terms of legality because they are in breach of fundamental human rights. The logic of these applications is that all twenty-five EU Member States are also bound by the ECHR and in particular its Articles 6 and 13 which guarantee the right to a fair trial and a remedy for breaches thereof. Therefore, the attempted strategy has encompassed a case against all EU Member States as co-defendants, arguing that the Member States cannot, through the medium of attributing competence and relinquishing sovereignty to a supranational organization, devalue the human rights commitments to which they have adhered. Neither of the two relevant cases in the EU context have been successful. The first case, *Segi*, was declared inadmissible on the ground that the applicants were not victims in the sense of Article 34 of the ECHR, 'it [Article 34] does not permit individuals to complain against a law in abstracto simply because they feel that it contravenes

---

[56] See P Craig and G De Búrca, *EU Law—Text, Cases and Materials* (3rd edn, 2003) 486–503 for a succinct but detailed overview of the relevant case law.

[57] Case 585/93 *Stichting Greenpeace Council (Greenpeace International) v Commission* [1995] ECR II 2205.

[58] See, *inter alia*, J Ziller 'La dialectique du contentieux européen: le cas des recours contre les actes normatifs' in *Les droits individuels et le juge en Europe—Mélanges en l'honneur de Michel Fromont* (2001) 443.

[59] A particular disappointment to commentators after the Treaty of Nice, see eg A Albors-Llorens 'Changes in the Jurisdiction of the European Court of Justice under the Treaty of Amsterdam' (1998) 35(6) CML Rev 1273, and J-V Louis 'La fonction juridictionnelle de Nice à Rome' (2003) 11 (103) *Journal des Tribunaux* 257.

the Convention'.[60] The second case, *Senator Lines*, was also declared inadmissible judged on the merits. Due to developments in the case at EU level the applicant could not, at the time of the admissibility review, be considered a victim for the purposes of Article 34 of the ECHR.[61] Yet another route may be used by litigants, as demonstrated in the *Bosphorus* case, ie in those cases where a piece of EC or EU legisltation creates an obligation on Member States to transpose it into their internal law, they may try to challenge the national legislation which transposed EU law.[62] In the *Bosphorus* case, however, the European Court of Human Rights withdrew from an appreciation upon merit, indicating that the EU system provided a level of protection equivalent to that of the ECHR. As this is not fully the case, the *Bosphorus* case may be read as pointing indirectly to the already discussed lacunae in the EU system. A number of recent judgments of the European Court of First Instance are also ambivalent on this matter, and point to another set of lacunae, ie the cases where EU decisions are merely implementing decisions of the United Nations Security Council. In the *Yusuf* and *Kadi* cases the Court of First Instance reserved the possibility to review the conformity to *jus cogens* of such a decision in a way that is not at all convincing,[63] and might still be challenged by the ECJ on appeal.[64] In the sanctions decisions of late 2005, the Court of First Instance reminded the Member States of procedural guarantees that they have to follow in such a situation, thus contributing to fill the gap a little. On the whole, the situation remains very unsatisfactory from the point of view of access to justice.

We can perhaps agree that this is not the proper way forward for achieving access to justice for litigants who challenge law on fundamental rights-related grounds. The Constitutional Treaty, in paragraph 2 of Article I-9, stipulates that the Union shall accede to the ECHR, which would naturally provide a recourse for these litigants. Another avenue which has not been carried through in the Constitutional Treaty would be the possibility of a specific remedy for the protection of fundamental rights before the ECJ, similar to the *Verffassungsbeschwerde* in Germany or *Amparo* in Spain.

---

[60] *Segi and Gestroas Pro-Amnistía v Germany and Ors* Application 6422/02 and 9916/02, Decision of 23 May 2002, European Court of Human Rights 2002-V.

[61] *Senator Lines GmbH v Austria and Ors*, Application 56672/00, Decision 10.3.2004, ECHR 2004-IV. A further third case before the European Court of Human Rights raised the same legality review argument against the NATO member states with regard to measures taken by NATO. This case, *Bankovic and Ors v Belgium and Ors* Application 52207/99, Decision of December 12 December 2001, European Court of Human Rights 2001-XII, was also declared inadmissible.

[62] *Bosphorus v Ireland*, Application 45036/98, Judgment of 30 June 2005 (2006) 42 EHRR 1.

[63] See D Simon and F Mariatte, 'The EC Court of First Instance: a Professor of International Law?' [Le Tribunal de première instance des Communautés: Professeur de droit international] *Europe*, December 2005, 6–10; and see also ch 1, section III D above (Francioni).

[64] Case T-306/01 *Yusuf and Al Barakaat v Council and Commission* and Case T-315/01 *Kadi v Council and Commission*, Judgments of 21 September 2005, not yet reported, both on appeal before the European Court of Justice as respectively Case C-402/05P and Case C-415/05P.

In summary, access to justice for individual litigants is the most acute lacuna in the EU legal structure. And, in addition, one cannot overlook the ever increasing volume of cases before the court and the subsequent incremental rise in the length of proceedings. Some of the more recent reforms within the court structure are intended to address this problem and very recently, similarly to national solutions, the setting up of the Civil Service Tribunal to deal with matters of employment law (staff cases) is one step in this direction.[65]

2. Cross-border cooperation mechanisms

A separate facet of access to justice in the European Union, which is more recent and currently still under development, is linked to the idea of free movement—on the one hand, as a fundamental freedom in the internal market for companies and economic actors and on the other hand, as a right of Union citizens in an area of freedom, security, and justice. Successive enlargements of the European Community and an increase in cross-border movement have highlighted the issue of national courts dealing more often with cross-border litigation comprising such elements as parties domiciled in different states or the need to serve documents in, as well as obtain evidence from, foreign jurisdictions.

The Council of Europe had for many years been aware of this field aspect of litigation and had elaborated projects, but these have not resulted in many mandatory conventions.[66] Similarly, under the auspices of the Hague Conference on Private International Law, several conventions were in force but these did not apply to all EU Member States.[67] Hence, within the European Union, as a consequence of the practical reality of economic actors and citizens moving across borders, subsequent Treaty amendments at Maastricht in 1992 and Amsterdam in 1997 created and extended the attributed competence in the field of cross-border judicial cooperation for both criminal and civil matters. This means, that there is scope for minimum level harmonizing of access to justice in these fields, albeit there are different and particular legislative procedures and instruments in place.[68] There has

---

[65] The Civil Service Tribunal was established by Council Decision 2004/752, [2004] OJ L33/7. Following the Decision of the President of the European Court of Justice, [2005] OJ 2005 L352/1, the Tribunal has been operational since December 2005. See website at <http://curia.eu.int/en/instit/presentationfr/index_tfp.htm>.

[66] Currently the Council of Europe projects include both improvement of the functioning of justice on the domestic level in the Member States and on the cross-border level, see <http://www.coe.int/cepej>.

[67] Among these, the Hague Convention on the Service of Documents 1965 and the Hague Convention on the Taking of Evidence 1970.

[68] For judicial cooperation in civil matters the legal basis is EC Treaty, Art 65; note the particular institutional rules in Arts 67 and 68. See also, *inter alia*, H Labayle, 'Un espace de liberté, de sécurité et de justice'(1997) *Revue Trimestrielle de Droit Européen* 813 and J Basedow, 'The Communitarization of the Conflict of Laws under the Treaty of Amsterdam'(2000) 37(3) CML Rev 687 for a comment on the legal basis and the institutional rules. For judicial cooperation in criminal matters the legal

been considerable activity in both the policy area of criminal cooperation and that of civil cooperation. The full breadth of that activity cannot be fully elaborated here and accordingly we have chosen one measure in each field to demonstrate the potential implications for access to justice in the European Union.

First, for judicial cooperation in criminal matters, the measure which is the most far reaching vis-à-vis procedural rules is the *Proposal for a Framework Decision on certain procedural rights in criminal proceedings throughout the European Union*.[69] The measure is currently at the stage of Commission proposal and is going through the legislative procedure, hence it is not final or binding yet. However, we can nevertheless glean worthwhile information and use it as a basis for projections of potential impact on access to justice if it enters into force.[70] Significantly, the proposal is not limited in its scope to transfrontier cases. Hence, if it enters into force it would apply to purely domestic cases too. The proposal is, however, strictly considered as a means of minimum harmonization and hence its non-regression clause in Article 17 specifically states that it shall not be construed as limiting Member State laws which provide a higher level of protection.

These two characteristics of the proposed Framework Decision clearly establish it as an espousal of mutual minimum standards which are nonetheless more elaborate than the shorter articles of the ECHR. Therefore, the proposal can be seen as an attempt to codify existing mutual principles. Since the proposed instrument is a Framework Decision, it needs to be implemented nationally. Therefore, despite its minimum nature it might *in casu* have an impact and necessitate national implementation measures where current protection is lower than that guaranteed in the proposal. The proposal includes several articles which are of significance to access to justice. With regard to the definition of criminal procedure, the scope of application elaborated in Article 1, it is relevant that 'all' proceedings which aim at establishing the guilt or innocence of a person suspected of a criminal offence are covered regardless of the way in which they are defined in the national context. Furthermore, appeal proceedings are also included in the definition, which allows broad protection. However, in some aspects the scope is narrow because it does not protect ancillary parties, for example the rights of witnesses who are giving evidence in a criminal trial.

---

basis is EU Treaty, Art 31; note the particular institutional rules in Arts 34 and 35. See also, *inter alia*, S Peers, *EU Justice and Home Affairs Law* (2000) for a comment on the legal basis and the institutional rules.

   [69] COM(2004)328, 28 April 2004. For a critical view, see R Lööf, 'Shooting from the Hip—Proposed Minimum Rights in Criminal Proceedings' 12 European Law Journal 421.

   [70] At the time of writing, early 2006, the decision of the Council is pending. The European Parliament has published its Report (A6–64/2005, 21 March 2005) and Opinion (T6–91/2005, 12 April 2005). However, as the European Parliament is only consulted, the more important step will be the negotiations in the Council of the EU. According to the European Parliament legislative tracking website, <http://www.europarl.europa.eu/oeil/> consulted on 21 February 2006, the Council dealt with the proposal in December 2005, and the final decision is pending.

The first protected right in the proposal is the right to legal advice, even before answering questions in relation to a charge.[71] Furthermore, the right to advice is not deemed adequate. In addition, Member States are under a positive obligation to ensure that legal advice is available, that it is effective and provided by a qualified lawyer, and that it is free if costs would cause undue financial hardship to the suspected person.[72] These provisions demonstrate a commitment to a high level of access to justice protection, but the Articles are, due to the nature of the document, quite vaguely worded and will be open to interpretation.

Access to justice is also guaranteed by the provisions in relation to language. Member States are obliged to provide free translation of all documents and free interpretation during proceedings. To secure fairness, the proposal goes even further and stipulates that Member States must ensure that service providers are sufficiently qualified and that an audio or video recording is made of the proceedings for quality control purposes.[73] Another interesting provision from the point of view of access to justice is the duty to inform suspected persons of their rights in writing, ie the duty to have a national 'Letter of Rights' with translations available in all the official Community languages. Enunciating these rights and others in the proposal forms one significant level of guaranteeing access to justice for individuals throughout the European Union. However, the implementation of these on the national level within the structures of the national legal systems will in the future show the reach and actual implications of the proposal.

Secondly, for judicial cooperation in civil matters, the measure chosen to depict the developments in the policy area is the already mentioned Directive on Legal Aid.[74] In comparison to the Framework Decision on certain procedural rights in criminal proceedings, it is more focused and detailed, not pertaining to all guarantees of fair proceedings but very specifically regulating the issue of legal aid. The scope of the measure is also narrower, since it applies exclusively to cross-border disputes.[75] There is no definition of 'civil and commercial' in the Directive but the Commission mentions that naturally included are employment and consumer matters, and we can further note that family matters also fall within its scope. However, it is noteworthy that the parties entitled to receive appropriate legal aid are solely natural persons, thus in practical terms excluding small businesses.[76]

From an access to justice perspective, the minimum standard of legal aid that the Member State in which the court is sitting is obliged to offer to natural persons

[71] Proposed Art 2.

[72] Proposed Art 3–5.

[73] Proposed Art 6–9.

[74] Council Directive (EC) 2003/8, [2003] OJ L26/41 and corrigendum [2003] OJ L32/15.

[75] Art 1 of the Directive. Note that Art 2 gives a definition of cross-border disputes which, for the purposes of the Directive, therefore encompasses disputes in which one party is domiciled or habitually resident in a Member State other than the Member State where the court is sitting or where the decision is to be enforced.

[76] ibid Art 3.

is significant. The obligation includes costs in relation to pre-litigation advice, the cost of legal representation in court, and an exemption from or assistance with the court fees.[77] The Directive also specifically obliges the Member State in which the court is sitting to grant legal aid for the particular cross-border related costs of language interpretation and translation, as well as travel costs.[78] At the end of proceedings, legal aid shall continue to be granted for the enforcement expenses and shall also continue in the event of an appeal.[79] In addition, the Member State of the legal aid recipient's domicile is obliged to provide legal aid covering assistance of a local lawyer before the legal aid application has been received by the Member State in which the court is sitting and also covering the costs of translation of the legal aid application.[80] A fundamental and important point is that Member States shall grant legal aid without discrimination to Union citizens and third-country nationals residing lawfully in a Member State.[81] However, these entitlements to legal aid can naturally be conditional upon an assessment of the economic situation of the applicant, based on objective factors.[82] One facet of the goal of transparency in the procedures is that the authorities dealing with applications must give reasons if they do not support a request and the applicant must have the right to appeal against that decision.[83]

The drafting of the Directive was based on the recognition that differences between national legal aid systems could create obstacles for the citizens and that a cross-border element would also generate additional expenditure for the citizens in question.[84] The above provisions show a clear commitment to address these issues and do advance the situation of cross-border litigants. Furthermore, from an access to justice perspective, the introduction of standard forms and a time limit for the

---

[77] ibid Art 3. Moreover, legal aid might also guarantee, depending on the national system in force, the costs of the opposing party in the event that the legal aid recipient loses the case.

[78] ibid Article 7.

[79] ibid Article 9.

[80] ibid Art 8. It specifically mentions that legal aid should be granted for alternative dispute resolution mechanisms if the parties are obliged by law to resort to these or if the parties have been ordered to do so by the court.

[81] ibid Art 4.

[82] ibid Art 5. Since there are marked differences in the living standards and cost of living in different Member States it was clearly not possible for the Directive to impose any kind of common European financial threshold for eligibility for legal aid, as is done by statute in several Member States. Thus, the Directive instead focuses on the fact that any factors taken into account in the assessment of the applicant's financial situation must be objective.

[83] ibid Art 15. States may also reject applications for actions which appear to be manifestly unfounded or take the nature of the action into account in defamation claims. The Member States are not obliged to provide legal aid cover at all if the proceedings are designed for litigants in person or if the applicant enjoys other alternative mechanisms that cover the cost of proceedings. In addition, the Member States may request that the recipients pay reasonable contributions towards the costs of proceedings or refund the sum in part or in whole if their financial situation has substantially improved.

[84] COM(2002)13,2.

transmitting authorities to send on applications for legal aid are welcome introductions, aiming to introduce simplicity and efficiency. Nevertheless, the system which is introduced is only a bare minimum and does not fundamentally address the heterogeneity among the Member States vis-à-vis the quality of the legal aid provided.[85] Therefore, as with the Framework Directive on certain procedural rights in criminal proceedings, the Legal Aid Directive for civil and commercial matters evidences the difficult balance between the supranational and the national levels in the practical implementation of achieving access to justice.

IV. CONCLUSION

Access to justice, as demonstrated by comparative and EU law, is a field where—as the saying goes—'the Devil is in the details'. On the one hand, supranational and international protection of access to justice might remain wishful thinking if lawyers do not take the pains to go into the details of provisions of procedural law, in order to check their compliance with the broad and generous proclamations of constitutional texts and international treaties. No system will ever achieve perfection, as there is an inevitable tension between the development of access to justice and the growth of litigation, which sometimes creates unbearable pressures on the budgets devoted to justice. The development of alternative modes of conflict resolution is only a partial answer to the problems, as are the efforts invested in better law-making. On the other hand, the pressure of international and supranational law has undoubtedly fostered reforms of civil and criminal procedure, which appear as immense progress when placed in a historical perspective. The evolution of access to international justice, limited as it remains, may also be seen as a reason for optimism, but it may face difficulties, especially as the number of potential litigants could grow exponentially.

---

[85] The Member States are left to organize the conditions for legal aid, eg they are allowed to keep or introduce financial thresholds for eligibility. Nor does the Directive deal with the quality of legal aid and, *inter alia,* leaves untouched typical national limitations on legal aid work, eg counsel may only work a certain number of hours or is remunerated at a rate significantly under market value.

7

Access to Justice for Victims of Torture

RORY STEPHEN BROWN[1]

I. INTRODUCTION

Mr Al-Adsani, a British citizen in Kuwait considered responsible for the circulation of videotapes of a sensitive nature by Sheikh Jaber Al-Sabah Al-Saud Al-Sabah, was forcibly abducted from his home and taken, at gunpoint, to the Kuwaiti State Security Prison where he was falsely imprisoned and repeatedly beaten. After three days, he was released (having signed a confession under duress) only to be transported, again at gunpoint, to the palace of the Emir of Kuwait's brother, where he suffered cruelty of almost inconceivable magnitude. This detestable torture included being held underwater in a swimming pool containing human corpses, and being dragged into a small room where his tormentor, the Sheikh, set fire to mattresses doused with petrol. Ten days later, upon his return to Britain, the victim was treated for serious burns, covering 25 per cent of his body, and for grave psychological damage.[2]

A British Court held that the state of Kuwait was entitled to 'immunity' from civil proceedings in Britain even in respect of acts of torture. Immunity may be understood as 'a bar against one state from sitting in judgement on another state'.[3] This left the victim, Mr Al-Adsani, with neither an opportunity to argue his case on the merits nor a remedy, diplomatic channels having borne no fruit due to the United Kingdom government's refusal to assist.[4] Half a decade later, this result was endorsed by a wafer-thin majority of the European Court of Human Rights as a legitimate, lawful exercise of judicial discretion consonant with the rights enshrined in the European Convention on Human Rights (ECHR).[5] Part of an obviously exasperated minority, Loucaides J called the decision of the majority a 'travesty of justice'.[6]

---

[1] I am indebted to Professor Francioni for his characteristically painstaking reading of previous drafts of this paper. Responsibility for all submissions and for the inevitable errors remains my own.

[2] *Al-Adsani v UK* [2001] Application 35763/97, paras 10–12. Facts as described by the Court.

[3] H Fox, *The Law of State Immunity* (Oxford, 2002) 4.

[4] *Al-Adsani v Government of Kuwait* [1996] 107 ILR 536 (CA).

[5] *Al-Adsani v UK* (n 2 above).

[6] ibid *per* Loucaides J, Dissenting Opinion, first sentence.

Simply put, the fact that many victims of such egregious maltreatment may go unheard and uncompensated, due to the immunity from foreign civil jurisdiction enjoyed by officials and their state, is of great concern to the present author. The lack of practical, realizable remedies for victims of torture is the matter addressed by this chapter. It should be noted at the offset that the analysis is restricted to the *civil* law of remedies for torture. It is not concerned with any aspects of the criminal law, though some criminal cases are cited where the judgments shed light on the civil regime. To begin with, this chapter sketches the present law. That law is then criticized for its failure to respect the right of access to justice. Finally, a suggestion is made for a workable, realistic, and principled legal framework for a transnational torture tort that can be put into immediate effect by judges of tribunals all over the world. The question asked by this chapter is not so much *why* torture victims should be secured access to justice (which is taken as a given) but *how* this is to work in practice. How can justice for victims of torture suffered at the hands of foreign governments be secured? Can plaintiffs claim for torture damages in courts of states outside the jurisdiction in which the torture occurred, and, if so, under what circumstances?

II. THE PRESENT LAW: AN OVERVIEW

The law pertaining to immunity in foreign civil proceedings for torture damages, being at the interface of public and private; domestic and international; civil and criminal law; and connected, as it is, with more fundamental structural considerations of the international legal order, is of perplexing complexity. Immunity law is of indeterminate nature, uncertain origins, and pliable content, all of which are disputed vociferously at the highest level.[7] Upendra Baxi describes this state of affairs in the following, colourful terms: 'Epistemic constructs such as *forum non conveniens*, comity, jurisdiction *in personam* and *in rem*, *profession juris* stipulations, *lex fori*, *lex loci delicti*, and even the seemingly flexible "public policy" are coated in an historical and dogmatic opacity that remains, as yet, impermeable to an activist gaze.'[8] So what is the law pertaining to access to justice for torture victims and state immunity? The following summary proceeds in rough chronological order.

It is noteworthy that a ban on torture occupies pride of place in the domestic criminal, civil, and constitutional law of the majority of developed civilizations around the world. It serves almost as a hallmark of legality.[9] Torture is prohibited

---

[7] See the dissents in *Al-Adsani v UK* (n 2 above) and *Case Concerning the Arrest Warrant of 11 April 2000 (Democratic Republic of Congo v Belgium)* [2002] <http://www.icj-cij.org/icjwww/idocket/iCOBE/iCOBEframe.htm>.

[8] U Baxi, 'Geographies of Injustice: Human Rights at the Altar of Convenience' in C Scott (ed), *Torture as Tort: Comparative Perspectives on the Development of Transnational Human Rights Litigation* (Oxford, 2001) 199.

[9] See, for an exploration of torture as a legal 'archetype', J Waldron, 'Torture and Positive Law: Jurisprudence for the White House' (2005) 105 Col LR 1681.

in international treaties, such as the Universal Declaration of Human Rights, 1948 (Article 5).[10] Its prohibition is also featured in regional human rights covenants; for example in Article 3 of the ECHR, 1950. Article 6 of that document, considered in detail below, sets out the right of access to justice.[11]

Though bilateral trade agreements lifting state immunity exist, the first attempt to regulate the matter in a multilateral convention resulted in the European Convention on State Immunity, 1972 (the 'Basle Convention').[12] The only tort exception to immunity in this document requires the tortious act or omission to have taken place in the *forum* state. At the time of writing, only eight states had ratified the Basle Convention.[13] It remains a somewhat ailing attempt 'to establish' common rules, presumably due to the absence of consensus.[14]

Under Section 2(3) of the International Covenant on Civil and Political Rights (ICCPR), which entered into force on 23 March 1976, each state party must ensure that victims of rights violations have an effective remedy determined and enforced by a competent authority, notwithstanding the official capacity of the violator of the right. It also obliges states to develop a judicial remedy.

In the landmark case of *Filártiga v Peña-Irala*,[15] a torture victim was allowed, following the teleological reincarnation of a dormant United States statute of 1789, to bring a suit for damages against an official of a foreign government for acts committed abroad in pursuance of government policy. The justification for this finding was that the torturer, for civil law purposes, had become, 'like the pirate and the slave trader' *hostis humani generis*, meaning 'an enemy of all mankind'.[16] Although considered groundbreaking, it is worth recalling that it 'is not extraordinary for a court to adjudicate a tort claim arising out of its territorial jurisdiction'.[17]

The most important document in the attempt to suppress torture is the Convention against Torture and Other Cruel, Inhuman or Degrading Treatment or Punishment, 1984, (UNCAT). In Article 1, it defines the heinous practice as:

... any act by which severe pain or suffering, whether physical or mental, is intentionally inflicted on a person for such purposes as obtaining from him or a third person information or a confession, punishing him for an act he or a third person has committed or is

---

[10] Universal Declaration of Human Rights, GA Res 217A(III), UN Doc A/810 1948.

[11] ECHR, 1950.

[12] European Convention on State Immunity, 1972. Good examples of bilateral agreements removing immunities for governments engaging in international trade are the Peace Treaties signed after the First World War: See, eg, 1919 Treaty of Versailles, Art 281; 1920 Treaty of Sévres, Art 268.

[13] Austria, Belgium, Cyprus, Germany, Luxembourg, the Netherlands, Switzerland, and the UK: Information from <http://conventions.coe.int/Treaty/Commun/ChercheSig.asp?NT=074&CM=8&DF=&CL=ENG> (last visited 26 February 2007).

[14] A Orakhelashvili, 'State Immunity in National and International Law: Three Recent Cases Before the European Court of Human Rights' (2002) 15 LJIL 703, 708.

[15] *Filártiga v Peña-Irala* 630 F 2d 876 (CA, 2 Cir 1980).

[16] ibid 890.

[17] ibid 885.

suspected of having committed, or intimidating or coercing him or a third person, or for any reason based on discrimination of any kind, when such pain or suffering is inflicted by or at the instigation of or with the consent or acquiescence of a public official or other person acting in an official capacity.

Article 14(1) demands that: 'Each State Party shall ensure in its legal system that the victim of an act of torture obtains redress and has an enforceable right to fair and adequate compensation.' An analysis of the meaning of this problematic provision is postponed until the next section which criticizes the present law.

In *Prinz v Federal Republic of Germany*[18] the defendant was granted sovereign immunity, barring the application of an American holocaust survivor. The following year, in *Xuncax v Gramajo*,[19] a Massachusetts court held that personal *civil* liability functioned retroactively against a Guatemalan military director by virtue of the twin facts that (a) universal condemnation of torture *preceded* United States legislation removing official immunity, and (b) that international condemnation of the practice *predated* the acts in issue.

Shortly thereafter, *Al-Adsani v Government of Kuwait* appeared,[20] the gruesome facts of which served as our introduction. In the same year, but in very different spirit, the Anti-terrorism and Effective Death Penalty Act 1996 (AEDPA) was enacted in the United States, removing immunity of those foreign states designated as 'State sponsors of terrorism' in proceedings for personal injury or death caused by an act of torture. Iran responded to this United States amendment to its previous scheme of immunity by enacting its own mirror legislation, enabling 'Iranian victims of United States "interference" to sue the United States in Iranian courts'.[21]

In *Prosecutor v Anto Furundzija*,[22] though peripheral to the *ratio decidendi*, the International Criminal Tribunal for the Former Yugoslavia (ICTY) held: 'Proceedings could be initiated by potential victims if they had *locus standi* before a competent international or national judicial body with a view to asking it to hold the national measure to be internationally unlawful; or the victim could bring a civil suit for damage in a foreign court, which would therefore be asked *inter alia* to disregard the legal value of the national authorising act.'[23]

In the landmark case of *R v Bow Street Metropolitan Stipendiary Magistrate and Ors, ex p Pinochet Ugarte (No 3)*,[24] the United Kingdom House of Lords denied a former head of state, present in England, immunity from an extradition request founded on allegations of torture. This was so even though the crimes were committed for the purposes of the state and whilst the erstwhile dictator was in office

---

[18] *Prinz v Federal Republic of Germany* [1994] 307 US App DC 102.
[19] *Xuncax v Gramajo* [1995] 886 F Supp 162.
[20] *Al-Adsani v Government of Kuwait* (n 4 above).
[21] K Sealing, 'State Sponsors of Terrorism' (2003) 38 Tex ILJ 119, 121.
[22] *Prosecutor v Anto Furundzija* (1998) IT-95-17/1.
[23] ibid para 155.
[24] *R v Bow Street Metropolitan Stipendiary Magistrate and Ors, ex p Pinochet Ugarte (No 3)* [1999] 2 All ER 97.

because *a denial of immunity could be justified where the conduct concerned constituted an international crime against humanity, triggering individual responsibility.* Somewhat illogically, in spite of having declared torture a *jus cogens* crime, the House of Lords unanimously preserved the immunity of the state itself and that of a serving head of state. In contradistinction to the *Furundzija* case, obiter dicta spoke to the continuing immunity of officials in *civil actions* for torture.[25]

In the same year, the Greek Areios Pagos, in *Prefecture of Voiotia v Federal Republic of Germany*,[26] held that the defendant state could not hide behind immunity in a civil claim based on alleged *jus cogens* violations during the second World War, because the crimes were not acts of, or were committed in abuse of, sovereign power. From a pecuniary viewpoint, this was a pyrrhic victory because the survivors' application for enforcement of the judgment, pursuant to Article 923 of the Greek Code of Civil Procedure, was refused by the competent Minister, a decision later approved by the Greek Supreme Court for its conformity with the ECHR.[27]

In *Al-Adsani v The United Kingdom*,[28] the well-known decision of the European Court of Human Rights, handed down on the same day as two other decisions of the same Court pertaining to state immunity, it was held that the British preservation of sovereign immunity pursued the legitimate aim of complying with international law to promote comity and good relations between states. Furthermore, and crucially, the interference with the right of access was considered proportionate to that aim by virtue of its congruence with international law. The result of the Court's finding was that the alleged perpetrators of the violation of a peremptory norm of international law went unpunished and the victim went unheard and uncompensated. It is important to note that this decision, though regrettable, does not in any way restrict the freedom of states to deny sovereign immunity to other states or their functionaries in civil proceedings.[29] Also noteworthy is that the case featured an impassioned dissent by eight of the judges, who, contrary to the majority, considered that Al-Adsani had been unduly deprived of his right of access to justice.

In the wake of that controversial decision, the Greek Special Supreme Court, seised of another war reparations case, held by a narrow majority that, as a result of customary international law, 'Germany enjoyed immunity without any restrictions or exceptions and therefore could not be sued before any Greek Civil Court for torts committed'.[30]

---

[25] ibid *per* Lords Millett at 273 and 278, Hutton at 264, Browne-Wilkinson at 205, and Phillips at 281.

[26] *Prefecture of Voiotia v Federal Republic of Germany (Aerios Pagos)* [2000] Case No 11/2000.

[27] *Federal Republic of Germany v Miltiadis Margellos (Decision of the Greek Special Supreme Court)* [2002] Case 6/17/9/2002.

[28] *Al-Adsani v UK* [2001] Application 35763/97.

[29] C Tams, 'Schwierigkeiten mit dem *ius cogens*' (2002) 40 *Archiv des Voelkerrechts* 331, 349.

[30] Case 6/17/9/2002 *Federal Republic of Germany v Miltiadis Margellos (Decision of the Greek Special Supreme Court)* [2002]. Pursuant to the Greek Constitution, art 87, this decision boasts only persuasive and not precedential value.

Another dramatic doctrinal division characterized the *Case Concerning the Arrest Warrant of 11 April 2000 (Democratic Republic of Congo v Belgium)*[31] before the International Court of Justice (ICJ), where the majority held that the issuance and international circulation by Belgium of an arrest warrant against Abdulaye Yerodia Ndombasi failed to respect the immunity from jurisdiction and the inviolability which the incumbent Minister for Foreign Affairs of the Congo enjoyed under international law, despite the allegations of crimes against humanity. This was a criminal law case but, importantly for present purposes, the dissentients, Higgins, Kooijmans, and Buergenthal JJ, argued from the ongoing erosion of immunity in civil and criminal law in support of the proposition that immunity does not enjoy intrinsic value, rather it is 'an exception to a normative rule which would otherwise apply'.[32]

In Canada, paying close attention to the absence of a human rights exception in the domestic statutory scheme, the Ontario Superior Court of Justice upheld Iran's immunity in the face of allegations of torture in *Bouzari v Islamic Republic of Iran*.[33] Following this decision, the Committee against Torture[34] rebuked the Canadians, stating that 'as a countermeasure permitted under international public law, a State could remove immunity from another State—a permitted action to respond to torture carried out by that State'.[35] Criticizing the 'absence of effective measures to provide civil compensation to victims of torture in all cases', the Committee recommended that Canada 'review its position under Article 14 of UNCAT to ensure the provision of compensation through its civil jurisdiction to *all* victims of torture'.[36]

In *Ferrini v Repubblica Federale di Germania*[37] the Italian Supreme Court case, pertaining to forcible deportation and forced labour perpetrated by the Nazis, it was held that transgressions of fundamental human rights 'offend universal values which transcend the interests of individual national communities'. Several months after the *Ferrini* decision, the United Kingdom Appeal Court in *Jones v Kingdom of Saudi Arabia*,[38] saw fit, in a judgment that was more courageous than it was

---

[31] *Case Concerning the Arrest Warrant of 11 April 2000 (Democratic Republic of Congo v Belgium)* [2002] <http://www.icj-cij.org/icjwww/idocket/iCOBE/iCOBEframe.htm>.

[32] ibid Joint Separate Opinion of Higgins *et al*, para 71.

[33] *Bouzari v Iran* [2002] 2002 OJ No 1624.

[34] The Committee is the body created to oversee the implementation of UNCAT.

[35] CAT, Summary Record of the Second Part (Public) of the 646th Meeting, 6 May 2005, Cat/C/SR. 646/Add.1 (2005).

[36] Committee Against Torture, 34th Session, Consideration of Article 19 Reports, CAT/C/CO/ CAN (2005) para D(5)(f) (emphasis added).

[37] *Ferrini v Repubblica Federale di Germania* [2004] Cas March 11, 2004 (Sez Un) published in (2004) 87 *Rivista di Diritto Internazionale* 589. For solid analysis of this case, see M Iovanne, 'The *Ferrini* Judgment of the Italian Supreme Court' (2004) XIV *Italian Yearbook of International Law* 165 and A Gianelli, 'Crimini internazionali ed immunità degli stati dalla giurisdizione nella sentenza *Ferrini*' (2004) 87 *Rivista di Diritto Internazionale* 643.

[38] *Jones v Kingdom of Saudi Arabia* [2004] EWCA Civ 1394.

convincing, to deny immunity to the impleaded officials whilst preserving the immunity of the defendant state.

Soon after this, the United Nations Convention on Jurisdictional Immunities of States and Their Property[39] (the 'United Nations Convention') was opened for signing and, though not yet in force, proved to have a strong influence in Saudi Arabia's appeal against the United Kingdom Appeal Court's finding, in which the House of Lords decided to reinstate the immunity of the Saudi officials and reaffirm that of the Saudi Arabian State.[40] For present purposes, the relevant provisions of the United Nations Convention are Articles 2(b)(vi), 5, 6(2)(b), and 12, which provide respectively: that state immunity extends to 'representatives of the state acting in that capacity'; for a general rule of immunity for states and their property from third country civil suits; that foreign proceedings shall be considered to have been instituted against a state even if it is unnamed in the action when the effect of the proceedings is 'to affect the property, rights, interests or activities' of the state; and for an exception to the general rule of immunity in the case of personal injuries and damage to property attributable to the state if such injury or damage occurred in the forum state. In the future, Article 12 may cast an interpretive shadow over the cases of *Ferrini*[41] and *Prefecture of Voiotia*[42] in both of which part of the tort occurred in the forum state.[43]

Although not logically exclusionary of an implied exception for transnational litigation stemming from *jus cogens* violations of human rights, the combined effect of Article 2(b)(vi)'s expansive definition of the state (to include anyone acting as its representative);[44] Article 5's broad general rule on immunity; the catch-all provision in Article 6(2)(b);[45] and the narrowly-drawn exception in Article 12 is to make such a plaintiff-friendly interpretation hard to reach.[46] It is worth recalling that it is easy—given the framing of immunity in the United Nations Convention, the Basle Convention, and various domestic statutes—to 'elevate sovereign immunity to a superior principle of international law and

[39] UN Convention on Jurisdictional Immunities of States and Their Property, 2004. REDRESS (an association seeking justice for torture victims) opposed ratification of this Convention due to the absence of a protocol excluding serious international crime from its ambit.

[40] *Jones v Kingdom of Saudi Arabia* [2006] UKHL 26.

[41] *Ferrini v Repubblica Federale di Germania* [2004] Cas March 11, 2004 (Sez Un) published in (2004) 87 *Rivista di Diritto Internazionale* 589.

[42] *Prefecture of Voiotia v Federal Republic of Germany (Aerios Pagos)* [2000] Case No 11/2000.

[43] Mr Ferrini was taken into German custody in Italy and then deported to Germany. In *Prefecture of Voiotia* the relevant tortious conduct occurred during German occupation of the forum state's territory.

[44] Christopher Hall somewhat chillingly points out that this definition would be wide enough to include intelligence services, paramilitary death squads, and private contractors in state *emploi*: CK Hall, 'UN Convention on State Immunity: The Need for a Human Rights Protocol' (2006) 55 ICLQ 411, 415.

[45] Presumably, Art 6(2) would militate against a finding of individual official liability, precluding a result such as that endorsed in the English Appeal Court in *Jones v Kingdom of Saudi Arabia* [2004] EWCA Civ 1394. On this point, see K Parlett, 'Immunity in Civil Proceedings for Torture: The Emerging Exception' (2006) 1 EHRLR 49, 63.

[46] Hall (n 44 above) 411.

to lose sight of the essential reality that it is an exception to the normal doctrine of juris-diction'.[47] The structure of various legal provisions reflects not the origins, nor the nature of immunity, but expeditious drafting. One must keep in mind the more fundamental question of whether or not jurisdiction is an illegitimate interference with another state's affairs (this is discussed below, see text accompanying footnote 70 *et seq*).

The influence of the United Nations Convention on the House of Lords (Lord Bingham calling it 'wholly inimical to the claimant's contention')[48] was stronger than might have been anticipated, given that the Working Group on Jurisdictional Immunities of States and their Properties, after consideration of developments up until 1999, regarded the matter of the relationship between *jus cogens* norms and state immunity as too embryonic for inclusion in a convention designed to be 'codificatory' of existing law.[49] Furthermore, it is difficult to resist Lorna McGregor's conclusion that the five-year delay in the adoption of the Convention since the Working Group's consideration of the rapidly changing relation-ship between *jus cogens* and state immunity renders the text outdated.[50] It is obvious that the Convention represents a leg in a journey rather than the final destination. It certainly should not have been used in support of a proposition in an area of law that it was not intended to cover and which its draughtsmen did not consider. The House of Lords deci-sion in the *Jones* case is sad testament to Christopher Hall's prediction that the 'numerous ambiguities' in the Convention may move domestic courts to interpret it as precluding compensation in such cases.[51] Contrariwise, given the United Kingdom's membership of UNCAT, one might have expected the House of Lords to have taken a less dismissive approach to the aforementioned explanatory comments by the Committee against Torture on the extent of a state party's obligations under Article 14.[52]

As a result of this latest word on state immunity, the following situation is typical for many countries: In theory, though not often in practice, proceedings can be brought by a victim against a governmental official of state A under the domestic (usually constitutional) law of state A for torture meted out on home turf (within state A).[53] If a foreign official (of state B) tortured a citizen in the latter's home country (state A), the victim can avail himself of the jurisdictional exception

---

[47] R Higgins, 'Certain Unresolved Aspects of the Law of State Immunity' (1982) 29 Netherlands International Law Review 265.

[48] *Jones v Kingdom of Saudi Arabia* [2006] UKHL 26, para 26.

[49] General Assembly, Sixth Committee, 'Convention on Jurisdictional Immunity of States and their Property: Report of the Chairman of the Working Group' (1999) paras 46–48; L McGregor, 'State Immunity and Jus Cogens' (2006) 55 ICLQ 437.

[50] McGregor (n 49 above) 437.

[51] Hall (n 44 above) 411. See also Parlett's view that the UN Convention might 'oblige a party to accord immunity to a foreign state in civil proceedings for torture', Parlett (n 45 above) 59.

[52] *Jones v Kingdom of Saudi Arabia* [2006] UKHL 26, para 23.

[53] In addition to being in probable violation of domestic constitutional guarantees, as Jennifer Orange points out, a state party to UNCAT, refusing to hear a claim for torture which occurred in its own territory would be in clear violation of Art 14. J Orange, 'Torture Tort Choice of Law and *Tolofson*' in C Scott (ed), *Torture as Tort: Comparative Perspectives on the Development of Transnational Human Rights Litigation* (2001) 310.

(generally expressed in statutory form) for torts occurring within the citizen's state (ie within the territory of state A). Further, if a soldier of state A tortured a person, irrespective of nationality, abroad in country B where A was an occupying force, the victim would have a cause of action in the courts of A.[54] However, a citizen of state A, tortured in state B, by an official of the latter's government has no claim against that official or as against state B in the domestic courts of state A after returning home.[55] It is this latter circumstance which is addressed by this chapter.

Having discussed jurisprudence and treaty law, it is now apt to consider how the competing normative imperatives of state immunity and access to justice rank in the roster of international law rules. To start with, it is by no means clear that states grant immunity out of a sense of legal obligation deriving from customary international law.[56] Furthermore, the Chairperson of the United Nations Committee against Torture was correct then (and would be correct now) to observe that, where torture has been committed by a state official, there was 'no peremptory norm of general international law that prevented states from withdrawing immunity from foreign states in such cases to claim for liability for torture'.[57] Similarly free from doubt is the proposition that 'international law does not simply permit, but affirmatively requires that states take action to protect [torture] victims and promote justice'.[58] Rather, the locus of controversy is the *extent* of the permission and of the requirement. Erika de Wet maintains—and, the *Furundzija* optimistic dicta notwithstanding, it is hard to disagree—that 'the consensus has not progressed to a level where it would include an optimization of the efficient enforcement of *jus cogens* norms, such as a peremptory obligation to grant the victims of torture a legal avenue for claiming compensation'.[59]

What then is the status of the mysterious rules on state immunity? The attentive reader will have noted that state immunity is largely the creation of national courts, though its development has been punctuated by bilateral and, more recently, multilateral treaties.[60] This realization colours the entire analysis, for it is difficult to

---

[54] Some courts have gone further, eg in the UK Appeal Court, Mance LJ saw it as the state's duty to afford civil redress in respect of torture committed abroad by one of its officers, irrespective of control or occupation: *Jones v Kingdom of Saudi Arabia* [2004] EWCA Civ 1394, para 20. Precisely this was an issue in the recent case of *Al-Skeini and Ors v Secretary of State for Defence* [2007] UKHL 26, where it was held that the relatives of an Iraqi citizen, tortured to death by British forces in Iraq, could bring a claim in courts in the UK for the latter's infringement of its human rights obligations.

[55] *Jones v The Kingdom of Saudi Arabia* [2006] UKHL 26.

[56] L McGregor, REDRESS, 'Immunity v. Accountability: Considering the Relationship between State Immunity and Accountability for Torture and other Serious International Crimes' (2005) 16.

[57] CAT, 'Summary Record of the Second Part (Public) of the 646th Meeting, 6 May 2005, Cat/C/SR. 646/Add.1' (2005) para 67.

[58] Orange (n 53 above) 306.

[59] E de Wet, 'The Prohibition of Torture as an International Norm of *jus cogens* and its Implications for National and Customary Law' (2004) 15 EJIL 97, 120.

[60] See generally, eg R Gardiner, 'UN Convention on State Immunity: Form and Function' (2006) 55 ICLQ 407; or E Denza, 'The 2005 UN Convention on State Immunity in Perspective' (2006) 55 ICLQ 395.

determine whether or not the correct exercise is in international or comparative law, or indeed, more broadly, whether these two disciplines can sensibly be described as *distinct*. However, as Lord Wilberforce remarked, 'to argue from the terms of a statute to establish what international law provides is to stand the accepted argument on its head'.[61] Having surveyed the various legal sources, Lord Denning (perhaps a little glibly) observed: 'There is no uniform practice. There is no uniform rule. So there is no help there.'[62] To compound the problem, the law of sovereign immunity is in flux, nuanced, and contested,[63] leading Alexander Orakhelashvili to argue that no rule of international law exists to delineate the scope of immunity, rather states act 'on the basis of considerations such as interest, comity and reciprocity'.[64] As a matter of law, it is undeniable that immunity rules originate from (and are part of the body of) international law. Orakhelashvili's observation does not detract from this point. Indeed, the *Tehran Hostages* case,[65] concerning Iran's responsibility to protect the inviolability of United States consular officials who had been taken hostage, is a good example of an *international* court applying *international* law rules on immunity. In that case the ICJ was of the opinion that the relevant rules on Iran's responsibilities derived not only from the 1961 Vienna Convention on Diplomatic Relations, but also from general international law.[66] As the late Sir Robert Jennings pointed out, 'the fact is that states do not give themselves unlimited discretion' in the determination of the reach of extraterritorial jurisdiction for the simple reason that all states are cognisant of the intolerable state of affairs entailed by the exorbitant unilateral exercise of jurisdiction'.[67] Returning to the more specific, narrower question in this chapter, it is contended that, *whatever the status of immunity rules, no international law norm exists that bestows immunity on officials or states that use torture.* Two main considerations evidence this proposition. First, there is no international treaty that legislates for the matter. Secondly, state practice, though more uniform in other fields (eg trade or warships), is diverse when it comes to torture—indeed state legislatures and sometimes judges clearly view it as a matter for national discretion whether or not they extend immunity to other states.

What then is the status of the right to access to justice? There is no space here for an extensive consideration of this issue.[68] In his authoritative chapter at the

---

[61]   *I Congreso del Partido* [1983] I AC 260.

[62]   *Rahimtoola v Nizam of Hyderabad* [1958] AC 379, 609.

[63]   M Reimann, 'A Human Rights Exception to Sovereign Immunity: Some Thoughts on *Prinz v Federal Republic of Germany*' (1994–1995) 16 Mich JIL 403, 420.

[64]   A Orakhelashvili, 'State Immunity and International Public Order' (2002) 45 German Yearbook of International Law 227, 249.

[65]   *United States Diplomatic and Consular Staff in Tehran* [1980] 1980 ICJ 3.

[66]   ibid para 62.

[67]   Jennings made this observation in the different context of antitrust law, nevertheless it applies with equal force here, R Jennings, 'Extraterritorial Jurisdiction and The United States Antitrust Laws (1957)' in *Collected Writings of Sir Robert Jennings* (1998) 820.

[68]   The reader interested in this fundamental question is directed to Professor Francioni's contribution to this volume, ch 1 above, which provides a comprehensive and detailed analysis of the right of access to justice in international law.

beginning of this volume, Professor Francioni maintains that it is now possible to acknowledge that access to justice is a right recognized by general international law. That said, he also recognizes that 'the practice of international tribunals is still very reluctant to accept an exception to immunity in respect of individual claims for alleged violations of human rights, even if the human rights are so fundamental as to be part of *jus cogens*'.[69] Here, it is submitted that *the right of access to justice in customary international law positively requires that practical and effective avenues for making claims are available to torture victims*. This is explored in greater detail shortly.

It is indisputable that *inherent limits exist on the power of a sovereign state vis-à-vis* human beings; that some actions lie beyond the pale of governmental authority even within its own jurisdiction.[70] Sovereignty 'never extends beyond the limits drawn by the unconditionally binding rules of international law'.[71] It is clear that a shift has taken place, away from the dogma of absolute immunity, towards the viewpoint that a state's acts are subject to external scrutiny; that there are limits on a state's sovereignty; and that a state can act, in a manner which is ultra vires its powers as sovereign.[72] The violation of *jus cogens* norms is the paradigm example of such illicit activity. This short analysis of the legal backdrop reveals that the current judicial tendency is to apply a restrictive theory of immunity in line with the distinction between acts *jure imperii* and *jure gestionis*. This shift is detectable in state practice, decisions of domestic and international tribunals, and by reference to international treaties, the United Nations Convention being the most prominent example. In fact, one of the most powerful arguments that states, immunity should not obtain in cases of torture is that *immunity has already been restricted in the commercial context*. It certainly seems unreasonable for states to restrict immunity in the commercial context for the benefit of companies whilst preserving immunity in cases of egregious violations of human rights that also constitute grave crimes of international law.[73] In summary, therefore, the question for courts, commentators, and claimants alike is not really *why* torture victims should enjoy the right of access to justice but *how* to make this normative imperative a reality.

---

[69] See p 48 above.

[70] A variant of this argument is that torture, being contrary to *jus cogens*, is not a sovereign act and hence does not attract immunity. See W Adams, 'In Search of a Defence of the Transnational Human Rights Paradigm: May Jus Cogens Norms be Invoked to Create Implied Exceptions in Domestic State Immunity Statutes?' in C Scott (ed) *Torture as Tor: Comparative Perspectives on the Development of Transnational Human Rights Litigation*, (2001) 253. However, it seems more natural to say that it *was* the act of a sovereign but was ultra vires its powers.

[71] Reimann (n 63 above) 421.

[72] As Lord Nicholls had it, in *R v Bow Street Metropolitan Stipendiary Magistrate, ex p Pinochet Ugarte (No 1)* (1998) 37 ILM 1302, 1333, international law 'has made it plain that certain types of conduct...are not acceptable on the part of anyone...the contrary conclusion would make a mockery of international law'.

[73] McGregor (n 56 above) 55.

III. A CRITIQUE OF THE PRESENT LAW

Reflecting on the international regime against torture, the majority in *Al-Adsani v The United Kingdom*[74] at the European Court of Human Rights, proclaimed that 'No legal loopholes have been left' in the suppression of 'any manifestation of torture by operating both at the interstate level and at the level of individuals'.[75] How is it then that Mr Al-Adsani was left without a remedy? Well, frequently, plaintiffs encounter problems caused by jurisdictional rules 'rooted in an outmoded conception of the world that emphasised sovereignty and independence often at the cost of fairness'.[76]

It has already been demonstrated that UNCAT provides no detailed guidance on the issue under consideration, other than to impose a duty on states to provide remedies for torture victims. Similarly, it has been shown that the United Nations Immunity Convention does not make the picture any clearer. International treaty law is therefore inadequate in this area and does not furnish us with either normative criteria or machinery to vindicate the right of access to justice for torture victims.

Furthermore, with notable exceptions, the judicial response to date has been disappointing because of a failure to apprehend that in cases for torture damages, the retention of civil immunity for states and their agents violates the customary international norm of access to justice, correctly understood. In short, courts have not found a satisfactory way to ensure that access to justice trumps immunity. Therefore, the contention here is that, *where no realistic alternative remedial avenues exist, the denial of hearings on the merits to torture victims in third country actions is a violation of the right of access to justice, correctly understood.*

The relationship between state immunity and access to justice is obvious. The denial of state immunity gives 'effect to the ever-growing recognition of human rights: in particular the right of access to an impartial court for the determination of one's civil rights and obligations'.[77]

The simple proposition of this section is that automatic state or official immunity from civil torture proceedings in foreign courts render UNCAT a hollow and futile proclamation, and violate the claimant's right of access to a court combined with his right to physical integrity. It is argued that 'closing the court doors would mean to inflict "another horrendous indignity" upon the plaintiff[s] who had already suffered enough'.[78] 'Denial of court access is especially serious when it occurs in the victim's home country [because] the very government that demands loyalty from, and thus owes protection to, the plaintiff, refuses to assist him in the vindication

[74] *Al-Adsani v UK* [2001] Application 35763/97.
[75] ibid para 30.
[76] *Hunt v T&N plc* [1993] 4 SCR 289, 309–10.
[77] *Holland v Lampen-Wolfe* [2000] 1 WLR 1573, *per* Lord Cooke at 1578.
[78] Reimann (n 63 above) 413, quoting from Sporkin J's judgment in the Federal District Court.

of his undisputed rights. As a result, the state deprives him of what is normally his only hope for compensation.'[79]

The present assertion that automatic immunity for torture in third country civil proceedings is inconsistent with access to justice, properly understood, is developed below by reference to two concepts, *symbiosis* and the *substance of procedure*. It is demonstrated that, at least when viewed from the perspective of access to justice, immunity and jurisdiction are inextricably linked. Before turning to these two concepts, a brief consideration of UNCAT is apposite.

A focal point of the debate has been whether or not the mandate contained in Article 14, of UNCAT that: 'Each state party shall ensure in its legal system that the victim of an act of torture obtains redress and has an enforceable right to fair and adequate compensation' is of extraterritorial application.[80] In the academic literature, not enough has been made of the fact that a natural reading of the section yields exactly this result: Each state shall ensure 'in its legal system', ie at home, that 'the victim of an act of torture obtains redress'; apparently notwithstanding the nationality of the torturer and of the victim and the geographical location of the act of torture. This conclusion is bolstered by the presence of a territorial qualifier in other provisions.[81] However Andrew Byrnes argues that 'the most plausible theory for the omission of the territorial qualifier from Article 14 of UNCAT remains that of inadvertence, given the lack of evidence in the *travaux* of an affirmative decision to remove the words "committed in any territory under its jurisdiction"'.[82] Though this is possible, it would require extreme inadvertence indeed, given the importance of UNCAT and of the provision on reparations, calling Byrnes' contention into doubt. However, given considerable disagreement on the effect of the subsection, he is on safe ground in concluding that 'it is difficult to argue unequivocally that Article 14 ... must be interpreted as requiring States parties to provide the same civil right to redress for torture which occurs outside its jurisdiction as it is obliged to provide for torture which is alleged to have occurred within its territorial and other jurisdiction'.[83] Consequently, Sandra Raponi is perhaps putting it too high, given the importance of the distinction between adjudicative and enforcement jurisdiction,[84] in her argument that states 'may actually have an international *obligation* to provide redress and compensation in transnational torture cases'.[85] That said, the

---

[79] ibid.

[80] A Byrnes, 'Civil Remedies for Torture Committed Abroad: An Obligation under the Convention against Torture?' in C Scott (ed), *Torture as Tort: Comparative Perspectives on the Development of Transnational Human Rights Litigation* (2001) 419.

[81] Article 31(2) of the Vienna Convention on the Law of Treaties states that any provision of a treaty shall be interpreted in the context of other relevant provisions.

[82] Byrnes (n 80 above) 548.

[83] ibid 549.

[84] ie in this context, the difference between the jurisdiction to hear a case and jurisdiction to make a damages award.

[85] S Raponi, 'Grounding a Cause of Action for Torture in Transnational Law' in C Scott (ed) *Torture as Tort: Comparative Perspectives on the Development of Transnational Human Rights Litigation* (2001) 398.

natural reading of Article 14, especially in the light of the recent Committee Against Torture comment to Canada (see above), makes it equally impossible to assume that its effect is territorially limited. Perhaps a more nuanced approach is required.

Moving to the crux of this section, the contention here is that once the *symbiotic* nature of the relationship between the right of access to justice and other rights is acknowledged, the *substance of procedure* is more easily understood. The notion of 'symbiosis' refers to the fact that the right of access to a court relies on other rights for its content, whilst they, in turn, rely on the right of access for their vindication. Put somewhat simply, an action is nothing without a cause. Equally, the other rights, to life, not to be tortured, etc would be toothless dogs, without the right of access to a court, without the opportunity for vindication of the guarantee in the right. The notion of symbiosis can be developed by reference to ECHR jurisprudence.

Article 6(1) of the ECHR provides: 'In the determination of his civil rights and obligations or of any criminal charge against him, everyone is entitled to a fair and public hearing within a reasonable time by an independent and impartial tribunal established by law.' Article 13 of the same document reads: 'Everyone whose rights and freedoms as set forth in this Convention are violated shall have an effective remedy before a national authority notwithstanding that the violation has been committed by persons acting in an official capacity.'

From these provisions, Graham Virgo argues that the ECHR should be interpreted as bestowing extra-territorial effect on domestic rules for the compensation of torture victims because of (a) its supranational nature, (b) its creation of a Eurozone of rights protection, and (c) because of the importance of the rights it contains.[86] These are not arguments that can lightly be dismissed but perhaps they require further elaboration and supplementation if we wish to ground a transnational torture tort of worldwide reach.

The main proposition here is that *it is folly to balance Article 6(1) against the rule of state immunity in isolation* because the content and, consequently, the importance of the right of access to the courts depends on the substantive right that has been infringed. Article 6(1) itself is empty of substantive content so will rarely, if ever, override an important public interest. It is only when the right of access to justice is considered as part of the armour that protects a worthwhile right, such as the right not to be tortured, that it acquires meaning, value, and the potential to trump public interest arguments like state immunity. Therefore the right of access to justice has a *symbiotic* relationship with other rights precisely because it means *nothing* if no other right or liberty has been violated, evoking the desire to access the courts. Conversely, without access to justice, none of the other rights that we purportedly enjoy could be vindicated. Consequently, the right of access gains importance in a directly *proportionate relationship* to the importance of the right(s) allegedly violated and the gravity of the alleged violation.

---

[86] G Virgo, 'Characterisation, Choice of Law and Human Rights' in C Scott (ed) *Torture as Tort: Comparative Perspectives on the Development of Transnational Human Rights Litigation*, (2001) 341.

Had the European Court of Human Rights in the *Al-Adsani* case considered Article 6 (access to justice) and Article 3 (banning torture) together in this light, rather than considering them in isolation, logic may have dictated a different conclusion. Article 3 is similarly inept on its own in the context of compensation for torture victims because it speaks to the *outlawing* of the practice, not to civil law repercussions of maltreatment. The Court's conclusion that Article 3 had not been violated by the United Kingdom because there was no causal connection between the alleged torture and United Kingdom authorities bordered on the facile. If a hollow promise (Article 3) and an empty right (Article 6) that relies on other rights for its content are considered separately from one another, the whole structure of the inquiry is biased against the claimant. This is because hollowness and emptiness are not values that will ever trump valid public interest arguments.

By way of example, in *Osman v United Kingdom*,[87] a case stemming from a teacher's unhealthy obsession with (and his subsequent violent attack on the life of) one of his pupils, the United Kingdom police, who were aware of the obsessional character of the teacher's behaviour, enjoyed immunity from civil suit in the United Kingdom. A unanimous European Court of Human Rights held the State responsible at the international level for having failed to provide in its legal system for a civil suit against the authorities in the wake of an incident of non-state violence resulting in the loss of life'.[88] The Court achieved this result, not by finding a violation of the right to life, but, tellingly, by finding a violation of the right of access to a court. However, it was the *gravity* of the infringement of the right to life (albeit by a non-state actor) that made the right of access to a court so important. In this way, the value of the right of access and, correspondingly, the legitimacy of any restriction on it, is indexed to the infringement of the right at stake. Access to a court is less important in the case of a parking ticket than in the case of torture. The more important the right violated, and the more flagrant the violation, the more important the right to be heard.[89] One might object to this analysis by saying that the Court in the *Osman* case was moved by the consideration that it was the responsibility of the police in the United Kingdom to protect United Kingdom citizens, whilst in the case of torture committed by officials abroad, the officials of another state are responsible. The response to this is simple. The victims in the *Osman* saga did not suffer or perish at the hands of the state, rather at those of a madman, just as the victim in *Al-Adsani* did not suffer at the hands of the forum state (the alleged torture having taken place at the hands of the Kuwaiti administration). From this

---

[87] *Osman v UK* [1998] ECHR (GC) Application 23452/94.

[88] A Clapham, 'Revisiting Human Rights in the Private Sphere: Using the European Convention on Human Rights to Protect the Right of Access to the Civil Courts' in C Scott (ed), *Torture as Tort: Comparative Perspectives on the Development of Transnational Human Rights Litigation* (2001) 523.

[89] In ch 1 above, Professor Francioni comes to a similar conclusion: 'The more severe the breach complained of...the more important it is to preserve the right of the victims or their descendants to have access to remedial measures and to effective investigation and prosecution of the responsible persons', see p 46 above.

observation, common ground can be reached. The conclusion can be drawn that, if human rights are effectively to be protected, a state's human rights obligations must extend beyond the actions or inactions of its own agents (and sometimes, as will be argued later, beyond its own territory).[90] In summary, except in a purely abstract context, it is folly (and potentially fatal for claimants) to consider access to justice as a stand-alone right.

The focus now moves to the 'substance of procedure'. Simply formulated, this term is intended to convey that procedural restrictions may operate to rob valid claims of substance. For torture victims, denial of access to a third country court can signal the end of the road for their hopes of justice.

The European Court of Human Rights has stated that, 'the grant of immunity is to be seen not as qualifying a substantive right but as a procedural bar on the national courts' power to determine the *right*'.[91] This smacks of contradiction because the same court seemed to recognize the import of the substance of procedure at the very beginning of the *Al-Adsani* judgment, reasoning that *any* restriction on admittance to a court implicated the right of access to justice. From the perspective of the ECHR, this latter proposition must be correct as it is consistent with the Court's fundamental jurisprudence to the effect that: 'The Convention is intended to guarantee not rights that are *theoretical or illusory* but rights that are *practical and effective*.'[92] (It is not a toothless dog.) More pertinently, it went on to say that, 'this is particularly so of the right of access to the courts in view of the prominent place held in a democratic society by the right to a fair trial'.[93] As Christian Tams points out, it makes little difference to the claimant whether the restriction on access is imposed on the court from within or from without.[94] Indeed, it would be absurd if a plaintiff's ability to vindicate his rights, turned on a national judge's cute distinction between externally and internally ordained restrictions on access.

It is submitted that Mance LJ was correct to hold in the *Jones* case that any blanket imposition of immunity deprives the right of access to justice of 'real meaning'.[95] Moreover, there is no escaping the fact that 'immunity from suit may enable avoidance of liability',[96] perhaps this will awaken tribunals to the injustice that is caused by a dogmatic, unreflective application of rules on immunity. In fact, once one accepts the 'systemic need of assuring the implementation of the values underlying peremptory norms' there is scope for denouncing oversimplistic and obstructive the argument that procedural rules as to the correct jurisdiction and the substantive cause of action are mutually exclusive as.[97]

---

[90] Clapham (n 88 above).
[91] *Al-Adsani v The UK* [2001] Application 35763/97, para 49.
[92] *Cordova v Italy (No 1)* [2003] Application 40877/98, para 58 (emphasis added).
[93] Ibid.
[94] Tams (n 29 above) 337.
[95] *Jones v Kingdom of Saudi Arabia* [2004] EWCA Civ 1394, para 92.
[96] Fox (n 3 above) 20.
[97] A Bianchi, '*Ferrini v Federal Republic of Germany*' (2005) 99 AJIL 242, 247.

Now that it has been established that the dichotomy between substance and procedure is often a fig leaf, *attention must turn to the balancing act* between the public benefits of preserving state immunity and the disbenefits of denying a plaintiff access to the court.

The European Court of Human Rights noted 'the legitimate aim of complying with international law to promote comity and good relations between states through the respect of another state's sovereignty'.[98] The intention here is not to dispute the obvious advantages of friendly relations between nation states, or that comity is a legitimate governmental aim, rather, it is to query whether or not the extension of state immunity in pursuit of that aim can be considered a *proportionate interference* with the individual's right (a) not to be tortured, combined with (b) to access to justice.[99] Correspondingly, it is not denied that, a 'destabilization' of international relations may result from the removal of sovereign immunity in transnational tort claims for torture.[100] On the contrary, what is argued here is that either, (a) the grave private and societal damage that results from refusing to hear about alleged violations of human rights is not proportionate to the aim of maintaining comity between states, or, alternatively, (b) that the gains to be had from the grant of immunity are so *nebulous and immeasurable* as to be impossible to balance against the *clear and quantifiable* violation of the victim's right to physical integrity and access to justice. The level of interference with a person's physical integrity in cases of torture need not be overemphasized. What should be made clear is that the dismissal of a transnational torture claim, more often than not, means the end of the line for the plaintiff,[101] it means, to use the Strasbourg Court's words, the 'impairment of the very essence of the right'.[102] It does not seem much to ask of a judge, where positive law is inconclusive as to the answer to a question, to choose a clear, morally palatable, individually and socially beneficial outcome over a result of little, debatable, or unquantifiable public moral worth.

With respect to this matter, Loucaides J's dissent in the *Al-Adsani* case merits separate mention. He maintained that, 'any form of blanket immunity, whether based on international law or national law, which is applied by a court in order to block completely the judicial determination of a civil right without balancing the competing interests' constituted a disproportionate infringement of the right of access to justice.[103] Vitally, as Mance LJ opined in the United Kingdom Court

---

[98] *Al-Adsani v UK* [2001] Application 35763/97, para 54.

[99] *Osman v UK* [1998] ECHR (GC) Application 23452/94 is authority for the proposition that an immunity from jurisdiction has to be proportionate to the government's aim.

[100] E de Wet, 'The Prohibition of Torture as an International Norm of *jus cogens* and its Implications for National and Customary Law' (2004) 15 EJIL 97, 120.

[101] C Scott, 'Introduction to Torture as Tort: From Sudan to Canada to Somalia' in C Scott (ed), *Torture as Tort: Comparative Perspectives on the Development of Transnational Human Rights Litigation* (2001) 1.

[102] *Al-Adsani v UK* [2001] Application 35763/97, para 7.

[103] ibid Dissenting Opinion of Loucaides J.

of Appeal in the *Jones* case, one of those competing interests must be 'whether the
state where any alleged torture has occurred provides an effective domestic remedy
for alleged systematic torture by its officials'.[104] Would it not be more consistent
with a system of human rights protection to assume a rebuttable presumption that
the automatic barring of a claim for the alleged violation of an absolute right is a
disproportionate infringement on that right, especially where no recourse to law
is available in the foreign jurisdiction, unless proven otherwise?

A final question about access for to how long torture victims should have access
to the courts. Should the availability of an action be temporally limited? There is a
strong argument to say that there should be no limitation periods for civil actions
stemming from torture allegations, due to the fact that no limitations apply to the
more draconian criminal punishments for such misbehaviour.[105] Further, social
oppression often delays the surfacing of reports of torture.

The emphasis so far has been on the meaning of 'access'. But what is the meaning of 'justice' in this context. The argument proffered here is that, even in the
absence of pecuniary compensation, there is massive symbolic and restorative value
in a victim's victory in foreign proceedings for torture; in fact: 'The remedial consequence of successfully bringing a case is often, or even usually, only a secondary concern.'[106] It is the day in court; the official declaration of wrongdoing; the
sober, curial contemplation of witness accounts of the terrible events; the collective
sympathy of the public gallery; and the scathing media outpourings that expunge
the claimant's sense of victimhood. Frankly, no sum of money, however trifling
or exorbitant can compensate a victim of torture for the appalling torment he has
endured. The reader will recall the helpful distinction between enforcement and
adjudication jurisdiction.

In reference to the rare recovery of damages in claims brought under United
States foreign torts legislation, John Terry correctly categorizes such actions as a
'cathartic ritual'; a vehicle for the vindication of the 'personhood' of the victim;
for the 'peoplehood of the victimized community'; and 'a means for providing
a measure of self-respect, vindication and recognition for the victims of serious
violations of international human rights'.[107] He contends (irrefutably) that the resonance of high-drama cases of the order of *Pinochet (No 3)*[108] and *Filártiga*[109] goes
beyond the (very important) symbolism involved in the official denunciation of the
actions of the oppressing state, rather, it extends to fortify the international law of

---

[104] *Jones v Kingdom of Saudi Arabia* [2004] EWCA Civ 1394, *per* Mance LJ, para 86.

[105] Scott (n 101 above) 42.

[106] Virgo (n 86 above) 335.

[107] J Terry, 'Taking *Filártiga* on the Road: Why Courts Outside the United States Should Accept
Jurisdiction Over Actions Involving Torture Committed Abroad' in C Scott (ed) *Torture as Tort:
Comparative Perspectives on the Development of Transnational Human Rights Litigation* (2001) 113.

[108] *R v Bow Street Metropolitan Stipendiary Magistrate and Ors, ex p Pinochet Ugarte (No 3)*
[1999] 2 All ER 97.

[109] *Filártiga v Peña-Irala* 630 F 2d 876 (CA, 2 Cir 1980).

human rights, by inspiring the judicial branch and potential plaintiffs alike, whilst rebuking the executive for its 'bunker mentality'.[110] In summary, the value of modes of restorative justice other than pecuniary compensation should not be discounted, including restitution; guarantees of non-repetition; and rehabilitation. This section has investigated the meaning and nature of the right of access to justice. The next section turns to the question of how this right is to be vindicated in practice.

IV. A PROPOSAL FOR REFORM

So far, though there are those in the academy who will maintain, albeit customarily by implication, that the sanctity of state immunity is of greater importance than the availability of avenues for redress to restore the integrity of individual torture survivors, they represent a minority.[111] This is largely because the positing of the symbolic value of sovereignty as a value of higher rank than human dignity is an indefensible and grotesquely old-fashioned stance. Instead, debate has largely centred on the formal question of *how* such foreign civil jurisdiction should function in practice, and several commentators plausibly maintain that legal chaos would ensue if domestic courts of one state were to judge upon the executive acts of another; that any extension of judicial jurisdiction into the territorial competence of foreign states would constitute an unworkable, not to mention illegitimate, encroachment into internal affairs.[112] This final part of the chapter takes up the challenge of constructing a legitimate platform for civil claims for redress pursuant to torture suffered abroad. It is argued (1) that judges should adopt a case-by-case approach based on the practical availability of alternative fora for torture victims to make their claims; (2) that neither states nor individuals should enjoy immunity from civil proceedings for torture damages; and (3) that judges should supply the omission of the (inter)national legislatures and ensure access to justice *proprio motu*.

A. A Case-by-Case Approach Based on the Practical Availability of Access to Justice

Massimo Iovane is correct to highlight that courts may have sometimes failed to check whether or not individuals have an 'alternative method' for satisfying their claims before upholding the jurisdictional immunity of a foreign state and

---

[110] D Golove and S Holmes, 'Terrorism and Accountability: Why Checks and Balances Apply Even in "The War on Terrorism"' (2004) 2 New York University Review of Law and Security 6.

[111] See eg H Fox *The Law of State Immunity* (2002). This viewpoint may also receive more support in the executive branch but this does not speak to its legitimacy.

[112] For a consideration of how a transnational tort of torture should function, see Scott (ed) (n 107 above).

its agents.[113] The main proposition here is that courts should adopt a *case-by-case* approach in their decisions on immunity, depending on whether or not access to justice was or is practically available in a more appropriate forum. Principles developed in the context of *exhaustion of local remedies* and *forum non conveniens* already exist and can be applied by the courts to achieve equitable results in each instance, which do not offend international law.

The aim of this section is to demonstrate that these two doctrines can usefully be deployed in the context of a transnational tort, allowing for the case-by-case consideration of the propriety of the exercise of jurisdiction in the forum state.[114]

The first principle—exhaustion of local remedies—dictates that, as a *sine qua non* of the pursuit of claims by an individual's state, the person concerned must avail herself of the avenues available in the alleged wrongdoer state.[115] The suggestion here is that the individual must attempt to exhaust local remedies, if it is practically possible to do so, before seeking justice in another forum in order to avoid unnecessary, illegitimate circumvention of local legal systems.[116] For instance, the European Court of Human Rights was correct in *McElhinney v United Kingdom*[117] to consider the plaintiff's failure to take the opportunity to bring an action in Northern Ireland as relevant when determining the gravity of the infringement to his right of access to justice.[118] This approach has the result, in cases where it is possible for the plaintiff to gain meaningful access the courts in the wrongdoer state,[119] that international disharmony is minimized. However, where the rule of law has disintegrated in the offending state to an extent where local remedies are unavailable, futile, or illusory, the plaintiff may turn to other jurisdictions. This would be the case where adequate remedies are absent; where proceedings are delayed unreasonably; or where factual reasons intervene, such as danger to the plaintiff.[120] As Ian Brownlie has it, the local remedies requirement evaporates where remedies are not available as a matter of reasonable possibility'.[121] Similarly, Iovane addresses the question of whether or

---

[113] M Iovanne, 'The Ferrini Judgment of the Italian Supreme Court' (2004) XIV IYIL 165, 193.

[114] For a similar suggestion, see R Garnett, 'State Immunity Triumphs in the European Court of Human Rights' (2002) 118 LQR 367.

[115] For a European case to this effect, see *McElhinney v Ireland and UK* [2000] Application 31253/96. For a comprehensive consideration of the doctrine of exhaustion of local remedies at a critical juncture in its development, see eg R Pisillo Mazzeschi, 'Exhaustion of Domestic Remedies and State Responsibility for Violation of Human Rights' (2000) X IYIL 17.

[116] Incidentally, this rule was preserved by the US Anti-terrorism and Effective Death Penalty Act 1996. For an exegesis on the importance of this rule, see F Hassan, 'A Conflict of Philosophies: The *Filártiga* Jurisprudence' (1983) 32 ICLQ 250.

[117] *McElhinney v Ireland and UK* [2000] Application 31253/96.

[118] ibid para 39.

[119] This is true at least where the torture is a one-off as opposed to part of a policy of state oppression.

[120] International Law Association, 'Report of the 69th Conference' (2000) 620–5.

[121] I Brownlie, *Principles of Public International Law* (3rd edn, 1979) 497.

not the denial of immunity in civil proceedings for torture can be considered an 'internationally wrongful act that is to say an exorbitant exercise of jurisdiction on the part of the forum state. He correctly concludes that 'cases must be evaluated from their inception to their conclusion and beyond'.[122] This involves taking into account the availability of remedies in the state where the tort occurred, any diplomatic avenues that have been pursued, and possible remedies in the international sphere. In his view, and it is a view shared by the present author, it is not, without more, wrongful for a foreign tribunal to offer access to justice where none has been made available in the state where the torture allegedly occurred.

A tricky question arises where the torturer has been the beneficiary of either an amnesty (which, as a legislative measure, would be an 'act of state') in her home country or the favourable arrangements sometimes provided for by so-called truth and reconciliation commissions. How should these devices affect the determination of whether or not there is a claim to be answered? Essentially, the questions remain the same, though they may be framed in the past tense: Did the claimant have access to justice? Did the claimant exhaust local remedies? As Jennifer Llewellyn remarks: 'Assessing legitimacy becomes a process of weeding out those amnesties inconsistent with the requirements for justice under international law.'[123] In the case of an amnesty or immunity, unilaterally provided for by the legislature of a state for its torturers and itself, which makes no or inadequate provision for the compensation of the regime's victims, the answer is simple: local remedies were not available, the plaintiff has not had access to justice and should be afforded such in the alternative forum. This conclusion is strengthened if either or both of the states concerned are parties to either the UNCAT (because of the mandate to provide a remedy in Article 14); or the ICCPR, (due to the aforementioned obligation in section2(3) to secure for victims of rights violations an effective remedy before a competent authority). Llewellyn argues that 'just amnesties' that provide 'investigation, accountability and redress' should operate to bar an action in foreign *fora*.[124] This is totally unobjectionable but it is unclear what is left of the 'amnesty' if perpetrators are held accountable and victims are compensated. Mance LJ neatly encapsulated the correct approach in the *Jones* case, finding that if a state can be shown to have failed to provide an effective domestic remedy for alleged torture, this must on any view weaken its position in insisting on a claim to state immunity in respect of such a claim against one of its officials elsewhere'.[125]

The second doctrine, *forum non conveniens*, usually operates along the following (similar) lines: 'The basic principle is that a stay will only be granted on the ground of *forum non conveniens* where the court is satisfied that there is some other

---

[122] Iovanne (n 113 above) 191.

[123] J Llewellyn, 'Just Amnesty and Private International Law' in Scott (ed) *Torture as Tort: Comparative Perspectives on the Development of Transnational Human Rights Litigation*, (2001) 592.

[124] ibid 598–9.

[125] *Jones v Kingdom of Saudi Arabia* [2004] EWCA Civ 1394, para 86.

226   *Rory Stephen Brown*

available forum, having competent jurisdiction, which is the appropriate forum for the trial of the action, i.e. in which the case may be tried more suitably for the interests of all the parties and the ends of justice.'[126]

Byrnes makes the eminently sensible suggestion that that 'the fact that a person may have been or would be unable to avail himself or herself of the right to redress under Article 14 in the *lex loci delicti* could be taken into account in determining whether an action should be stayed on the basis of the doctrine of *forum non conveniens*, on the ground that the plaintiff cannot obtain justice in the natural forum'.[127] Conversely, no objection is made here to the possibility of a defendant state moving to stay an action on the grounds that justice would be available in the plaintiff's home state. To be sure, if this were the case, then a claimant should be dissuaded from vexatious forum shopping with a stay.

As Lord Browne-Wilkinson observed, the provision for judicial review of its shortcomings is not the hallmark of a totalitarian regime.[128] If the torture occurred in a regime of this nature, the court should resist a defendant state's request for a stay but, it is submitted, such a request should also be denied in the event that other 'insurmountable barriers' have the effect of preventing access to justice, for example, where there is cogent evidence of 'police complicity with the torturers, judicial bias, or intimidation by government officials or non-governmental actors'[129] or even, grounded fears for personal safety if the claimant were to return to the wrongdoer state.[130] In the determination of the quality of access to justice in the venue, there is also no objection to other practicalities that affect the administration of justice being taken into account, such as the place of residence of the parties; whether or not the claimant suffered effects of the torture since arriving in the forum; the costs involved in the adduction of evidence, etc. However, these factors, relating to convenience and cost, pale into insignificance if there is no real chance of a plaintiff asserting his rights in the ostensibly more natural forum.[131] Impaired or imperfect hearings are to be preferred to none at all. Courts should attempt to concentrate their analysis on whether or not there are alternative available fora for the claimant to present her case. This approach was adopted by the Italian Corte di Cassazione in *Pistelli v European University Institute* where the Court was influenced by the fact that an alternative forum existed (namely, the European judicature) in its decision to affirm the Institute's immunity from Italian civil jurisdiction.[132]

---

[126] *Spiliada Maritime Corp v Cansulex Ltd* [1987] 1 UKAC 460, 476.

[127] Byrnes (n 80 above) 549.

[128] *R v Bow Street Metropolitan Stipendiary Magistrate and others, ex p Pinochet Ugarte (No 3)* [1999] 2 All ER 97, 109.

[129] Terry (n 106 above) 122–3.

[130] *Oppenheimer v Louis Rosenthal & Co* [1937] 1 All ER 23.

[131] *Connelly v RTZ Corp plc* [1998] AC 854 (HL). See *per* Lord Goff, 866.

[132] *Pistelli v European University Institute* [2005] Corte di Cassazione (Sezioni Unite Civili), 28 October 2005, No 20995.

It might be objected that the *forum non conveniens* approach increases uncertainty in transnational adjudication due to the necessity of a case-by-case approach.[133] However, this criticism is misplaced for two reasons: First, there is already a great amount of case law on the operation of the doctrine, which would help to guide judges in its application, and in the setting of new precedents leading to relative precision in its application. Secondly, a degree of uncertainty in the initial application of the law is an acceptable price to pay for the effective vindication of human rights.

B. Neither States Nor Their Agents Should Enjoy Immunity for Torture

This section argues that *neither state nor agent* should be shielded by immunity rules from civil liability for torture. On the contrary, they should be jointly and severally liable.

In terms of the individual civil responsibility of the official, it is a salutary discipline briefly to consider the developments in international law. The dissentients in the *Arrest Warrant* case, and this is a proposition with which the majority probably would not have taken issue, stated that 'a trend is discernible that, in a world which increasingly rejects impunity for the most repugnant of offences, *the attribution of responsibility and accountability is becoming firmer*, the possibility for the assertion of jurisdiction wider and the availability of immunity as a shield more limited'.[134]

In 1994, Arthur Watts declared: 'The idea that individuals who commit international crimes are *internationally* accountable for them has now become an accepted part of international law.'[135] Furthermore, as the Nuremberg Tribunal stated: 'The authors of these acts cannot shelter themselves behind their official position in order to be freed from punishment in appropriate proceedings.'[136] In the context of criminal law, the ICTY held that it was indisputably declaratory of customary international law, that individuals of whatever rank were personally responsible for acts of torture.[137] If the imposition of criminal liability on individuals is acceptable in the case of torture, involving as it does punishment, and often incarceration, then *a fortiori*, the less onerous consequences of civil liability can no longer be objectionable.

---

[133] Garnett (n 114 above) 372.

[134] *Case Concerning the Arrest Warrant of 11 April 2000 (Democratic Republic of Congo v Belgium)* [2002] <http://www.icj-cij.org/icjwww/idocket/iCOBE/iCOBEframe.htm>, Joint Separate Opinion of Higgins, Kooijmans and Buergentahl, para 75 (emphasis added).

[135] W Arthur, at The Hague Lectures, The Legal Position in International Law of Heads of State, Heads of Government and Foreign Ministers (1994-III 247 *Recueil des Cours*), 82.

[136] N J Kritz, *Transnational Justice: How emerging democracies reckon with former regimes* (1995) vol III, 462.

[137] *Prosecutor v Anto Furundzija* (1998) IT-95–17/1, para 140.

The question here—answered in the negative—is whether or not the Appeal Court in *Jones* got it right, holding that an official did not enjoy immunity for torture, even if the torture was committed outside the state of suit but that: 'There is no basis on which the state could be made liable to indemnify one of its officials proved to have committed systematic torture.'[138] The Appeal Court was shackled by the English rules of precedent, by virtue of which the Court in *Jones* was bound to follow its decision in *Al-Adsani*, which, as will be recalled, preserved a foreign *state's* immunity from civil suit in England for torture.[139] The Appeal Court was not, therefore, in a position to assert the liability of the state as well as that of the official.

Traditionally, one of the reasons cited by courts for extending immunity to officials is that the removal of such immunity would undermine the state's own immunity.[140] Hence, if it is accepted, as is argued here, that state immunity for torture is misconceived, the justifications for protecting the individual disappear too.

Contrary to recent authority, it is argued that neither the state nor the official should benefit from the protection of immunity from civil claims based on allegations of acts in violation of the prohibition on torture; in the parlance of tort law, they are jointly and severally liable. The rank of the official should bear no relevance whatsoever.

Though attractive from the point of view of reconciling the competing considerations of adequate recompense for the victim and admonition of the heinous act, with the preservation of diplomatic relations and the desire to avoid the condemnation of an entire state,[141] Fox is correct in her claim that the sacrifice of an official scapegoat in total ignorance of the systemic institutional backdrop to torture will not offer a solution to the problem of systematic state torture.[142]

But if the individual is liable, as contended here, why should the state also be liable? Or is this notion 'absurd', as asserted by Lord Phillips in the Appeal Court in the *Jones* case?[143] Obviously, the offering up of one, usually lowly, official does nothing to address the culpability of the state *qua* governmental apparatus. This obfuscation should be dissuaded not encouraged in the name of accountability. In this connexion, it should be remembered that a government does not act, except through its agents. In this way, individual and state responsibility coincide. Properly understood, the torture is both an individual act and an act of state. Furthermore, actions against individuals are unlikely to satisfy the victim in the overwhelming majority of cases—either because the perpetrator is obfuscated by

---

[138] *Jones v Kingdom of Saudi Arabia* [2004] EWCA Civ 1394, *per* Mance LJ, para 76.

[139] ibid *per* Lord Phillips MR, para 102.

[140] *Propend Finance v Alan Sing and The Commissioner of the Australian Federal Police* [1997] 111 ILR 611, 699.

[141] A Cassese, *International Law in a Divided World* (1986) 275.

[142] H Fox, 'Where Does the Buck Stop? State Immunity from Civil Jurisdiction and Torture?' (2005) 121 LQR 353, 359.

[143] *Jones* (n 138 above) para 126.

official machinery and unidentifiable, due to his lack of (attachable) assets, or due to his demise (as was the case in *Prinz*).[144] On the other hand, foreign sovereigns are much more amenable, affluent, and present defendants.

The next question is whether or not state liability should be based on a fault element or a knowledge requirement. Several interrelated reasons seem to compel the conclusion that *a state should be strictly liable for torture*: On one view, the raison d'être of the state is the protection of citizens and visitors. It seems that, should one of its agents directly contradict this purpose by violating an individual in a manner as horrific as torture, its liability should be strict. Relatedly, the state possesses vast financial resources, largely provided by its citizens as a quid pro quo for the benefits of settled government. If those benefits are completely negated by the State's preference for brutality over legality, there is a strong argument that the individual should be compensated or *reimbursed* (for the brazen violation of the social contract). An adjunct of this argument is that the rule of law is, at least to some extent, *repaired* in the act of recompense. The state's repayment signifies a broken (often constitutional) promise and there is great symbolic resonance in this act of remorseful redress. More practically, in order to readjust the asymmetric power relationship between the state and the individual in terms, *inter alia*, of resources for legal proceedings, the evidential hurdles facing the plaintiff should not be exaggeratedly high. Again, on a practical level, the quality of institutional competence and responsibility of the state is improved by the imposition of strict vicarious liability for the misdemeanours of its agents. The final and perhaps most compelling reason in favour of vicarious liability of the state derives from the terms of the Draft Articles on State Responsibility, which provide for a broad approach to official capacity and for the irrelevance of an official's contravention of instructions or the impropriety or ulterior nature of his motives in the determination of the liability of the state.[145]

Having discussed *why* the state should be strictly liable for torturous practices of its officials, under what doctrine of law can this liability be asserted? In a timely contribution to the debate on transnational torture,[146] Valerie Oosterveld and Alejandra Flah assessed the suitability of various frameworks of derivative civil liability for the tort of torture, including *respondeat superior* (whereby principals are liable for agents' tortious conduct occurring within the scope of

---

[144] Reimann (n 63 above).

[145] Draft Articles on Responsibility of States for Internationally Wrongful Acts 2001, Art 4 and 7.

[146] V Oosterveld and A Flah, 'Holding Leaders Liable for Torture by Others: Command Responsibility and Respondeat Superior as Frameworks for Derivative Civil Liability' in Scott (ed) *Torture as Tort: Comparative Perspectives on the Development of Transnational Human Rights Litigation* (2001) 453. See also, for a discussion of the defence of superior orders, P de Sena, 'Immunity of State Organs and Defence of Superior Orders as an Obstacle to the Domestic Enforcement of International Human Rights' in B Conforti and F Francioni (eds), *Enforcing International Human Rights in Domestic Courts* (1997).

their employment); *command responsibility* (under which a military commander is criminally responsible for crimes of his subordinates); and *enterprise liability* (strict liability for employers irrespective of whether or not the agent's conduct was undertaken for personal purposes and regardless of the prohibition of that conduct by the employer).

There is no space here for a discussion of all of these doctrines. Nevertheless, the latter, enterprise liability, presents itself as the most suitable vehicle for deriving liability of the state from the acts of its agents. The Californian case of *Mary M v City of Los Angeles*,[147] concerning a police officer who raped a woman in a twisted bargain in exchange for letting her off a speeding violation, provides an example of the merits of the enterprise liability approach. In that case, it was held that, 'employers may be held liable even if the employee's conduct is prohibited by the employer, is intentional or malicious, and does not benefit the employer'.[148] Oosterveld and Flah tell us that 'the doctrine of "enterprise liability"...broadens the "scope of employment" test in two ways: (1) the liability of a superior will not only extend to the actual or possible control over his employees, but also to the risks *inherent in or created by the enterprise*; and (2) the employee's conduct need not be for the benefit of the superior in order for the latter to be found liable'.[149]

Important for present purposes is that a state may not escape liability by complaining that the officials' acts were banned in internal law or they were of a private rather than public nature or that it was not at fault due to the absence of real or constructive knowledge of the torture.[150] Ergo, the doctrine of enterprise liability seems perfectly suited to this task. Such a construct, familiar to all developed legal systems across the globe, is well-suited to slicing through the layers of command in both the military and government that tend to deflect responsibility onto inferior officers, lowly scapegoats, and obliging functionaries, pinning the blame on the broad chest of the state. This approach enjoys the additional advantage of being consonant with the International Law Commission's Commentary on Article 4 of the Draft Articles on the International Responsibility of States, which states that: 'It is irrelevant for this purpose that the person concerned may have had ulterior or improper motives or may be abusing public power. Where such a person acts in an apparently official capacity, or under colour of authority, the actions in question will be attributable to the State.'

Another advantage of the notion of enterprise liability is that it avoids one of the traps awaiting advocates attempting to pin civil liability on officials for torture. As we have seen, the definition of torture requires it to be undertaken, instigated by, acquiesced in, or consented to by an official.[151] Traditionally, that same official

---

[147] *Mary M v City of Los Angeles* 814 P 2d 1341 (Cal Sup Ct) (1991).

[148] Oosterveld and Flah (n 145 above) 452.

[149] ibid (emphasis added).

[150] This construction also avoids nice questions as to how one imputes knowledge to a state.

[151] Convention against Torture and Other Cruel, Inhuman or Degrading Treatment or Punishment, 1984, Art 1.

flavour of the act has triggered sovereign immunity. Advocates normally argue that the act is official for the purposes of UNCAT and then *un*official to avoid the operation of immunity. Officiality is therefore a double-edged sword upon which the plaintiff falls, defeating his own claim.[152] The notion of enterprise liability advocated here avoids this self-defeating circularity. Thus the official nature of the act of torture 'does no more...than identify the author and the public context in which the author must be acting'.[153] The 'officiality' does not then trigger state or official immunity, because such protection only shields acts that fall within a sovereign's competence in international law. This intuition simply voices the truism that the fact that a government or official has acted tells us nothing about the legality of that act. An official *can* though he *may* not torture. Formulated differently, such maltreatment is within the *factual* but not the *legal* capacity of a state agent.

Having decided that the state and the agent of torture should be jointly and severally liable, how can we expect states to react to a finding of civil liability? Keeping in mind the distinction between immunity from jurisdiction and immunity from enforcement, it seems that the defendant state has one of three options: Either it can (a) recognize the legal effect of the judgment, pay up and, in so doing, contribute to the development of an exception to the 'general' rule on state immunity, or (b) denounce the judgment as an exercise of illegitimate exorbitant jurisdiction over matters subject only to the jurisdiction of the defendant's courts, or (c) it can deny the court's jurisdiction and yet pay compensation *ex gratia* as set out in the judgment (or some other sum) as a means of expressing its remorse whilst reserving its position on any purported exception to the rule on state immunity. In any event, the finding of liability is *res judicata* and, as such (subject to the appeals process) precludes a reconsideration of the matter in another jurisdiction.[154]

C. A Judicial Regime

The contention of this section is that the system of justice for torture victims proposed above can and should be administered by judges in the absence of (inter)national legislative initiative.

It is fair to say that one of the main aims of UNCAT is the compensation of victims of torture,[155] whilst it would not be *un*fair to say that purposive interpretation of national legislation and international covenants in the light of this aim has been conspicuously absent from judicial consideration of this matter. With respect, criticism aimed at the minority judgment in the *Al-Adsani* case and the court in

---

[152] See *Jones v Kingdom of Saudi Arabia* [2006] UKHL 26, *per* Lord Bingham, para 19.

[153] *Jones v Kingdom of Saudi Arabia* [2004] EWCA Civ 1394, *per* Mance LJ, para 71.

[154] The diplomatic machinations subsequent to the *Letelier v Republic of Chile* 488 F Supp 665 (DDC 1980) litigation provide a good example of these issues.

[155] P Burns and S McBurney, 'Impunity and the United Nations Convention against Torture: A shadow play without an Ending', in C Scott (ed), *Torture as Tort: Comparative Perspectives on the Development of Transnational Human Rights Litigation* (2001) 287.

the *Ferrini* case regarding their usage of moral rather than legal concepts,[156] their
utopian or idealistic approaches to the law, fall short of the mark. [157] What these
judgments may lack in terms of legal precision and analysis of conflict of law
issues, they more than make up for in purposive and teleological reasoning aimed
at achieving a coherent international law system based on a clear, normative hier-
archy, the spirit and intention behind UNCAT, and the fundamental goals of the
international legal order.[158] Notably, if one reconceptualizes the *jus cogens* ban on
torture as a *principle*, it does not dictate an 'end-result' to the debate about transnational torture actions, but it serves instead to 'offer a substantive reason why a
particular end-result should be preferred'.[159]

With increasing frequency, national courts and international tribunals seek
guidance *inter se*,[160] meaning that the effect of a decision of a constitutional
or supreme court reproduces itself around the world; the unthinking, repeated
reinforcement of the normative conclusions extending the longevity of the original
judgment beyond its deserved lifespan.[161] In short, judges of constitutional and
supranational courts should underestimate neither their enormous responsibility
for the development of international law nor the potentially stultifying effects of
a backwards-facing finding.

It is time now to consider the respective merits and demerits of judicial initiative,
as opposed to action by state legislatures and/or international treaties. Despite the
advantages of treaties in terms of clarity, they can have a stifling effect on international law if their timing is ill-fated and if judges are not prepared to interpret
them as 'living instruments' capable of bearing different meanings over time.[162]
For example, Lorna McGregor criticizes the United Nations Convention in the
following terms: 'the combination of the general provision for immunity; the exclusion of criminal but not civil proceedings; and the removal of the provision allowing for future developments in international law, collectively risk the ossification of

---

[156] H Fox, 'State Immunity and the International Crime of Torture' (2006) 2 EHRLR 142,
156.

[157] See, eg Tams (n 29 above).

[158] For similar argument, see Bianchi (n 97 above).

[159] E Voyiakis, 'Access to Court v State Immunity' (2003) 52 ICLQ 297, 322.

[160] ibid 285.

[161] For better or worse, the influence of House of Lords judgment is wide-ranging and powerful.
The *Jones* case is now authority, internationally, for the proposition that a victim of torture perpetrated abroad should be denied access to the courts by dint of the law on state immunity: *Jones v The
Kingdom of Saudi Arabia* [2006] UKHL 26. The importance of statements by constitutional courts on
international law cannot be understated, particularly in the field of immunity. The House of Lords,
especially, shoulders great responsibility for the development of world jurisprudence. As the supreme
court of a previous hegemon and the central court of a commonwealth of nations, it punches above
its weight, in terms of the persuasive sway of its determinations: See, for the effects of historic hegemonic status, C Campbell, ' "Wars on Terror" and vicarious hegemons: The UK, International Law
and the Northern Ireland Conflict' (2005) 54 ICLQ 321.

[162] Byrnes (n 80 above) 548.

the development of the relationship between state immunity and *jus cogens* norms under international law'.[163]

Though it is conceded that, 'aggrieved individuals need more uniformity than can possibly be provided even by far-sighted judges acting alone',[164] John Terry is correct in his contention that judges should, in accordance with settled principles of international law, allow transnational tort claims for torture until the third country remedy is 'sanctioned by treaty or authorised by domestic legislation'.[165] In this connection, it is argued that court judgments apparently interfering with foreign sovereign discretion would swiftly precipitate long overdue official consideration of the matter of civil immunity for *jus cogens* violations.

Even though ultimately, some form of legislative action would be desirable in order to bring clarity and certainty to this area of the law, a sovereign legislative act declaring that foreign sovereigns do not enjoy immunity in domestic courts, would be functionally pointless. The nature of *jus cogens* is such that it overrides conflicting domestic provisions. Hence, a national enactment purporting to remove an immunity that does not exist would be a mere utterance of the obvious; namely that a state cannot expect protection when it steps outside the clearly drawn bounds of international law.

Furthermore, there is something counter-intuitive in a sovereign taking legislative action to remove state immunity for acts committed by a foreign state ultra vires, or in otherwords outside its competence as sovereign. Given that these limits on states' supremacy derive not from consensus (according to conventional wisdom) but rather from fundamental, dare-we-say, *constitutional* and purportedly immutable norms of the international legal order, national legislatures seem to be inappropriate fora. Put simply, sovereigns may not determine their own competences; they do not enjoy *kompetenz-kompetenz* in these matters. Contrariwise, national courts, by dint of their separation and independence from the sovereign law-giver and law-enforcer, are much more natural venues for the delineation of the periphery of state power.

The next issue relating to the proposed judicial regime goes to which courts are the appropriate fora for the determination of civil actions for torture. Scott helpfully recalls that 'the existence of norms within a legal order does not in and of itself decide the question of allocation of institutional authority to judge those norms'.[166] Nor should it. In the present context, in which (1) international human rights enforcement mechanisms are limited,[167] and (2) values exist that are common and fundamental to all nation states, there is a strong argument that municipal courts

---

[163] McGregor (n 49 above) 445.

[164] Denza (n 60 above) 398.

[165] Terry (n 107 above) 133.

[166] C Scott, 'Translating Torture into Transnational Tort: Conceptual Divides in the Debate on Corporate Accountability for Human Rights Harms' in Scott (ed) (n 53 above) 56.

[167] International Law Association Human Rights Committee, 'Report on Civil Actions in the English Courts for Serious Human Rights Violations Abroad' (2001) abstract.

are well situated to facilitate enforcement.[168] Indeed, if, upon consideration of an international human rights treaty, it is established that no international mechanism has been set up for the realization of the rights captured in the text, then, it is submitted, the natural presumption would be that the vision of the draughtsmen involved a delegation of responsibility to domestic tribunals. In the present context, Raponi points out that the procedures linked to UNCAT are neither comprehensive nor effective, the responsibility clearly resting with the organs of the state parties to implement and breathe life into the rights it contains.[169]

In the jurisprudence of the European Court of Human Rights, great emphasis has been placed on the 'special character of the Convention as a treaty for the *collective* enforcement of human rights and fundamental freedoms'.[170] It is submitted that this approach, rather than the reliance on international tribunals, is the only way to ensure effective vindication of human rights. Andrew Clapham correctly maintains that: 'If international human rights law is to be effective and to fulfil the promise of the rule of law, it must also extend to foreign torturers—in other words, into a transnational private sphere'.[171] Clearly, without the cooperation of domestic tribunals, the attempt to protect international human rights will remain futile.[172]

Moreover, in relation to effective vindication of the rights of individuals, national courts enjoy significant advantages over their handicapped international cousins. The ICJ is a poor forum for human rights claimants for the simple reason that individuals lack standing. States may bring claims on behalf of aggrieved citizens but history tells us that they are not fain to do so for reasons of political expediency. The International Criminal Court (ICC) is similarly ailing (despite torture falling within its competence) because its jurisdiction derives from the consent of either the state of the accused or the state in which the alleged violations occurred or from the Security Council.[173]

Typically, it is objected that the neutrality of national courts is at least questionable. This grumble carries no weight. Accustomed to finding against the incumbent government on home territory, at least in states where justice is not a euphemism for politics, there is no apparent reason why a national court would

---

[168] A Bianchi, 'Immunity *versus* Human Rights: The *Pinochet* Case' (1999) 10(2) EJIL 237, 238.

[169] Raponi (n 85 above) 394–5.

[170] *Loizidou v Turkey (Preliminary Objections)* [1995] ECHR (1995) Series A, No 310, para 70 (emphasis added).

[171] A Clapham, 'Postscript: Developments Related to Pinochet as of January 2001' in C Scott (ed), *Torture as Tort: Comparative Perspectives on the Development of Transnational Human Rights Litigation* (2001) 534.

[172] See, on this topic, Conforti and Francioni (eds) (n 146 above). It is in light of the fact that immunity often results in both remediless victims and unpunished perpetrators that Principle 19 of the *Principles to Combat Impunity* recommends 'a distribution of jurisdiction between national, foreign, international and internationalized courts'. See D Orentlicher, 'Report of independent expert to update the Set of principles to combat impunity—Updated Set of principles for the protection and promotion of human rights through action to combat impunity' (2005).

[173] Rome Statute of the ICC, 1998, Art 12 and 13.

be predisposed to bias in the adjudication of claims where another state features as a party. Furthermore, national courts are familiar with claims involving foreign governments in commercial contexts where traditional immunity has eroded. Correspondingly, there is no reason to expect prejudice in civil proceedings for torture (statutorily enshrined politics notwithstanding).

It could also be argued that the cultural differences in the understanding of the notion of torture, inhuman, and degrading treatment form a reason why claims should only be heard in the jurisdiction where the alleged maltreatment occurred.[174] The most important retorts to this argument are as follows. First, if a state does not provide in its legal system, access to justice for someone who alleges maltreatment at the hands of government officials, that state, it is submitted, waives its right to object if the victim seeks a hearing elsewhere. Remember, we are dealing with hearing the case on the merits, merely allowing the claimant in court. The determination that torture has occurred comes later. Secondly, the cultural differences with respect to what is torture, inhuman, or degrading treatment can be taken into account in the assessment of damages, if it is established that such practices have been utilized.

In summary, it may be argued that practical hurdles and an absence of political will to establish effective international enforcement apparatus militate for domestic, transnational application of international norms, though there is nothing preventing domestic courts surveying the institutional landmarks on the international plane to ascertain whether or not a transnational action might be incompatible with existing enforcement modalities.[175] Where, as one pragmatic commentator points out, international law provides the 'normativity', domestic courts can be expected to supply the 'machinery'.[176]

V. CONCLUSION

It is suggested that the flexible system of transnational tortious jurisdiction proposed here, based on case-by-case appraisal of the practical availability of alternative avenues of justice, would serve to reconcile the goals of securing justice for victims of torture; the desirability to locate a claim in the most appropriate location and with the most effective procedural structure; the protection of a defendant state's legitimate interests; and the necessity to act in accordance with, and contribute to, a coherent system of international law.[177]

---

[174] I am grateful to Professor Francioni for highlighting this matter.

[175] Raponi (n 85 above) 399; A McConville, 'Taking Jurisdiction in Transnational Human Rights Tort Litigation' in Scott (ed) (n 53 above) 176.

[176] M Moran, 'An Uncivil Action: The Tort of Torture and Cosmopolitan Private Law' in C Scott (ed) *Torture as Tort: Comparative Perspectives on the Development of Transnational Human Rights Litigation* (2001) 668.

[177] As set out by the International Law Association Human Rights Committee, 'Report on Civil Actions in the English Courts for Serious Human Rights Violations Abroad' (2001).

Index